EVERYMAN, I will go with thee,

and be thy guide,

In thy most need to go by thy side

FRANCIS BEAUMONT

Born 1584 (?), and educated at Oxford. Married in 1613 or 1614, Ursula Isley, a Kentish heiress, and retired from playwriting. Died 1616, and is buried in Westminster Abbey.

JOHN FLETCHER

Born 1579, and educated at Cambridge. Died 1625, and is buried in St Mary Overy (now Southwark Cathedral). Beaumont and Fletcher collaborated between 1608 and 1613.

Beaumont & Fletcher
Select Plays

INTRODUCTION BY

M. C. BRADBROOK

*Mistress of Girton College, and Professor of English
in the University of Cambridge*

DENT: LONDON

EVERYMAN'S LIBRARY

DUTTON: NEW YORK

© Introduction, J. M. Dent & Sons Ltd, 1962
All rights reserved
Made in Great Britain
at the
Aldine Press · Letchworth · Herts
for
J. M. DENT & SONS LTD
Aldine House · Bedford Street · London
First included in Everyman's Library 1911
Last reprinted 1970

PR2422
S4
L962

NO. 506

ISBN: 0 460 00506 5

INTRODUCTION

THE fifty-two plays ascribed to Beaumont and Fletcher would not have represented an unduly large output for the working life of even one man; their contemporary, Thomas Heywood, claimed to have had a hand in two hundred and twenty. Only five years, however (1608–13), can be reckoned as the period of their collaboration, after which Beaumont retired from the stage. The work of these five years sufficed to establish a type of play which remained influential throughout the century, and which was long considered superior to Shakespeare's. In his *Essay of Dramatic Poesy*, Dryden observes that two of Beaumont and Fletcher's plays were acted for every one by Shakespeare or Jonson; later he recognized that 'Shakespeare had an universal mind, which comprehended all characters and passions; Fletcher a more confined and limited . . . he was a limb of Shakespeare' (*Grounds of Criticism in Tragedy*, 1679).

This judgment, given in the year when the Second Folio of Beaumont and Fletcher's plays appeared, rightly mentions Fletcher alone; for not only had he much the larger share in the writing, but it is his characteristic tone and attitude that prevail. The problem of deciding which plays belong to Beaumont, which to Fletcher, which to both and which contain works by other men is hardly susceptible of final solution; however, the linguistic studies of Cyrus Hoy have brought out clearly Fletcher's share in the plays. Two plays in the present volume are entirely Fletcher's—*The Faithful Shepherdess* and *The Wild Goose Chase*; *Bonduca* is probably so. *The Knight of the Burning Pestle* is now ascribed to Beaumont, while *The Maid's Tragedy* and *A King and No King* remain collaborative, as they purport to be.

Some plays were written for the choristers' troupe, the Children of Blackfriars; others for Shakespeare's company, the King's Men, who in 1608 took over the small select theatre at the Blackfriars for their winter quarters. Fletcher became one of the leading writers for this company, and seems briefly to have collaborated with Shakespeare; *The Two Noble Kinsmen*, on the title-page of 1634, is claimed for 'the memorable Worthies of their time, Mr John Fletcher

v

6 2 4 0 2

and Mr William Shakespeare, Gent.'. They are also supposed to have shared the writing of the lost *Cardenio*, and of *King Henry VIII*.

Beaumont died in 1616, the same year as Shakespeare; Fletcher in 1625, the same year as King James I. The writings of the two dramatists, as distinct from all that has been ascribed to them, supply a characteristic example of the most important kind of Jacobean poetry, the baroque.

Baroque art, which in the early seventeenth century developed all over Europe, is an art of distortion. The term *barocco* was originally applied by Portuguese jewellers to pearls of irregular form. In baroque art, whether sculpture, painting or poetry, the human form is shown in violent emotion, while it is at the same time naturalistically displayed, and not formalized by convention. Baroque poetry has been defined as

> ... poetry in which, although the problems of the age are reflected, the perfect poise between intelligence and sensibility is either destroyed or not achieved or not attempted, with the result that the poet has a distorted view of life, distorted through imagination and sensibility, without any care for apparent proportion or balance.... The baroque poet thus depends on his power to carry his reader into his own world, which is often a sort of surreality, and to light up for him those strange vistas which such baroque sensibility can open up, both in the concrete world of nature and in the recesses of man's sensibility.
>
> Odette de Mourgues, *Metaphysical, Baroque and Précieux Poetry* (Oxford, 1953), page 74.[1]

In Fletcher's plays extraordinary situations provide distortion, while the easy simplicity of the language provides the naturalism which contrasts with it. The first description of these plays as baroque came from Sofia, in studies courageously begun by Marco Mincoff during the last war.[2] The more recent work of Eugene Waith in America and Clifford Leech in England develops this view. Leech speaks of

> ... a more relaxed drama, which in its character types mirrored a stable world, and yet in its language maintained and indeed further developed the informality of the earliest Jacobean years. The essential property of the new Beaumont and Fletcher drama consists in its dislocation.... There is no firm ground for reverence, or for a cosmic scheme, in the great majority of plays which

---

[1] See the bibliography in this book for works on the baroque.
[2] Marco Mincoff, *Verbal Repetition in Elizabethan Tragedy* (St Clement Okridsky University of Sofia, 1944), pages 98–103. See his *Shakespeare, Fletcher and Baroque Tragedy* in *Shakespeare Survey* 20 (1967).

deeply bear John Fletcher's impress. Neither Fletcher nor Beaumont was ever a declared revolutionary, yet few dramatists can have written plays as fully destructive by implication.

Clifford Leech, *The John Fletcher Plays* (1962), page 32.

A little later he refers to this drama's 'inherent and largely non-explicit scepticism' (page 40).

Beaumont and Fletcher, succeeding the greater dramatists, Shakespeare and Jonson, could most readily outgo their predecessors by blending sophistication with violence. In these plays of genuine power the still unspent force of the language is diverted to virtuoso display; in tragedy as inflated rhetoric that sweeps along torrentially, and is used to present the most extreme and most extraordinary situations. These are often taken from classical exercises in the law, especially from Seneca and Suetonius, whose works would be familiar to the most intelligent and lively part of the select audience at Blackfriars, the young students from the Inns of Court. To this gentlemanly group the playwrights themselves belonged; Beaumont was the son of a judge. To hold back the vital piece of evidence till the end, as the playwrights often do, would be to invite the young lawyers to exercise their wits upon the plot.

In comedy the gay irresponsibility of rakes and spendthrifts, anticipating the mood of the Restoration stage, might be expected to appeal in wit, sophistication and successful impudence to such young men. All surrender to feeling is mocked; the pleasures of fortune-hunting and the reckless baffling of fools supply the staple of many plays, of which *The Wild Goose Chase* is the best. Mirabel is the first of a line of heroes culminating in his namesake, the hero of Congreve's *The Way of the World* (1700). Like Don Juan, Mirabel carries round his catalogue of seductions, but is captured in the end by the witty huntress Oriana, after a series of stratagems which include a wooing by her own brother, a scene in which she feigns to be mad for love, and finally the disguise of a rich heiress which, after she has secured him, Mirabel claims to have penetrated. 'Baffling', the sportive torment of an eccentric, is often practised by Fletcher's ladies on their lovers; for though love figures so prominently as motive, it is always seen as a comic madness. This can lead to some very horsy language, when for instance, in *Bonduca*, a Roman captain falls madly in love with the memory of Bonduca's daughter because of the firm

constancy of her death; such language is destructive of the
sentiment it claims to portray.

> What do I ail, i' th' name of heaven? I did but see her,
> And see her die; she stinks by this time strongly,
> Abominably stinks. . . .
> A pox upon the bots, the love-bots! Hang me! . . .
>
> v. ii. 1 ff.

Here can be heard the pounding, blustering tones of
asseveration that belong to all Fletcher's noble boobies in
love—beginning with Arbaces, hero of *A King and No King*,
whose notions of honour are inflexible and simple as a
schoolboy's, while his surrender to passions betray a depth
of self-ignorance that almost puts him on a level with the
comic coward of the play, Captain Bessus.

The theme is the incestuous love of Arbaces for his
supposed sister, eventually found not to be his sister at all.
Plentiful hints of a mystery are dropped—the title itself
would supply one—but not till the end does the wise old
counsellor tell his enraged offspring: 'If you kill me—know
—you kill your father!' The design of this play has been
strongly defended, and is indeed very ingenious; but the
passions of Arbaces, which unking him before he is unkinged
by Gobrias, reduce him to comic proportions, and with him
the simple heroic virtues he stands for. Arbaces is a much
better example than Othello of the critical devaluation of the
simple soldierly hero; and those inclined to see Othello in the
way suggested by T. S. Eliot and F. R. Leavis would do well
to look first at Arbaces.

In *The Maid's Tragedy* the violent, amoral and ruthless
Evadne, whose delicate air deceives even her lover the King,
is a fitting sister for the ruthless if devoted Melantius; each
despises and uses weaker creatures for a personal end. The
play offers a series of brilliantly planned scenes, fast moving
and lurid, built round the frozen grief of the betrayed
Aspatia, who gives the play its title. In the lament, where
she sees herself in a 'tapestry of woe', can be found for once
the full maturity of tragic speech, at the dead and motionless
centre of all the fury:

> Suppose I stand upon the sea-beach now,
> Mine arms thus, and my hair blown with the wind,
> Wild as that desert . . . and the trees about me
> Let them be dry and leafless; let the rocks
> Groan with continual surges; and behind me
> Make all a desolation. Look, look, wenches!   II. ii.

It is no accident that T. S. Eliot chose these lines to set before one of his own most controlled and yet violent poems, 'Sweeney Erect'.

At the centre of the pastoral, *The Faithful Shepherdess*, lies the unappeased grief of Clorin for her buried shepherd. Yet here, too, with characteristic 'dislocation', Clorin is allowed to play at being inconstant, and by this therapeutic device release from his love-sickness a shepherd who has fallen in love with her virtue. Varieties of love-sickness give the theme, and Clorin cures them all.

The play is set in old-fashioned pastoral style, with four 'places' shown together—Clorin's bower, the holy well, a dale and a hollow tree. Such scenes had been familiar thirty years before, in plays by Lyly or Peele; but here Fletcher, drawing on Guarini's *Pastor Fido*, aims at deliberate contrast with the old merriments of 'Whitsun ales and cream', of 'country hired shepherds ... with curtailed dogs in strings, sometimes laughing together and sometimes killing one another'. Yet once again the central feeling is deeply ambiguous; Pan, the shepherd's god, protects chastity but seems to practise lust; the shape-changing by which lustful Amaryllis takes on the form of faithful Amoret, the comic lubricity of Cloe, and the chaste disgust of Thenot and Perigot make up a strange blend of libertine freedom and slightly mawkish virtue. Twice the hero stabs the heroine; this sexual violence, like the similar wounding of Aspatia and Arethusa, a perversity forced upon a highly moral character by circumstances, is typical of Fletcher's plays. Like other baroque writers, he explores the morbid, the macabre, the taboo; he loves to set a character in extremes, yet to keep familiarity by a natural turn of speech. *The Faithful Shepherdess* is a delicate piece of artifice; its fragility and limitations are part of its charm.

In *The Knight of the Burning Pestle* Beaumont recalls older drama by the mode of burlesque. The historic perspective strengthens the perspective that separates the play world from reality—a perspective that the more innocent characters do not see. Ralph, the 'prentice who has 'played Jeronimo with a shoemaker for a wager', dies in a speech that echoes *The Spanish Tragedy*; he has been fired by reading old romances, full of people, 'sometimes laughing and sometimes killing one another', and he brings in the Whitsun-ale festivities of the City when he appears as a

May Lord, decked in scarves and rings. His mistress interrupts the play to admonish or advise, calls for actors as readily as she calls for beer, and has never seen anything but fairground shows before. Ignoring the music provided (reputed among the best in Europe), her husband George proudly pays for 'the Waits of Southwark', asking particularly for that vulgar instrument, the shawm.

This burlesque, dedicated to Keysar, manager of the children's troupe and himself a Citizen and Goldsmith of London, does not seem to distinguish between the rant of Kyd's *Spanish Tragedy* and that of Hotspur in Shakespeare's *Henry IV*. The main butt was intended to be Thomas Heywood, whom Lamb called 'a prose Shakespeare', and his popular play *The Four Prentices of London*. Heywood really was very naïve, yet perhaps Beaumont did not realize how far, by this mockery, he was displaying his own disinheritance.

The printer finds it necessary to say that the play is 'elder above a year' to *Don Quixote*; but Cervantes's wry and tender story left the chivalric virtues as noble, if not quite as realistic as before; his irony brings an adjustment of view, not a change of values. Don Quixote, like Hotspur, may be rapt with visions; he is not subjected to indulgent belittlement, like Arbaces.

The irony of Jacobean baroque, however, should be comprehensible to the present age; for the 'sick' humour of comedy, the notion of 'l'absurde' in tragedy provide insights highly relevant to the deeply disturbed, powerful, yet seemingly light-hearted work of those who have been called 'entertainers to the Jacobean gentry'.

M. C. BRADBROOK.

Girton College, Cambridge.
1962.

SELECT BIBLIOGRAPHY

QUARTO EDITIONS. *The Faithful Shepherdess*, n.d. (1609?); *The Knight of the Burning Pestle*, 1613; *The Maid's Tragedy*, 1619; *A King and No King*, 1619; *The Wild Goose Chase*, 1652. Ten other plays were also published in quarto.

FOLIO EDITIONS. *Bonduca* appeared in the First Folio of 1647, which included the remainder of the plays; the Second Folio of 1679 added those previously issued in quarto, making fifty-two plays in all.

LATER EDITIONS. The plays were edited by Theobalds, by Seward and Simpson and by Colman in the eighteenth century; by Weber, by Dyce and by Darley in the nineteenth. There is an incomplete Variorum Edition (20 plays, 4 vols.) by A. H. Bullen, 1904–10; Arnold Glover and A. R. Waller (10 vols., Cambridge 1905–12) reproduce the text of the Second Folio. Fredson Bowers edits a critical old-spelling edition of which two volumes have appeared, *The Dramatic Works in the Beaumont and Fletcher Canon* (Cambridge 1966, 1970). Individual plays have appeared in the Belles Lettres Series, the Malone Society Reprints, the Revels Plays, the Regents Renaissance Drama Series.

Two plays partly by Fletcher, *The Jeweller of Amsterdam* and *Cardenio*, are lost. One play generally ascribed to Fletcher and Massinger, *Sir John Van Olden Barnevelt*, was first printed by A. H. Bullen in *A Collection of Old English Plays*, 1882–5. *The Two Noble Kinsmen*, ascribed to Fletcher and Shakespeare, is reprinted in *The Shakespeare Apocrypha*, ed. C. F. Tucker Brooke, Oxford, 1908.

CRITICAL STUDIES. Ashley H. Thorndike, *The Influence of Beaumont and Fletcher on Shakespeare*, Worcester, Mass., n.d. (1901); O. L. Hatcher, *John Fletcher*, 1905; C. M. Gayley, *Beaumont the Dramatist*, 1914; A. C. Sprague, *Beaumont and Fletcher on the Restoration Stage*, Cambridge, Mass., 1926; U. Ellis-Fermor, *Jacobean Drama*, 1936, contains an essay; L. B. Wallis, *Fletcher, Beaumont and Company, Entertainers to the Jacobean Gentry*, New York, 1947; E. M. Waith, *The Pattern of Tragicomedy in Beaumont and Fletcher*, 1952; W. W. Appleton, *Beaumont and Fletcher, a Critical Study*, 1956; Clifford Leech, *The John Fletcher Plays*, 1962; John Danby, *Poets on Fortune's Hill*, 1952, contains an essay, and *The Jacobean Theatre* (ed. J. R. Brown and B. Harris), 1960, contains an essay by Philip Edwards.

STUDIES OF AUTHORSHIP AND BIBLIOGRAPHY. Maurice Chelli, *Études sur la collaboration de Massinger avec Fletcher et son groupe*, 1926; E. H. C. Oliphant, *The Plays of Beaumont and Fletcher*, 1927; R. C. Bald, *Bibliographical Studies in the Beaumont and Fletcher Folio of 1647*, 1938; D. M. McKeithan, *The Debt to Shakespeare in the Beaumont and Fletcher Plays*, Austen, Texas, 1939; Baldwin Maxwell, *Studies in Beaumont, Fletcher and Massinger*, Chapel Hill, 1939; Cyrus Hoy, *The Share of Fletcher and his Collaborators in the Beaumont and Fletcher Canon*, Parts I–VII; *Studies in Bibliography*, University of Virginia, vols. viii–xv (1954–62). Kenneth Muir, *Shakespeare as Collaborator*, 1960, deals with the Fletcher-Shakespeare group of plays.

CONTENTS

THE KNIGHT OF THE BURNING PESTLE

TO HIS MANY WAYS ENDEARED FRIEND,
MASTER ROBERT KEYSAR

Sir,—This unfortunate child, who, in eight days (as lately I have learned), was begot and born, soon after was by his parents (perhaps because he was so unlike his brethren) exposed to the wide world, who, for want of judgment, or not understanding the privy mark of irony about it (which shewed it was no offspring of any vulgar brain), utterly rejected it; so that, for want of acceptance, it was even ready to give up the ghost, and was in danger to have been smothered in perpetual oblivion, if you (out of your direct antipathy to ingratitude) had not been moved both to relieve and cherish it: wherein I must needs commend both your judgment, understanding, and singular love to good wits. You afterwards sent it to me, yet being an infant and somewhat ragged: I have fostered it privately in my bosom these two years; and now, to shew my love, return it to you, clad in good lasting clothes, which scarce memory will wear out, and able to speak for itself; and withal, as it telleth me, desirous to try his fortune in the world, where, if yet it be welcome, father, foster-father, nurse, and child all have their desired end. If it be slighted or traduced, it hopes his father will beget him a younger brother, who shall revenge his quarrel, and challenge the world either of fond and merely literal interpretation or illiterate misprision. Perhaps it will be thought to be of the race of Don Quixote; we both may confidently swear it his elder above a year; and therefore may (by virtue of his birthright) challenge the wall of him. I doubt not but they will meet in their adventures, and I hope the breaking of one staff will make them friends; and perhaps they will combine themselves, and travel through the world to seek their adventures. So I commit him to his good fortune, and myself to your love. Your assured friend,

W. B[URRE].

3

TO THE READERS OF THIS COMEDY

GENTLEMEN,—The world is so nice in these our times, that for apparel there is no fashion; for music (which is a rare art, though now slighted) no instrument; for diet, none but the French kickshaws that are delicate; and for plays, no invention but that which now runneth an invective way, touching some particular persons, or else it is contemned before it is thoroughly understood. This is all that I have to say: that the author had no intent to wrong any one in this comedy; but, as a merry passage, here and there interlaced it with delight, which he hopes will please all, and be hurtful to none.

PROLOGUE

WHERE the bee can suck no honey, she leaves her sting behind; and where the bear cannot find origanum to heal his grief, he blasteth all other leaves with his breath. We fear it is like to fare so with us; that, seeing you cannot draw from our labours sweet content, you leave behind you a sour mislike, and with open reproach blame our good meaning, because you cannot reap the wonted mirth. Our intent was at this time to move inward delight, not outward lightness; and to breed (if it might be) soft smiling, not loud laughing; knowing it, to the wise, to be a great pleasure to hear counsel mixed with wit, as to the foolish, to have sport mingled with rudeness. They were banished the theatre of Athens, and from Rome hissed, that brought parasites on the stage with apish actions, or fools with uncivil habits, or courtezans with immodest words. We have endeavoured to be as far from unseemly speeches, to make your ears glow, as we hope you will be free from unkind reports, or mistaking the authors' intention (who never aimed at any one particular in this play), to make our cheeks blush. And thus I leave it, and thee to thine own censure, to like or dislike.—VALE.

DRAMATIS PERSONÆ

SPEAKER OF THE PROLOGUE
A CITIZEN.
HIS WIFE.
RALPH, *his Apprentice.*
Boys.

VENTUREWELL, *a Merchant.*
HUMPHREY.
MERRYTHOUGHT.
JASPER,
MICHAEL, } *his Sons.*
TIM,
GEORGE, } *Apprentices.*
Host.
Tapster.
Barber.
Three Men, *supposed captives.*
Sergeant.
WILLIAM HAMMERTON.
GEORGE GREENGOOSE.
Soldiers, and Attendants.

LUCE, *Daughter of Venturewell.*
MISTRESS MERRYTHOUGHT.
Woman, *supposed a captive.*
POMPIONA, *Daughter of the King of Moldavia.*

SCENE: *London and the neighbouring Country, excepting
Act IV. Scene ii., where it is in Moldavia*

THE KNIGHT OF THE BURNING
PESTLE

INDUCTION

Several Gentlemen *sitting on Stools upon the Stage. The*
Citizen, *his* Wife, *and* RALPH *sitting below among the
audience.*

Enter Speaker of the Prologue.

S. of Prol. " From all that's near the court, from all that's
  great,
    Within the compass of the city-walls—
    We now have brought our scene——"

Citizen *leaps on the Stage.*

Cit. Hold your peace, goodman boy!
S. of Prol. What do you mean, sir?
Cit. That you have no good meaning: this seven years there
  hath been plays at this house, I have observed it, you
  have still girds at citizens; and now you call your play
  " The London Merchant." Down with your title, boy!
  down with your title!
S. of Prol. Are you a member of the noble city?
Cit. I am.
S. of Prol. And a freeman?
Cit. Yea, and a grocer.
S. of Prol. So, grocer, then, by your sweet favour, we intend
  no abuse to the city.
Cit. No, sir! yes, sir: if you were not resolved to play the
  Jacks, what need you study for new subjects, purposely
  to abuse your betters? why could not you be contented,
  as well as others, with " The legend of Whittington," or
  " The Life and Death of Sir Thomas Gresham, with the
  building of the Royal Exchange," or " The story of
  Queen Eleanor, with the rearing of London Bridge upon
  woolsacks? "

7

S. of Prol. You seem to be an understanding man: what would you have us do, sir?

Cit. Why, present something notably in honour of the commons of the city.

S. of Prol. Why, what do you say to " The Life and Death of fat Drake, or the Repairing of Fleet-privies? "

Cit. I do not like that; but I will have a citizen, and he shall be of my own trade.

S. of Prol. Oh, you should have told us your mind a month since; our play is ready to begin now.

Cit. 'Tis all one for that; I will have a grocer, and he shall do admirable things.

S. of Prol. What will you have him do?

Cit. Marry, I will have him——

Wife. [*below.*] Husband, husband!

Ralph. [*below.*] Peace, mistress.

Wife. [*below.*] Hold thy peace, Ralph; I know what I do, I warrant ye.—Husband, husband!

Cit. What sayest thou, cony?

Wife. [*below.*] Let him kill a lion with a pestle, husband! let him kill a lion with a pestle!

Cit. So he shall.—I'll have him kill a lion with a pestle.

Wife. [*below.*] Husband! shall I come up, husband?

Cit. Ay, cony.—Ralph, help your mistress this way.—Pray, gentlemen, make her a little room.—I pray you, sir, lend me your hand to help up my wife: I thank you, sir.—So. [*Wife comes on the Stage.*

Wife. By your leave, gentlemen all; I'm something troublesome: I'm a stranger here; I was ne'er at one of these plays, as they say, before; but I should have seen " Jane Shore " once; and my husband hath promised me, any time this twelvemonth, to carry me to " The Bold Beauchamps," but in truth he did not. I pray you, bear with me.

Cit. Boy, let my wife and I have a couple of stools and then begin; and let the grocer do rare things.

[*Stools are brought.*

S. of Prol. But, sir, we have never a boy to play him: every one hath a part already.

Wife. Husband, husband, for God's sake, let Ralph play him! beshrew me, if I do not think he will go beyond them all.

Cit. Well remembered, wife.—Come up, Ralph.—I'll tell you, gentlemen; let them but lend him a suit of reparel and necessaries, and, by gad, if any of them all blow wind in the tail on him, I'll be hanged.

[*Ralph comes on the Stage.*

Wife. I pray you, youth, let him have a suit of reparel!— I'll be sworn, gentlemen, my husband tells you true: he will act you sometimes at our house, that all the neighbours cry out on him; he will fetch you up a couraging part so in the garret, that we are all as feared, I warrant you, that we quake again: we'll fear our children with him; if they be never so unruly, do but cry, " Ralph comes, Ralph comes ! " to them, and they'll be as quiet as lambs.—Hold up thy head, Ralph; show the gentlemen what thou canst do; speak a huffing part; I warrant you, the gentlemen will accept of it.

Cit. Do, Ralph, do.

Ralph. " By Heaven, methinks, it were an easy leap
   To pluck bright honour from the pale-faced moon;
   Or dive into the bottom of the sea,
   Where never fathom-line touched any ground,
   And pluck up drowned honour from the lake of hell."

Cit. How say you, gentlemen, is it not as I told you?

Wife. Nay, gentlemen, he hath played before, my husband says, Mucedorus, before the wardens of our company.

Cit. Ay, and he should have played Jeronimo with a shoe-maker for a wager.

S. of Prol. He shall have a suit of apparel, if he will go in.

Cit. In, Ralph, in, Ralph; and set out the grocery in their kind, if thou lovest me.   [*Exit Ralph.*

Wife. I warrant, our Ralph will look finely when he's dressed.

S. of Prol. But what will you have it called?

Cit. " The Grocer's Honour."

S. of Prol. Methinks " The Knight of the Burning Pestle " were better.

Wife. I'll be sworn, husband, that's as good a name as can be.

Cit. Let it be so.—Begin, begin; my wife and I will sit down.

S. of Prol. I pray you, do.

Cit. What stately music have you? you have shawms?

S. of Prol. Shawms! no.

Cit. No! I'm a thief, if my mind did not give me so.   Ralph plays a stately part, and he must needs have shawms: I'll be at the charge of them myself, rather than we'll be without them.

S. of Prol. So you are like to be.

Cit. Why, and so I will be: there's two shillings;—[*Gives money.*]—let's have the waits of Southwark; they are as rare fellows as any are in England; and that will fetch them all o'er the water with a vengeance, as if they were mad.

S. of Prol. You shall have them. Will you sit down, then?

Cit. Ay.—Come, wife.

Wife. Sit you merry all, gentlemen; I'm bold to sit amongst you for my ease. [*Citizen and Wife sit down.*

S. of Prol. "From all that's near the court, from all that's
    great,
Within the compass of the city-walls,
We now have brought our scene. Fly far from hence
All private taxes, immodest phrases,
Whatever may but show like vicious!
For wicked mirth never true pleasure brings,
But honest minds are pleased with honest things."—
Thus much for that we do; but for Ralph's part you
must answer for yourself.

Cit. Take you no care for Ralph; he'll discharge himself, I
warrant you. [*Exit Speaker of Prologue.*

Wife. I'faith, gentlemen, I'll give my word for Ralph.

ACT I

SCENE I.—*A Room in the House of Venturewell.*

Enter VENTUREWELL *and* JASPER.

Vent. Sirrah, I'll make you know you are my prentice,
And whom my charitable love redeemed
Even from the fall of fortune; gave thee heat
And growth, to be what now thou art, new-cast thee;
Adding the trust of all I have, at home,
In foreign staples, or upon the sea,
To thy direction; tied the good opinions
Both of myself and friends to thy endeavours;
So fair were thy beginnings. But with these,
As I remember, you had never charge
To love your master's daughter, and even then
When I had found a wealthy husband for her;
I take it, sir, you had not: but, however,

  I'll break the neck of that commission,
  And make you know you are but a merchant's factor.
Jasp. Sir, I do liberally confess I am yours,
  Bound both by love and duty to your service,
  In which my labour hath been all my profit:
  I have not lost in bargain, nor delighted
  To wear your honest gains upon my back;
  Nor have I given a pension to my blood,
  Or lavishly in play consumed your stock;
  These, and the miseries that do attend them,
  I dare with innocence proclaim are strangers
  To all my temperate actions. For your daughter,
  If there be any love to my deservings
  Borne by her virtuous self, I cannot stop it;
  Nor am I able to refrain her wishes,
  She's private to herself, and best of knowledge
  Whom she will make so happy as to sigh for:
  Besides, I cannot think you mean to match her
  Unto a fellow of so lame a presence,
  One that hath little left of nature in him.
Vent. 'Tis very well, sir: I can tell your wisdom
  How all this shall be cured.
Jasp. Your care becomes you.
Vent. And thus it shall be, sir: I here discharge you
  My house and service; take your liberty;
  And when I want a son, I'll send for you. *[Exit.*
Jasp. These be the fair rewards of them that love!
  Oh, you that live in freedom, never prove
  The travail of a mind led by desire!

Enter Luce.

Luce. Why, how now, friend? struck with my father's
  thunder!
Jasp. Struck, and struck dead, unless the remedy
  Be full of speed and virtue; I am now,
  What I expected long, no more your father's.
Luce. But mine.
Jasp. But yours, and only yours, I am;
  That's all I have to keep me from the statute.
  You dare be constant still?
Luce. Oh, fear me not!
  In this I dare be better than a woman:
  Nor shall his anger nor his offers move me,

Were they both equal to a prince's power.

Jasp. You know my rival!

Luce. Yes, and love him dearly;
 Even as I love an ague or foul weather:
 I prithee, Jasper, fear him not.

Jasp. Oh, no!
 I do not mean to do him so much kindness.
 But to our own desires: you know the plot
 We both agreed on?

Luce. Yes, and will perform
 My part exactly.

Jasp. I desire no more.
 Farewell, and keep my heart; 'tis yours.

Luce. I take it;
 He must do miracles makes me forsake it.

           [Exeunt severally.

[*Cit.* Fie upon 'em, little infidels! what a matter's here now!
 Well, I'll be hanged for a halfpenny, if there be not some
 abomination knavery in this play. Well; let 'em look
 to't; Ralph must come, and if there be any tricks
 a-brewing——

Wife. Let 'em brew and bake too, husband, a' God's name;
 Ralph will find all out, I warrant you, an they were older
 than they are.—[*Enter Boy.*]—I pray, my pretty youth,
 is Ralph ready?

Boy. He will be presently.

Wife. Now, I pray you, make my commendations unto him,
 and withal carry him this stick of liquorice: tell him his
 mistress sent it to him; and bid him bite a piece; 'twill
 open his pipes the better, say.]   [*Exit Boy.*

SCENE II.—*Another Room in the House of Venturewell.*

Enter VENTUREWELL *and* HUMPHREY.

Vent. Come, sir, she's yours; upon my faith, she's yours;
 You have my hand: for other idle lets
 Between your hopes and her, thus with a wind
 They are scattered and no more. My wanton prentice,
 That like a bladder blew himself with love,
 I have let out, and sent him to discover
 New masters yet unknown.

Hum. I thank you, sir,
 Indeed, I thank you, sir; and, ere I stir,

It shall be known, however you do deem,
    I am of gentle blood, and gentle seem.
Vent. Oh, sir, I know it certain.
Hum. Sir, my friend,
    Although, as writers say, all things have end,
    And that we call a pudding hath his two,
    Oh, let it not seem strange, I pray, to you,
    If in this bloody simile I put
    My love, more endless than frail things or gut!
[*Wife.* Husband, I prithee, sweet lamb, tell me one thing;
    but tell me truly.—Stay, youths, I beseech you, till I
    question my husband.
Cit. What is it, mouse?
Wife. Sirrah, didst thou ever see a prettier child? how it
    behaves itself, I warrant ye, and speaks and looks,
    and perts up the head!—I pray you, brother, with your
    favour, were you never none of Master Moncaster's
    scholars?
Cit. Chicken, I prithee heartily, contain thyself: the childer
    are pretty childer; but when Ralph comes, lamb——
Wife. Ay, when Ralph comes, cony!—Well, my youth, you
    may proceed.]
Vent. Well, sir, you know my love, and rest, I hope,
    Assured of my consent; get but my daughter's,
    And wed her when you please.   You must be bold,
    And clap in close unto her: come, I know
    You have language good enough to win a wench.
[*Wife.* A whoreson tyrant! h'as been an old stringer in's
    days, I warrant him.]
Hum. I take your gentle offer, and withal
    Yield love again for love reciprocal.
Vent. What, Luce! within there!

Enter Luce.

Luce. Called you, sir?
Vent. I did:
    Give entertainment to this gentleman;
    And see you be not froward.—To her, sir:
    My presence will but be an eye-sore to you.   [*Exit.*
Hum. Fair Mistress Luce, how do you? are you well?
    Give me your hand, and then I pray you tell
    How doth your little sister and your brother;
    And whether you love me or any other.

Luce. Sir, these are quickly answered.

Hum. So they are,
> Where women are not cruel.   But how far
> Is it now distant from the place we are in,
> Unto that blessèd place, your father's warren?

Luce. What makes you think of that, sir?

Hum. Even that face;
> For, stealing rabbits whilom in that place,
> God Cupid, or the keeper, I know not whether,
> Unto my cost and charges brought you thither,
> And there began——

Luce. Your game, sir.

Hum. Let no game,
> Or any thing that tendeth to the same,
> Be ever more remembered, thou fair killer,
> For whom I sate me down, and brake my tiller.

[*Wife.* There's a kind gentleman, I warrant you: when will
you do as much for me, George?]

Luce. Beshrew me, sir, I am sorry for your losses,
> But, as the proverb says, I cannot cry:
> I would you had not seen me!

Hum. So would I,
> Unless you had more maw to do me good.

Luce. Why, cannot this strange passion be withstood;
> Send for a constable, and raise the town.

Hum. Oh, no! my valiant love will batter down
> Millions of constables, and put to flight
> Even that great watch of Midsummer-day at night.

Luce. Beshrew me, sir, 'twere good I yielded, then;
> Weak women cannot hope, where valiant men
> Have no resistance.

Hum. Yield, then; I am full
> Of pity, though I say it, and can pull
> Out of my pocket thus a pair of gloves.
> Look, Lucé, look; the dog's tooth nor the dove's
> Are not so white as these; and sweet they be,
> And whipt about with silk, as you may see.
> If you desire the price, shoot from your eye
> A beam to this place, and you shall espy
> F S, which is to say, my sweetest honey,
> They cost me three and twopence, or no money.

Luce. Well, sir, I take them kindly, and I thank you:
> What would you more?

Hum. Nothing.

Luce. Why, then, farewell.

Hum. Nor so, nor so; for, lady, I must tell,
    Before we part, for what we met together:
    God grant me time and patience and fair weather!

Luce. Speak, and declare your mind in terms so brief.

Hum. I shall: then, first and foremost, for relief
    I call to you, if that you can afford it;
    I care not at what price, for, on my word, it
    Shall be repaid again, although it cost me
    More than I'll speak of now; for love hath tost me
    In furious blanket like a tennis-ball,
    And now I rise aloft, and now I fall.

Luce. Alas, good gentleman, alas the day!

Hum. I thank you heartily; and, as I say,
    Thus do I still continue without rest,
    I' the morning like a man, at night a beast,
    Roaring and bellowing mine own disquiet,
    That much I fear, forsaking of my diet
    Will bring me presently to that quandary,
    I shall bid all adieu.

Luce. Now, by St. Mary,
    That were great pity!

Hum. So it were, beshrew me;
    Then, ease me, lusty Luce, and pity show me.

Luce. Why, sir, you know my will is nothing worth
    Without my father's grant; get his consent,
    And then you may with assurance try me.

Hum. The worshipful your sire will not deny me;
    For I have asked him, and he hath replied,
    " Sweet Master Humphrey, Luce shall be thy bride."

Luce. Sweet Master Humphrey, then I am content.

Hum. And so am I, in truth.

Luce. Yet take me with you;
    There is another clause must be annexed,
    And this it is: I swore, and will perform it,
    No man shall ever joy me as his wife
    But he that stole me hence. If you dare venture,
    I am yours (you need not fear; my father loves you);
    If not, farewell for ever!

Hum. Stay, nymph, stay:
    I have a double gelding, coloured bay,
    Sprung by his father from Barbarian kind;

    Another for myself, though somewhat blind,
    Yet true as trusty tree.
Luce. I am satisfied;
    And so I give my hand.   Our course must lie
    Through Waltham forest, where I have a friend
    Will entertain us.   So, farewell, Sir Humphrey,
    And think upon your business.   *[Exit.*
Hum. Though I die,
    I am resolved to venture life and limb
    For one so young, so fair, so kind, so trim.   *[Exit.*
[*Wife.* By my faith and troth, George, and as I am virtuous,
    it is e'en the kindest young man that ever trod on shoe-
    leather.—Well, go thy ways; if thou hast her not, 'tis
    not thy fault, i'faith.
Cit. I prithee, mouse, be patient; 'a shall have her, or I'll
    make some of 'em smoke for't.
Wife. That's my good lamb, George.—Fie, this stinking
    tobacco kills me! would there were none in England!—
    Now, I pray, gentlemen, what good does this stinking
    tobacco do you? nothing, I warrant you: make chim-
    neys o' your faces!]

SCENE III.—*A Grocer's Shop.*

Enter RALPH, *as a Grocer, reading* Palmerin of England,
with TIM *and* GEORGE.

[*Wife.* Oh, husband, husband, now, now! there's Ralph,
    there's Ralph.
Cit. Peace, fool! let Ralph alone.—Hark you, Ralph; do
    not strain yourself too much at the first.—Peace!—
    Begin, Ralph.]
Ralph. [*Reads.*] Then Palmerin and Trineus, snatching their
    lances from their dwarfs, and clasping their helmets,
    galloped amain after the giant; and Palmerin, having
    gotten a sight of him, came posting amain, saying,
    " Stay, traitorous thief! for thou mayst not so carry
    away her, that is worth the greatest lord in the world; "
    and, with these words, gave him a blow on the shoulder,
    that he struck him besides his elephant. And Trineus,
    coming to the knight that had Agricola behind him, set
    him soon besides his horse, with his neck broken in the
    fall; so that the princess, getting out of the throng, between
    joy and grief, said, " All happy knight, the mirror of all

such as follow arms, now may I be well assured of the love thou bearest me." I wonder why the kings do not raise an army of fourteen or fifteen hundred thousand men, as big as the army that the Prince of Portigo brought against Rosicleer, and destroy these giants; they do much hurt to wandering damsels, that go in quest of their knights.

[*Wife*. Faith, husband, and Ralph says true; for they say the King of Portugal cannot sit at his meat, but the giants and the ettins will come and snatch it from him.

Cit. Hold thy tongue.—On, Ralph!]

Ralph. And certainly those knights are much to be commended, who, neglecting their possessions, wander with a squire and a dwarf through the deserts to relieve poor ladies.

[*Wife*. Ay, by my faith, are they, Ralph; let 'em say what they will, they are indeed. Our knights neglect their possessions well enough, but they do not the rest.]

Ralph. There are no such courteous and fair well-spoken knights in this age: they will call one " the son of a whore," that Palmerin of England would have called " fair sir; " and one that Rosicleer would have called " right beauteous damsel," they will call " damned bitch."

[*Wife*. I'll be sworn will they, Ralph; they have called me so an hundred times about a scurvy pipe of tobacco.]

Ralph. But what brave spirit could be content to sit in his shop, with a flappet of wood, and a blue apron before him, selling mithridatum and dragon's-water to visited houses, that might pursue feats of arms, and, through his noble achievements, procure such a famous history to be written of his heroic prowess?

[*Cit*. Well said, Ralph; some more of those words, Ralph!

Wife. They go finely, by my troth.]

Ralph. Why should not I, then, pursue this course, both for the credit of myself and our company? for amongst all the worthy books of achievements, I do not call to mind that I yet read of a grocer-errant: I will be the said knight.—Have you heard of any that hath wandered unfurnished of his squire and dwarf? My elder prentice Tim shall be my trusty squire, and little George my dwarf. Hence, my blue apron! Yet, in remembrance of my former trade, upon my shield shall be portrayed a Burning Pestle, and I will be called the Knight of the Burning Pestle.

[*Wife.* Nay, I dare swear thou wilt not forget thy old trade; thou wert ever meek.]

Ralph. Tim!

Tim. Anon.

Ralph. My beloved squire, and George my dwarf, I charge you that from henceforth you never call me by any other name but "the right courteous and valiant Knight of the Burning Pestle;" and that you never call any female by the name of a woman or wench, but "fair lady," if she have her desires, if not, "distressed damsel;" that you call all forests and heaths "deserts," and all horses "palfreys."

[*Wife.* This is very fine, faith.—Do the gentleman like Ralph, think you, husband?

Cit. Ay, I warrant thee; the players would give all the shoes in their shop for him.]

Ralph. My beloved squire Tim, stand out. Admit this were a desert, and over it a knight-errant pricking, and I should bid you inquire of his intents, what would you say?

Tim. Sir, my master sent me to know whither you are riding?

Ralph. No, thus: "Fair sir, the right courteous and valiant Knight of the Burning Pestle commanded me to inquire upon what adventure you are bound, whether to relieve some distressed damsel, or otherwise."

[*Cit.* Whoreson blockhead, cannot remember!

Wife. I'faith, and Ralph told him on't before: all the gentlemen heard him.—Did he not, gentlemen? did not Ralph tell him on't?]

George. Right courteous and valiant Knight of the Burning Pestle, here is a distressed damsel to have a halfpenny-worth of pepper.

[*Wife.* That's a good boy! see, the little boy can hit it; by my troth, it's a fine child.]

Ralph. Relieve her, with all courteous language. Now shut up shop; no more my prentices, but my trusty squire and dwarf. I must bespeak my shield and arming pestle. [*Exeunt Tim and George.*

[*Cit.* Go thy ways, Ralph! As I'm a true man, thou art the best on 'em all.

Wife. Ralph, Ralph!
Ralph. What say you, mistress?
Wife. I prithee, come again quickly, sweet Ralph.
Ralph. By and by.]   [*Exit.*

SCENE IV.—*A Room in Merrythought's House.*

Enter Mistress MERRYTHOUGHT *and* JASPER.

Mist. Mer. Give thee my blessing! no, I'll ne'er give thee
   my blessing; I'll see thee hanged first; it shall ne'er
   be said I gave thee my blessing.   Thou art thy father's
   own son, of the right blood of the Merrythoughts.   I
   may curse the time that e'er I knew thy father; he hath
   spent all his own and mine too; and when I tell him of
   it, he laughs, and dances, and sings, and cries, " A merry
   heart lives long-a."   And thou art a wastethrift, and
   art run away from thy master that loved thee well, and
   art come to me; and I have laid up a little for my
   younger son Michael, and thou thinkest to bezzle that,
   but thou shalt never be able to do it.—Come hither,
   Michael!

Enter MICHAEL.

Come, Michael, down on thy knees; thou shalt have
   my blessing.
Mich. [*Kneels.*] I pray you, mother, pray to God to bless me.
Mist. Mer. God bless thee! but Jasper shall never have my
   blessing; he shall be hanged first: shall he not, Michael?
   how sayest thou?
Mich. Yes, forsooth, mother, and grace of God.
Mist. Mer. That's a good boy!
[*Wife.* I'faith, it's a fine-spoken child.]
Jasp. Mother, though you forget a parent's love
   I must preserve the duty of a child.
   I ran not from my master, nor return
   To have your stock maintain my idleness.
[*Wife.* Ungracious child, I warrant him; hark, how he chops
   logic with his mother!—Thou hadst best tell her she
   lies; do, tell her she lies.
Cit. If he were my son, I would hang him up by the heels,
   and flay him, and salt him, whoreson haltersack.]
Jasp. My coming only is to beg your love,
   Which I must ever, though I never gain it;

And, howsoever you esteem of me,
There is no drop of blood hid in these veins
But, I remember well, belongs to you
That brought me forth, and would be glad for you
To rip them all again, and let it out.

Mist. Mer. I'faith, I had sorrow enough for thee, God knows;
but I'll hamper thee well enough.   Get thee in, thou
vagabond, get thee in, and learn of thy brother Michael.

[*Exeunt Jasper and Michael.*

Mer. [*Singing within.*]

> Nose, nose, jolly red nose,
> And who gave thee this jolly red nose?

Mist. Mer. Hark, my husband! he's singing and hoiting;
and I'm fain to cark and care, and all little enough.—
Husband! Charles! Charles Merrythought!

Enter MERRYTHOUGHT.

Mer. [*Sings.*]

> Nutmegs and ginger, cinnamon and cloves;
> And they gave me this jolly red nose.

Mist. Mer. If you would consider your state, you would have
little list to sing, i-wis.

Mer. It should never be considered, while it were an estate,
if I thought it would spoil my singing.

Mist. Mer. But how wilt thou do, Charles? thou art an old
man, and thou canst not work, and thou hast not forty
shillings left, and thou eatest good meat, and drinkest
good drink, and laughest.

Mer. And will do.

Mist. Mer. But how wilt thou come by it, Charles?

Mer. How! why, how have I done hitherto these forty years?
I never came into my dining room, but, at eleven and
six o'clock, I found excellent meat and drink o' the
table; my clothes were never worn out, but next morning a tailor brought me a new suit: and without question
it will be so ever; use makes perfectness.   If all should
fail, it is but a little straining myself extraordinary, and
laugh myself to death.

[*Wife.* It's a foolish old man this; is not he, George?
Cit. Yes, cony.
Wife. Give me a penny i' the purse while I live, George.
Cit. Ay, by lady, cony, hold thee there.]

Mist. Mer. Well, Charles; you promised to provide for

Jasper, and I have laid up for Michael. I pray you, pay Jasper his portion: he's come home, and he shall not consume Michael's stock; he says his master turned him away, but, I promise you truly, I think he ran away.

[*Wife.* No, indeed, Mistress Merrythought; though he be a notable gallows, yet I'll assure you his master did turn him away, even in this place; 'twas, i'faith, within this half-hour, about his daughter; my husband was by.

Cit. Hang him, rogue! he served him well enough: love his master's daughter! By my troth, cony, if there were a thousand boys, thou wouldst spoil them all with taking their parts; let his mother alone with him.

Wife. Ay, George; but yet truth is truth.]

Mer. Where is Jasper? he's welcome, however. Call him in; he shall have his portion. Is he merry?

Mist. Mer. Ah, foul chive him, he is too merry!—Jasper! Michael!

Re-enter JASPER *and* MICHAEL.

Mer. Welcome, Jasper! though thou runnest away, welcome! God bless thee! 'Tis thy mother's mind thou shouldst receive thy portion; thou hast been abroad, and I hope hast learned experience enough to govern it; thou art of sufficient years; hold thy hand—one, two, three, four, five, six, seven, eight, nine, there is ten shillings for thee. [*Gives money.*] Thrust thyself into the world with that, and take some settled course: if fortune cross thee, thou hast a retiring place; come home to me; I have twenty shillings left. Be a good husband; that is, wear ordinary clothes, eat the best meat, and drink the best drink; be merry, and give to the poor, and, believe me, thou hast no end of thy goods.

Jasp. Long may you live free from all thought of ill,
And long have cause to be thus merry still!
But, father——

Mer. No more words, Jasper; get thee gone.
Thou hast my blessing; thy father's spirit upon thee!
Farewell, Jasper!   [*Sings.*

But yet, or ere you part (oh, cruel!)
Kiss me, kiss me, sweeting, mine own dear jewel!

So, now begone; no words.   [*Exit Jasper.*

Mist. Mer. So, Michael, now get thee gone too.

Mich. Yes, forsooth, mother; but I'll have my father's blessing first.

Mist. Mer. No, Michael; 'tis no matter for his blessing; thou hast my blessing; begone. I'll fetch my money and jewels, and follow thee; I'll stay no longer with him, I warrant thee. [*Exit Michael.*]—Truly, Charles, I'll be gone too.

Mer. What! you will not?

Mist. Mer. Yes, indeed will I.

Mer. [*Sings.*]

> Heigh-ho, farewell, Nan!
> I'll never trust wench more again, if I can.

Mist. Mer. You shall not think, when all your own is gone, to spend that I have been scraping up for Michael.

Mer. Farewell, good wife; I expect it not: all I have to do in this world, is to be merry; which I shall, if the ground be not taken from me; and if it be,   [*Sings.*

> When earth and seas from me are reft,
> The skies aloft for me are left.

[*Exeunt severally.*

[*Wife.* I'll be sworn he's a merry old gentleman for all that. [*Music.*] Hark, hark, husband, hark! fiddles, fiddles! now surely they go finely. They say 'tis present death for these fiddlers, to tune their rebecks before the great Turk's grace; it's not, George? [*Enter a Boy and dances.*] But, look, look! here's a youth dances!— Now, good youth, do a turn o' the toe.—Sweetheart, i'faith, I'll have Ralph come and do some of his gambols. —He'll ride the wild mare, gentlemen, 'twould do your hearts good to see him.—I thank you, kind youth; pray, bid Ralph come.

Cit. Peace, cony!—Sirrah, you scurvy boy, bid the players send Ralph; or, by God's——an they do not, I'll tear some of their periwigs beside their heads: this is all riff-raff.]

[*Exit Boy.*

ACT II

SCENE I.—*A Room in the House of Venturewell.*

Enter VENTUREWELL *and* HUMPHREY.

Vent. And how, faith, how goes it now, son Humphrey?

Hum. Right worshipful, and my belovèd friend
And father dear, this matter's at an end.

Vent. 'Tis well: it should be so: I'm glad the girl
Is found so tractable.

Hum. Nay, she must whirl
From hence (and you must wink; for so, I say,
The story tells,) to-morrow before day.

[*Wife.* George, dost thou think in thy conscience now 'twill
be a match? tell me but what thou thinkest, sweet
rogue. Thou seest the poor gentleman, dear heart,
how it labours and throbs, I warrant you, to be at rest!
I'll go move the father for't.

Cit. No, no; I prithee, sit still, honeysuckle; thou'lt spoil
all. If he deny him, I'll bring half-a-dozen good fellows
myself, and in the shutting of an evening, knock't up,
and there's an end.

Wife. I'll buss thee for that, i'faith, boy. Well, George,
well, you have been a wag in your days, I warrant
you; but God forgive you, and I do with all my heart.]

Vent. How was it, son? you told me that to-morrow
Before day-break, you must convey her hence.

Hum. I must, I must; and thus it is agreed:
Your daughter rides upon a brown-bay steed,
I on a sorrel, which I bought of Brian,
The honest host of the Red roaring Lion,
In Waltham situate. Then, if you may,
Consent in seemly sort; lest, by delay,
The Fatal Sisters come, and do the office,
And then you'll sing another song.

Vent. Alas,
Why should you be thus full of grief to me,
That do as willing as yourself agree
To any thing, so it be good and fair?
Then, steal her when you will, if such a pleasure
Content you both; I'll sleep and never see it,
To make your joys more full. But tell me why

You may not here perform your marriage?

[*Wife.* God's blessing o' thy soul, old man! i'faith, thou art
loath to part true hearts. I see 'a has her, George; and
I'm as glad on't!—Well, go thy ways, Humphrey, for a
fair-spoken man; I believe thou hast not thy fellow
within the walls of London; an I should say the suburbs
too, I should not lie.—Why dost not rejoice with me,
George?

Cit. If I could but see Ralph again, I were as merry as mine
host, i'faith.]

Hum. The cause you seem to ask, I thus declare—
Help me, O Muses nine! Your daughter sware
A foolish oath, and more it was the pity;
Yet no one but myself within this city
Shall dare to say so, but a bold defiance
Shall meet him, were he of the noble science;
And yet she sware, and yet why did she sware?
Truly, I cannot tell, unless it were
For her own ease; for, sure, sometimes an oath,
Being sworn thereafter, is like cordial broth;
And this it was she swore, never to marry
But such a one whose mighty arm could carry
(As meaning me, for I am such a one)
Her bodily away, through stick and stone,
Till both of us arrive, at her request,
Some ten miles off, in the wild Waltham forest.

Vent. If this be all, you shall not need to fear
Any denial in your love: proceed;
I'll neither follow, nor repent the deed.

Hum. Good night, twenty good nights, and twenty more,
And twenty more good nights,—that makes three-score!
[*Exeunt severally.*

SCENE II.—*Waltham Forest.*

Enter Mistress MERRYTHOUGHT *and* MICHAEL.

Mist. Mer. Come, Michael; art thou not weary, boy?

Mich. No, forsooth, mother, not I.

Mist. Mer. Where be we now, child?

Mich. Indeed, forsooth, mother, I cannot tell, unless we be
at Mile-End: Is not all the world Mile-End, mother?

Mist. Mer. No, Michael, not all the world, boy; but I can
assure thee, Michael, Mile End is a goodly matter: there

has been a pitchfield, my child, between the naughty
Spaniels and the Englishmen; and the Spaniels ran
away, Michael, and the Englishmen followed: my
neighbour Coxstone was there, boy, and killed them all
with a birding-piece.

Mich. Mother, forsooth——

Mist. Mer. What says my white boy?

Mich. Shall not my father go with us too?

Mist. Mer. No, Michael, let thy father go snick-up; he
shall never come between a pair of sheets with me again
while he lives; let him stay at home, and sing for his
supper, boy. Come, child, sit down, and I'll show my
boy fine knacks, indeed. [*They sit down: and she takes
out a casket.*] Look here, Michael; here's a ring, and
here's a brooch, and here's a bracelet, and here's two
rings more, and here's money and gold by th'eye, my boy.

Mich. Shall I have all this, mother?

Mist. Mer. Ay, Michael, thou shalt have all, Michael.

[*Cit.* How likest thou this, wench?

Wife. I cannot tell; I would have Ralph, George; I'll see
no more else, indeed, la; and I pray you, let the youths
understand so much by word of mouth; for, I tell you
truly, I'm afraid o' my boy. Come, come, George, let's
be merry and wise: the child's a fatherless child; and
say they should put him into a strait pair of gaskins,
'twere worse than knot-grass; he would never grow
after it.]

Enter RALPH, TIM, *and* GEORGE.

[*Cit.* Here's Ralph, here's Ralph!

Wife. How do you do, Ralph? you are welcome, Ralph, as
I may say; it's a good boy, hold up thy head, and be
not afraid; we are thy friends, Ralph; the gentlemen
will praise thee, Ralph, if thou playest thy part with
audacity. Begin, Ralph, a' God's name!]

Ralph. My trusty squire, unlace my helm: give me my hat.
Where are we, or what desert may this be?

George. Mirror of knighthood, this is, as I take it, the perilous
Waltham-down; in whose bottom stands the enchanted
valley.

Mist. Mer. Oh, Michael, we are betrayed, we are betrayed!
here be giants! Fly, boy! fly, boy, fly!
               [*Exit with Michael leaving the casket.*

Ralph. Lace on my helm again.   What noise is this?
　　A gentle lady, flying the embrace
　　Of some uncourteous knight!   I will relieve her.
　　Go, squire, and say, the Knight, that wears this Pestle
　　In honour of all ladies, swears revenge
　　Upon that recreant coward that pursues her;
　　Go, comfort her, and that same gentle squire
　　That bears her company.
Tim. I go, brave knight.　　　　　　　　　　　　*[Exit.*
Ralph. My trusty dwarf and friend, reach me my shield;
　　And hold it while I swear.   First, by my knighthood;
　　Then by the soul of Amadis de Gaul,
　　My famous ancestor;   then by my sword
　　The beauteous Brionella girt about me;
　　By this bright burning Pestle, of mine honour
　　The living trophy;   and by all respect
　　Due to distressèd damsels;   here I vow
　　Never to end the quest of this fair lady
　　And that forsaken squire till by my valour
　　I gain their liberty!
George. Heaven bless the knight
　　That thus relieves poor errant gentlewomen!   *[Exeunt.*
[*Wife.* Ay, marry, Ralph, this has some savour in't; I would
　　see the proudest of them all offer to carry his books after
　　him.   But, George, I will not have him go away so soon;
　　I shall be sick if he go away, that I shall: call Ralph
　　again, George, call Ralph again; I prithee, sweetheart,
　　let him come fight before me, and let's ha' some drums
　　and some trumpets, and let him kill all that comes near
　　him, an thou lovest me, George!
Cit. Peace a little, bird: he shall kill them all, an they were
　　twenty more on 'em than there are.]

Enter JASPER.

Jasp. Now, Fortune, if thou be'st not only ill,
　　Show me thy better face, and bring about
　　Thy desperate wheel, that I may climb at length,
　　And stand.   This is our place of meeting,
　　If love have any constancy.   Oh, age,
　　Where only wealthy men are counted happy!
　　How shall I please thee, how deserve thy smiles,
　　When I am only rich in misery?
　　My father's blessing and this little coin

Is my inheritance; a strong revénue!
From earth thou art, and to the earth I give thee:
                              [*Throws away the money.*
There grow and multiply, whilst fresher air
Breeds me a fresher fortune.—How! illusion?
                              [*Sees the casket.*
What, hath the devil coined himself before me?
'Tis metal good, it rings well; I am waking,
And taking too, I hope.   Now, God's dear blessing
Upon his heart that left it here! 'tis mine;
These pearls, I take it, were not left for swine.
                              [*Exit with the casket.*

[*Wife.* I do not like that this unthrifty youth should embezzle away the money; the poor gentlewoman his
mother will have a heavy heart for it, God knows.

Cit. And reason good, sweetheart.

Wife. But let him go; I'll tell Ralph a tale in's ear shall
fetch him again with a wanion, I warrant him, if he be
above ground; and besides, George, here are a number
of sufficient gentlemen can witness, and myself, and
yourself, and the musicians, if we be called in question.

SCENE III.—*Another part of the Forest.*

Enter RALPH *and* GEORGE.

But here comes Ralph, George; thou shalt hear him
speak as he were an emperal.]

Ralph. Comes not sir squire again?

George. Right courteous knight,
    Your squire doth come, and with him comes the lady,
    For and the Squire of Damsels, as I take it.

Enter TIM, Mistress MERRYTHOUGHT, *and* MICHAEL.

Ralph. Madam, if any service or devoir
    Of a poor errant knight may right your wrongs,
    Command it; I am prest to give you succour;
    For to that holy end I bear my armour.

Mist. Mer. Alas, sir, I am a poor gentlewoman, and I have
    lost my money in this forest!

Ralph. Desert, you would say, lady; and not lost
    Whilst I have sword and lance.   Dry up your tears,
    Which ill befit the beauty of that face,

And tell the story, if I may request it,
Of your disastrous fortune.

Mist. Mer. Out, alas! I left a thousand pound, a thousand
pound, e'en all the money I had laid up for this youth,
upon the sight of your mastership; you looked so grim,
and, as I may say it, saving your presence, more like
a giant than a mortal man.

Ralph. I am as you are, lady; so are they;
All mortal. But why weeps this gentle squire?

Mist. Mer. Has he not cause to weep, do you think, when
he hath lost his inheritance?

Ralph. Young hope of valour, weep not; I am here
That will confound thy foe, and pay it dear
Upon his coward head, that dares deny
Distressèd squires and ladies equity.
I have but one horse, on which shall ride
This fair lady behind me, and before
This courteous squire: fortune will give us more
Upon our next adventure. Fairly speed
Beside us, squire and dwarf, to do us need! [*Exeunt.*

[*Cit.* Did not I tell you, Nell, what your man would do? by
the faith of my body, wench, for clean action and good
delivery, they may all cast their caps at him.

Wife. And so they may, i'faith; for I dare speak it boldly,
the twelve companies of London cannot match him,
timber for timber. Well, George, an he be not inveigled
by some of these paltry players, I ha' much marvel: but,
George, we ha' done our parts, if the boy have any grace
to be thankful.

Cit. Yes, I warrant thee, duckling.]

SCENE IV.—*Another part of the Forest.*

Enter HUMPHREY *and* LUCE.

Hum. Good Mistress Luce, however I in fault am
For your lame horse, you're welcome unto Waltham;
But which way now to go, or what to say,
I know not truly, till it be broad day.

Luce. Oh, fear not, Master Humphrey; I am guide
For this place good enough.

Hum. Then, up and ride;
Or, if it please you, walk, for your repose,
Or sit, or, if you will, go pluck a rose;

Either of which shall be indifferent
To your good friend and Humphrey, whose consent
Is so entangled ever to your will,
As the poor harmless horse is to the mill.

Luce. Faith, an you say the word, we'll e'en sit down,
And take a nap.

Hum. 'Tis better in the town,
Where we may nap together; for, believe me,
To sleep without a snatch would mickle grieve me.

Luce. You're merry, Master Humphrey.

Hum. So I am,
And have been ever merry from my dam.

Luce. Your nurse had the less labour.

Hum. Faith, it may be,
Unless it were by chance I did beray me.

Enter JASPER.

Jasp. Luce! dear friend Luce!

Luce. Here, Jasper.

Jasp. You are mine.

Hum. If it be so, my friend, you use me fine:
What do you think I am?

Jasp. An arrant noddy.

Hum. A word of obloquy! Now, by God's body,
I'll tell thy master; for I know thee well.

Jasp. Nay, an you be so forward for to tell,
Take that, and that; and tell him, sir, I gave it:
And say, I paid you well.   [*Beats him.*

Hum. Oh, sir, I have it,
And do confess the payment! Pray, be quiet.

Jasp. Go, get you to your night-cap and the diet,
To cure your beaten bones.

Luce. Alas, poor Humphrey;
Get thee some wholesome broth, with sage and comfrey;
A little oil of roses and a feather
To 'noint thy back withal.

Hum. When I came hither,
Would I had gone to Paris with John Dory!

Luce. Farewell, my pretty nump; I am very sorry I cannot
bear thee company.

Hum. Farewell:
The devil's dam was ne'er so banged in hell.
                        [*Exeunt Luce and Jasper.*

[*Wife*. This young Jasper will prove me another thing, o'
my conscience, an he may be suffered. George, dost
not see, George, how 'a swaggers, and flies at the very
heads o' folks, as he were a dragon? Well, if I do not
do his lesson for wronging the poor gentleman, I am no
true woman. His friends that brought him up might
have been better occupied, i-wis, than have taught him
these fegaries: he's e'en in the high way to the gallows,
God bless him!

Cit. You're too bitter, cony; the young man may do well
enough for all this.

Wife. Come hither, Master Humphrey; has he hurt you?
now, beshrew his fingers for't! Here, sweetheart, here's
some green ginger for thee. Now, beshrew my heart,
but 'a has peppernel in's head, as big as a pullet's egg!
Alas, sweet lamb, how thy temples beat! Take the
peace on him, sweetheart, take the peace on him.

Cit. No, no; you talk like a foolish woman: I'll ha' Ralph
fight with him, and swinge him up well-favouredly.—
Sirrah boy, come hither. [*Enter Boy*.] Let Ralph
come in and fight with Jasper.

Wife. Ay, and beat him well; he's an unhappy boy.

Boy. Sir, you must pardon; the plot of our play lies contrary; and 'twill hazard the spoiling of our play.

Cit. Plot me no plots! I'll ha' Ralph come out; I'll make
your house too hot for you else.

Boy. Why, sir, he shall; but if any thing fall out of order,
the gentlemen must pardon us.

Cit. Go your ways, goodman boy! [*Exit Boy*.] I'll hold
him a penny, he shall have his bellyful of fighting now.
Ho, here comes Ralph! no more!]

SCENE V.—*Another part of the Forest.*

Enter RALPH, Mistress MERRYTHOUGHT, MICHAEL,
TIM, *and* GEORGE.

Ralph. What knight is that, squire? ask him if he keep
  The passage, bound by love of lady fair,
  Or else but prickant.

Hum. Sir, I am no knight,
  But a poor gentleman, that this same night
  Had stolen from me, on yonder green,
  My lovely wife, and suffered (to be seen

Yet extant on my shoulders) such a greeting,
That whilst I live I shall think of that meeting.
[*Wife.* Ay, Ralph, he beat him unmercifully, Ralph; an
thou sparest him, Ralph, I would thou wert hanged.
Cit. No more, wife, no more.]
Ralph. Where is the caitiff-wretch hath done this deed?
Lady, your pardon; that I may proceed
Upon the quest of this injurious knight.—
And thou, fair squire, repute me not the worse,
In leaving the great venture of the purse
And the rich casket, till some better leisure.
Hum. Here comes the broker hath purloined my treasure.

Enter JASPER *and* LUCE.

Ralph. Go, squire, and tell him I am here,
An errant knight-at-arms, to crave delivery
Of that fair lady to her own knight's arms.
If he deny, bid him take choice of ground,
And so defy him.
Tim. From the Knight that bears
The Golden Pestle, I defy thee, knight,
Unless thou make fair restitution
Of that bright lady.
Jasp. Tell the knight that sent thee,
He is an ass; and I will keep the wench,
And knock his head-piece.
Ralph. Knight, thou art but dead,
If thou recall not thy uncourteous terms.
[*Wife.* Break's pate, Ralph; break's pate, Ralph, soundly!]
Jasp. Come, knight; I am ready for you.   Now your Pestle
                              [*Snatches away his pestle.*
Shall try what temper, sir, your mortar's of.
With that he stood upright in his stirrups, and gave the
Knight of the calf-skin such a knock [*Knocks Ralph
down.*] that he forsook his horse, and down he fell; and
then he leaped upon him, and plucking off his helmet——
Hum. Nay, an my noble knight be down so soon,
Though I can scarcely go, I needs must run.   [*Exit.*
[*Wife.* Run, Ralph, run, Ralph; run for thy life, boy;
Jasper comes, Jasper comes!]   [*Exit Ralph.*
Jasp. Come, Luce, we must have other arms for you:
Humphrey, and Golden Pestle, both adieu! [*Exeunt.*
[*Wife.* Sure the devil (God bless us!) is in this springald!

Why, George, didst ever see such a fire-drake? I am
afraid my boy's miscarried: if he be, though he were
Master Merrythought's son a thousand times, if there be
any law in England, I'll make some of them smart for't.

Cit. No, no; I have found out the matter, sweetheart; as
sure as we are here, he is enchanted: he could no more
have stood in Ralph's hands than I can in my lord
mayor's. I'll have a ring to discover all enchantments,
and Ralph shall beat him yet: be no more vexed, for it
shall be so.]

SCENE VI.—*Before the Bell Inn, Waltham.*

Enter RALPH, Mistress MERRYTHOUGHT, MICHAEL,
TIM, *and* GEORGE.

[*Wife.* Oh, husband, here's Ralph again!—Stay, Ralph
again, let me speak with thee. How dost thou, Ralph?
art thou not shrewdly hurt? the foul great lungies laid
unmercifully on thee: there's some sugar-candy for
thee. Proceed; thou shalt have another bout with him.

Cit. If Ralph had him at the fencing-school, if he did not
make a puppy of him, and drive him up and down the
school, he should ne'er come in my shop more.]

Mist. Mer. Truly, Master Knight of the Burning Pestle, I
am weary.

Mich. Indeed, la, mother, and I am very hungry.

Ralph. Take comfort, gentle dame, and you, fair squire;
For in this desert there must needs be placed
Many strong castles, held by courteous knights;
And till I bring you safe to one of those,
I swear by this my order ne'er to leave you.

[*Wife.* Well said, Ralph!—George, Ralph was ever comfortable, was he not?

Cit. Yes, duck.

Wife. I shall ne'er forget him. When he had lost our child,
(you know it was strayed almost alone to Puddle Wharf,
and the criers were abroad for it, and there it had
drowned itself but for a sculler,) Ralph was the most
comfortablest to me: " Peace, mistress," says he, " let
it go; I'll get you another as good." Did he not,
George, did he not say so?

Cit. Yes, indeed did he, mouse.]

George. I would we had a mess of pottage and a pot of drink,
    squire, and were going to bed!

Tim. Why, we are at Waltham town's end, and that's the
    Bell Inn.

George. Take courage, valiant knight, damsel, and squire!
    I have discovered, not a stone's cast off,
    An ancient castle, held by the old knight
    Of the most holy order of the Bell,
    Who gives to all knights-errant entertain:
    There plenty is of food, and all prepared
    By the white hands of his own lady dear.
    He hath three squires that welcome all his guests;
    The first, hight Chamberlino, who will see
    Our beds prepared, and bring us snowy sheets,
    Where never footman stretched his buttered hams;
    The second, hight Tapstero, who will see
    Our pots full filled, and no froth therein;
    The third, a gentle squire, Ostlero hight,
    Who will our palfreys slick with wisps of straw,
    And in the manger put them oats enough,
    And never grease their teeth with candle-snuff.

[*Wife.* That same dwarf's a pretty boy, but the squire's a
    groutnol.]

Ralph. Knock at the gates, my squire, with stately lance.
                  [*Tim knocks at the door.*

Enter Tapster.

Tap. Who's there?—You're welcome, gentlemen: will you
    see a room?

George. Right courteous and valiant Knight of the Burning
    Pestle, this is the Squire Tapstero.

Ralph. Fair Squire Tapstero, I a wandering knight,
    Hight of the Burning Pestle, in the quest
    Of this fair lady's casket and wrought purse,
    Losing myself in this vast wilderness,
    Am to this castle well by fortune brought;
    Where, hearing of the goodly entertain
    Your knight of holy order of the Bell
    Gives to all damsels and all errant knights,
    I thought to knock, and now am bold to enter.

Tap. An't please you see a chamber, you are very welcome.
                     [*Exeunt.*

[*Wife.* George, I would have something done, and I cannot
　　tell what it is.

Cit. What is it, Nell?

Wife. Why, George, shall Ralph beat nobody again? prithee,
　　sweetheart, let him.

Cit. So he shall, Nell; and if I join with him, we'll knock
　　them all.]

SCENE VII.—*A Room in the House of Venturewell.*

Enter HUMPHREY *and* VENTUREWELL.

[*Wife.* Oh, George, here's Master Humphrey again now that
　　lost Mistress Luce, and Mistress Luce's father.　Master
　　Humphrey will do somebody's errand, I warrant him.]

Hum. Father, it's true in arms I ne'er shall clasp her;
　　For she is stoln away by your man Jasper.

[*Wife.* I thought he would tell him.]

Vent. Unhappy that I am, to lose my child!
　　Now I begin to think on Jasper's words,
　　Who oft hath urged to me thy foolishness:
　　Why didst thou let her go? thou lov'st her not,
　　That wouldst bring home thy life, and not bring her.

Hum. Father, forgive me.　Shall I tell you true?
　　Look on my shoulders, they are black and blue:
　　Whilst to and fro fair Luce and I were winding,
　　He came and basted me with a hedge-binding.

Vent. Get men and horses straight: we will be there
　　Within this hour.　You know the place again!

Hum. I know the place where he my loins did swaddle;
　　I'll get six horses, and to each a saddle.

Vent. Meantime I will go talk with Jasper's father.

　　　　　　　　　　　　　　　　[*Exeunt severally.*

[*Wife.* George, what wilt thou lay with me now, that Master
　　Humphrey has not Mistress Luce yet? speak, George,
　　what wilt thou lay with me?

Cit. No, Nell; I warrant thee, Jasper is at Puckeridge with
　　her by this.

Wife. Nay, George, you must consider Mistress Luce's feet
　　are tender; and besides 'tis dark; and, I promise you
　　truly, I do not see how he should get out of Waltham
　　forest with her yet.

Cit. Nay, cony, what wilt thou lay with me, that Ralph has
　　her not yet?

Wife. I will not lay against Ralph, honey, because I have
   not spoken with him.]

SCENE VIII.—*A Room in Merrythought's House.*

Enter MERRYTHOUGHT.

[*Wife.* But look, George, peace! here comes the merry old
   gentleman again.]
Mer. [*Sings.*]

> When it was grown to dark midnight,
>   And all were fast asleep,
> In came Margaret's grimly ghost,
>   And stood at William's feet.

I have money, and meat, and drink beforehand, till
to-morrow at noon; why should I be sad? methinks I
have half-a-dozen jovial spirits within me!   [*Sings.*]

> I am three merry men, and three merry men!

To what end should any man be sad in this world? give
me a man that when he goes to hanging cries,

> Troul the black bowl to me!

and a woman that will sing a catch in her travail! I
have seen a man come by my door with a serious face,
in a black cloak, without a hat-band, carrying his head
as if he looked for pins in the street; I have looked out
of my window half a year after, and have spied that
man's head upon London Bridge. 'Tis vile: never trust
a tailor that does not sing at his work; his mind is of
nothing but filching.
[*Wife.* Mark this, George; 'tis worth noting; Godfrey my
   tailor, you know, never sings, and he had fourteen yards
   to make this gown: and I'll be sworn, Mistress Penistone
   the draper's wife had one made with twelve.]
Mer. [*Sings.*]

> 'Tis mirth that fills the veins with blood,
> More than wine, or sleep, or food;
> Let each man keep his heart at ease,
> No man dies of that disease.
> He that would his body keep
> From diseases, must not weep;
> But whoever laughs and sings,
> Never he his body brings
> Into fevers, gouts, or rheums,
> Or lingeringly his lungs consumes,

> Or meets with achès in the bone,
> Or catarrhs or griping stone;
> But contented lives for aye;
> The more he laughs, the more he may.

[*Wife.* Look, George; how sayst thou by this, George? is't not a fine old man?—Now, God's blessing o' thy sweet lips!—When wilt thou be so merry, George? faith, thou art the frowningest little thing, when thou art angry, in a country.

Cit. Peace, cony; thou shalt see him taken down too, I warrant thee.

Enter VENTUREWELL.

Here's Luce's father come now.]

Mer. [*Sings.*]

> As you came from Walsingham,
> From that holy land,
> There met you not with my true love
> By the way as you came?

Vent. Oh, Master Merrythought, my daughter's gone!
This mirth becomes you not; my daughter's gone!

Mer. [*Sings.*]

> Why, an if she be, what care I?
> Or let her come, or go, or tarry.

Vent. Mock not my misery; it is your son
(Whom I have made my own, when all forsook him)
Has stoln my only joy, my child, away.

Mer. [*Sings.*]

> He set her on a milk-white steed,
> And himself upon a grey;
> He never turned his face again,
> But he bore her quite away.

Vent. Unworthy of the kindness I have shown
To thee and thine! too late I well perceive
Thou art consenting to my daughter's loss.

Mer. Your daughter! what a stir's here wi' your daughter?
Let her go, think no more on her, but sing loud. If
both my sons were on the gallows, I would sing, [*Sings.*

> Down, down, down they fall;
> Down, and arise they never shall.

Vent. Oh, might I behold her once again,
And she once more embrace her aged sire!

Mer. Fie, how scurvily this goes! "And she once more
embrace her aged sire?" You'll make a dog on her,

will ye? she cares much for her aged sire, I warrant you.
[Sings.

> She cares not for her daddy, nor
> She cares not for her mammy,
> For she is, she is, she is, she is
> My lord of Lowgave's lassy.

Vent. For this thy scorn I will pursue that son
Of thine to death.

Mer. Do; and when you ha' killed him,   [*Sings.*

> Give him flowers enow, palmer, give him flowers enow.
> Give him red, and white, and blue, green, and yellow.

Vent. I'll fetch my daughter——

Mer. I'll hear no more o' your daughter; it spoils my mirth.

Vent. I say, I'll fetch my daughter.

Mer. [*Sings.*]

> Was never man for lady's sake,
> Down, down,
> Tormented as I poor Sir Guy,
> De derry down,
> For Lucy's sake, that lady bright,
> Down, down,
> As ever men beheld with eye,
> De derry down.

Vent. I'll be revenged, by Heaven!   [*Exeunt severally.*

[*Wife.* How dost thou like this, George?

Cit. Why, this is well, cony; but if Ralph were hot once,
thou shouldst see more.   [*Music.*

Wife. The fiddlers go again, husband.

Cit. Ay, Nell; but this is scurvy music.   I gave the whoreson
gallows money, and I think he has not got me the waits
of Southwark: if I hear 'em not anon, I'll twinge him
by the ears.—You musicians, play Baloo!

Wife. No, good George, let's ha' Lachrymæ!

Cit. Why, this is it, cony.

Wife. It's all the better, George.   Now, sweet lamb, what
story is that painted upon the cloth? the Confutation
of St. Paul?

Cit. No, lamb; that's Ralph and Lucrece.

Wife. Ralph and Lucrece! which Ralph? our Ralph?

Cit. No, mouse; that was a Tartarian.

Wife. A Tartarian!   Well, I would the fiddlers had done,
that we might see our Ralph again!]

ACT III

SCENE I.—*Waltham Forest.*

Enter JASPER *and* LUCE.

Jasp. Come, my dear dear; though we have lost our way
We have not lost ourselves. Are you not weary
With this night's wandering, broken from your rest,
And frighted with the terror that attends
The darkness of this wild unpeopled place?
Luce. No, my best friend; I cannot either fear,
Or entertain a weary thought, whilst you
(The end of all my full desires) stand by me:
Let them that lose their hopes, and live to languish
Amongst the number of forsaken lovers,
Tell the long weary steps, and number time,
Start at a shadow, and shrink up their blood,
Whilst I (possessed with all content and quiet)
Thus take my pretty love, and thus embrace him.
Jasp. You have caught me, Luce, so fast, that, whilst I live,
I shall become your faithful prisoner,
And wear these chains for ever. Come, sit down,
And rest your body, too, too delicate
For these disturbances.—[*They sit down.*] So: will you
sleep?
Come, do not be more able than you are;
I know you are not skilful in these watches,
For women are no soldiers: be not nice,
But take it; sleep, I say.
Luce. I cannot sleep;
Indeed, I cannot, friend.
Jasp. Why, then, we'll sing,
And try how that will work upon our senses.
Luce. I'll sing, or say, or any thing but sleep.
Jasp. Come, little mermaid, rob me of my heart
With that enchanting voice.
Luce. You mock me, Jasper. [*They sing.*

> *Jasp.* Tell me, dearest, what is love?
> *Luce.* 'Tis a lightning from above;
>   'Tis an arrow, 'tis a fire,
>   'Tis a boy they call Desire;
>   'Tis a smile
>   Doth beguile
> *Jasp.* The poor hearts of men that prove.

Tell me more, are women true?
Luce. Some love change, and so do you.
Jasp.   Are they fair and never kind?
Luce.   Yes, when men turn with the wind.
Jasp.   Are they froward?
Luce.   Ever toward
Those that love, to love anew.

Jasp. Dissemble it no more; I see the god
Of heavy sleep lay on his heavy mace
Upon your eyelids.
Luce. I am very heavy.   [*Sleeps.*
Jasp. Sleep, sleep; and quiet rest crown thy sweet thoughts!
Keep from her fair blood distempers, startings,
Horrors, and fearful shapes! let all her dreams
Be joys, and chaste delights, embraces, wishes,
And such new pleasures as the ravished soul
Gives to the senses!—So; my charms have took.—
Keep her, you powers divine, whilst I contemplate
Upon the wealth and beauty of her mind!
She is only fair and constant, only kind,
And only to thee, Jasper. Oh, my joys!
Whither will you transport me? let not fulness
Of my poor buried hopes come up together
And overcharge my spirits! I am weak.
Some say (however ill) the sea and women
Are governed by the moon; both ebb and flow,
Both full of changes; yet to them that know,
And truly judge, these but opinions are,
And heresies, to bring on pleasing war
Between our tempers, that without these were
Both void of after-love and present fear,
Which are the best of Cupid. Oh, thou child
Bred from despair, I dare not entertain thee,
Having a love without the faults of women,
And greater in her perfect goods than men!
Which to make good, and please myself the stronger,
Though certainly I am certain of her love,
I'll try her, that the world and memory
May sing to after-times her constancy.—
                              [*Draws his sword.*

Luce! Luce! awake!
Luce. Why do you fright me, friend,
With those distempered looks? what makes your sword
Drawn in your hand? who hath offended you?

I prithee, Jasper, sleep; thou art wild with watching.

Jasp. Come, make your way to Heaven, and bid the world,
    With all the villanies that stick upon it,
    Farewell; you're for another life.

Luce. Oh, Jasper,
    How have my tender years committed evil,
    Especially against the man I love,
    Thus to be cropped untimely?

Jasp. Foolish girl,
    Canst thou imagine I could love his daughter
    That flung me from my fortune into nothing?
    Dischargèd me his service, shut the doors
    Upon my poverty, and scorned my prayers,
    Sending me, like a boat without a mast,
    To sink or swim?　Come; by this hand you die;
    I must have life and blood, to satisfy
    Your father's wrongs.

[*Wife.* Away, George, away! raise the watch at Ludgate,
and bring a mittimus from the justice for this desperate
villain!—Now, I charge you, gentlemen, see the king's
peace kept!—Oh, my heart, what a varlet's this, to offer
manslaughter upon the harmless gentlewoman!

Cit. I warrant thee, sweetheart, we'll have him hampered.]

Luce. Oh, Jasper, be not cruel!
    If thou wilt kill me, smile, and do it quickly,
    And let not many deaths appear before me;
    I am a woman, made of fear and love,
    A weak, weak woman; kill not with thy eyes,
    They shoot me through and through: strike, I am
      ready;
    And, dying, still I love thee.

Enter VENTUREWELL, HUMPHREY, *and* Attendants.

Vent. Whereabouts?

Jasp. No more of this; now to myself again.　　[*Aside.*

Hum. There, there he stands, with sword, like martial
    knight,
    Drawn in his hand; therefore beware the fight,
    You that be wise; for, were I good Sir Bevis,
    I would not stay his coming, by your leavès.

Vent. Sirrah, restore my daughter!

Jasp. Sirrah, no.

Vent. Upon him, then!

            [*They attack Jasper, and force Luce from him.*

[*Wife.* So; down with him, down with him, down with him!
    cut him i' the leg, boys, cut him i' the leg!]

Vent. Come your ways, minion: I'll provide a cage
    For you, you're grown so tame.—Horse her away.

Hum. Truly, I'm glad your forces have the day.

               [*Exeunt all except Jasper.*

Jasp. They are gone, and I am hurt; my love is lost,
    Never to get again.   Oh, me unhappy!
    Bleed, bleed and die!   I cannot.   Oh, my folly,
    Thou hast betrayed me!   Hope, where art thou fled?
    Tell me, if thou be'st anywhere remaining,
    Shall I but see my love again?   Oh, no!
    She will not deign to look upon her butcher,
    Nor is it fit she should; yet I must venture.
    Oh, Chance, or Fortune, or whate'er thou art,
    That men adore for powerful, hear my cry,
    And let me loving live, or losing die!   [*Exit.*

[*Wife.* Is 'a gone, George?

Cit. Ay, cony.

Wife. Marry, and let him go, sweetheart.   By the faith o'
    my body, 'a has put me into such a fright, that I tremble
    (as they say) as 'twere an aspen-leaf.   Look o' my little
    finger, George, how it shakes.   Now, in truth, every
    member of my body is the worse for't.

Cit. Come, hug in mine arms, sweet mouse; he shall not
    fright thee any more.   Alas, mine own dear heart, how
    it quivers!]

       SCENE II.—*A Room in the Bell Inn, Waltham.*

   Enter Mistress MERRYTHOUGHT, RALPH, MICHAEL,
      TIM, GEORGE, Host, *and* Tapster.

[*Wife.* Oh, Ralph! how dost thou, Ralph?   How hast thou
    slept to-night?   has the knight used thee well?

Cit. Peace, Nell; let Ralph alone.]

Tap. Master, the reckoning is not paid.

Ralph. Right courteous knight, who, for the order's sake
    Which thou hast ta'en, hang'st out the holy Bell,
    As I this flaming Pestle bear about,
    We render thanks to your puissant self,
    Your beauteous lady, and your gentle squires,

For thus refreshing of our wearied limbs,
Stiffened with hard achievements in wild desert.

Tap. Sir, there is twelve shillings to pay.

Ralph. Thou merry Squire Tapstero, thanks to thee
For comforting our souls with double jug:
And, if adventurous fortune prick thee forth,
Thou jovial squire, to follow feats of arms,
Take heed thou tender every lady's cause,
Every true knight, and every damsel fair;
But spill the blood of treacherous Saracens,
And false enchanters that with magic spells
Have done to death full many a noble knight.

Host. Thou valiant Knight of the Burning Pestle, give ear
to me; there is twelve shillings to pay, and, as I am a
true knight, I will not bate a penny.

[*Wife.* George, I prithee, tell me, must Ralph pay twelve
shillings now?

Cit. No, Nell, no; nothing but the old knight is merry with
Ralph.

Wife. Oh, is't nothing else? Ralph will be as merry as he.]

Ralph. Sir Knight, this mirth of yours becomes you well;
But, to requite this liberal courtesy,
If any of your squires will follow arms,
He shall receive from my heroic hand
A knighthood, by the virtue of this Pestle.

Host. Fair knight, I thank you for your noble offer:
Therefore, gentle knight,
Twelve shillings you must pay, or I must cap you.

[*Wife.* Look, George! did not I tell thee as much? the
knight of the Bell is in earnest. Ralph shall not be
beholding to him: give him his money, George, and let
him go snick up.

Cit. Cap Ralph! no.—Hold your hand, Sir Knight of the
Bell; there's your money [*gives money*]: have you anything to say to Ralph now? Cap Ralph!

Wife. I would you should know it, Ralph has friends that
will not suffer him to be capt for ten times so much, and
ten times to the end of that.—Now take thy course,
Ralph.]

Mist. Mer. Come, Michael; thou and I will go home to thy
father; he hath enough left to keep us a day or two,
and we'll set fellows abroad to cry our purse and our
casket: shall we, Michael?

Mich. Ay, I pray, mother; in truth my feet are full of
chilblains with travelling.

[*Wife.* Faith, and those chilblains are a foul trouble.
Mistress Merrythought, when your youth comes home,
let him rub all the soles of his feet, and his heels, and his
ankles with a mouse-skin; or, if none of your people can
catch a mouse, when he goes to bed, let him roll his feet
in the warm embers, and, I warrant you, he shall be
well; and you may make him put his fingers between
his toes, and smell to them; it's very sovereign for his
head, if he be costive.]

Mist. Mer. Master Knight of the Burning Pestle, my son
Michael and I bid you farewell: I thank your worship
heartily for your kindness.

Ralph. Farewell, fair lady, and your tender squire.
If pricking through these deserts, I do hear
Of any traitorous knight, who through his guile
Hath light upon your casket and your purse,
I will despoil him of them, and restore them.

Mist. Mer. I thank your worship.   [*Exit with Michael.*

Ralph. Dwarf, bear my shield; squire, elevate my lance:—
And now farewell, you Knight of holy Bell.

[*Cit.* Ay, ay, Ralph, all is paid.]

Ralph. But yet, before I go, speak, worthy knight,
Of aught you do of sad adventures know,
Where errant knight may through his prowess win
Eternal fame, and free some gentle souls
From endless bonds of steel and lingering pain.

Host. Sirrah, go to Nick the barber, and bid him prepare
himself, as I told you before, quickly.

Tap. I am gone, sir.   [*Exit.*

Host. Sir Knight, this wilderness affordeth none
But the great venture, where full many a knight
Hath tried his prowess, and come off with shame;
And where I would not have you lose your life
Against no man, but furious fiend of hell.

Ralph. Speak on, Sir Knight; tell what he is and where:
For here I vow, upon my blazing badge,
Never to blaze a day in quietness,
But bread and water will I only eat,
And the green herb and rock shall be my couch,
Till I have quelled that man, or beast, or fiend,
That works such damage to all errant knights.

Host. Not far from hence, near to a craggy cliff,
    At the north end of this distressèd town,
    There doth stand a lowly house,
    Ruggedly builded, and in it a cave
    In which an ugly giant now doth won,
    Ycleped Barbarossa: in his hand
    He shakes a naked lance of purest steel,
    With sleeves turned up; and him before he wears
    A motley garment, to preserve his clothes
    From blood of those knights which he massacres
    And ladies gent: without his door doth hang
    A copper basin on a prickant spear;
    At which no sooner gentle knights can knock,
    But the shrill sound fierce Barbarossa hears,
    And rushing forth, brings in the errant knight,
    And sets him down in an enchanted chair;
    Then with an engine, which he hath prepared,
    With forty teeth, he claws his courtly crown;
    Next makes him wink, and underneath his chin
    He plants a brazen piece of mighty bord,
    And knocks his bullets round about his cheeks;
    Whilst with his fingers, and an instrument
    With which he snaps his hair off, he doth fill
    The wretch's ears with a most hideous noise:
    Thus every knight-adventurer he doth trim,
    And now no creature dares encounter him.
Ralph. In God's name, I will fight with him. Kind sir,
    Go but before me to this dismal cave,
    Where this huge giant Barbarossa dwells,
    And, by that virtue that brave Rosicleer
    That damnèd brood of ugly giants slew,
    And Palmerin Frannarco overthrew,
    I doubt not but to curb this traitor foul,
    And to the devil send his guilty soul.
Host. Brave-sprighted knight, thus far I will perform
    This your request; I'll bring you within sight
    Of this most loathsome place, inhabited
    By a more loathsome man; but dare not stay,
    For his main force swoops all he sees away.
Ralph. Saint George, set on before! march squire and page!
                               [Exeunt.
[*Wife.* George, dost think Ralph will confound the giant?
Cit. I hold my cap to a farthing he does: why, Nell, I saw

him wrestle with the great Dutchman, and hurl
him.

Wife. Faith, and that Dutchman was a goodly man, if all
things were answerable to his bigness. And yet they
say there was a Scotchman higher than he, and that
they two and a knight met, and saw one another for
nothing. But of all the sights that ever were in London,
since I was married, methinks the little child that was so
fair grown about the members was the prettiest; that
and the hermaphrodite.

Cit. Nay, by your leave, Nell, Ninivie was better.

Wife. Ninivie! oh, that was the story of Jone and the wall,
was it not, George?

Cit. Yes, lamb.]

SCENE III.—*The Street before Merrythought's House.*

Enter Mistress MERRYTHOUGHT.

[*Wife.* Look, George, here comes Mistress Merrythought
again! and I would have Ralph come and fight with
the giant; I tell you true, I long to see't.

Cit. Good Mistress Merrythought, begone, I pray you, for
my sake; I pray you, forbear a little; you shall have
audience presently; I have a little business.

Wife. Mistress Merrythought, if it please you to refrain your
passion a little, till Ralph have despatched the giant
out of the way, we shall think ourselves much bound
to you. [*Exit Mistress Merrythought.*] I thank you,
good Mistress Merrythought.

Cit. Boy, come hither. [*Enter Boy.*] Send away Ralph
and this whoreson giant quickly.

Boy. In good faith, sir, we cannot; you'll utterly spoil our
play, and make it to be hissed; and it cost money; you
will not suffer us to go on with our plot.—I pray, gentlemen, rule him.

Cit. Let him come now and despatch this, and I'll trouble
you no more.

Boy. Will you give me your hand of that?

Wife. Give him thy hand, George, do; and I'll kiss him. I
warrant thee, the youth means plainly.

Boy. I'll send him to you presently.

Wife. [*Kissing him.*] I thank you, little youth. [*Exit Boy.*]

Faith, the child hath a sweet breath, George; but I
think it be troubled with the worms; carduus benedictus
and mare's milk were the only thing in the world for't.

SCENE IV.—*Before a Barber's Shop, Waltham.*

Enter RALPH, HOST, TIM, *and* GEORGE.

Wife. Oh, Ralph's here, George!—God send thee good luck,
Ralph!]
Host. Puissant knight, yonder his mansion is.
Lo, where the spear and copper basin are!
Behold that string, on which hangs many a tooth,
Drawn from the gentle jaw of wandering knights!
I dare not stay to sound; he will appear. [*Exit.*
Ralph. Oh, faint not, heart! Susan, my lady dear,
The cobbler's maid in Milk Street, for whose sake
I take these arms, oh, let the thought of thee
Carry thy knight through all adventurous deeds;
And, in the honour of thy beauteous self,
May I destroy this monster Barbarossa!—
Knock, squire, upon the basin, till it break
With the shrill strokes, or till the giant speak.
                    [*Tim knocks upon the basin.*

Enter Barber.

[*Wife.* Oh, George, the giant, the giant!—Now, Ralph, for
thy life!]
Bar. What fond unknowing wight is this, that dares
So rudely knock at Barbarossa's cell,
Where no man comes but leaves his fleece behind?
Ralph. I, traitorous caitiff, who am sent by fate
To punish all the sad enormities
Thou hast committed against ladies gent
And errant knights. Traitor to God and men,
Prepare thyself; this is the dismal hour
Appointed for thee to give strict account
Of all thy beastly treacherous villanies.
Bar. Fool-hardy knight, full soon thou shalt aby
This fond reproach: thy body will I bang;
                    [*Takes down his pole.*
And, lo, upon that string thy teeth shall hang!
Prepare thyself, for dead soon shalt thou be.

Ralph. Saint George for me!   [*They fight.*
Bar. Gargantua for me!
[*Wife.* To him, Ralph, to him! hold up the giant; set out
    thy leg before, Ralph!
Cit. Falsify a blow, Ralph, falsify a blow! the giant lies open
    on the left side.
Wife. Bear't off, bear't off still! there, boy!—
    Oh, Ralph's almost down, Ralph's almost down!]
Ralph. Susan, inspire me! now have up again.
[*Wife.* Up, up, up, up, up! so, Ralph! down with him, down
    with him, Ralph!
Cit. Fetch him o'er the hip, boy!
                        [*Ralph knocks down the Barber.*
Wife. There, boy! kill, kill, kill, kill, kill, Ralph!
Cit. No, Ralph; get all out of him first.]
Ralph. Presumptuous man, see to what desperate end
    Thy treachery hath brought thee! The just gods,
    Who never prosper those that do despise them,
    For all the villanies which thou hast done
    To knights and ladies, now have paid thee home
    By my stiff arm, a knight adventurous.
    But say, vile wretch, before I send thy soul
    To sad Avernus, (whither it must go)
    What captives holdst thou in thy sable cave?
Bar. Go in, and free them all; thou hast the day.
Ralph. Go, squire and dwarf, search in this dreadful cave,
    And free the wretched prisoners from their bonds.
                        [*Exeunt Tim and George*
Bar. I crave for mercy, as thou art a knight,
    And scorn'st to spill the blood of those that beg.
Ralph. Thou show'd'st no mercy, nor shalt thou have any;
    Prepare thyself, for thou shalt surely die.

Re-enter Tim *leading a* Man *winking, with a Basin
        under his Chin.*

Tim. Behold, brave knight, here is one prisoner,
    Whom this vile man hath uséd as you see.
[*Wife.* This is the first wise word I heard the squire speak.]
Ralph. Speak what thou art, and how thou hast been used,
    That I may give him condign punishment.
Man. I am a knight that took my journey post
    Northward from London; and in courteouswise

This giant trained me to his loathsome den,
Under pretence of killing of the itch;
And all my body with a powder strewed,
That smarts and stings; and cut away my beard,
And my curled locks wherein were ribands tied;
And with a water washed my tender eyes,
(Whilst up and down about me still he skipt,)
Whose virtue is, that, till my eyes be wiped
With a dry cloth, for this my foul disgrace,
I shall not dare to look a dog i' the face.

[*Wife.* Alas, poor knight!—Relieve him, Ralph; relieve poor
    knights, whilst you live.]

Ralph. My trusty squire, convey him to the town,
    Where he may find relief.—Adieu, fair knight.
               [*Exeunt Man with Tim, who presently re-enters.*

Re-enter GEORGE, *leading a second* Man, *with a patch
over his nose.*

George. Puissant Knight, of the Burning Pestle hight,
    See here another wretch, whom this foul beast
    Hath scotched and scored in this inhuman wise.

Ralph. Speak me thy name, and eke thy place of birth,
    And what hath been thy usage in this cave.

2nd Man. I am a knight, Sir Pockhole is my name,
    And by my birth I am a Londoner,
    Free by my copy, but my ancestors
    Were Frenchmen all; and riding hard this way
    Upon a trotting horse, my bones did ache;
    And I, faint knight, to ease my weary limbs,
    Light at this cave; when straight this furious fiend,
    With sharpest instrument of purest steel,
    Did cut the gristle of my nose away,
    And in the place this velvet plaster stands:
    Relieve me, gentle knight, out of his hands!

[*Wife.* Good Ralph, relieve Sir Pockhole, and send him away;
    for in truth his breath stinks.]

Ralph. Convey him straight after the other knight.—Sir
    Pockhole, fare you well.

2nd Man. Kind sir, good night.
             [*Exit with George, who presently re-enters.*

3rd Man [*within*].   Deliver us!   [*Cries within.*
Woman [*within*].   Deliver us!

[*Wife.* Hark, George, what a woeful cry there is! I think
    some woman lies-in there.]
3rd Man [*within*]. Deliver us!
Women [*within*]. Deliver us!
Ralph. What ghastly noise is this? Speak, Barbarossa,
    Or, by this blazing steel, thy head goes off!
Bar. Prisoners of mine, whom I in diet keep.
    Send lower down into the cave,
    And in a tub that's heated smoking hot,
    There may they find them, and deliver them.
Ralph. Run, squire and dwarf; deliver them with speed.
                        [*Exeunt Tim and George.*
[*Wife.* But will not Ralph kill this giant? Surely I am
    afraid, if he let him go, he will do as much hurt as ever
    he did.
Cit. Not so, mouse, neither, if he could convert him.
Wife. Ay, George, if he could convert him; but a giant is
    not so soon converted as one of us ordinary people.
    There's a pretty tale of a witch, that had the devil's
    mark about her, (God bless us!) that had a giant to her
    son, that was called Lob-lie-by-the-fire; didst never hear
    it, George?
Cit. Peace, Nell, here comes the prisoners.]

Re-enter Tim, *leading a third* Man, *with a glass of lotion in
his hand, and* George *leading a* Woman, *with diet-bread
and drink in her hand.*

George. Here be these pinèd wretches, manful knight,
    That for this six weeks have not seen a wight.
Ralph. Deliver what you are, and how you came
    To this sad cave, and what your usage was?
3rd Man. I am an errant knight that followed arms
    With spear and shield; and in my tender years
    I stricken was with Cupid's fiery shaft,
    And fell in love with this my lady dear,
    And stole her from her friends in Turnbull Street,
    And bore her up and down from town to town,
    Where we did eat and drink, and music hear;
    Till at the length at this unhappy town
    We did arrive, and coming to this cave,
    This beast us caught, and put us in a tub,
    Where we this two months sweat, and should have done

Another month, if you had not relieved us.

Woman. This bread and water hath our diet been,
 Together with a rib cut from a neck
 Of burned mutton; hard hath been our fare:
 Release us from this ugly giant's snare!

3rd Man. This hath been all the food we have received;
 But only twice a-day, for novelty,
 He gave a spoonful of this hearty broth
 To each of us, through this same slender quill.
            [Pulls out a syringe.

Ralph. From this infernal monster you shall go,
 That useth knights and gentle ladies so!—
 Convey them hence.
     *[3rd Man and Woman are led off by Tim and
      George, who presently re-enter.*

[*Cit.* Cony, I can tell thee, the gentlemen like Ralph.

Wife. Ay, George, I see it well enough.—Gentlemen, I thank
 you all heartily for gracing my man Ralph; and I
 promise you, you shall see him oftener.]

Bar. Mercy, great knight! I do recant my ill,
 And henceforth never gentle blood will spill.

Ralph. I give thee mercy; but yet shalt thou swear,
 Upon my Burning Pestle, to perform
 Thy promise utterèd.

Bar. I swear and kiss.   *[Kisses the Pestle.*

Ralph. Depart, then and amend.—   *[Exit Barber.*
 Come, squire and dwarf; the sun grows towards his set,
 And we have many more adventures yet. *[Exeunt.*

[*Cit.* Now Ralph is in this humour, I know he would ha'
 beaten all the boys in the house, if they had been set
 on him.

Wife. Ay, George, but it is well as it is: I warrant you, the
 gentlemen do consider what it is to overthrow a giant.]

SCENE V.—*The Street before Merrythought's House.*

Enter Mistress MERRYTHOUGHT *and* MICHAEL.

[*Wife.* But, look, George; here comes Mistress Merrythought,
 and her son Michael.—Now you are welcome, Mistress
 Merrythought; now Ralph has done, you may go on.]

Mist. Mer. Mick, my boy——

Mich. Ay, forsooth, mother.

Mist. Mer. Be merry, Mick; we are at home now; where,
I warrant you, you shall find the house flung out of
the windows. [*Music within.*] Hark! hey, dogs, hey!
this is the old world, i'faith, with my husband. If I get
in among them, I'll play them such a lesson, that they
shall have little list to come scraping hither again—
Why, Master Merrythought! husband! Charles Merrythought!

Mer. [*Appearing above, and singing.*]

> If you will sing, and dance, and laugh,
>   And hollow, and laugh again,
> And then cry, " there, boys, there! " why, then,
>   One, two, three, and four,
>   We shall be merry within this hour.

Mist. Mer. Why, Charles, do you not know your own natural
wife? I say, open the door, and turn me out those
mangy companions; 'tis more than time that they were
fellow and fellow-like with you. You are a gentleman,
Charles, and an old man, and father of two children;
and I myself, (though I say it) by my mother's side niece
to a worshipful gentleman and a conductor; he has been
three times in his majesty's service at Chester, and is
now the fourth time, God bless him and his charge, upon
his journey.

Mer. [*Sings.*]

> Go from my window, love, go;
> Go from my window, my dear!
>   The wind and the rain
>   Will drive you back again;
> You cannot be lodged here.

Hark you, Mistress Merrythought, you that walk upon
adventures, and forsake your husband, because he sings
with never a penny in his purse; what, shall I think
myself the worse? Faith, no, I'll be merry. You come
not here; here's none but lads of mettle, lives of a
hundred years and upwards; care never drunk their
bloods, nor want made them warble " Heigh-ho, my
heart is heavy."

Mist. Mer. Why, Master Merrythought, what am I, that you
should laugh me to scorn thus abruptly? am I not your
fellow-feeler, as we may say, in all our miseries? your
comforter in health and sickness? have I not brought
you children? are they not like you, Charles? look upon
C 506

thine own image, hard-hearted man! and yet for all
this——

Mer. [*Sings.*]

Begone, begone, my juggy, my puggy,
Begone, my love, my dear!
The weather is warm,
'Twill do thee no harm:
Thou canst not be lodged here.——

Be merry, boys! some light music, and more wine!

[*Exit above.*

[*Wife.* He's not in earnest, I hope, George, is he?

Cit. What if he be, sweetheart?

Wife. Marry, if he be, George, I'll make bold to tell him he's
an ingrant old man to use his bedfellow so scurvily.

Cit. What! how does he use her, honey?

Wife. Marry, come up, sir saucebox! I think you'll take his
part, will you not? Lord, how hot you have grown!
you are a fine man, an' you had a fine dog; it becomes
you sweetly!

Cit. Nay, prithee, Nell, chide not; for, as I am an honest man
and a true Christian grocer, I do not like his doings.

Wife. I cry you mercy, then, George! you know we are all
frail and full of infirmities.—D'ye hear, Master Merrythought? may I crave a word with you?]

Mer. [*Appearing above.*] Strike up lively, lads!

[*Wife.* I had not thought, in truth, Master Merrythought,
that a man of your age and discretion, as I may say,
being a gentleman, and therefore known by your gentle
conditions, could have used so little respect to the weakness of his wife; for your wife is your own flesh, the staff
of your age, your yoke-fellow, with whose help you draw
through the mire of this transitory world; nay, she's
your own rib: and again——]

Mer. [*Sings.*]

I came not hither for thee to teach,
I have no pulpit for thee to preach,
I would thou hadst kissed me under the breech,
As thou art a lady gay.

[*Wife.* Marry, with a vengeance! I am heartily sorry for the
poor gentlewoman: but if I were thy wife, i'faith, grey-
beard, i'faith——

Cit. I prithee, sweet honeysuckle, be content.

Wife. Give me such words, that am a gentlewoman born!
hang him, hoary rascal! Get me some drink, George;

I am almost molten with fretting: now, beshrew his
knave's heart for it!]   [*Exit Citizen.*
Mer. Play me a light lavolta. Come, be frolic.
    Fill the good fellows wine.
Mist. Mer. Why, Master Merrythought, are you disposed to
    make me wait here? You'll open, I hope; I'll fetch
    them that shall open else.
Mer. Good woman, if you will sing, I'll give you something;
    if not——   [*Sings.*

> You are no love for me, Margaret,
> I am no love for you.—

Come aloft, boys, aloft!   [*Exit above.*
Mist. Mer. Now a churl's fart in your teeth, sir!—Come,
    Mick, we'll not trouble him; 'a shall not ding us i'
    the teeth with his bread and his broth, that he shall
    not. Come, boy; I'll provide for thee, I warrant thee.
    We'll go to Master Venturewell's, the merchant: I'll get
    his letter to mine host of the Bell in Waltham; there I'll
    place thee with the tapster: will not that do well for
    thee, Mick? and let me alone for that old cuckoldly
    knave your father; I'll use him in his kind, I warrant
    ye.   [*Exeunt.*

Re-enter Citizen with Beer.

[*Wife.* Come, George, where's the beer?
Cit. Here, love.
Wife. This old fornicating fellow will not out of my mind
    yet.—Gentlemen, I'll begin to you all; and I desire more
    of your acquaintance with all my heart. [*Drinks.*] Fill
    the gentlemen some beer, George. [*Enter Boy.*] Look,
    George, the little boy's come again: methinks he looks
    something like the Prince of Orange in his long stocking,
    if he had a little harness about his neck. George, I will
    have him dance fading.—Fading is a fine jig, I'll assure
    you, gentlemen.—Begin, brother. [*Boy dances.*] Now
    'a capers, sweetheart!—Now a turn o' the toe, and then
    tumble! cannot you tumble, youth?
Boy. No, indeed, forsooth.
Wife. Nor eat fire?
Boy. Neither.
Wife. Why, then, I thank you heartily; there's twopence to
    buy you points withal.]

ACT IV

SCENE I.—*A Street*.

Enter Jasper *and* Boy.

Jasp. There, boy, deliver this; but do it well.
    Hast thou provided me four lusty fellows,
                                     [Gives a letter.
    Able to carry me? and art thou perfect
    In all thy business?
Boy. Sir, you need not fear;
    I have my lesson here, and cannot miss it:
    The men are ready for you, and what else
    Pertains to this employment.
Jasp. There, my boy;
    Take it, but buy no land.   *[Gives money.*
Boy. Faith, sir, 'twere rare
    To see so young a purchaser. I fly,
    And on my wings carry your destiny.
Jasp. Go, and be happy! [*Exit Boy.*] Now, my latest hope,
    Forsake me not, but fling thy anchor out,
    And let it hold! Stand fixed, thou rolling stone,
    Till I enjoy my dearest! Hear me, all
    You powers, that rule in men, celestial!   *[Exit.*
[*Wife.* Go thy ways; thou art as crooked a sprig as ever
    grew in London. I warrant him, he'll come to some
    naughty end or other; for his looks say no less: besides,
    his father (you know, George) is none of the best; you
    heard him take me up like a flirt-gill, and sing bawdy
    songs upon me; but, i'faith, if I live, George,——
Cit. Let me alone, sweetheart: I have a trick in my head
    shall lodge him in the Arches for one year, and make
    him sing *peccavi* ere I leave him; and yet he shall never
    know who hurt him neither.
Wife. Do, my good George, do!
Cit. What shall we have Ralph do now, boy?
Boy. You shall have what you will, sir.
Cit. Why, so, sir; go and fetch me him then, and let the
    Sophy of Persia come and christen him a child.

Boy. Believe me, sir, that will not do so well; 'tis stale; it
 has been had before at the Red Bull.

Wife. George, let Ralph travel over great hills, and let him
 be very weary, and come to the King of Cracovia's house,
 covered with black velvet; and there let the king's
 daughter stand in her window, all in beaten gold, comb-
 ing her golden locks with a comb of ivory; and let her
 spy Ralph, and fall in love with him, and come down to
 him, and carry him into her father's house; and then
 let Ralph talk with her.

Cit. Well said, Nell; it shall be so.—Boy, let's ha't done
 quickly.

Boy. Sir, if you will imagine all this to be done already, you
 shall hear them talk together; but we cannot present
 a house covered with black velvet, and a lady in beaten
 gold.

Cit. Sir boy, let's ha't as you can, then.

Boy. Besides, it will show ill-favouredly to have a grocer's
 prentice to court a king's daughter.

Cit. Will it so, sir? you are well read in histories! I pray
 you, what was Sir Dagonet? was not he prentice to a
 grocer in London? Read the play of "The Four
 Prentices of London," where they toss their pikes so.
 I pray you, fetch him in, sir, fetch him in.

Boy. It shall be done.—It is not our fault, gentlemen. [*Exit.*

Wife. Now we shall see fine doings, I warrant ye, George.]

SCENE II.—*A Hall in the King of Moldavia's Court.*

Enter POMPIONA, RALPH, TIM, *and* GEORGE.

[*Wife.* Oh, here they come! how prettily the King of
 Cracovia's daughter is dressed!

Cit. Ay, Nell, it is the fashion of that country, I warrant ye.]

Pomp. Welcome, Sir Knight, unto my father's court,
 King of Moldavia; unto me Pompiona,
 His daughter dear! But, sure, you do not like
 Your entertainment, that will stay with us
 No longer but a night.

Ralph.   Damsel right fair,
 I am on many sad adventures bound,
 That call me forth into the wilderness;
 Besides, my horse's back is something galled;

Which will enforce me ride a sober pace.
But many thanks, fair lady, be to you
For using errant knight with courtesy!

Pomp. But say, brave knight, what is your name and birth?

Ralph. My name is Ralph; I am an Englishman
(As true as steel, a hearty Englishman),
And prentice to a grocer in the Strand
By deed indent, of which I have one part:
But fortune calling me to follow arms,
On me this only order I did take
Of Burning Pestle, which in all men's eyes
I bear, confounding ladies' enemies.

Pomp. Oft have I heard of your brave countrymen,
And fertile soil and store of wholesome food;
My father oft will tell me of a drink
In England found, and nipitato called,
Which driveth all the sorrow from your hearts.

Ralph. Lady, 'tis true; you need not lay your lips
To better nipitato than there is.

Pomp. And of a wild fowl he will often speak,
Which powdered-beef-and-mustard callèd is:
For there have been great wars 'twixt us and you;
But truly, Ralph, it was not 'long of me.
Tell me then, Ralph, could you contented be
To wear a lady's favour in your shield?

Ralph. I am a knight of a religious order,
And will not wear a favour of a lady
That trusts in Antichrist and false traditions.

[*Cit.* Well said, Ralph! convert her, if thou canst.]

Ralph. Besides, I have a lady of my own
In merry England, for whose virtuous sake
I took these arms; and Susan is her name,
A cobbler's maid in Milk Street; whom I vow
Ne'er to forsake whilst life and Pestle last.

Pomp. Happy that cobbling dame, whoe'er she be,
That for her own, dear Ralph, hath gotten thee!
Unhappy I, that ne'er shall see the day
To see thee more, that bear'st my heart away!

Ralph. Lady, farewell; I needs must take my leave.

Pomp. Hard-hearted Ralph, that ladies dost deceive!

[*Cit.* Hark thee, Ralph: there's money for thee [*Gives money*];
give something in the King of Cracovia's house; be not
beholding to him.]

Ralph. Lady, before I go, I must remember
   Your father's officers, who truth to tell,
   Have been about me very diligent:
   Hold up thy snowy hand, thou princely maid!
   There's twelve-pence for your father's chamberlain;
   And another shilling for his cook,
   For, by my troth, the goose was roasted well;
   And twelve-pence for your father's horse-keeper,
   For 'nointing my horse-back, and for his butter
   There is another shilling; to the maid
   That washed my boot-hose there's an English groat
   And two-pence to the boy that wiped my boots;
   And last, fair lady, there is for yourself
   Three-pence, to buy you pins at Bumbo-fair.
Pomp. Full many thanks; and I will keep them safe
   Till all the heads be off, for thy sake, Ralph.
Ralph. Advance, my squire and dwarf! I cannot stay.
Pomp. Thou kill'st my heart in passing thus away.
                                        [*Exeunt.*
[*Wife.* I commend Ralph yet, that he will not stoop to a
   Cracovian; there's properer women in London than any
   are there, I-wis.]

SCENE III.—*A Room in the House of Venturewell.*

Enter Venturewell, Humphrey, Luce, *and* Boy.

[*Wife.* But here comes Master Humphrey and his love again
   now, George.
Cit. Ay, cony; peace.]
Vent. Go, get you up; I will not be entreated;
   And, gossip mine, I'll keep you sure hereafter
   From gadding out again with boys and unthrifts:
   Come, they are women's tears; I know your fashion.—
   Go, sirrah, lock her in, and keep the key
   Safe as you love your life.   [*Exeunt Luce and Boy.*
                              Now, my son Humphrey,
   You may both rest assurèd of my love
   In this, and reap your own desire.
Hum. I see this love you speak of, through your daughter,
   Although the hole be little; and hereafter
   Will yield the like in all I may or can,
   Fitting a Christian and a gentleman.

Vent. I do believe you, my good son, and thank you;
　　For 'twere an impudence to think you flattered.
Hum. It were, indeed; but shall I tell you why?
　　I have been beaten twice about the lie.
Vent. Well, son, no more of compliment.　My daughter
　　Is yours again: appoint the time and take her;
　　We'll have no stealing for it; I myself
　　And some few of our friends will see you married.
Hum. I would you would, i'faith! for, be it known,
　　I ever was afraid to lie alone.
Vent. Some three days hence, then.
Hum. Three days! let me see:
　　'Tis somewhat of the most; yet I agree,
　　Because I mean against the appointed day
　　To visit all my friends in new array.

Enter Servant.

Serv. Sir, there's a gentlewoman without would speak with
　　your worship.
Vent. What is she?
Serv. Sir, I asked her not.
Vent. Bid her come in.　　　　　　　　　*[Exit Servant.*

Enter Mistress MERRYTHOUGHT *and* MICHAEL.

Mist. Mer. Peace be to your worship!　I come as a poor
　　suitor to you, sir, in the behalf of this child.
Vent. Are you not wife to Merrythought?
Mist. Mer. Yes, truly.　Would I had ne'er seen his eyes! he
　　has undone me and himself and his children; and there
　　he lives at home, and sings and hoits and revels among
　　his drunken companions! but, I warrant you, where to
　　get a penny to put bread in his mouth he knows not:
　　and therefore, if it like your worship, I would entreat
　　your letter to the honest host of the Bell in Waltham,
　　that I may place my child under the protection of his
　　tapster, in some settled course of life.
Vent. I'm glad the heavens have heard my prayers.　Thy
　　husband,
　　When I was ripe in sorrows, laughed at me;
　　Thy son, like an unthankful wretch, I having
　　Redeemed him from his fall, and made him mine,
　　To show his love again, first stole my daughter,

Then wronged this gentleman, and, last of all,
Gave me that grief had almost brought me down
Unto my grave, had not a stronger hand
Relieved my sorrows.   Go, and weep as I did,
And be unpitied; for I here profess
An everlasting hate to all thy name.

Mist. Mer. Will you so, sir? how say you by that?—Come,
Mick; let him keep his wind to cool his pottage.   We'll
go to thy nurse's, Mick: she knits silk stockings, boy;
and we'll knit too, boy, and be beholding to none of
them all.   [*Exit with Michael.*

Enter Boy.

Boy. Sir, I take it you are the master of this house.
Vent. How then, boy!
Boy. Then to yourself, sir, comes this letter.   [*Gives letter.*
Vent. From whom, my pretty boy?
Boy. From him that was your servant; but no more
Shall that name ever be, for he is dead:
Grief of your purchased anger broke his heart.
I saw him die, and from his hand received
This paper, with a charge to bring it hither:
Read it, and satisfy yourself in all.

Vent. [*Reads.*] Sir, that I have wronged your love I must
confess; in which I have purchased to myself, besides
mine own undoing, the ill opinion of my friends.   Let
not your anger, good sir, outlive me, but suffer me to
rest in peace with your forgiveness: let my body (if a
dying man may so much prevail with you) be brought to
your daughter, that she may truly know my hot flames
are now buried, and withal receive a testimony of the
zeal I bore her virtue.   Farewell for ever, and be ever
happy!   Jasper.

God's hand is great in this: I do forgive him;
Yet I am glad he's quiet, where I hope
He will not bite again.—Boy, bring the body,
And let him have his will, if that be all.

Boy. 'Tis here without, sir.
Vent. So, sir; if you please,
You may conduct it in; I do not fear it.
Hum. I'll be your usher, boy; for, though I say it,
He owed me something once, and well did pay it.
                                        [*Exeunt.*

SCENE IV.—*Another Room in the House of Venturewell.*

Enter Luce.

Luce. If there be any punishment inflicted
    Upon the miserable, more than yet I feel,
    Let it together seize me, and at once
    Press down my soul! I cannot bear the pain
    Of these delaying tortures.—Thou that art
    The end of all, and the sweet rest of all,
    Come, come, oh, Death! bring me to thy peace,
    And blot out all the memory I nourish
    Both of my father and my cruel friend!—
    Oh, wretched maid, still living to be wretched,
    To be a say to Fortune in her changes,
    And grow to number times and woes together!
    How happy had I been, if, being born,
    My grave had been my cradle!

Enter Servant.

Serv. By your leave,
    Young mistress; here's a boy hath brought a coffin:
    What 'a would say, I know not; but your father
    Charged me to give you notice. Here they come.
                            [*Exit.*

Enter Boy, *and two* Men *bearing a Coffin.*

Luce. For me I hope 'tis come, and 'tis most welcome.
Boy. Fair mistress, let me not add greater grief
    To that great store you have already. Jasper
    (That whilst he lived was yours, now dead
    And here enclosed) commanded me to bring
    His body hither, and to crave a tear
    From those fair eyes (though he deserved not pity),
    To deck his funeral; for so he bid me
    Tell her for whom he died.
Luce. He shall have many.—
    Good friends, depart a little, whilst I take
    My leave of this dead man, that once I loved.
                  [*Exeunt Boy and Men.*

Hold yet a little, life! and then I give thee
To thy first heavenly being. Oh, my friend!
Hast thou deceived me thus, and got before me?
I shall not long be after.   But, believe me,
Thou wert too cruel, Jasper, 'gainst thyself,
In punishing the fault I could have pardoned,
With so untimely death: thou didst not wrong me
But ever wert most kind, most true, most loving;
And I the most unkind, most false, most cruel!
Didst thou but ask a tear?   I'll give thee all,
Even all my eyes can pour down, all my sighs,
And all myself, before thou goest from me:
These are but sparing rites; but if thy soul
Be yet about this place, and can behold
And see what I prepare to deck thee with,
It shall go up, borne on the wings of peace,
And satisfied.   First will I sing thy dirge,
Then kiss thy pale lips, and then die myself,
And fill one coffin and one grave together.   [*Sings.*

> Come, you whose loves are dead,
>   And, whiles I sing,
>   Weep, and wring
> Every hand, and every head
> Bind with cypress and sad yew;
> Ribands black and candles blue
> For him that was of men most true!
>
> Come with heavy moaning,
>   And on his grave
>   Let him have
> Sacrifice of sighs and groaning;
> Let him have fair flowers enow,
> White and purple, green and yellow,
> For him that was of men most true!

Thou sable cloth, sad cover of my joys,
I lift thee up, and thus I meet with death.
       [*Removes the Cloth, and Jasper rises out of the Coffin.*
Jasp. And thus you meet the living.
Luce. Save me, Heaven!
Jasp. Nay, do not fly me, fair; I am no spirit:
    Look better on me; do you know me yet?
Luce. Oh, thou dear shadow of my friend!
Jasp. Dear substance;
    I swear I am no shadow; feel my hand,
    It is the same it was; I am your Jasper,
    Your Jasper that's yet living, and yet loving.

Pardon my rash attempt, my foolish proof
I put in practice of your constancy;
For sooner should my sword have drunk my blood,
And set my soul at liberty, than drawn
The least drop from that body: for which boldness
Doom me to anything; if death, I take it,
And willingly.

Luce. This death I'll give you for it;   [*Kisses him.*
So, now I am satisfied you are no spirit,
But my own truest, truest, truest friend:
Why do you come thus to me?

Jasp. First, to see you;
Then to convey you hence.

Luce. It cannot be;
For I am locked up here, and watched at all hours,
That 'tis impossible for me to scape.

Jasp. Nothing more possible.   Within this coffin
Do you convey yourself: let me alone,
I have the wits of twenty men about me;
Only I crave the shelter of your closet
A little, and then fear me not.   Creep in,
That they may presently convey you hence:
Fear nothing, dearest love; I'll be your second;
                    [*Luce lies down in the Coffin, and Jasper
                        covers her with the cloth.*
Lie close: so; all goes well yet.—Boy!

Re-enter Boy *and* Men.

Boy. At hand, sir.
Jasp. Convey away the coffin, and be wary.
Boy. 'Tis done already.   [*Exeunt Men with the Coffin.*
Jasp. Now must I go conjure.   [*Exit into a Closet.*

Enter VENTUREWELL.

Vent. Boy, boy!
Boy. Your servant, sir.
Vent. Do me this kindness, boy; (hold, here's a crown;)
Before thou bury the body of this fellow,
Carry it to his old merry father, and salute him
From me, and bid him sing; he hath cause.
Boy. I will, sir.
Vent. And then bring me word what tune he is in,

And have another crown; but do it truly.
I have fitted him a bargain now will vex him.
Boy. God bless your worship's health, sir!
Vent. Farewell, boy!   [*Exeunt severally.*

SCENE V.—*A Street before Merrythought's House.*

Enter MERRYTHOUGHT.

[*Wife.* Ah, old Merrythought, art thou there again? let's hear some of thy songs.]
Mer. [*Sings.*]

> Who can sing a merrier note
> Than he that cannot change a groat?

Not a denier left, and yet my heart leaps: I do wonder yet, as old as I am, that any man will follow a trade, or serve, that may sing and laugh, and walk the streets. My wife and both my sons are I know not where; I have nothing left, nor know I how to come by meat to supper; yet am I merry still, for I know I shall find it upon the table at six o'clock; therefore, hang thought!   [*Sings.*

> I would not be a serving-man
>   To carry the cloak-bag still,
> Nor would I be a falconer
>   The greedy hawks to fill;
> But I would be in a good house,
>   And have a good master too;
> But I would eat and drink of the best,
>   And no work would I do.

This it is that keeps life and soul together, mirth; this is the philosopher's stone that they write so much on, that keeps a man ever young.

Enter Boy.

Boy. Sir, they say they know all your money is gone, and they will trust you for no more drink.
Mer. Will they not? let 'em choose! The best is, I have mirth at home, and need not send abroad for that; let them keep their drink to themselves.   [*Sings.*

> For Julian of Berry, she dwells on a hill,
> And she hath good beer and ale to sell,
> And of good fellows she thinks no ill;
>   And thither will we go now, now, now,
>   And thither will we go now.

And when you have made a little stay,
You need not ask what is to pay,
But kiss your hostess, and go your way;
   And thither will we go now, now, now,
   And thither will we go now.

Enter another Boy.

2nd Boy. Sir, I can get no bread for supper.

Mer. Hang bread and supper! let's preserve our mirth, and
   we shall never feel hunger, I'll warrant you.   Let's have
   a catch, boys; follow me, come.   [*They sing.*

Ho, ho, nobody at home!
Meat, nor drink, nor money ha' we none.
Fill the pot, Eedy,
Never more need I.

Mer. So, boys; enough.   Follow me: Let's change our place,
   and we shall laugh afresh.   [*Exeunt.*

[*Wife.* Let him go, George; 'a shall not have any countenance
   from us, nor a good word from any i' the company, if I
   may strike stroke in't.

Cit. No more 'a sha'not, love.   But, Nell, I will have Ralph
   do a very notable matter now, to the eternal honour and
   glory of all grocers.—Sirrah! you there, boy!   Can none
   of you hear?

Enter Boy.

Boy. Sir, your pleasure?

Cit. Let Ralph come out on May-day in the morning, and
   speak upon a conduit, with all his scarfs about him, and
   his feathers, and his rings, and his knacks.

Boy. Why, sir, you do not think of our plot; what will
   become of that, then?

Cit. Why, sir, I care not what become on't: I'll have him
   come out, or I'll fetch him out myself; I'll have something done in honour of the city: besides, he hath been
   long enough upon adventures.   Bring him out quickly;
   or, if I come in amongst you——

Boy. Well, sir, he shall come out, but if our play miscarry,
   sir, you are like to pay for't.

Cit. Bring him away then!   [*Exit Boy.*

Wife. This will be brave, i'faith!   George, shall not he dance
   the morris too, for the credit of the Strand?

Cit. No, sweetheart, it will be too much for the boy.   Oh,
   there he is, Nell! he's reasonable well in reparel: but he
   has not rings enough.]

Enter RALPH, *dressed as a May-lord.*

Ralph. London, to thee I do present the merry month of
 May;
 Let each true subject be content to hear me what I say:
 For from the top of conduit-head, as plainly may appear,
 I will both tell my name to you, and wherefore I came
  here.
 My name is Ralph, by due descent though not ignoble I
 Yet far inferior to the stock of gracious grocery;
 And by the common counsel of my fellows in the Strand,
 With gilded staff and crossèd scarf, the May-lord here I
  stand.
 Rejoice, oh, English hearts, rejoice! rejoice, oh, lovers
  dear!
 Rejoice, oh, city, town, and country! rejoice, eke every
  shere!
 For now the fragrant flowers do spring and sprout in
  seemly sort,
 The little birds do sit and sing, the lambs do make fine
  sport;
 And now the birchen-tree doth bud, that makes the
  schoolboy cry;
 The morris rings, while hobby-horse doth foot it
  feateously;
 The lords and ladies now abroad, for their disport and
  play,
 Do kiss sometimes upon the grass, and sometimes in the
  hay;
 Now butter with a leaf of sage is good to purge the
  blood;
 Fly Venus and phlebotomy, for they are neither good;
 Now little fish on tender stone begin to cast their bellies,
 And sluggish snails, that erst were mewed, do creep out
  of their shellies;
 The rumbling rivers now do warm, for little boys to
  paddle;
 The sturdy steed now goes to grass, and up they hang
  his saddle;
 The heavy hart, the bellowing buck, the rascal, and the
  pricket,
 Are now among the yeoman's peas, and leave the fearful
  thicket:

And be like them, oh, you, I say, of this same noble
town,
And lift aloft your velvet heads, and slipping off your
gown,
With bells on legs, and napkins clean unto your shoulders
tied,
With scarfs and garters as you please, and " Hey for our
town ! " cried.
March out, and show your willing minds, by twenty and
by twenty,
To Hogsdon or to Newington, where ale and cakes are
plenty;
And let it ne'er be said for shame, that we the youths of
London
Lay thrumming of our caps at home, and left our custom
undone.
Up, then, I say, both young and old, both man and
maid a-maying,
With drums, and guns that bounce aloud, and merry
tabor playing!
Which to prolong, God save our king, and send his
country peace,
And root out treason from the land! and so, my friends,
I cease. [*Exit.*

ACT V

SCENE I.—*A Room in the House of Venturewell.*

Enter VENTUREWELL.

Vent. I will have no great store of company at the wedding;
a couple of neighbours and their wives; and we will have
a capon in stewed broth, with marrow, and a good piece
of beef stuck with rosemary.

Enter JASPER, *with his Face mealed.*

Jasp. Forbear thy pains, fond man! it is too late.
Vent. Heaven bless me! Jasper!
Jasp. Ay, I am his ghost,
Whom thou hast injured for his constant love;
Fond worldly wretch! who dost not understand
In death that true hearts cannot parted be.

First know, thy daughter is quite borne away
On wings of angels, through the liquid air,
To far out of thy reach, and never more
Shalt thou behold her face: but she and I
Will in another world enjoy our loves;
Where neither father's anger, poverty,
Nor any cross that troubles earthly men,
Shall make us sever our united hearts.
And never shalt thou sit or be alone
In any place, but I will visit thee
With ghastly looks, and put into thy mind
The great offences which thou didst to me:
When thou art at thy table with thy friends,
Merry in heart, and filled with swelling wine,
I'll come in midst of all thy pride and mirth,
Invisible to all men but thyself,
And whisper such a sad tale in thine ear
Shall make thee let the cup fall from thy hand,
And stand as mute and pale as death itself.

Vent. Forgive me, Jasper! Oh, what might I do,
    Tell me, to satisfy thy troubled ghost?

Jasp. There is no means; too late thou think'st of this.

Vent. But tell me what were best for me to do?

Jasp. Repent thy deed, and satisfy my father,
    And beat fond Humphrey out of thy doors.   [*Exit.*

[*Wife.* Look, George; his very ghost would have folks
    beaten.]

Enter HUMPHREY.

Hum. Father, my bride is gone, fair Mistress Luce:
    My soul's the fount of vengeance, mischief's sluice.

Vent. Hence, fool, out of my sight with thy fond passion!
    Thou hast undone me.   [*Beats him.*

Hum. Hold, my father dear,
    For Luce thy daughter's sake, that had no peer!

Vent. Thy father, fool! there's some blows more; begone.—
                                        [*Beats him.*
    Jasper, I hope thy ghost be well appeased
    To see thy will performed. Now will I go
    To satisfy thy father for thy wrongs.   [*Aside and exit.*

Hum. What shall I do? I have been beaten twice,
    And Mistress Luce is gone. Help me, device
    Since my true love is gone, I never more,

Whilst I do live, upon the sky will pore;
But in the dark will wear out my shoe-soles
In passion in Saint Faith's church under Paul's.   [*Exit.*
[*Wife.* George, call Ralph hither; if you love me, call Ralph
    hither: I have the bravest thing for him to do, George;
    prithee, call him quickly.
Cit. Ralph! why, Ralph, boy!

Enter RALPH.

Ralph. Here, sir.
Cit. Come hither, Ralph; come to thy mistress, boy.
Wife. Ralph, I would have thee call all the youths together
    in battle-ray, with drums, and guns, and flags, and march
    to Mile-End in pompous fashion, and there exhort your
    soldiers to be merry and wise, and to keep their beards
    from burning, Ralph; and then skirmish, and let your
    flags fly, and cry, "Kill, kill, kill!" My husband shall
    lend you his jerkin, Ralph, and there's a scarf; for the
    rest, the house shall furnish you, and we'll pay for't. Do
    it bravely, Ralph; and think before whom you perform,
    and what person you represent.
Ralph. I warrant you, mistress; if I do it not, for the honour
    of the city and the credit of my master, let me never
    hope for freedom!
Wife. 'Tis well spoken, i'faith. Go thy ways; thou art a
    spark indeed.
Cit. Ralph, Ralph, double your files bravely, Ralph!
Ralph. I warrant you, sir.   [*Exit.*
Cit. Let him look narrowly to his service; I shall take him
    else. I was there myself a pikeman once, in the hottest
    of the day, wench; had my feather shot sheer away, the
    fringe of my pike burnt off with powder, my pate broken
    with a scouring-stick, and yet, I thank God, I am here.
                                              [*Drums within.*
Wife. Hark, George, the drums!
Cit. Ran, tan, tan, tan, tan, tan! Oh, wench, an thou hadst
    but seen little Ned of Aldgate, Drum-Ned, how he made
    it roar again, and laid on like a tyrant, and then struck
    softly till the ward came up, and then thundered again,
    and together we go! "Sa, sa, sa, bounce!" quoth the
    guns; "Courage, my hearts!" quoth the captains;
    "Saint George!" quoth the pikemen; and withal, here

they lay: and there they lay: and yet for all this I am
here, wench.

Wife. Be thankful for it, George; for indeed 'tis wonderful.]

SCENE II.—*A Street (and afterwards Mile End).*

Enter Ralph *and Company of* Soldiers (*among whom are*
William Hammerton *and* George Greengoose),
with drums and colours.

Ralph. March fair, my hearts! Lieutenant, beat the rear
up.—Ancient, let your colours fly; but have a great care
of the butcher's hooks at Whitechapel; they have been
the death of many a fair ancient.—Open your files, that
I may take a view both of your persons and munition.
—Sergeant, call a muster.

Serg. A stand!—William Hammerton, pewterer!

Ham. Here, captain!

Ralph. A corselet and a Spanish pike; 'tis well: can you
shake it with a terror?

Ham. I hope so, captain.

Ralph. Charge upon me. [*He charges on Ralph.*]—'Tis with
the weakest: but more strength, William Hammerton,
more strength. As you were again!—Proceed, Sergeant.

Serg. George Greengoose, poulterer!

Green. Here!

Ralph. Let me see your piece, neighbour Greengoose: when
was she shot in?

Green. An't like you, master captain, I made a shot even
now, partly to scour her, and partly for audacity.

Ralph. It should seem so certainly, for her breath is yet
inflamed; besides, there is a main fault in the touch-
hole, it runs and stinketh; and I tell you moreover, and
believe it, ten such touch-holes would breed the pox in
the army. Get you a feather, neighbour, get you a
feather, sweet oil, and paper, and your piece may do well
enough yet. Where's your powder?

Green. Here.

Ralph. What, in a paper! as I am a soldier and a gentleman,
it craves a martial court! you ought to die for't. Where's
your horn? answer me to that.

Green. An't like you, sir, I was oblivious.

Ralph. It likes me not you should be so; 'tis a shame for

you, and a scandal to all our neighbours, being a man of worth and estimation, to leave your horn behind you: I am afraid 'twill breed example. But let me tell you no more on't.—Stand, till I view you all.—What's become o' the nose of your flask?

1st Sold. Indeed, la, captain, 'twas blown away with powder.

Ralph. Put on a new one at the city's charge.—Where's the stone of this piece?

2nd Sold. The drummer took it out to light tobacco.

Ralph. 'Tis a fault, my friend; put it in again.—You want a nose,—and you a stone.—Sergeant, take a note on't, for I mean to stop it in the pay.—Remove, and march! [*They march.*] Soft and fair, gentlemen, soft and fair! double your files! as you were! faces about! Now, you with the sodden face, keep in there! Look to your match, sirrah, it will be in your fellow's flask anon. So; make a crescent now; advance your pikes; stand and give ear!—Gentlemen, countrymen, friends, and my fellow-soldiers, I have brought you this day, from the shops of security and the counters of content, to measure out in these furious fields honour by the ell, and prowess by the pound. Let it not, oh, let it not, I say, be told hereafter, the noble issue of this city fainted; but bear yourselves in this fair action like men, valiant men, and free men! Fear not the face of the enemy, nor the noise of the guns, for, believe me, brethren, the rude rumbling of a brewer's cart is far more terrible, of which you have a daily experience; neither let the stink of powder offend you, since a more valiant stink is nightly with you.

To a resolvèd mind his home is everywhere:
I speak not this to take away
The hope of your return; for you shall see
(I do not doubt it) and that very shortly
Your loving wives again and your sweet children,
Whose care doth bear you company in baskets.
Remember, then, whose cause you have in hand,
And, like a sort of true-born scavengers,
Scour me this famous realm of enemies.
I have no more to say but this: stand to your tacklings, lads, and show to the world you can as well brandish a sword as shake an apron. Saint George, and on, my hearts!

All. Saint George, Saint George!   [*Exeunt.*

[*Wife.* 'Twas well done, Ralph! I'll send thee a cold capon a-field and a bottle of March beer; and, it may be, come myself to see thee.

Cit. Nell, the boy hath deceived me much; I did not think it had been in him. He has performed such a matter, wench, that, if I live, next year I'll have him captain of the galley-foist, or I'll want my will.]

SCENE III.—*A Room in Merrythought's House.*

Enter Merrythought.

Mer. Yet, I thank God, I break not a wrinkle more than I had. Not a stoop, boys? Care, live with cats: I defy thee! My heart is as sound as an oak; and though I want drink to wet my whistle, I can sing;   [*Sings.*

Come no more there, boys, come no more there;
For we shall never whilst we live come any more there.

Enter Boy, *and two* Men *bearing a Coffin.*

Boy. God save you, sir!

Mer. It's a brave boy. Canst thou sing?

Boy. Yes, sir, I can sing; but 'tis not so necessary at this time.

Mer. [*Sings.*]

Sing we, and chant it;
Whilst love doth grant it.

Boy. Sir, sir, if you knew what I have brought you, you would have little list to sing.

Mer. [*Sings.*]

Oh, the Mimon round,
Full long I have thee sought,
And now I have thee found,
And what hast thou here brought?

Boy. A coffin, sir, and your dead son Jasper in it.

[*Exit with Men.*

Mer. Dead! [*Sings.*]

Why, farewell he!
Thou wast a bonny boy,
And I did love thee.

Enter JASPER.

Jasp. Then, I pray you, sir, do so still.
Mer. Jasper's ghost!   [*Sings.*

> Thou art welcome from Stygian lake so soon;
> Declare to me what wondrous things in Pluto's court are done.

Jasp. By my troth, sir, I ne'er came there; 'tis too hot for
    me, sir.
Mer. A merry ghost, a very merry ghost!   [*Sings.*

> And where is your true love?   Oh, where is yours?

Jasp. Marry, look you, sir!
      [*Removes the cloth, and Luce rises out of the Coffin.*
Mer. Ah, ha! art thou good at that, i'faith?   [*Sings.*

> With hey, trixy, terlery-whiskin,
> The world it runs on wheels;
> When the young man's ——,
> Up goes the maiden's heels.

Mistress MERRYTHOUGHT *and* MICHAEL *within.*

Mist. Mer. [*within.*] What, Master Merrythought! will you
    not let's in? what do you think shall become of us?
Mer. [*Sings.*]

> What voice is that that calleth at our door?

Mist. Mer. [*within.*] You know me well enough; I am sure I
    have not been such a stranger to you.
Mer. [*Sings.*]

> And some they whistled, and some they sung,
> Hey, down, down!
> And some did loudly say,
> Ever as the Lord Barnet's horn blew,
> Away, Musgrave, away!

Mist. Mer. [*within.*] You will not have us starve here, will
    you, Master Merrythought?
Jasp. Nay, good sir, be persuaded; she is my mother:
    If her offences have been great against you,
    Let your own love remember she is yours,
    And so forgive her.
Luce. Good Master Merrythought,
    Let me entreat you; I will not be denied.
Mist. Mer. [*within.*] Why, Master Merrythought, will you be
    a vexed thing still?

Mer. Woman, I take you to my love again; but you shall
    sing before you enter; therefore despatch your song and
    so come in.

Mist. Mer. [*within.*] Well, you must have your will, when
    all's done.—Mick, what song canst thou sing, boy?

Mich. [*within.*] I can sing none, forsooth, but " A Lady's
    Daughter, of Paris properly,"   [*Sings within.*

          It was a lady's daughter, etc.

Merrythought *opens the Door ; enter* Mistress
    Merrythought *and* Michael.

Mer. Come, you're welcome home again.   [*Sings.*

      If such danger be in playing,
        And jest must to earnest turn,
      You shall go no more a-maying——

Vent. [*within.*] Are you within, sir? Master Merrythought!

Jasp. It is my master's voice: good sir, go hold him
    In talk, whilst we convey ourselves into
    Some inward room.   [*Exit with Luce.*

Mer. What are you? are you merry?
    You must be very merry, if you enter.

Vent. [*within.*] I am, sir.

Mer. Sing, then.

Vent. [*within.*] Nay, good sir, open to me.

Mer. Sing, I say,
    Or, by the merry heart, you come not in!

Vent. [*within.*] Well, sir, I'll sing.   [*Sings.*

         Fortune, my foe, etc.

Merrythought *opens the Door :* Enter Venturewell.

Mer. You are welcome, sir, you are welcome: you see your
    entertainment; pray you, be merry.

Vent. Oh, Master Merrythought, I'm come to ask you
    Forgiveness for the wrongs I offered you,
    And your most virtuous son! they're infinite;
    Yet my contrition shall be more than they:
    I do confess my hardness broke his heart,
    For which just Heaven hath given me punishment
    More than my age can carry; his wandering spirit,
    Nor yet at rest, pursues me everywhere,
    Crying, " I'll haunt thee for thy cruelty."

My daughter, she is gone, I know not how,
Taken invisible, and whether living
Or in the grave, 'tis yet uncertain to me.
Oh, Master Merrythought, these are the weights
Will sink me to my grave! forgive me, sir.

Mer. Why, sir, I do forgive you; and be merry;
And if the wag in's lifetime played the knave,
Can you forgive him too?

Vent. With all my heart, sir.

Mer. Speak it again, and heartily.

Vent. I do, sir;
Now, by my soul, I do.

Re-enter LUCE *and* JASPER.

Mer. [*Sings.*]

> With that came out his paramour;
> She was as white as the lily flower:
> Hey, troul, troly, loly!
> With that came out her own dear knight;
> He was as true as ever did fight, etc.

Sir, if you will forgive 'em, clap their hands together;
there's no more to be said i' the matter.

Vent. I do, I do.

[*Cit.* I do not like this. Peace, boys! Hear me, one of you:
everybody's part is come to an end but Ralph's, and
he's left out.

Boy. 'Tis 'long of yourself, sir; we have nothing to do with
his part.

Cit. Ralph, come away!—Make an end on him, as you have
done of the rest, boys; come.

Wife. Now, good husband, let him come out and die.

Cit. He shall, Nell.—Ralph, come away quickly, and die, boy!

Boy. 'Twill be very unfit he should die, sir, upon no occasion
—and in a comedy too.

Cit. Take you no care of that, sir boy; is not his part at an
end, think you, when he's dead?—Come away, Ralph!]

Enter RALPH, *with a forked Arrow through his Head.*

Ralph. When I was mortal, this my costive corps
Did lap up figs and raisins in the Strand;
Where sitting, I espied a lovely dame,
Whose master wrought with lingel and with awl,

And underground he vampèd many a boot.
Straight did her love prick forth me, tender sprig,
To follow feats of arms in warlike wise
Through Waltham desert; where I did perform
Many achievements, and did lay on ground
Huge Barbarossa, that insulting giant,
And all his captives soon set at liberty.
Then honour pricked me from my native soil
Into Moldavia, where I gained the love
Of Pompiona, his belovèd daughter;
But yet proved constant to the black thumbed maid
Susan, and scornèd Pompiona's love;
Yet liberal I was, and gave her pins,
And money for her father's officers.
I then returnèd home, and thrust myself
In action, and by all men chosen was
Lord of the May, where I did flourish it,
With scarfs and rings, and posy in my hand.
After this action I preferrèd was,
And chosen city-captain at Mile End,
With hat and feather, and with leading-staff,
And trained my men, and brought them all off clear,
Save one man that berayed him with the noise.
But all these things I Ralph did undertake
Only for my belovèd Susan's sake.
Then coming home, and sitting in my shop
With apron blue, Death came into my stall
To cheapen *aquavitæ ;* but ere I
Could take the bottle down and fill a taste,
Death caught a pound of pepper in his hand,
And sprinkled all my face and body o'er
And in an instant vanishèd away.
[*Cit.* 'Tis a pretty fiction, i'faith.]
Ralph. Then took I up my bow and shaft in hand,
And walked into Moorfields to cool myself:
But there grim cruel Death met me again,
And shot this forkèd arrow through my head;
And now I faint; therefore be warned by me,
My fellows every one, of forkèd heads!
Farewell, all you good boys in merry London!
Ne'er shall we more upon Shrove Tuesday meet,
And pluck down houses of iniquity;—
My pain increaseth;—I shall never more

Hold open, whilst another pumps both legs,
Nor daub a satin gown with rotten eggs;
Set up a stake, oh, never more I shall!
I die! fly, fly, my soul, to Grocers' Hall!
Oh, oh, oh, etc.

[*Wife.* Well said, Ralph! do your obeisance to the gentlemen, and go your ways: well said, Ralph!]

[*Ralph rises, makes obeisance, and exit.*

Mer. Methinks all we, thus kindly and unexpectedly re-
conciled, should not depart without a song.

Vent. A good motion.

Mer. Strike up, then!

Song.

Better music ne'er was known
Than a quire of hearts in one.
Let each other, that hath been
Troubled with the gall or spleen,
Learn of us to keep his brow
Smooth and plain, as ours are now:
Sing, though before the hour of dying;
He shall rise, and then be crying,
" Hey, ho, 'tis nought but mirth
That keeps the body from the earth!"

[*Exeunt.*

Cit. Come, Nell, shall we go? the play's done.

Wife. Nay, by my faith, George, I have more manners than
so; I'll speak to these gentlemen first.—I thank you all,
gentlemen, for your patience and countenance to Ralph,
a poor fatherless child; and if I might see you at my
house, it should go hard but I would have a bottle of
wine and a pipe of tobacco for you: for, truly, I hope
you do like the youth, but I would be glad to know the
truth; I refer it to your own discretions, whether you
will applaud him or no; for I will wink, and whilst you
shall do what you will.   I thank you with all my heart.
God give you good night!—Come, George.   [*Exeunt.*

THE MAID'S TRAGEDY

KING.
LYSIPPUS, *Brother to the King.*
AMINTOR, *a noble Gentleman.*
MELANTIUS, ⎱ *Brothers to Evadne.*
DIPHILUS, ⎰
CALIANAX, *an old humorous Lord, and Father to Aspatia.*
CLEON, ⎱ *Gentlemen.*
STRATO, ⎰
DIAGORAS, *a Servant to Calianax.*

EVADNE, *Sister to Melantius.*

ASPATIA, *troth-plight Wife to Amintor*
ANTIPHILA, ⎱ *Waiting-Gentle-*
OLYMPIAS, ⎰ *women to Aspatia.*
DULA, *Waiting-Woman to Evadne.*
Ladies.

NIGHT,
CYNTHIA,
NEPTUNE, ⎱ *Masquers.*
ÆOLUS,
Sea Gods,

SCENE.—THE CITY OF RHODES.

ACT I

SCENE I.—*An Apartment in the Palace.*

Enter CLEON, STRATO, LYSIPPUS, *and* DIPHILUS.

Cleon. The rest are making ready, sir.
Lys. So let them;
　　There's time enough.
Diph. You are the brother to the king, my lord;
　　We'll take your word.
Lys. Strato, thou hast some skill in poetry:
　　What think'st thou of the masque? will it be well?
Strat. As well as masque can be.
Lys. As masque can be?
Strat. Yes; they must commend their king, and speak in
　　　　praise
　　Of the assembly; bless the bride and bridegroom
　　In person of some god. They are tied to rules
　　Of flattery.
Cle. See, good my lord, who is return'd!

Enter MELANTIUS.

Lys. Noble Melantius! the land, by me,
　　Welcomes thy virtues home to Rhodes.

Thou, that with blood abroad buy'st us our peace!
The breath of kings is like the breath of gods;
My brother wish'd thee here, and thou art here.
He will be too kind, and weary thee
With often welcomes.   But the time doth give thee
A welcome above his, or all the world's.

Mel. My lord, my thanks; but these scratch'd limbs of mine
Have spoke my love and truth unto my friends,
More than my tongue e'er could.   My mind's the same
It ever was to you: Where I find worth,
I love the keeper till he let it go,
And then I follow it.

Diph. Hail, worthy brother!
He, that rejoices not at your return
In safety, is mine enemy for ever.

Mel. I thank thee, Diphilus.   But thou art faulty;
I sent for thee to exercise thine arms
With me at Patria: Thou camest not, Diphilus;
'Twas ill.

Diph. My noble brother, my excuse
Is my king's strict command; which you, my lord,
Can witness with me.

Lys. 'Tis true, Melantius;
He might not come, till the solemnity
Of this great match was past.

Diph. Have you heard of it?

Mel. Yes.   I have given cause to those that envy
My deeds abroad, to call me gamesome:
I have no other business here at Rhodes.

Lys. We have a masque to-night, and you must tread
A soldier's measure.

Mel. These soft and silken wars are not for me:
The music must be shrill, and all confused,
That stirs my blood; and then I dance with arms.
But is Amintor wed?

Diph. This day.

Mel. All joys upon him! for he is my friend.
Wonder not that I call a man so young my friend:
His worth is great; valiant he is, and temperate;
And one that never thinks his life his own,
If his friend need it.   When he was a boy,
As oft as I returned (as, without boast,
I brought home conquest) he would gaze upon me,

And view me round, to find in what one limb
The virtue lay to do those things he heard.
Then would he wish to see my sword, and feel
The quickness of the edge, and in his hand
Weigh it: He oft would make me smile at this.
His youth did promise much, and his ripe years
Will see it all perform'd.

Enter ASPATIA.

Hail, maid and wife!
Thou fair Aspatia, may the holy knot
That thou hast tied to-day, last till the hand
Of age undo it! may'st thou bring a race
Unto Amintor, that may fill the world
Successively with soldiers!

Asp. My hard fortunes
Deserve not scorn; for I was never proud
When they were good.   [*Exit.*

Mel. How's this?

Lys. You are mistaken,
For she is not married.

Mel. You said Amintor was.

Diph. 'Tis true; but——

Mel. Pardon me, I did receive
Letters at Patria from my Amintor,
That he should marry her.

Diph. And so it stood
In all opinion long; but your arrival
Made me imagine you had heard the change.

Mel. Who hath he taken then?

Lys. A lady, sir,
That bears the light about her, and strikes dead
With flashes of her eye: the fair Evadne,
Your virtuous sister.

Mel. Peace of heart betwixt them!
But this is strange.

Lys. The king my brother did it
To honour you; and these solemnities
Are at his charge.

Mel. 'Tis royal, like himself. But I am sad
My speech bears so unfortunate a sound
To beautiful Aspatia. There is rage

Hid in her father's breast, Calianax,
Bent long against me; and he should not think,
If I could call it back, that I would take
So base revenges, as to scorn the state
Of his neglected daughter.   Holds he still
His greatness with the king?

Lys. Yes.   But this lady
Walks discontented, with her watery eyes
Bent on the earth.   The unfrequented woods
Are her delight; and when she sees a bank
Stuck full of flowers, she with a sigh will tell
Her servants what a pretty place it were
To bury lovers in; and make her maids
Pluck 'em, and strew her over like a corse.
She carries with her an infectious grief,
That strikes all her beholders; she will sing
The mournful'st things that ever ear hath heard,
And sigh, and sing again; and when the rest
Of our young ladies, in their wanton blood,
Tell mirthful tales in course, that fill the room
With laughter, she will, with so sad a look,
Bring forth a story of the silent death
Of some forsaken virgin, which her grief
Will put in such a phrase, that, ere she end,
She'll send them weeping, one by one, away.

Mel. She has a brother under my command,
Like her; a face as womanish as hers;
But with a spirit that hath much outgrown
The number of his years.

Enter AMINTOR.

Cle. My lord, the bridegroom!

Mel. I might run fiercely, not more hastily,
Upon my foe.   I love thee well, Amintor;
My mouth is much too narrow for my heart;
I joy to look upon those eyes of thine;
Thou art my friend, but my disorder'd speech
Cuts off my love.

Amin. Thou art Melantius;
All love is spoke in that.   A sacrifice,
To thank the gods Melantius is return'd
In safety!   Victory sits on his sword,

As she was wont: May she build there and dwell;
And may thy armour be, as it hath been,
Only thy valour and thine innocence!
What endless treasures would our enemies give,
That I might hold thee still thus!

Mel. I am but poor
In words; but credit me, young man, thy mother
Could do no more but weep for joy to see thee
After long absence: All the wounds I have
Fetch'd not so much away, nor all the cries
Of widowed mothers. But this is peace,
And that was war.

Amin. Pardon, thou holy god
Of marriage bed, and frown not, I am forced,
In answer of such noble tears as those,
To weep upon my wedding-day.

Mel. I fear thou'rt grown too fickle; for I hear
A lady mourns for thee; men say, to death;
Forsaken of thee; on what terms I know not.

Amin. She had my promise; but the king forbade it,
And made me make this worthy change, thy sister,
Accompanied with graces far above her;
With whom I long to lose my lusty youth,
And grow old in her arms.

Mel. Be prosperous!

Enter Messenger.

Mess. My lord, the masquers rage for you.

Lys. We are gone. Cleon, Strato, Diphilus—
             [*Exeunt Lysippus, Cleon, Strato, and Diphilus.*

Amin. We'll all attend you.—We shall trouble you
With our solemnities.

Mel. Not so, Amintor:
But if you laugh at my rude carriage
In peace, I'll do as much for you in war,
When you come thither. Yet I have a mistress
To bring to your delights; rough though I am,
I have a mistress, and she has a heart
She says; but, trust me, it is stone, no better;
There is no place that I can challenge in't.
But you stand still, and here my way lies.
                              [*Exeunt severally*

SCENE II.—*A large Hall in the same, with a Gallery full of Spectators.*

Enter CALIANAX, *with* DIAGORAS *at the Door.*

Cal. Diagoras, look to the doors better for shame; you let in all the world, and anon the king will rail at me—why, very well said—by Jove, the king will have the show i' th' court.

Diag. Why do you swear so, my lord? You know, he'll have it here.

Cal. By this light, if he be wise, he will not.

Diag. And if he will not be wise, you are forsworn.

Cal. One may wear out his heart with swearing, and get thanks on no side. I'll be gone—look to't who will.

Diag. My lord, I shall never keep them out. Pray, stay; your looks will terrify them.

Cal. My looks terrify them, you coxcombly ass, you! I'll be judged by all the company whether thou hast not a worse face than I.

Diag. I mean, because they know you and your office.

Cal. Office! I would I could put it off; I am sure I sweat quite through my office. I might have made room at my daughter's wedding: they have near kill'd her among them; and now I must do service for him that hath forsaken her. Serve that will. [*Exit.*

Diag. He's so humorous since his daughter was forsaken— Hark, hark! there, there! so, so! Codes, codes! [*Knock within.*] What now?

Mel. [*within.*] Open the door.

Diag. Who's there?

Mel. [*within.*] Melantius.

Diag. I hope your lordship brings no troop with you; for, if you do, I must return them.

[*Opens the door. Persons endeavour to rush in.*

Enter MELANTIUS *and a* Lady.

Mel. None but this lady, sir.

Diag. The ladies are all placed above, save those that come in the king's troop: The best of Rhodes sit there, and there's room.

Mel. I thank you, sir.—When I have seen you placed,

madam, I must attend the king; but, the masque done,
I'll wait on you again.

> [*Exit with the Lady into the gallery.*

Diag. Stand back there!—Room for my lord Melantius!—
pray, bear back—this is no place for such youths and
their trulls—let the doors shut again.—No!—do your
heads itch? I'll scratch them for you. [*Shuts the
door.*]—So, now thrust and hang. [*Knocking.*] Again!
who is't now?—I cannot blame my lord Calianax for
going away: 'Would he were here! he would run raging
among them, and break a dozen wiser heads than his
own, in the twinkling of an eye.—What's the news now?
[*Within.*] I pray you, can you help me to the speech of the
master-cook?

Diag. If I open the door, I'll cook some of your calves-heads.
Peace, rogues! [*Knocking.*]—Again! who is't?

Mel. [*within.*] Melantius.

Enter CALIANAX.

Cal. Let him not in.

Diag. O, my lord, I must.—Make room there for my lord.

Enter MELANTIUS.

Is your lady placed?   [*To Melantius.*

Mel. Yes, sir.
I thank you.—My Lord Calianax, well met.
Your causeless hate to me, I hope, is buried.

Cal. Yes, I do service for your sister here,
That brings my own poor child to timeless death;
She loves your friend Amintor; such another
False-hearted lord as you.

Mel. You do me wrong,
A most unmanly one, and I am slow
In taking vengeance! But be well advised.

Cal. It may be so.—Who placed the lady there,
So near the presence of the king?

Mel. I did.

Cal. My lord, she must not sit there.

Mel. Why?

Cal. The place is kept for women of more worth.

Mel. More worth than she? It misbecomes your age,
And place, to be thus womanish. Forbear!

What you have spoke, I am content to think
The palsy shook your tongue to.

Cal. Why, 'tis well
If I stand here to place men's wenches.

Mel. I shall forget this place, thy age, my safety,
And, thorough all, cut that poor sickly week,
Thou hast to live, away from thee.

Cal. Nay, I know you can fight for your whore.

Mel. Bate the king, and be he flesh and blood,
He lies, that says it! Thy mother at fifteen
Was black and sinful to her.

Diag. Good my lord!

Mel. Some god pluck threescore years from that fond man,
That I may kill him and not stain mine honour.
It is the curse of soldiers, that in peace
They shall be braved by such ignoble men,
As, if the land were troubled, would with tears
And knees beg succour from 'em. 'Would, that blood,
That sea of blood, that I have lost in fight,
Were running in thy veins, that it might make thee
Apt to say less, or able to maintain,
Should'st thou say more! This Rhodes, I see, is nought
But a place privileged to do men wrong.

Cal. Ay, you may say your pleasure.

Enter AMINTOR.

Amin. What vile injury
Has stirr'd my worthy friend, who is as slow
To fight with words as he is quick of hand?

Mel. That heap of age, which I should reverence
If it were temperate; but testy years
Are most contemptible.

Amin. Good sir, forbear.

Cal. There is just such another as yourself.

Amin. He will wrong you, or me, or any man,
And talk as if he had no life to lose,
Since this our match. The king is coming in:
I would not for more wealth than I enjoy,
He should perceive you raging. He did hear
You were at difference now, which hastened him.

Cal. Make room there!   [*Hautboys play within.*

Enter KING, EVADNE, ASPATIA, Lords, *and* Ladies.

King. Melantius, thou art welcome, and my love
    Is with thee still: But this is not a place
    To brabble in.   Calianax, join hands.
Cal. He shall not have my hand.
King. This is no time
    To force you to it.   I do love you both:
    Calianax, you look well to your office;
    And you, Melantius, are welcome home.—
    Begin the masque!
Mel. Sister, I joy to see you, and your choice.
    You look'd with my eyes when you took that man:
    Be happy in him!   [*Recorders play.*
Evad. O, my dearest brother!
    Your presence is more joyful than this day
    Can be unto me.

THE MASQUE.

NIGHT *rises in mists.*

Night. Our reign is come; for in the raging sea
    The sun is drown'd, and with him fell the Day.
    Bright Cynthia, hear my voice; I am the Night,
    For whom thou bear'st about thy borrow'd light.
    Appear; no longer thy pale visage shroud,
    But strike thy silver horns quite through a cloud
    And send a beam upon my swarthy face;
    By which I may discover all the place
    And persons, and how many longing eyes
    Are come to wait on our solemnities.

Enter CYNTHIA.

    How dull and black am I! I could not find
    This beauty without thee, I am so blind.
    Methinks, they show like to those eastern streaks
    That warn us hence, before the morning breaks!
    Back, my pale servant, for these eyes know how
    To shoot far more and quicker rays than thou.
Cynth. Great queen, they be a troop for whom alone
    One of my clearest moons I have put on;
    A troop, that looks as if thyself and I

Had pluck'd our reins in, and our whips laid by,
To gaze upon these mortals, that appear
Brighter than we.

Night. Then let us keep 'em here;
And never more our chariots drive away,
But hold our places and outshine the day.

Cynth. Great queen of shadows, you are pleased to speak
Of more than may be done: We may not break
The gods' decrees; but, when our time is come,
Must drive away, and give the day our room.
Yet, while our reign lasts, let us stretch our power
To give our servants one contented hour,
With such unwonted solemn grace and state,
As may for ever after force them hate
Our brother's glorious beams; and wish the night
Crown'd with a thousand stars, and our cold light:
For almost all the world their service bend
To Phœbus, and in vain my light I lend;
Gazed on unto my setting from my rise
Almost of none, but of unquiet eyes.

Night. Then shine at full, fair queen, and by thy power
Produce a birth, to crown this happy hour,
Of nymphs and shepherds: Let their songs discover,
Easy and sweet, who is a happy lover.
Or, if thou woo't, then call thine own Endymion,
From the sweet flowery bed he lies upon,
On Latmus' top, thy pale beams drawn away,
And of this long night let him make a day.

Cynth. Thou dream'st, dark queen; that fair boy was not
mine,
Nor went I down to kiss him. Ease and wine
Have bred these bold tales: Poets, when they rage,
Turn gods to men, and make an hour an age.
But I will give a greater state and glory,
And raise to time a noble memory
Of what these lovers are. Rise, rise, I say,
Thou power of deeps; thy surges laid away,
Neptune, great king of waters, and by me
Be proud to be commanded.

NEPTUNE *rises.*

Nept. Cynthia, see,
Thy word hath fetch'd me hither: Let me know

Why I ascend?
Cynth. Doth this majestic show
    Give thee no knowledge yet?
Nept. Yes, now I see
    Something intended, Cynthia, worthy thee.
    Go on: I'll be a helper.
Cynth. Hie thee then,
    And charge the wind fly from his rocky den.
    Let loose thy subjects; only Boreas,
    Too foul for our intention, as he was,
    Still keep him fast chain'd: we must have none here
    But vernal blasts, and gentle winds appear;
    Such as blow flowers, and through the glad boughs sing
    Many soft welcomes to the lusty spring:
    These are our music.   Next, thy watery race
    Bring on in couples (we are pleased to grace
    This noble night), each in their richest things
    Your own deeps, or the broken vessel, brings.
    Be prodigal, and I shall be as kind,
    And shine at full upon you.
Nept. Ho! the wind-
    Commanding Æolus!

Enter ÆOLUS *out of a Rock.*

Æol. Great Neptune?
Nept. He.
Æol. What is thy will?
Nept. We do command thee free
    Favonius, and thy milder winds, to wait
    Upon our Cynthia; but tie Boreas straight;
    He's too rebellious.
Æol. I shall do it.
Nept. Do.——   [*Exit Æolus into the rock and re-enters.*
Æol. Great master of the flood, and all below,
    Thy full command has taken.—Ho! the Main!
    Neptune!
Nept. Here.
Æol. Boreas has broke his chain,
    And, struggling, with the rest has got away.
Nept. Let him alone, I'll take him up at sea;
    He will not long be thence.   Go once again,
    And call out of the bottoms of the main

Blue Proteus, and the rest; charge them put on
Their greatest pearls, and the most sparkling stone
The beaten rock breeds; till this night is done
By me a solemn honour to the moon.
Fly, like a full sail.
Æol. I am gone.
Cynth. Dark Night,
Strike a full silence; do a thorough right
To this great chorus; that our music may
Touch high as Heaven, and make the east break day
At mid-night.   [*Music.*

SONG.

Cynthia, to thy power and thee,
    We obey.
Joy to this great company!
    And no day
Come to steal this night away,
  Till the rites of love are ended;
And the lusty bridegroom say,
    Welcome, light, of all befriended.

Pace out, you watery powers below;
    Let your feet,
Like the gallies when they row,
    Even beat.
Let your unknown measures, set
  To the still winds, tell to all,
That gods are come, immortal, great,
  To honour this great nuptial.
          [*The Measure by the Sea-gods.*

SECOND SONG.

Hold back thy hours, dark Night, till we have done:
  The day will come too soon;
Young maids will curse thee if thou steal'st away,
And leav'st their losses open to the day;
    Stay, stay, and hide
    The blushes of the bride!
Stay, gentle Night, and with thy darkness cover
    The kisses of her lover.
Stay, and confound her tears, and her shrill cryings,
Her weak denials, vows, and often dyings;
    Stay, and hide all:
    But help not, though she call.

Nept. Great queen of us and Heaven,
Hear what I bring to make this hour a full one,
If not o'ermeasure.
Cynth. Speak, sea's king.
Nept. The tunes my Amphitrite joys to have,

When they will dance upon the rising wave,
And court me as she sails. My Tritons, play
Music to lead a storm; I'll lead the way.   [*Measure.*

SONG.

To bed, to bed; come, Hymen, lead the bride,
  And lay her by her husband's side;
    Bring in the virgins every one,
    That grieve to lie alone;
That they may kiss while they may say, a maid;
To-morrow, 'twill be other, kiss'd, and said.
    Hesperus be long a-shining,
    Whilst these lovers are a-twining.

Æol. Ho! Neptune!
Nept. Æolus!
Æol. The sea goes high,
    Boreas hath raised a storm: Go and apply
    Thy trident; else, I prophesy, ere day
    Many a tall ship will be cast away.
    Descend with all the gods, and all their power,
    To strike a calm.
Cynth. A thanks to every one, and to gratulate
    So great a service, done at my desire,
    Ye shall have many floods, fuller and higher
    Than you have wished for; no ebb shall dare
    To let the day see where your dwellings are.
    Now back unto your government in haste,
    Lest your proud charge should swell above the waste,
    And win upon the island.
Nept. We obey.   [*Neptune descends, and the Sea-gods.*
Cynth. Hold up thy head, dead Night; see'st thou not Day?
    The east begins to lighten: I must down,
    And give my brother place.
Night. Oh, I could frown
    To see the Day, the Day that flings his light
    Upon my kingdom, and contemns old Night!
    Let him go on and flame! I hope to see
    Another wild-fire in his axletree;
    And all fall drench'd. But I forgot; speak, queen.
    The day grows on; I must no more be seen.
Cynth. Heave up thy drowsy head again, and see
    A greater light, a greater majesty,
    Between our set and us! Whip up thy team!
    The day-break's here, and yon sun-flaring beam

Shot from the south.   Say, which way wilt thou go?
Night. I'll vanish into mists.
Cynth. I into day.   [*Exeunt.*

THE MASQUE ENDS.

King. Take lights there!—Ladies, get the bride to bed.—
    We will not see you laid.   Good-night, Amintor;
    We'll ease you of that tedious ceremony.
    Were it my case, I should think time run slow.
    If thou be'st noble, youth, get me a boy,
    That may defend my kingdom from my foes.
Amin. All happiness to you.
King. Good night, Melantius.   [*Exeunt.*

ACT II

SCENE I.—*Antechamber to Evadne's Bedroom in the Palace.*

Enter EVADNE, ASPATIA, DULA, *and other* Ladies.

Dula. Madam, shall we undress you for this fight?
    The wars are nak'd that you must make to-night.
Evad. You are very merry, Dula.
Dula. *I should be merrier far, if 'twere*
        With me as 'tis with you.
Evad. How's that?
Dula.   *That I might go to bed with him*
        With the credit that you do.
Evad. Why, how now, wench?
Dula. Come, ladies, will you help?
Evad. I am soon undone.
Dula. And as soon done:
    Good store of clothes will trouble you at both.
Evad. Art thou drunk, Dula?
Dula. Why, here's none but we.
Evad. Thou think'st belike, there is no modesty
    When we're alone.
Dula. Ay, by my troth, you hit my thoughts aright.
Evad. You prick me, lady.
Dula. 'Tis against my will.
    Anon you must endure more, and lie still;
    You're best to practise.

Evad. Sure, this wench is mad.

Dula. No, 'faith, this is a trick that I have had
 Since I was fourteen.

Evad. 'Tis high time to leave it.

Dula. Nay, now I'll keep it, till the trick leave me.
 A dozen wanton words, put in your head,
 Will make you livelier in your husband's bed.

Evad. Nay, 'faith, then take it.

Dula. Take it, madam? where?
 We all, I hope, will take it, that are here.

Evad. Nay, then, I'll give you o'er.

Dula. So will I make
 The ablest man in Rhodes, or his heart ache.

Evad. Wilt take my place to-night?

Dula. I'll hold your cards 'gainst any two I know.

Evad. What wilt thou do?

Dula. Madam, we'll do't, and make 'em leave play too.

Evad. Aspatia, take her part.

Dula. I will refuse it.
 She will pluck down a side; she does not use it.

Evad. Why, do.

Dula. You will find the play
 Quickly, because your head lies well that way.

Evad. I thank thee, Dula. 'Would thou could'st instil
 Some of thy mirth into Aspatia!
 Nothing but sad thoughts in her breast do dwell:
 Methinks, a mean betwixt you would do well.

Dula. She is in love: Hang me, if I were so,
 But I could run my country. I love, too,
 To do those things that people in love do.

Asp. It were a timeless smile should prove my cheek:
 It were a fitter hour for me to laugh,
 When at the altar the religious priest
 Were pacifying the offended powers
 With sacrifice, than now. This should have been
 My night; and all your hands have been employed
 In giving me a spotless offering
 To young Amintor's bed, as we are now
 For you. Pardon, Evadne; 'would my worth
 Were great as yours, or that the king, or he,
 Or both, thought so! Perhaps he found me worthless:
 But, till he did so, in these ears of mine,
 These credulous ears, he pour'd the sweetest words

That art or love could frame.   If he were false,
Pardon it, Heaven! and if I did want
Virtue, you safely may forgive that too;
For I have lost none that I had from you.

Evad. Nay, leave this sad talk, madam.

Asp. Would I could!
Then should I leave the cause.

Evad. See, if you have not spoil'd all Dula's mirth.

Asp. Thou think'st thy heart hard; but if thou be'st caught,
Remember me; thou shalt perceive a fire
Shot suddenly into thee.

Dula. That's not so good; let 'em shoot anything
But fire, I fear 'em not.

Asp. Well, wench, thou may'st be taken.

Evad. Ladies, good-night: I'll do the rest myself.

Dula. Nay, let your lord do some.

Asp. [*Sings.*] *Lay a garland on my hearse,*
Of the dismal yew.

Evad. That's one of your sad songs, madam.

Asp. Believe me, 'tis a very pretty one.

Evad. How is it, madam?

SONG.

> *Asp.* Lay a garland on my hearse,
>   Of the dismal yew;
>   Maidens, willow branches bear;
>   Say I died true:
>   My love was false, but I was firm
>   From my hour of birth.
>   Upon my buried body lie
>   Lightly, gentle earth!

Evad. Fie on't, madam!   The words are so strange, they are
able to make one dream of hobgoblins.   " I could never
have the power:"   Sing that, Dula.

SONG.

> *Dula.* I could never have the power
>   To love one above an hour,
>   But my heart would prompt mine eye
>   On some other man to fly;
>   Venus, fix mine eyes fast,
> Or if not, give me all that I shall see at last.

Evad. So, leave me now.

Dula. Nay, we must see you laid.

Asp. Madam, good-night.   May all the marriage joys

That longing maids imagine in their beds,
Prove so unto you!   May no discontent
Grow 'twixt your love and you!   But, if there do,
Inquire of me, and I will guide your moan;
Teach you an artificial way to grieve,
To keep your sorrow waking.   Love your lord
No worse than I: but if you love so well,
Alas, you may displease him; so did I.
This is the last time you shall look on me.—
Ladies, farewell.   As soon as I am dead,
Come all, and watch one night about my hearse;
Bring each a mournful story, and a tear,
To offer at it when I go to earth.
With flatt'ring ivy clasp my coffin round;
Write on my brow my fortune; let my bier
Be borne by virgins that shall sing, by course,
The truth of maids, and perjuries of men.

Evad. Alas, I pity thee.   [*Exit Evadne.*
All. Madam, good-night.
1 *Lady.* Come, we'll let in the bridegroom.
Dula. Where's my lord?

Enter AMINTOR.

1 *Lady.* Here, take this light.
Dula. You'll find her in the dark.
1 *Lady.* Your lady's scarce a-bed yet; you must help her.
Asp. Go, and be happy in your lady's love.
    May all the wrongs, that you have done to me,
    Be utterly forgotten in my death!
    I'll trouble you no more; yet I will take
    A parting kiss, and will not be denied.
    You'll come, my lord, and see the virgins weep
    When I am laid in earth, though you yourself
    Can know no pity.   Thus I wind myself
    Into this willow garland, and am prouder
    That I was once your love, though now refused,
    Than to have had another true to me.
    So with my prayers I leave you, and must try
    Some yet-unpractised way to grieve and die.   [*Exit.*
Dula. Come, ladies, will you go?
All. Good-night, my lord.
Amin. Much happiness unto you all!—   [*Exeunt Ladies.*

I did that lady wrong: Methinks, I feel
Her grief shoot suddenly through all my veins.
Mine eyes run: This is strange at such a time.
It was the king first moved me to't;—but he
Has not my will in keeping.—Why do I
Perplex myself thus? Something whispers me,
" Go not to bed."   My guilt is not so great
As mine own conscience, too sensible,
Would make me think: I only break a promise,
And 'twas the king that forced me.—Timorous flesh,
Why shak'st thou so?—Away, my idle fears!

Enter EVADNE.

Yonder she is, the lustre of whose eye
Can blot away the sad remembrance
Of all these things.—Oh, my Evadne, spare
That tender body; let it not take cold.
The vapours of the night will not fall here:
To bed, my love.   Hymen will punish us
For being slack performers of his rites.
Cam'st thou to call me?
Evad. No.
Amin. Come, come, my love,
    And let us lose ourselves to one another.
    Why art thou up so long?
Evad. I am not well.
Amin. To bed, then; let me wind thee in these arms,
    Till I have banish'd sickness.
Evad. Good my lord,
    I cannot sleep.
Amin. Evadne, we will watch;
    I mean no sleeping.
Evad. I'll not go to bed.
Amin. I pr'ythee do.
Evad. I will not for the world.
Amin. Why, my dear love?
Evad. Why? I have sworn I will not.
Amin. Sworn!
Evad. Ay.
Amin. How! sworn, Evadne?
Evad. Yes, sworn, Amintor; and will swear again,
    If you will wish to hear me.

Amin. To whom have you sworn this?

Evad. If I should name him, the matter were not great.

Amin. Come, this is but the coyness of a bride.

Evad. The coyness of a bride?

Amin. How prettily that frown becomes thee!

Evad. Do you like it so?

Amin. Thou canst not dress thy face in such a look,
　　But I shall like it.

Evad. What look likes you best?

Amin. Why do you ask?

Evad. That I may show you one less pleasing to you.

Amin. How's that?

Evad. That I may show you one less pleasing to you.

Amin. I pr'ythee, put thy jests in milder looks;
　　It shows as thou wert angry.

Evad. So, perhaps,
　　I am indeed.

Amin. Why, who has done thee wrong?
　　Name me the man, and by thyself I swear,
　　Thy yet-unconquer'd self, I will revenge thee.

Evad. Now I shall try thy truth. If thou dost love me,
　　Thou weigh'st not anything compared with me:
　　Life, honour, joys eternal, all delights
　　This world can yield, or hopeful people feign,
　　Or in the life to come, are light as air
　　To a true lover when his lady frowns,
　　And bids him *do this*. Wilt thou kill this man?
　　Swear, my Amintor, and I'll kiss the sin
　　Off from thy lips.

Amin. I will not swear, sweet love,
　　Till I do know the cause.

Evad. I would thou would'st.
　　Why, it is thou that wrong'st me; I hate thee;
　　Thou should'st have kill'd thyself.

Amin. If I should know that, I should quickly kill
　　The man you hated.

Evad. Know it then, and do't.

Amin. Oh, no; what look soe'er thou shalt put on
　　To try my faith, I shall not think thee false:
　　I cannot find one blemish in thy face,
　　Where falsehood should abide. Leave, and to bed.
　　If you have sworn to any of the virgins,
　　That were your old companions, to preserve

    Your maidenhead a night, it may be done
    Without this means.

Evad. A maidenhead, Amintor,
    At my years?

Amin. Sure, she raves!—This cannot be
    Thy natural temper. Shall I call thy maids?
    Either thy healthful sleep hath left thee long,
    Or else some fever rages in thy blood.

Evad. Neither, Amintor: Think you I am mad,
    Because I speak the truth?

Amin. Will you not lie with me to-night?

Evad. To-night! you talk as if I would hereafter.

Amin. Hereafter! yes, I do.

Evad. You are deceived.
    Put off amazement, and with patience mark
    What I shall utter; for the oracle
    Knows nothing truer: 'tis not for a night,
    Or two, that I forbear thy bed, but for ever.

Amin. I dream! Awake, Amintor!

Evad. You hear right.
    I sooner will find out the beds of snakes,
    And with my youthful blood warm their cold flesh,
    Letting them curl themselves about my limbs,
    Than sleep one night with thee. This is not feign'd,
    Nor sounds it like the coyness of a bride.

Amin. Is flesh so earthly to endure all this?
    Are these the joys of marriage? Hymen, keep
    This story (that will make succeeding youth
    Neglect thy ceremonies) from all ears;
    Let it not rise up, for thy shame and mine,
    To after-ages: We will scorn thy laws,
    If thou no better bless them. Touch the heart
    Of her that thou hast sent me, or the world
    Shall know, there's not an altar that will smoke
    In praise of thee; we will adopt us sons;
    Then virtue shall inherit, and not blood.
    If we do lust, we'll take the next we meet,
    Serving ourselves as other creatures do;
    And never take note of the female more,
    Nor of her issue.—I do rage in vain;
    She can but jest. O, pardon me, my love!
    So dear the thoughts are that I hold of thee,
    That I must break forth. Satisfy my fear;

It is a pain, beyond the hand of death,
To be in doubt: Confirm it with an oath,
If this be true.

Evad. Do you invent the form:
Let there be in it all the binding words
Devils and conjurers can put together,
And I will take it.   I have sworn before,
And here, by all things holy, do again,
Never to be acquainted with thy bed.
Is your doubt over now?

Amin. I know too much.   Would I had doubted still!
Was ever such a marriage night as this!
Ye powers above, if you did ever mean
Man should be used thus, you have thought a way
How he may bear himself, and save his honour.
Instruct me in it; for to my dull eyes
There is no mean, no moderate course to run:
I must live scorn'd, or be a murderer.
Is there a third?   Why is this night so calm?
Why does not Heaven speak in thunder to us,
And drown her voice?

Evad. This rage will do no good.

Amin. Evadne, hear me: Thou hast ta'en an oath,
But such a rash one, that, to keep it, were
Worse than to swear it: Call it back to thee;
Such vows as those never ascend the Heaven;
A tear or two will wash it quite away.
Have mercy on my youth, my hopeful youth,
If thou be pitiful; for, without boast,
This land was proud of me.   What lady was there,
That men call'd fair and virtuous in this isle,
That would have shunn'd my love?   It is in thee
To make me hold this worth.   Oh! we vain men,
That trust out all our reputation,
To rest upon the weak and yielding hand
Of feeble woman!   But thou art not stone;
Thy flesh is soft, and in thine eyes doth dwell
The spirit of love; thy heart cannot be hard.
Come, lead me from the bottom of despair,
To all the joys thou hast; I know thou wilt;
And make me careful, lest the sudden change
O'ercome my spirits.

Evad. When I call back this oath,

The pains of hell environ me!

Amin. I sleep, and am too temperate! Come to bed!
  Or by those hairs, which, if thou hadst a soul
  Like to thy locks, were threads for kings to wear
  About their arms——

Evad. Why, so, perhaps, they are.

Amin. I'll drag thee to my bed, and make thy tongue
  Undo this wicked oath, or on thy flesh
  I'll print a thousand wounds to let out life!

Evad. I fear thee not. Do what thou dar'st to me!
  Every ill-sounding word, or threat'ning look,
  Thou show'st to me, will be revenged at full.

Amin. It will not, sure, Evadne?

Evad. Do not you hazard that.

Amin. Have you your champions?

Evad. Alas, Amintor, think'st thou I forbear
  To sleep with thee, because I have put on
  A maiden's strictness? Look upon these cheeks,
  And thou shalt find the hot and rising blood
  Unapt for such a vow. No; in this heart
  There dwells as much desire, and as much will
  To put that wish'd act in practice, as ever yet
  Was known to woman; and they have been shown,
  Both. But it was the folly of thy youth
  To think this beauty, to what land soe'er
  It shall be call'd, shall stoop to any second.
  I do enjoy the best, and in that height
  Have sworn to stand or die: You guess the man.

Amin. No: let me know the man that wrongs me so,
  That I may cut his body into motes,
  And scatter it before the northern wind.

Evad. You dare not strike him.

Amin. Do not wrong me so.
  Yes, if his body were a poisonous plant,
  That it were death to touch, I have a soul
  Will throw me on him.

Evad. Why, it is the king.

Amin. The king!

Evad. What will you do now?

Amin. 'Tis not the king!

Evad. What did he make this match for, dull Amintor?

Amin. Oh, thou hast named a word, that wipes away
  All thoughts revengeful! In that sacred name,

" The king," there lies a terror.   What frail man
Dares lift his hand against it?   Let the gods
Speak to him when they please: till when let us
Suffer, and wait.

Evad. Why should you fill yourself so full of heat,
And haste so to my bed? I am no virgin.

Amin. What devil put it in thy fancy, then,
To marry me?

Evad. Alas, I must have one
To father children, and to bear the name
Of husband to me, that my sin may be
More honourable.

Amin. What a strange thing am I!

Evad. A miserable one; one that myself
Am sorry for.

Amin. Why, show it then in this:
If thou hast pity, though thy love be none,
Kill me; and all true lovers, that shall live
In after-ages cross'd in their desires,
Shall bless thy memory, and call thee good;
Because such mercy in thy heart was found,
To rid a ling'ring wretch.

Evad. I must have one
To fill thy room again, if thou wert dead;
Else, by this night, I would: I pity thee.

Amin. These strange and sudden injuries have fallen
So thick upon me, that I lose all sense
Of what they are.   Methinks I am not wrong'd:
Nor is it aught, if from the censuring world
I can but hide it.   Reputation!
Thou art a word, no more.—But thou hast shown
An impudence so high, that to the world,
I fear, thou wilt betray or shame thyself.

Evad. To cover shame, I took thee; never fear
That I would blaze myself.

Amin. Nor let the king
Know I conceive he wrongs me; then mine honour
Will thrust me into action, though my flesh
Could bear with patience.   And it is some ease
To me in these extremes, that I knew this
Before I touch'd thee; else had all the sins
Of mankind stood betwixt me and the king,
I had gone through 'em to his heart and thine.

I have left one desire: 'tis not his crown
Shall buy me to thy bed, now I resolve,
He has dishonoured thee.   Give me thy hand;
Be careful of thy credit, and sin close;
'Tis all I wish.   Upon thy chamber-floor
I'll rest to-night, that morning-visitors
May think we did as married people use.
And, pr'ythee, smile upon me when they come,
And seem to toy, as if thou hadst been pleased
With what we did.
Evad. Fear not; I will do this.
Amin. Come, let us practise: and as wantonly
As ever loving bride and bridegroom met,
Let's laugh and enter here.
Evad. I am content.
Amin. Down all the swellings of my troubled heart!
When we walk thus intwined, let all eyes see
If ever lovers better did agree.   [*Exeunt.*

SCENE II.—*An Apartment in the Citadel.*

Enter ASPATIA, ANTIPHILA, *and* OLYMPIAS.

Asp. Away, you are not sad; force it no further.
Good Gods, how well you look!   Such a full colour
Young bashful brides put on.   Sure, you are new married!
Ant. Yes, madam, to your grief.
Asp. Alas, poor wenches!
Go learn to love first; learn to lose yourselves;
Learn to be flatter'd, and believe, and bless
The double tongue that did it.   Make a faith
Out of the miracles of ancient lovers,
Such as speak truth, and died in't; and, like me,
Believe all faithful, and be miserable.
Did you ne'er love yet, wenches?   Speak, Olympias;
Thou hast an easy temper, fit for stamp.
Olym. Never.
Asp. Nor you, Antiphila?
Ant. Nor I.
Asp. Then, my good girls, be more than women, wise:
At least be more than I was; and be sure
You credit anything the light gives light to,
Before a man.   Rather believe the sea

Weeps for the ruin'd merchant, when he roars;
Rather, the wind courts but the pregnant sails,
When the strong cordage cracks; rather, the sun
Comes but to kiss the fruit in wealthy autumn,
When all falls blasted.   If you needs must love,
(Forced by ill fate) take to your maiden bosoms
Two dead-cold aspicks, and of them make lovers:
They cannot flatter, nor forswear; one kiss
Makes a long peace for all.   But man,
Oh, that beast man!   Come, let's be sad, my girls!
That down-cast of thine eye, Olympias,
Shows a fine sorrow.   Mark, Antiphila;
Just such another was the nymph Œnone,
When Paris brought home Helen.   Now, a tear;
And then thou art a piece expressing fully
The Carthage queen, when, from a cold sea-rock,
Full with her sorrow, she tied fast her eyes
To the fair Trojan ships; and, having lost them,
Just as thine eyes do, down stole a tear.   Antiphila,
What would this wench do, if she were Aspatia?
Here she would stand, till some more pitying god
Turn'd her to marble!   'Tis enough, my wench!
Show me the piece of needlework you wrought.

Ant. Of Ariadne, madam?

Asp. Yes, that piece.—
This should be Theseus; he has a cozening face:
You meant him for a man?

Ant. He was so, madam.

Asp. Why, then, 'tis well enough.   Never look back:
You have a full wind, and a false heart, Theseus!
Does not the story say, his keel was split,
Or his masts spent, or some kind rock or other
Met with his vessel?

Ant. Not as I remember.

Asp. It should have been so.   Could the gods know this,
And not, of all their number, raise a storm?
But they are all as ill!   This false smile
Was well express'd; just such another caught me!
You shall not go [on] so, Antiphila:
In this place work a quicksand,
And over it a shallow smiling water,
And his ship ploughing it; and then a Fear:
Do that Fear to the life, wench.

Ant. 'Twill wrong the story.

Asp. 'Twill make the story, wrong'd by wanton.poets,
Live long, and be believed. But where's the lady?

Ant. There, madam.

Asp. Fie! you have miss'd it here, Antiphila;
You are much mistaken, wench:
These colours are not dull and pale enough
To show a soul so full of misery
As this sad lady's was. Do it by me;
Do it again, by me, the lost Aspatia,
And you shall find all true but the wild island.
Suppose I stand upon the sea-beach now,
Mine arms thus, and mine hair blown with the wind,
Wild as that desart; and let all about me
Be teachers of my story. Do my face
(If thou hadst ever feeling of a sorrow)
Thus, thus, Antiphila: Strive to make me look
Like Sorrow's monument! And the trees about me,
Let them be dry and leafless; let the rocks
Groan with continual surges; and, behind me,
Make all a desolation. Look, look, wenches!
A miserable life of this poor picture!

Olym. Dear madam!

Asp. I have done. Sit down; and let us
Upon that point fix all our eyes; that point there.
Make a dull silence, till you feel a sudden sadness
Give us new souls.

Enter CALIANAX.

Cal. The king may do this, and he may not do it:
My child is wrong'd, disgraced.—Well, how now,
huswives!
What, at your ease? Is this a time to sit still?
Up, you young lazy whores, up, or I'll swinge you!

Olym. Nay, good my lord.

Cal. You'll lie down shortly. Get you in, and work!
What, are you grown so resty you want heats?
We shall have some of the court-boys heat you shortly.

Ant. My lord, we do no more than we are charged.
It is the lady's pleasure we be thus
In grief: she is forsaken.

Cal. There's a rogue too!

A young dissembling slave! Well, get you in!
I'll have a bout with that boy. 'Tis high time
Now to be valiant; I confess my youth
Was never prone that way. What, made an ass?
A court-stale? Well, I will be valiant,
And beat some dozen of these whelps; I will!
And there's another of 'em, a trim cheating soldier;
I'll maul that rascal; he has out-braved me twice:
But now, I thank the gods, I am valiant.—
Go, get you in! I'll take a course with all.   [*Exeunt.*

ACT III

SCENE I.—*Antechamber to Evadne's Bedroom in the Palace.*

Enter Cleon, Strata, *and* Diphilus.

Cle. Your sister is not up yet.

Diph. Oh, brides must take their morning's rest; the night is troublesome.

Stra. But not tedious.

Diph. What odds, he has not my sister's maidenhead to-night?

Stra. No; it's odds, against any bridegroom living, he ne'er gets it while he lives.

Diph. You're merry with my sister; you'll please to allow me the same freedom with your mother.

Stra. She's at your service.

Diph. Then she's merry enough of herself; she needs no tickling. Knock at the door.

Stra. We shall interrupt them.

Diph. No matter; they have the year before them.—Good-morrow, sister! Spare yourself to-day; the night will come again.

Enter Amintor.

Amin. Who's there? my brother! I'm no readier yet.
Your sister is but now up.

Diph. You look as you had lost your eyes to-night:
I think you have not slept.

Amin. I'faith I have not.

Diph. You have done better, then.

Amin. We ventured for a boy: When he is twelve,
    He shall command against the foes of Rhodes.
    Shall we be merry?

Stra. You cannot; you want sleep.

Amin. 'Tis true.—But she,   *[Aside.*
    As if she had drank Lethe, or had made
    Even with Heaven, did fetch so still a sleep,
    So sweet and sound——

Diph. What's that?

Amin. Your sister frets
    This morning; and does turn her eyes upon me,
    As people on their headsman. She does chafe,
    And kiss, and chafe again, and clap my cheeks;
    She's in another world.

Diph. Then I had lost: I was about to lay
    You had not got her maidenhead to-night.

Amin. Ha! he does not mock me? *[Aside.]*—You had lost,
    indeed;
    I do not use to bungle.

Cleo. You do deserve her.

Amin. I laid my lips to hers, and that wild breath,
    That was so rude and rough to me last night,
    Was sweet as April.—I'll be guilty too,
    If these be the effects.   *[Aside.*

Enter MELANTIUS.

Mel. Good day, Amintor! for, to me, the name
    Of brother is too distant: We are friends.
    And that is nearer.

Amin. Dear Melantius!
    Let me behold thee. Is it possible?

Mel. What sudden gaze is this?

Amin. 'Tis wond'rous strange!

Mel. Why does thine eye desire so strict a view
    Of that it knows so well? There's nothing here
    That is not thine.

Amin. I wonder, much, Melantius,
    To see those noble looks, that make me think
    How virtuous thou art: And, on the sudden,
    'Tis strange to me thou shouldst have worth and honour;
    Or not be base, and false, and treacherous,
    And every ill. But——

Mel. Stay, stay, my friend;
 I fear this sound will not become our loves.
 No more; embrace me.
Amin. Oh, mistake me not:
 I know thee to be full of all those deeds
 That we frail men call good; but, by the course
 Of nature, thou shouldst be as quickly changed
 As are the winds; dissembling as the sea,
 That now wears brows as smooth as virgins' be,
 Tempting the merchant to invade his face,
 And in an hour calls his billows up,
 And shoots 'em at the sun, destroying all
 He carries on him.—Oh, how near am I
 To utter my sick thoughts!   [*Aside.*
Mel. But why, my friend, should I be so by nature?
Amin. I have wed thy sister, who hath virtuous thoughts
 Enough for one whole family; and, 'tis strange
 That you should feel no want.
Mel. Believe me, this compliment's too cunning for me.
Diph. What should I be then, by the course of nature,
 They having both robb'd me of so much virtue?
Stra. Oh, call the bride, my lord Amintor,
 That we may see her blush, and turn her eyes down:
 'Tis the prettiest sport!
Amin. Evadne!
Evad. [*within.*] My lord!
Amin. Come forth, my love!
 Your brothers do attend to wish you joy.
Evad. I am not ready yet.
Amin. Enough, enough.
Evad. They'll mock me.
Amin. 'Faith, thou shalt come in.

Enter EVADNE.

Mel. Good-morrow, sister! He that understands
 Whom you have wed, need not to wish you joy;
 You have enough: Take heed you be not proud.
Diph. Oh, sister, what have you done?
Evad. I done! why, what have I done?
Stra. My lord Amintor swears you are no maid now.
Evad. Pish!
Stra. I'faith, he does.
Evad. I knew I should be mock'd.

Diph. With a truth.

Evad. If 'twere to do again,
    In faith, I would not marry.

Amin. Nor I, by heaven!   [*Aside.*

Diph. Sister, Dula swears
    She heard you cry two rooms off.

Evad. Fie, how you talk!

Diph. Let's see you walk, Evadne.   By my troth,
    You are spoil'd.

Mel. Amintor!

Amin. Ha?

Mel. Thou art sad.

Amin. Who, I?   I thank you for that.
    Shall Diphilus, thou, and I, sing a catch?

Mel. How!

Amin. Pr'ythee, let's.

Mel. Nay, that's too much the other way.

Amin. I am so lightened with my happiness!
    How dost thou, love? kiss me.

Evad. I cannot love you, you tell tales of me.

Amin. Nothing but what becomes us.—Gentlemen,
    'Would you had all such wives, and all the world,
    That I might be no wonder!   You are all sad:
    What, do you envy me?   I walk, methinks,
    On water, and ne'er sink, I am so light.

Mel. 'Tis well you are so.

Amin. Well? how can I be other,
    When she looks thus?—Is there no music there?
    Let's dance.

Mel. Why, this is strange, Amintor!

Amin. I do not know myself; yet I could wish
    My joy were less.

Diph. I'll marry too, if it will make one thus.

Evad. Amintor, hark.   [*Aside.*

Amin. What says my love?—I must obey.

Evad. You do it scurvily, 'twill be perceived. [*Apart to him.*

Cleo. My lord, the king is here.

Enter KING *and* LYSIPPUS.

Amin. Where?

Stra. And his brother.

King. Good morrow, all!—
    Amintor, joy on joy fall thick upon thee

And, madam, you are alter'd since I saw you;
 I must salute you; you are now another's.
 How liked you your night's rest?

Evad. Ill, sir.

Amin. Ay, 'deed,
 She took but little.

Lys. You'll let her take more,
 And thank her too, shortly.

King. Amintor, wert
 Thou truly honest till thou wert married.

Amin. Yes, sir.

King. Tell me, then, how shows the sport unto thee?

Amin. Why, well.

King. What did you do?

Amin. No more, nor less, than other couples use;
 You know what 'tis; it has but a coarse name.

King. But, pr'ythee, I should think, by her black eye,
 And her red cheek, she should be quick and stirring
 In this same business; ha?

Amin. I cannot tell;
 I ne'er try'd other, sir; but I perceive
 She is as quick as you delivered.

King. Well, you will trust me then, Amintor,
 To chuse a wife for you again?

Amin. No, never, sir.

King. Why? like you this so ill?

Amin. So well I like her.
 For this I bow my knee in thanks to you,
 And unto heaven will pay my grateful tribute
 Hourly; and do hope we shall draw out
 A long contented life together here,
 And die both, full of grey hairs, in one day:
 For which the thanks are yours. But if the powers
 That rule us please to call her first away,
 Without pride spoke, this world holds not a wife
 Worthy to take her room.

King. I do not like this.—All forbear the room,
 But you, Amintor, and your lady.
    [Exeunt all but the King, Amintor, and Evadne.
 I have some speech with you, that may concern
 Your after living well.

Amin. [*aside.*] He will not tell me that he lies with her?
 If he do, something heavenly stay my heart,

> For I shall be apt to thrust this arm of mine
> To acts unlawful!

King. You will suffer me to talk with her,
> Amintor, and not have a jealous pang?

Amin. Sir, I dare trust my wife with whom she dares
> To talk, and not be jealous.

> *[Evadne and the King speak apart.*

King. How do you like
> Amintor?

Evad. As I did, sir.

King. How is that?

Evad. As one that, to fulfil your will and pleasure,
> I have given leave to call me wife and love.

King. I see there is no lasting faith in sin;
> They, that break word with heaven, will break again
> With all the world, and so dost thou with me.

Evad. How, sir?

King. This subtle woman's ignorance
> Will not excuse you: thou hast taken oaths,
> So great, methought, they did not well become
> A woman's mouth, that thou wouldst ne'er enjoy
> A man but me.

Evad. I never did swear so;
> You do me wrong.

King. Day and night have heard it.

Evad. I swore indeed, that I would never love
> A man of lower place; but, if your fortune
> Should throw you from this height, I bade you trust
> I would forsake you, and would bend to him
> That won your throne: I love with my ambition,
> Not with my eyes. But, if I ever yet
> Touch'd any other, leprosy light here
> Upon my face; which for your royalty
> I would not stain!

King. Why, thou dissemblest, and it is
> In me to punish thee.

Evad. Why, 'tis in me,
> Then, not to love you, which will more afflict
> Your body than your punishment can mine.

King. But thou hast let Amintor lie with thee.

Evad. I have not.

King. Impudence! he says himself so.

Evad. He lies.

King. He does not.
Evad. By this light he does,
    Strangely and basely! and I'll prove it so.
    I did not shun him for a night; but told him,
    I would never close with him.
King. Speak lower; 'tis false.
Evad. I am no man
    To answer with a blow; or, if I were,
    You are the king! But urge me not; 'tis most true.
King. Do not I know the uncontrolled thoughts
    That youth brings with him, when his blood is high
    With expectation, and desire of that
    He long hath waited for? Is not his spirit,
    Though he be temperate, of a valiant strain
    As this our age hath known? What could he do,
    If such a sudden speech had met his blood,
    But ruin thee for ever, if he had not kill'd thee?
    He could not bear it thus. He is as we,
    Or any other wrong'd man.
Evad. 'Tis dissembling.
King. Take him! farewell! henceforth I am thy foe;
    And what disgraces I can blot thee with look for.
Evad. Stay, sir!—Amintor!—You shall hear.—Amintor!
Amin. [*coming forward.*] What, my love?
Evad. Amintor, thou hast an ingenuous look,
    And shouldst be virtuous: It amazeth me,
    That thou canst make such base malicious lies!
Amin. What, my dear wife!
Evad. Dear wife! I do despise thee.
    Why, nothing can be baser than to sow
    Dissension amongst lovers.
Amin. Lovers! who?
Evad. The king and me.
Amin. O, God!
Evad. Who should live long, and love without distaste,
    Were it not for such pickthanks as thyself.
    Did you lie with me? Swear now, and be punish'd
    In hell for this!
Amin. The faithless sin I made
    To fair Aspatia, is not yet revenged;
    It follows me.—I will not lose a word
    To this vile woman: But to you, my king,
    The anguish of my soul thrusts out this truth,

You are a tyrant!   And not so much to wrong
An honest man thus, as to take a pride
In talking with him of it.

Evad. Now, sir, see
How loud this fellow lied.

Amin. You that can know to wrong, should know how men
Must right themselves: What punishment is due
From me to him that shall abuse my bed?
Is it not death?   Nor can that satisfy,
Unless I send your limbs through all the land,
To show how nobly I have freed myself.

King. Draw not thy sword: thou know'st I cannot fear
A subject's hand; but thou shalt feel the weight
Of this, if thou dost rage.

Amin. The weight of that!
If you have any worth, for Heaven's sake, think
I fear not swords; for as you are mere man,
I dare as easily kill you for this deed,
As you dare think to do it.   But there is
Divinity about you, that strikes dead
My rising passions: As you are my king,
I fall before you, and present my sword
To cut mine own flesh, if it be your will.
Alas! I am nothing but a multitude
Of walking griefs!   Yet, should I murder you,
I might before the world take the excuse
Of madness: For, compare my injuries,
And they will well appear too sad a weight
For reason to endure!   But, fall I first
Amongst my sorrows, ere my treacherous hand
Touch holy things!   But why (I know not what
I have to say) why did you chuse out me
To make thus wretched?   There were thousand fools
Easy to work on, and of state enough,
Within the island.

Evad. I would not have a fool;
It were no credit for me.

Amin. Worse and worse!
Thou, that dar'st talk unto thy husband thus,
Profess thyself a whore, and, more than so,
Resolve to be so still——It is my fate
To bear and bow beneath a thousand griefs,
To keep that little credit with the world!

But there were wise ones too; you might have ta'en
Another.
King. No; for I believe thee honest,
As thou wert valiant.
Amin. All the happiness
Bestowed upon me turns into disgrace.
Gods, take your honesty again, for I
Am loaden with it!—Good my lord the king,
Be private in it.
King. Thou may'st live, Amintor,
Free as thy king, if thou wilt wink at this,
And be a means that we may meet in secret.
Amin. A bawd! Hold, hold, my breast! A bitter curse
Seize me, if I forget not all respects
That are religious, on another word
Sounded like that; and, through a sea of sins,
Will wade to my revenge, though I should call
Pains here, and after life, upon my soul!
King. Well, I am resolute you lay not with her;
And so I leave you.   [*Exit King.*
Evad. You must needs be prating;
And see what follows.
Amin. Pr'ythee, vex me not!
Leave me: I am afraid some sudden start
Will pull a murder on me.
Evad. I am gone;
I love my life well.   [*Exit Evadne.*
Amin. I hate mine as much.—
This 'tis to break a troth! I should be glad,
If all this tide of grief would make me mad.   [*Exit.*

SCENE II.—*A Room in the Palace.*

Enter MELANTIUS.

Mel. I'll know the cause of all Amintor's griefs,
Or friendship shall be idle.

Enter CALIANAX.

Cal. O Melantius,
My daughter will die.
Mel. Trust me, I am sorry.
Would thou hadst ta'en her room!

Cal. Thou art a slave,
    A cut-throat slave, a bloody treacherous slave!

Mel. Take heed, old man; thou wilt be heard to rave,
    And lose thine offices.

Cal. I am valiant grown,
    At all these years, and thou art but a slave!

Mel. Leave! Some company will come, and I respect
    Thy years, not thee, so much, that I could wish
    To laugh at thee alone.

Cal. I'll spoil your mirth:
    I mean to fight with thee.   There lie, my cloak!
    This was my father's sword, and he durst fight.
    Are you prepared?

Mel. Why wilt thou dote thyself
    Out of thy life?   Hence, get thee to bed!
    Have careful looking-to, and eat warm things,
    And trouble not me: My head is full of thoughts,
    More weighty than thy life or death can be.

Cal. You have a name in war, where you stand safe
    Amongst a multitude; but I will try
    What you dare do unto a weak old man
    In single fight.   You will give ground, I fear.
    Come, draw.

Mel. I will not draw, unless thou pull'st thy death
    Upon thee with a stroke.   There's no one blow,
    That thou canst give, hath strength enough to kill me.
    Tempt me not so far then: The power of earth
    Shall not redeem thee.

Cal. [*aside.*] I must let him alone:
    He's stout and able; and, to say the truth,
    However I may set a face, and talk,
    I am not valiant.   When I was a youth,
    I kept my credit with a testy trick
    I had, 'mongst cowards, but durst never fight.

Mel. I will not promise to preserve your life,
    If you do stay.

Cal. I would give half my land
    That I durst fight with that proud man a little.
    If I had men to hold him, I would beat him
    Till he ask'd me mercy.

Mel. Sir, will you be gone?

Cal. I dare not stay; but I'll go home, and beat
    My servants all over for this.   [*Exit Calianax.*

Mel. This old fellow haunts me!
     But the distracted carriage of my Amintor
     Takes deeply on me: I will find the cause.
     I fear his conscience cries, he wrong'd Aspatia.

Enter AMINTOR.

Amin. Men's eyes are not so subtle to perceive
     My inward misery: I bear my grief
     Hid from the world.   How art thou wretched then?
     For aught I know, all husbands are like me;
     And every one I talk with of his wife,
     Is but a well dissembler of his woes,
     As I am.   'Would I knew it! for the rareness
     Afflicts me now.
Mel. Amintor, we have not enjoy'd our friendship of late,
     For we were wont to change our souls in talk.
Amin. Melantius, I can tell thee a good jest
     Of Strato and a lady the last day.
Mel. How was't?
Amin. Why, such an odd one!
Mel. I have long'd to speak with you;
     Not of an idle jest, that's forced, but of matter
     You are bound to utter to me.
Amin. What is that, my friend?
Mel. I have observed your words
     Fall from your tongue wildly; and all your carriage
     Like one that strove to show his merry mood,
     When he were ill disposed: You were not wont
     To put such scorn into your speech, or wear
     Upon your face ridiculous jollity.
     Some sadness sits here, which your cunning would
     Cover o'er with smiles, and 'twill not be.
     What is it?
Amin. A sadness here! what cause
     Can fate provide for me, to make me so?
     Am I not loved through all this isle?   The king
     Rains greatness on me.   Have I not received
     A lady to my bed, that in her eye
     Keeps mounting fire, and on her tender cheeks
     Inevitable colour, in her heart
     A prison for all virtue?   Are not you,
     Which is above all joys, my constant friend?
     What sadness can I have?   No; I am light,

And feel the courses of my blood more warm
And stirring than they were. 'Faith, marry too:
And you will feel so unexpress'd a joy
In chaste embraces, that you will indeed
Appear another.

Mel. You may shape, Amintor,
Causes to cozen the whole world withal,
And yourself too: but 'tis not like a friend,
To hide your soul from me. 'Tis not your nature
To be thus idle: I have seen you stand
As you were blasted, 'midst of all your mirth;
Call thrice aloud, and then start, feigning joy
So coldly!—World, what do I hear? a friend
Is nothing. Heaven, I would have told that man
My secret sins! I'll search an unknown land,
And there plant friendship; all is wither'd here.
Come with a compliment! I would have fought,
Or told my friend " he lied," ere sooth'd him so.
Out of my bosom!

Amin. But there is nothing——

Mel. Worse and worse! farewell!
From this time have acquaintance, but no friend.

Amin. Melantius, stay: You shall know what it is.

Mel. See, how you play'd with friendship! Be advised
How you give cause unto yourself to say,
You have lost a friend.

Amin. Forgive what I have done;
For I am so o'ergone with injuries
Unheard of, that I lose consideration
Of what I ought to do. Oh, oh!

Mel. Do not weep.
What is it? May I once but know the man
Hath turn'd my friend thus!

Amin. I had spoke at first,
But that——

Mel. But what?

Amin. I held it most unfit
For you to know. 'Faith, dc not know it yet.

Mel. Thou see'st my love, that will keep company
With thee in tears! hide nothing, then, from me:
For when I know the cause of thy distemper,
With mine old armour I'll adorn myself,
My resolution, and cut through my foes,

      Unto thy quiet; till I place thy heart
      As peaceable as spotless innocence.
      What is it?
Amin. Why, 'tis this——It is too big
      To get out——Let my tears make way awhile.
Mel. Punish me strangely, Heaven, if he 'scape
      Of life or fame, that brought this youth to this!
Amin. Your sister——
Mel. Well said.
Amin. You will wish't unknown,
      When you have heard it.
Mel. No.
Amin. Is much to blame,
      And to the king has given her honour up,
      And lives in whoredom with him.
Mel. How is this?
      Thou art run mad with injury, indeed;
      Thou couldst not utter this else.   Speak again;
      For I forgive it freely; tell thy griefs.
Amin. She's wanton: I am loth to say, " a whore,"
      Though it be true.
Mel. Speak yet again, before mine anger grow
      Up, beyond throwing down: What are thy griefs?
Amin. By all our friendship, these.
Mel. What, am I tame?
      After mine actions, shall the name of friend
      Blot all our family, and stick the brand
      Of whore upon my sister, unrevenged?
      My shaking flesh, be thou a witness for me,
      With what unwillingness I go to scourge
      This railer, whom my folly hath called friend!—
      I will not take thee basely; thy sword
      Hangs near thy hand; draw it, that I may whip
      Thy rashness to repentance.   Draw thy sword!
Amin. Not on thee, did thine anger swell as high
      As the wild surges. Thou shouldst do me ease
      Here, and eternally, if thy noble hand
      Would cut me from my sorrows.
Mel. This is base
      And fearful.   They, that use to utter lies,
      Provide not blows, but words, to qualify
      The men they wrong'd.   Thou hast a guilty cause.
Amin. Thou pleasest me; for so much more like this

Will raise my anger up above my griefs,
(Which is a passion easier to be borne)
And I shall then be happy.

Mel. Take then more,
To raise thine anger: 'Tis mere cowardice
Makes thee not draw; and I will leave thee dead,
However. But if thou art so much press'd
With guilt and fear, as not to dare to fight,
I'll make thy memory loath'd, and fix a scandal
Upon thy name for ever.

Amin. Then I draw,
As justly as our magistrates their swords
To cut offenders off. I knew before,
'Twould grate your ears; but it was base in you
To urge a weighty secret from your friend,
And then rage at it. I shall be at ease,
If I be kill'd; and if you fall by me,
I shall not long out-live you.

Mel. Stay awhile.—
The name of friend is more than family,
Or all the world besides: I was a fool!
Thou searching human nature, that didst wake
To do me wrong, thou art inquisitive,
And thrust'st me upon questions that will take
My sleep away! 'Would I had died, ere known
This sad dishonour!—Pardon me, my friend!
If thou wilt strike, here is a faithful heart;
Pierce it, for I will never heave my hand
To thine. Behold the power thou hast in me!
I do believe my sister is a whore,
A leprous one! Put up thy sword, young man.

Amin. How shall I bear it then, she being so?
I fear, my friend, that you will lose me shortly;
And I shall do a foul act on myself,
Through these disgraces.

Mel. Better half the land
Were buried quick together. No, Amintor;
Thou shalt have ease. Oh, this adulterous king,
That drew her to it! Where got he the spirit
To wrong me so?

Amin. What is it then to me,
If it be wrong to you?

Mel. Why, not so much:

    The credit of our house is thrown away.
    But from his iron den I'll waken Death,
    And hurl him on this king! My honesty
    Shall steel my sword; and on its horrid point
    I'll wear my cause, that shall amaze the eyes
    Of this proud man, and be too glittering
    For him to look on.

Amin. I have quite undone my fame.

Mel. Dry up thy watery eyes,
    And cast a manly look upon my face;
    For nothing is so wild as I, thy friend,
    Till I have freed thee. Still this swelling breast!
    I go thus from thee, and will never cease
    My vengeance, till I find thy heart at peace.

Amin. It must not be so. Stay!—Mine eyes would tell
    How loth I am to this; but, love and tears,
    Leave me awhile; for I have hazarded
    All that this world calls happy.—Thou hast wrought
    A secret from me, under name of friend,
    Which art could ne'er have found, nor torture wrung
    From out my bosom: Give it me again,
    For I will find it, wheresoe'er it lies,
    Hid in the mortal'st part! Invent a way
    To give it back.

Mel. Why would you have it back?
    I will to death pursue him with revenge.

Amin. Therefore I call it back from thee; for I know
    Thy blood so high, that thou wilt stir in this,
    And shame me to posterity.
    Take to thy weapon!

Mel. Hear thy friend, that bears
    More years than thou.

Amin. I will not hear! but draw,
    Or I——

Mel. Amintor!

Amin. Draw then; for I am full as resolute
    As fame and honour can inforce me be!
    I cannot linger. Draw!

Mel. I do. But is not
    My share of credit equal with thine,
    If I do stir?

Amin. No; for it will be call'd
    Honour in thee to spill thy sister's blood,

If she her birth abuse; and, on the king,
A brave revenge: But on me, that have walk'd
With patience in it, it will fix the name
Of fearful cuckold. Oh, that word! Be quick.

Mel. Then join with me.

Amin. I dare not do a sin, or else I would.
Be speedy.

Mel. Then dare not fight with me; for that's a sin.—
His grief distracts him.—Call thy thoughts again,
And to thyself pronounce the name of friend,
And see what that will work. I will not fight.

Amin. You must.

Mel. I will be kill'd first. Though my passions
Offer'd the like to you, 'tis not this earth
Shall buy my reason to it. Think awhile,
For you are (I must weep when I speak that)
Almost besides yourself.

Amin. Oh, my soft temper!
So many sweet words from thy sister's mouth,
I am afraid, would make me take her
To embrace, and pardon her. I am mad indeed,
And know not what I do. Yet, have a care
Of me in what thou dost.

Mel. Why, thinks my friend
I will forget his honour? or, to save
The bravery of our house, will lose his fame,
And fear to touch the throne of majesty?

Amin. A curse will follow that; but rather live
And suffer with me.

Mel. I'll do what worth shall bid me, and no more.

Amin. Faith, I am sick, and desperately I hope;
Yet, leaning thus, I feel a kind of ease.

Mel. Come, take again your mirth about you.

Amin. I shall never do't.

Mel. I warrant you; look up; we'll walk together;
Put thine arm here; all shall be well again.

Amin. Thy love (oh, wretched!) ay, thy love, Melantius!
Why, I have nothing else.

Mel. Be merry then. [*Exeunt.*

Re-enter MELANTIUS.

Mel. This worthy young man may do violence
Upon himself; but I have cherish'd him

To my best power, and sent him smiling from me,
To counterfeit again.   Sword, hold thine edge;
My heart will never fail me.

Enter DIPHILUS.

Diphilus! Thou com'st as sent.
Diph. Yonder has been such laughing.
Mel. Betwixt whom?
Diph. Why, our sister and the king;
I thought their spleens would break; they laugh'd us all
Out of the room.
Mel. They must weep, Diphilus.
Diph. Must they?
Mel. They must.
Thou art my brother; and if I did believe
Thou hadst a base thought, I would rip it out,
Lie where it durst.
Diph. You should not; I would first
Mangle myself and find it.
Mel. That was spoke
According to our strain.   Come, join thy hands to mine,
And swear a firmness to what project I
Shall lay before thee.
Diph. You do wrong us both:
People hereafter shall not say, there pass'd
A bond, more than our loves, to tie our lives
And deaths together.
Mel. It is as nobly said as I would wish.
Anon I'll tell you wonders: We are wrong'd.
Diph. But I will tell you now, we'll right ourselves.
Mel. Stay not: Prepare the armour in my house;
And what friends you can draw unto our side,
Not knowing of the cause, make ready too.
Haste, Diphilus, the time requires it, haste!—
[*Exit Diphilus.*
I hope my cause is just; I know my blood
Tells me it is; and I will credit it.
To take revenge, and lose myself withal,
Were idle; and to 'scape impossible,
Without I had the fort, which (misery!)
Remaining in the hands of my old enemy
Calianax——But I must have it.   See,

Enter CALIANAX.

Where he comes shaking by me.—Good my lord,
Forget your spleen to me; I never wrong'd you,
But would have peace with every man.

Cal. 'Tis well;
If I durst fight, your tongue would lie at quiet.

Mel. You are touchy without all cause.

Cal. Do, mock me.

Mel. By mine honour I speak truth.

Cal. Honour? where is it?

Mel. See, what starts
You make into your hatred, to my love
And freedom to you.　I come with resolution
To obtain a suit of you.

Cal. A suit of me!
'Tis very like it should be granted, sir.

Mel. Nay, go not hence:
'Tis this; you have the keeping of the fort,
And I would wish you, by the love you ought
To bear unto me, to deliver it
Into my hands.

Cal. I am in hope thou'rt mad,
To talk to me thus.

Mel. But there is a reason
To move you to it: I would kill the king,
That wrong'd you and your daughter.

Cal. Out, traitor!

Mel. Nay,
But stay: I cannot 'scape, the deed once done,
Without I have this fort.

Cal. And should I help thee?
Now thy treacherous mind betrays itself.

Mel. Come, delay me not;
Give me a sudden answer, or already
Thy last is spoke! refuse not offer'd love,
When it comes clad in secrets.

Cal. If I say　　　　　　　　　　　[*Aside.*
I will not, he will kill me; I do see't
Writ in his looks; and should I say I will,
He'll run and tell the king.—I do not shun
Your friendship, dear Melantius, but this cause
Is weighty; give me but an hour to think.

Mel. Take it.—I know this goes unto the king;
    But I am arm'd.   [*Exit Melantius.*
Cal. Methinks I feel myself
    But twenty now again! this fighting fool
    Wants policy: I shall revenge my girl,
    And make her red again. I pray, my legs
    Will last that pace that I will carry them:
    I shall want breath, before I find the king.   [*Exit.*

ACT IV

SCENE I.—*The Apartment of Evadne in the Palace.*

Enter MELANTIUS, EVADNE, *and* Ladies.

Mel. Save you!
Evad. Save you, sweet brother!
Mel. In my blunt eye, methinks, you look, Evadne——
Evad. Come, you will make me blush.
Mel. I would, Evadne;
    I shall displease my ends else.
Evad. You shall, if you commend me; I am bashful.
    Come, sir, how do I look?
Mel. I would not have your women hear me
    Break into commendation of you; 'tis not seemly.
Evad. Go, wait in the gallery.—Now speak. [*Exeunt Ladies.*
Mel. I'll lock the door first.
Evad. Why?
Mel. I will not have your gilded things, that dance
    In visitation with their Milan skins,
    Choke up my business.
Evad. You are strangely disposed, sir.
Mel. Good madam, not to make you merry.
Evad. No; if you praise me it will make me sad.
Mel. Such a sad commendation I have for you.
Evad. Brother, the court hath made you witty,
    And learn to riddle.
Mel. I praise the court for't: Has it learnt you nothing?
Evad. Me?
Mel. Ay, Evadne; thou art young and handsome,
    A lady of a sweet complexion,
    And such a flowing carriage, that it cannot
    Chuse but inflame a kingdom.

Evad. Gentle brother!

Mel. 'Tis yet in thy repentance, foolish woman,
    To make me gentle.

Evad. How is this?

Mel. 'Tis base;
    And I could blush, at these years, thorough all
    My honour'd scars, to come to such a parley.

Evad. I understand you not.

Mel. You dare not, fool!
    They, that commit thy faults, fly the remembrance.

Evad. My faults, sir! I would have you know, I care not
    If they were written here, here in my forehead.

Mel. Thy body is too little for the story;
    The lusts of which would fill another woman,
    Though she had twins within her.

Evad. This is saucy:
    Look you intrude no more! There lies your way.

Mel. Thou art my way, and I will tread upon thee,
    Till I find truth out.

Evad. What truth is that you look for?

Mel. Thy long-lost honour. 'Would the gods had set me
    Rather to grapple with the plague, or stand
    One of their loudest bolts! Come, tell me quickly,
    Do it without enforcement, and take heed
    You swell me not above my temper.

Evad. How, sir.
    Where got you this report?

Mel. Where there were people,
    In every place.

Evad. They, and the seconds of it are base people:
    Believe them not, they lied.

Mel. Do not play with mine anger, do not, wretch!
                                  [*Seizes her.*
    I come to know that desperate fool that drew thee
    From thy fair life: Be wise and lay him open.

Evad. Unhand me, and learn manners! Such another
    Forgetfulness forfeits your life.

Mel. Quench me this mighty humour, and then tell me
    Whose whore you are; for you are one, I know it.
    Let all mine honours perish, but I'll find him,
    Though he lie lock'd up in thy blood! Be sudden;
    There is no facing it, and be not flatter'd!
    The burnt air, when the Dog reigns, is not fouler

Than thy contagious name, till thy repentance
(If the gods grant thee any) purge thy sickness.

Evad. Be gone! you are my brother; that's your safety.

Mel. I'll be a wolf first! 'Tis, to be thy brother,
An infamy below the sin of coward.
I am as far from being part of thee,
As thou art from thy virtue: Seek a kindred
'Mongst sensual beasts, and make a goat thy brother?
A goat is cooler. Will you tell me yet?

Evad. If you stay here and rail thus, I shall tell you,
I'll have you whipp'd! Get you to your command,
And there preach to your sentinels, and tell them
What a brave man you are: I shall laugh at you.

Mel. You are grown a glorious whore! Where be your
fighters?
What mortal fool durst raise thee to this daring,
And I alive! By my just sword, he had safer
Bestride a billow, when the angry North
Plows up the sea, or made Heaven's fire his food!
Work me no higher. Will you discover yet?

Evad. The fellow's mad: Sleep, and speak sense.

Mel. Force my swoll'n heart no further: I would save thee.
Your great maintainers are not here, they dare not:
Would they were all, and arm'd! I would speak loud;
Here's one should thunder to 'em! will you tell me?
Thou hast no hope to 'scape: He that dares most,
And damns away his soul to do thee service,
Will sooner snatch meat from a hungry lion,
Than come to rescue thee; thou hast death about thee.
Who has undone thine honour, poison'd thy virtue,
And, of a lovely rose, left thee a canker?

Evad. Let me consider.

Mel. Do, whose child thou wert,
Whose honour thou hast murder'd, whose grave open'd,
And so pull'd on the gods, that in their justice
They must restore him flesh again, and life,
And raise his dry bones to revenge this scandal.

Evad. The gods are not of my mind; they had better
Let 'em lie sweet still in the earth; they'll stink here.

Mel. Do you raise mirth out of my easiness?   [*Draws.*
Forsake me, then, all weaknesses of nature,
That make men women! Speak, you whore, speak truth!
Or, by the dear soul of thy sleeping father,

This sword shall be thy lover! Tell, or I'll kill thee;
And, when thou hast told all, thou wilt deserve it.
Evad. You will not murder me?
Mel. No; 'tis a justice, and a noble one,
To put the light out of such base offenders.
Evad. Help!
Mel. By thy foul self, no human help shall help thee,
If thou criest! When I have kill'd thee as I
Have vow'd to do if thou confess not, naked,
As thou hast left thine honour, will I leave thee;
That on thy branded flesh the world may read
Thy black shame, and my justice. Wilt thou bend yet?
Evad. Yes.
Mel. Up, and begin your story.
Evad. Oh, I am miserable!
Mel. 'Tis true, thou art. Speak truth still.
Evad. I have offended: Noble sir, forgive me.
Mel. With what secure slave?
Evad. Do not ask me, sir:
Mine own remembrance is a misery
Too mighty for me.
Mel. Do not fall back again:
My sword's unsheathed yet.
Evad. What shall I do?
Mel. Be true, and make your fault less.
Evad. I dare not tell.
Mel. Tell, or I'll be this day a-killing thee.
Evad. Will you forgive me then?
Mel. Stay; I must ask mine honour first.—
I have too much foolish nature in me: Speak.
Evad. Is there none else here?
Mel. None but a fearful conscience; that's too many.
Who is't?
Evad. Oh, hear me gently. It was the king.
Mel. No more. My worthy father's and my services
Are liberally rewarded.—King, I thank thee!
For all my dangers and my wounds, thou hast paid me
In my own metal: These are soldiers' thanks!—
How long have you lived thus, Evadne?
Evad. Too long.
Mel. Too late you find it. Can you be sorry?
Evad. Would I were half as blameless.
Mel. Evadne, thou wilt to thy trade again!

Evad. First to my grave.

Mel. 'Would gods thou hadst been so blest.
　　　Dost thou not hate this king now? pr'ythee hate him.
　　　Couldst thou not curse him? I command thee, curse
　　　　him.
　　　Curse till the gods hear, and deliver him
　　　To thy just wishes! Yet, I fear, Evadne,
　　　You had rather play your game out.

Evad. No; I feel
　　　Too many sad confusions here, to let in
　　　Any loose flame hereafter.

Mel. Dost thou not feel, 'mongst all those, one brave anger
　　　That breaks out nobly, and directs thine arm
　　　To kill this base king?

Evad. All the gods forbid it!

Mel. No; all the gods require it:
　　　They are dishonour'd in him.

Evad. 'Tis too fearful.

Mel. You are valiant in his bed, and bold enough
　　　To be a stale whore, and have your madam's name
　　　Discourse for grooms and pages; and, hereafter,
　　　When his cool majesty hath laid you by,
　　　To be at pension with some needy sir,
　　　For meat and coarser clothes; Thus far you know
　　　No fear. Come, you shall kill him.

Evad. Good sir!

Mel. An 'twere to kiss him dead, thou shouldst smother him.
　　　Be wise, and kill him. Canst thou live, and know
　　　What noble minds shall make thee, see thyself
　　　Found out with every finger, made the shame
　　　Of all successions, and in this great ruin
　　　Thy brother and thy noble husband broken?
　　　Thou shalt not live thus. Kneel, and swear to help me,
　　　When I shall call thee to it; or, by all
　　　Holy in Heaven and earth, thou shalt not live
　　　To breathe a full hour longer; not a thought!
　　　Come, 'tis a righteous oath. Give me thy hands,
　　　And, both to Heaven held up, swear, by that wealth
　　　This lustful thief stole from thee, when I say it,
　　　To let his foul soul out.

Evad. Here I swear it;
　　　And, all you spirits of abused ladies,
　　　Help me in this performance!

Mel. Enough. This must be known to none
　　But you and I, Evadne; not to your lord,
　　Though he be wise and noble, and a fellow
　　Dares step as far into a worthy action
　　As the most daring: ay, as far as justice.
　　Ask me not why. Farewell. [*Exit Melantius.*
Evad. 'Would I could say so to my black disgrace!
　　Oh, where have I been all this time? how 'friended,
　　That I should lose myself thus desperately,
　　And none for pity show me how I wandered?
　　There is not in the compass of the light
　　A more unhappy creature: Sure, I am monstrous!
　　For I have done those follies, those mad mischiefs,
　　Would dare a woman. Oh, my loaden soul,
　　Be not so cruel to me; choke not up
　　The way to my repentance! Oh, my lord!

Enter AMINTOR.

Amin. How now?
Evad. My much-abused lord! [*Kneels.*
Amin. This cannot be!
Evad. I do not kneel to live; I dare not hope it;
　　The wrongs I did are greater. Look upon me,
　　Though I appear with all my faults.
Amin. Stand up.
　　This is a new way to beget more sorrow:
　　Heaven knows I have too many! Do not mock me:
　　Though I am tame, and bred up with my wrongs,
　　Which are my foster-brothers, I may leap,
　　Like a hand-wolf, into my natural wildness,
　　And do an outrage. Pr'ythee, do not mock me.
Evad. My whole life is so leprous, it infects
　　All my repentance. I would buy your pardon,
　　Though at the highest set; even with my life.
　　That slight contrition, that's no sacrifice
　　For what I have committed.
Amin. Sure I dazzle:
　　There cannot be a faith in that foul woman,
　　That knows no god more mighty than her mischiefs.
　　Thou dost still worse, still number on thy faults,
　　To press my poor heart thus. Can I believe
　　There's any seed of virtue in that woman
　　Left to shoot up, that dares go on in sin,

Known, and so known as thine is. Oh, Evadne!
'Would there were any safety in thy sex,
That I might put a thousand sorrows off,
And credit thy repentance! But I must not:
Thou hast brought me to that dull calamity,
To that strange misbelief of all the world,
And all things that are in it, that I fear
I shall fall like a tree, and find my grave,
Only remembering that I grieve.

Evad. My lord,
  Give me your griefs: You are an innocent,
A soul as white as heaven; let not my sins
Perish your noble youth. I do not fall here
To shadow, by dissembling with my tears,
(As, all say, women can), or to make less,
What my hot will hath done, which Heaven and you
Know to be tougher than the hand of time
Can cut from man's remembrance. No, I do not:
I do appear the same, the same Evadne,
Drest in the shames I lived in: the same monster!
But these are names of honour, to what I am:
I do present myself the foulest creature,
Most poisonous, dangerous, and despised of men,
Lerna e'er bred, or Nilus! I am hell,
Till you, my dear lord, shoot your light into me,
The beams of your forgiveness. I am soul-sick,
And wither with the fear of one condemn'd,
Till I have got your pardon.

Amin. Rise, Evadne.
  Those heavenly powers that put this good into thee,
Grant a continuance of it! I forgive thee:
Make thyself worthy of it; and take heed,
Take heed, Evadne, this be serious.
Mock not the powers above, that can and dare
Give thee a great example of their justice
To all ensuing eyes, if thou playest
With thy repentance, the best sacrifice.

Evad. I have done nothing good to win belief,
My life hath been so faithless. All the creatures,
Made for Heaven's honours, have their ends, and good
    ones,
All but the cozening crocodiles, false women!
They reign here like those plagues, those killing sores,

Men pray against; and when they die, like tales
Ill told and unbelieved, they pass away
And go to dust forgotten! But, my lord,
Those short days I shall number to my rest
(As many must not see me) shall, though too late,
Though in my evening, yet perceive a will;
Since I can do no good, because a woman,
Reach constantly at something that is near it:
I will redeem one minute of my age,
Or, like another Niobe, I'll weep
Till I am water.

Amin. I am now dissolved:
My frozen soul melts. May each sin thou hast
Find a new mercy! Rise; I am at peace.
Hadst thou been thus, thus excellently good,
Before that devil king tempted thy frailty,
Sure thou hadst made a star! Give me thy hand.
From this time I will know thee; and, as far
As honour gives me leave, be thy Amintor.
When we meet next, I will salute thee fairly,
And pray the gods to give thee happy days.
My charity shall go along with thee,
Though my embraces must be far from thee.
I should have kill'd thee, but this sweet repentance
Locks up my vengeance; for which thus I kiss thee—
The last kiss we must take! And 'would to Heaven
The holy priest, that gave our hands together,
Had given us equal virtues! Go, Evadne;
The Gods thus part our bodies. Have a care
My honour falls no farther: I am well then.

Evad. All the dear joys here, and, above, hereafter,
Crown thy fair soul! Thus I take leave, my lord;
And never shall you see the foul Evadne,
Till she have tried all honour'd means, that may
Set her in rest, and wash her stains away.   [*Exeunt.*

SCENE II.--*The Presence Chamber.*

Banquet—Enter KING *and* CALIANAX—*Hautboys play within.*

King. I cannot tell how I should credit this
From you, that are his enemy.
Cal. I am sure

He said it to me; and I'll justify it
What way he dares oppose—but with my sword.

King. But did he break, without all circumstance,
 To you, his foe, that he would have the fort,
 To kill me, and then 'scape?

Cal. If he deny it,
 I'll make him blush.

King. It sounds incredibly.

Cal. Ay, so does everything I say of late.

King. Not so, Calianax.

Cal. Yes, I should sit
 Mute, whilst a rogue with strong arms cuts your throat.

King. Well, I will try him; and, if this be true,
 I'll pawn my life I'll find it. If't be false,
 And that you clothe your hate in such a lie,
 You shall hereafter dote in your own house,
 Not in the court.

Cal. Why, if it be a lie,
 Mine ears are false; for, I'll be sworn, I heard it.
 Old men are good for nothing: You were best
 Put me to death for hearing, and free him
 For meaning it. You would have trusted me
 Once, but the time is alter'd.

King. And will still,
 Where I may do with justice to the world:
 You have no witness?

Cal. Yes, myself.

King. No more,
 I mean, there were that heard it.

Cal. How! no more?
 Would you have more? why, am not I enough
 To hang a thousand rogues?

King. But, so, you may
 Hang honest men too, if you please.

Cal. I may!
 'Tis like I will do so: There are a hundred
 Will swear it for a need too, if I say it——

King. Such witnesses we need not.

Cal. And 'tis hard
 If my word cannot hang a boisterous knave.

King. Enough.—Where's Strato?

Enter STRATO.

Stra. Sir!
King. Why, where's all the company?   Call Amintor in;
         Evadne.   Where's my brother, and Melantius?
         Bid him come too; and Diphilus.   Call all
         That are without there.   [*Exit Strato.*
         If he should desire
         The combat of you, 'tis not in the power
         Of all our laws to hinder it, unless
         We mean to quit 'em.
Cal.   Why, if you do think
         'Tis fit an old man, and a counsellor,
         Do fight for what he says, then you may grant it.

Enter AMINTOR, EVADNE, MELANTIUS, DIPHILUS,
         LYSIPPUS, CLEON, STRATO, DIAGORAS.

King. Come, sirs!—Amintor, thou art yet a bridegroom,
         And I will use thee so: Thou shalt sit down.—
         Evadne, sit; and you, Amintor, too:
         This banquet is for you, sir.—Who has brought
         A merry tale about him, to raise laughter
         Amongst our wine?   Why, Strato, where art thou?
         Thou wilt chop out with them unseasonably,
         When I desire them not.
Stra. 'Tis my ill luck, sir, so to spend them then.
King. Reach me a bowl of wine.—Melantius, thou
         Art sad.
Mel.   I should be, sir, the merriest here,
         But I have ne'er a story of my own
         Worth telling at this time.
King. Give me the wine.
         Melantius, I am now considering
         How easy 'twere, for any man we trust,
         To poison one of us in such a bowl.
Mel.   I think it were not hard, sir, for a knave.
Cal.   Such as you are.   [*Aside.*
King. I'faith, 'twere easy: It becomes us well
         To get plain-dealing men about ourselves;
         Such as you all are here.—Amintor, to thee;
         And to thy fair Evadne.
Mel.   Have you thought
         Of this, Calianax?   [*Apart to him.*

Cal. Yes, marry, have I.

Mel. And what's your resolution?

Cal. You shall have it,—
　　Soundly, I warrant you.

King. Reach to Amintor, Strato.

Amin. Here, my love,
　　This wine will do thee wrong, for it will set
　　Blushes upon thy cheeks; and, till thou dost
　　A fault, 'twere pity.

King. Yet, I wonder much
　　At the strange desperation of these men,
　　That dare attempt such acts here in our state:
　　He could not 'scape, that did it.

Mel. Were he known,
　　Impossible.

King. It would be known, Melantius.

Mel. It ought to be: If he got then away,
　　He must wear all our lives upon his sword.
　　He need not fly the island; he must leave
　　No one alive.

King. No; I should think no man
　　Could kill me, and 'scape clear, but that old man.

Cal. But I! heaven bless me! I! should I, my liege?

King. I do not think thou would'st; but yet thou might'st;
　　For thou hast in thy hands the means to 'scape,
　　By keeping of the fort.—He has, Melantius,
　　And he has kept it well.

Mel. From cobwebs, sir,
　　'Tis clean swept: I can find no other art
　　In keeping of it now: 'Twas ne'er besieged
　　Since he commanded it.

Cal. I shall be sure
　　Of your good word: But I have kept it safe
　　From such as you.

Mel. Keep your ill temper in:
　　I speak no malice.　Had my brother kept it,
　　I should have said as much.

King. You are not merry.
　　Brother, drink wine.　Sit you all still:—Calianax,
　　　　　　　　　　　　　　[*Apart to him.*
　　I cannot trust thus: I have thrown out words,
　　That would have fetch'd warm blood upon the cheeks
　　Of guilty men, and he is never moved:

He knows no such thing.

Cal. Impudence may 'scape,
When feeble virtue is accused.

King. He must,
If he were guilty, feel an alteration
At this our whisper, whilst we point at him:
You see he does not.

Cal. Let him hang himself:
What care I what he does? This he did say.

King. Melantius, you can easily conceive
What I have meant; for men that are in fault
Can subtly apprehend, when others aim
At what they do amiss: But I forgive
Freely, before this man. Heaven do so too!
I will not touch thee, so much as with shame
Of telling it. Let it be so no more.

Cal. Why, this is very fine.

Mel. I cannot tell
What 'tis you mean; but I am apt enough
Rudely to thrust into an ignorant fault.
But let me know it: Happily, 'tis nought
But misconstruction; and, where I am clear,
I will not take forgiveness of the gods,
Much less of you.

King. Nay, if you stand so stiff,
I shall call back my mercy.

Mel. I want smoothness
To thank a man for pardoning of a crime
I never knew.

King. Not to instruct your knowledge, but to show you
My ears are everywhere, you meant to kill me,
And get the fort to 'scape.

Mel. Pardon me, sir;
My bluntness will be pardoned: You preserve
A race of idle people here about you,
Facers and talkers, to defame the worth
Of those that do things worthy. The man that utter'd
this
Had perish'd without food, be't who it will,
But for this arm, that fenced him from the foe.
And if I thought you gave a faith to this,
The plainness of my nature would speak more.
Give me a pardon (for you ought to do't)

To kill him that spake this.

Cal. Ay, that will be
The end of all: Then I am fairly paid
For all my care and service.

Mel. That old man,
Who calls me enemy, and of whom I
(Though I will never match my hate so low)
Have no good thought, would yet, I think, excuse me,
And swear he thought me wrong'd in this.

Cal. Who—I?
Thou shameless fellow! Didst thou not speak to me
Of it thyself?

Mel. Oh, then it came from him?

Cal. From me! who should it come from, but from me?

Mel. Nay, I believe your malice is enough:
But I have lost my anger.—Sir, I hope
You are well satisfied.

King. Lysippus, cheer
Amintor and his lady; there's no sound
Comes from you; I will come and do't myself.

Amin. You have done already, sir, for me,
I thank you.   [*Apart.*

King. Melantius, I do credit this from him,
How slight soe'er you make't.

Mel. 'Tis strange you should.

Cal. 'Tis strange he should believe an old man's word
That never lied in's life.

Mel. I talk not to thee!—
Shall the wild words of this distemper'd man,
Frantic with age and sorrow, make a breach
Betwixt your majesty and me? 'Twas wrong
To hearken to him; but to credit him,
As much, at least, as I have power to bear.
But pardon me—whilst I speak only truth,
I may commend myself—I have bestow'd
My careless blood with you, and should be loth
To think an action that would make me lose
That, and my thanks too. When I was a boy,
I thrust myself into my country's cause,
And did a deed that pluck'd five years from time,
And styled me man then. And for you, my king,
Your subjects all have fed by virtue of
My arm. This sword of mine hath plough'd the ground,

And reapt the fruit in peace;
And you yourself have lived at home in ease.
So terrible I grew, that, without swords,
My name hath fetch'd you conquest: And my heart
And limbs are still the same: my will as great
To do you service. Let me not be paid
With such a strange distrust.

King. Melantius,
I held it great injustice to believe
Thine enemy, and did not; if I did,
I do not; let that satisfy.—What, struck
With sadness all? More wine!

Cal. A few fine words
Have overthrown my truth. Ah, thou'rt a villain!

Mel. Why, thou wert better let me have the fort,
                                        [*Apart to him.*
Dotard! I will disgrace thee thus for ever:
There shall no credit lie upon thy words.
Think better, and deliver it.

Cal. My liege,
He's at me now again to do it.—Speak;
Deny it, if thou canst.—Examine him
While he is hot; for if he cool again,
He will forswear it.

King. This is lunacy,
I hope, Melantius.

Mel. He hath lost himself
Much, since his daughter miss'd the happiness
My sister gain'd; and, though he call me foe,
I pity him.

Cal. Pity? a pox upon you!

Mel. Mark his disordered words! And, at the masque,
Diagoras knows, he raged, and rail'd at me,
And call'd a lady whore, so innocent
She understood him not. But it becomes
Both you and me too to forgive distraction:
Pardon him, as I do.

Cal. I'll not speak for thee,
For all thy cunning.—If you will be safe,
Chop off his head; for there was never known
So impudent a rascal.

King. Some, that love him,
Get him to bed. Why, pity should not let

Age make itself contemptible; we must be
All old; have him away.

Mel. Calianax,   *[Apart to him.*
The king believes you; come, you shall go home,
And rest; you have done well. You'll give it up
When I have used you thus a month, I hope.

Cal. Now, now, 'tis plain, sir; he does move me still.
He says, he knows I'll give him up the fort,
When he has used me thus a month. I am mad,
Am I not, still?

All. Ha, ha, ha!

Cal. I shall be mad indeed, if you do thus!
Why should you trust a sturdy fellow there
(That has no virtue in him; all's in his sword)
Before me? Do but take his weapons from him,
And he's an ass; and I'm a very fool,
Both with him, and without him, as you use me.

All. Ha, ha, ha!

King. 'Tis well, Calianax. But if you use
This once again, I shall entreat some other
To see your offices be well discharged.
Be merry, gentlemen; it grows somewhat late.—
Amintor, thou wouldst be a-bed again.

Amin. Yes, sir.

King. And you, Evadne.—Let me take
Thee in my arms, Melantius, and believe
Thou art, as thou deserv'st to be, my friend
Still, and for ever.—Good Calianax,
Sleep soundly; it will bring thee to thyself.

               [Exeunt all but Melantius and Calianax.

Cal. Sleep soundly! I sleep soundly now, I hope;
I could not be thus else.—How darest thou stay
Alone with me, knowing how thou hast used me?

Mel. You cannot blast me with your tongue, and that's
The strongest part you have about you.

Cal. I
Do look for some great punishment for this;
For I begin to forget all my hate,
And take't unkindly that mine enemy
Should use me so extraordinarily scurvily.

Mel. I shall melt too, if you begin to take
Unkindnesses: I never meant you hurt.

Cal. Thou'lt anger me again. Thou wretched rogue,

Meant me no hurt! Disgrace me, with the king;
Lose all my offices! This is no hurt,
Is it? I pr'ythee, what dost thou call hurt?

Mel. To poison men, because they love me not;
To call the credit of men's wives in question;
To murder children betwixt me and land;
This is all hurt.

Cal. All this thou think'st is sport;
For mine is worse: But use thy will with me;
For, betwixt grief and anger, I could cry.

Mel. Be wise then, and be safe; thou may'st revenge.

Cal. Ay, o' the king? I would revenge o' thee.

Mel. That you must plot yourself.

Cal. I'm a fine plotter.

Mel. The short is, I will hold thee with the king
In this perplexity, till peevishness
And thy disgrace have laid thee in thy grave.
But if thou wilt deliver up the fort,
I'll take thy trembling body in my arms,
And bear thee over dangers: Thou shalt hold
Thy wonted state.

Cal. If I should tell the king,
Canst thou deny't again?

Mel. Try, and believe.

Cal. Nay, then, thou canst bring anything about.
Thou shalt have the fort.

Mel. Why, well;
Here let our hate be buried; and this hand
Shall right us both. Give me thy aged breast
To compass.

Cal. Nay, I do not love thee yet;
I cannot well endure to look on thee:
And, if I thought it were a courtesy,
Thou should'st not have it. But I am disgraced;
My offices are to be ta'en away;
And, if I did but hold this fort a day,
I do believe, the king would take it from me,
And give it thee, things are so strangely carried.
Ne'er thank me for't; but yet the king shall know
There was some such thing in't I told him of;
And that I was an honest man.

Mel. He'll buy
That knowledge very dearly.—Diphilus,

Enter DIPHILUS.

What news with thee?
Diph. This were a night indeed
 To do it in: The king hath sent for her.
Mel. She shall perform it then.—Go, Diphilus,
 And take from this good man, my worthy friend,
 The fort; he'll give it thee.
Diph. Have you got that?
Cal. Art thou of the same breed? Canst thou deny
 This to the king too?
Diph. With a confidence
 As great as his.
Cal. 'Faith, like enough.
Mel. Away, and use him kindly.
Cal. Touch not me;
 I hate the whole strain. If thou follow me,
 A great way off, I'll give thee up the fort;
 And hang yourselves.
Mel. Be gone.
Diph. He's finely wrought. [*Exeunt Calianax and Diphilus.*
Mel. This is a night, 'spite of astronomers,
 To do the deed in. I will wash the stain,
 That rests upon our house, off with his blood.

Enter AMINTOR.

Amin. Melantius, now assist me: If thou be'st
 That which thou say'st, assist me. I have lost
 All my distempers, and have found a rage
 So pleasing! Help me.
Mel. Who can see him thus,
 And not swear vengeance?—What's the matter, friend?
Amin. Out with thy sword; and, hand in hand with me,
 Rush to the chamber of this hated king:
 And sink him, with the weight of all his sins,
 To hell for ever.
Mel. 'Twere a rash attempt,
 Not to be done with safety. Let your reason
 Plot your revenge, and not your passion.
Amin. If thou refusest me in these extremes,
 Thou art no friend: He sent for her to me;
 By Heaven, to me, myself! And, I must tell you,
 I love her, as a stranger; there is worth

In that vile woman, worthy things, Melantius;
And she repents. I'll do't myself alone,
Though I be slain. Farewell.

Mel. He'll overthrow
My whole design with madness.—Amintor,
Think what thou dost: I dare as much as Valour;
But 'tis the king, the king, the king, Amintor,
With whom thou fightest!—I know he's honest,
And this will work with him. [*Aside.*

Amin. I cannot tell
What thou hast said; but thou hast charm'd my sword
Out of my hand, and left me shaking here,
Defenceless.

Mel. I will take it up for thee.

Amin. What a wild beast is uncollected man!
The thing, that we call honour, bears us all
Headlong to sin, and yet itself is nothing.

Mel. Alas, how variable are thy thoughts!

Amin. Just like my fortunes: I was run to that
I purposed to have chid thee for. Some plot,
I did distrust, thou hadst against the king,
By that old fellow's carriage. But take heed;
There's not the least limb growing to a king
But carries thunder in it.

Mel. I have none
Against him.

Amin. Why, come then; and still remember,
We may not think revenge.

Mel. I will remember. [*Exeunt.*

ACT V

SCENE I.—*A Room in the Palace.*

Enter EVADNE *and a* Gentleman.

Evad. Sir, is the king a-bed?

Gent. Madam, an hour ago.

Evad. Give me the key then, and let none be near;
'Tis the king's pleasure.

Gent. I understand you, madam; 'would 'twere mine.
I must not wish good rest unto your ladyship.

Evad. You talk, you talk.

Gent. 'Tis all I dare do, madam; but the king
    Will wake, and then——
Evad. Saving your imagination, pray, good night, sir.
Gent. A good night be it then, and a long one, madam.
    I am gone.   [*Exeunt.*

SCENE II.—*The Bedchamber.   The* KING *discovered in Bed,*
sleeping.

Enter EVADNE.

Evad. The night grows horrible; and all about me
    Like my black purpose.   Oh, the conscience
    Of a lost virgin! whither wilt thou pull me?
    To what things, dismal as the depth of hell,
    Wilt thou provoke me?   Let no woman dare
    From this hour be disloyal, if her heart be flesh,
    If she have blood, and can fear: 'Tis a daring
    Above that desperate fool's that left his peace,
    And went to sea to fight.   'Tis so many sins,
    An age cannot repent 'em; and so great,
    The gods want mercy for!   Yet I must through 'em.
    I have begun a slaughter on my honour,
    And I must end it there.—He sleeps.   Good Heavens!
    Why give you peace to this untemperate beast,
    That hath so long transgress'd you; I must kill him,
    And I will do it bravely: The mere joy
    Tells me, I merit in it.   Yet I must not
    Thus tamely do it, as he sleeps; that were
    To rock him to another world: My vengeance
    Shall take him waking, and then lay before him
    The number of his wrongs and punishments.
    I'll shake his sins like furies, till I waken
    His evil angel, his sick conscience;
    And then I'll strike him dead.   King, by your leave:
                          [*Ties his arms to the bed.*
    I dare not trust your strength.   Your grace and I
    Must grapple upon even terms no more.
    So.   If he rail me not from my resolution,
    I shall be strong enough.—My lord the king! !
    My lord!—He sleeps, as if he meant to wake
    No more.—My lord!—Is he not dead already?
    Sir! My lord!

King. Who's that?

Evad. Oh, you sleep soundly, sir!

King. My dear Evadne,
    I have been dreaming of thee. Come to bed.

Evad. I am come at length, sir; but how welcome?

King. What pretty new device is this, Evadne?
    What, do you tie me to you? By my love,
    This is a quaint one. Come, my dear, and kiss me.
    I'll be thy Mars; to bed, my queen of love:
    Let us be caught together, that the gods
    May see, and envy our embraces.

Evad. Stay, sir, stay;
    You are too hot, and I have brought you physic
    To temper your high veins.

King. Pr'ythee, to bed then; let me take it warm;
    There thou shalt know the state of my body better.

Evad. I know you have a surfeited foul body;
    And you must bleed.

King. Bleed!

Evad. Ay, you shall bleed! Lie still; and, if the devil,
    Your lust, will give you leave, repent. This steel
    Comes to redeem the honour that you stole,
    King, my fair name; which nothing but thy death
    Can answer to the world.

King. How's this, Evadne?

Evad. I am not she; nor bear I in this breast
    So much cold spirit to be call'd a woman.
    I am a tiger; I am anything
    That knows not pity. Stir not! If thou dost,
    I'll take thee unprepared; thy fears upon thee,
    That make thy sins look double; and so send thee
    (By my revenge, I will) to look those torments
    Prepared for such black souls.

King. Thou dost not mean this; 'tis impossible:
    Thou art too sweet and gentle.

Evad. No, I am not.
    I am as foul as thou art, and can number
    As many such hells here. I was once fair,
    Once I was lovely; not a blowing rose
    More chastely sweet, till thou, thou, thou foul canker,
    (Stir not) didst poison me. I was a world of virtue,
    Till your curst court and you (Hell bless you for't!)
    With your temptations on temptations,

Made me give up mine honour; for which, king,
I'm come to kill thee.

King. No!

Evad. I am.

King. Thou art not!
I pr'ythee speak not these things: Thou art gentle,
And wert not meant thus rugged.

Evad. Peace, and hear me.
Stir nothing but your tongue, and that for mercy
To those above us; by whose lights I vow,
Those blessed fires that shot to see our sin,
If thy hot soul had substance with thy blood,
I would kill that too; which, being past my steel,
My tongue shall reach. Thou art a shameless villain!
A thing out of the overcharge of nature;
Sent, like a thick cloud, to disperse a plague
Upon weak catching women! such a tyrant,
That for his lust would sell away his subjects!
Ay, all his Heaven hereafter!

King. Hear, Evadne,
Thou soul of sweetness, hear! I am thy king.

Evad. Thou art my shame! Lie still, there's none about you,
Within your cries: All promises of safety
Are but deluding dreams. Thus, thus, thou foul man,
Thus I begin my vengeance!   [*Stabs him.*

King. Hold, Evadne!
I do command thee, hold.

Evad. I do not mean, sir,
To part so fairly with you; we must change
More of these love-tricks yet.

King. What bloody villain
Provoked thee to this murder?

Evad. Thou, thou monster.

King. Oh!

Evad. Thou kept'st me brave at court, and whor'd'st me,
            king;
Then married me to a young noble gentleman,
And whor'd'st me still.

King. Evadne, pity me.

Evad. Hell take me then! This for my lord Amintor!
This for my noble brother! and this stroke
For the most wrong'd of women!   [*Kills him.*

King. Oh! I die.
Evad. Die all our faults together! I forgive thee.　　　[*Exit.*

Enter *two* Gentlemen *of the Bedchamber.*

1 *Gent.* Come, now she's gone, let's enter; the king expects
　　it, and will be angry.
2 *Gent.* 'Tis a fine wench; we'll have a snap at her one of
　　these nights, as she goes from him.
1 *Gent.* Content. How quickly he had done with her! I
　　see, kings can do no more that way than other mortal
　　people.
2 *Gent.* How fast he is! I cannot hear him breathe.
1 *Gent.* Either the tapers give a feeble light,
　　Or he looks very pale.
2 *Gent.* And so he does:
　　Pray Heaven he be well; let's look.—Alas!
　　He's stiff, wounded and dead: Treason, treason!
1 *Gent.* Run forth and call.
2 *Gent.* Treason, treason!　　　　　　　　　　　[*Exit.*
1 *Gent.* This will be laid on us:
　　Who can believe a woman could do this?

Enter CLEON *and* LYSIPPUS.

Cleon. How now! Where's the traitor?
1 *Gent.* Fled, fled, away; but there her woful act lies still.
Cleon. Her act! a woman!
Lys. Where's the body?
1 *Gent.* There.
Lys. Farewell, thou worthy man! There were two bonds
　　That tied our loves, a brother and a king;
　　The least of which might fetch a flood of tears:
　　But such the misery of greatness is,
　　They have no time to mourn; then pardon me!—

Enter STRATO.

　　Sirs, which way went she?
Stra. Never follow her;
　　For she, alas! was but the instrument.
　　News is now brought in, that Melantius
　　Has got the fort, and stands upon the wall;
　　And with a loud voice calls those few, that pass

At this dead time of night, delivering
The innocence of this act.

Lys. Gentlemen,
I am your king.

Stra. We do acknowledge it.

Lys. I would I were not! Follow, all; for this
Must have a sudden stop. [*Exeunt.*

SCENE III.—*Before the Citadel.*

Enter MELANTIUS, DIPHILUS, *and* CALIANAX, *on the
Walls.*

Mel. If the dull people can believe I am arm'd,
(Be constant, Diphilus!) now we have time,
Either to bring our banish'd honours home,
Or create new ones in our ends.

Diph. I fear not;
My spirit lies not that way.—Courage, Calianax.

Cal. 'Would I had any! you should quickly know it.

Mel. Speak to the people: Thou art eloquent.

Cal. 'Tis a fine eloquence to come to the gallows!
You were born to be my end.   The devil take you!
Now must I hang for company.   'Tis strange,
I should be old, and neither wise nor valiant.

Enter below, LYSIPPUS, DIAGORAS, CLEON, STRATO,
and Guard.

Lys. See where he stands, as boldly confident
As if he had his full command about him.

Stra. He looks as if he had the better cause, sir;
Under your gracious pardon, let me speak it!
Though he be mighty-spirited, and forward
To all great things; to all things of that danger
Worse men shake at the telling of; yet, certainly,
I do believe him noble; and this action
Rather pull'd on, than sought: his mind was ever
As worthy as his hand

Lys. 'Tis my fear, too.
Heaven forgive all! Summon him, lord Cleon.

Cleon. Ho, from the walls there!

Mel. Worthy Cleon, welcome.
We could have wish'd you here, lord.   You are honest.

Cal. Well, thou art as flattering a knave, though
    I dare not tell thee so——   [*Aside.*

Lys. Melantius!

Mel. Sir?

Lys. I am sorry that we meet thus; our old love
    Never required such distance. Pray Heaven,
    You have not left yourself, and sought this safety
    More out of fear than honour! You have lost
    A noble master; which your faith, Melantius,
    Some think, might have preserved: Yet you know best.

Cal. When time was, I was mad; some, that dares fight,
    I hope will pay this rascal.

Mel. Royal young man, whose tears look lovely on thee;
    Had they been shed for a deserving one,
    They had been lasting monuments! Thy brother,
    While he was good, I call'd him king; and served him
    With that strong faith, that most unwearied valour,
    Pull'd people from the farthest sun to seek him,
    And beg his friendship. I was then his soldier.
    But since his hot pride drew him to disgrace me,
    And brand my noble actions with his lust
    (That never-cured dishonour of my sister,
    Base stain of whore! and, which is worse,
    The joy to make it still so) like myself,
    Thus I have flung him off with my allegiance;
    And stand here mine own justice, to revenge
    What I have suffered in him; and this old man,
    Wronged almost to lunacy.

Cal. Who—I?
    You would draw me in. I have had no wrong,
    I do disclaim ye all.

Mel. The short is this:
    'Tis no ambition to lift up myself
    Urgeth me thus; I do desire again
    To be a subject, so I may be free.
    If not, I know my strength, and will unbuild
    This goodly town. Be speedy and be wise,
    In a reply.

Stra. Be sudden, sir, to tie
    All up again: What's done is past recall,
    And past you to revenge; and there are thousands,
    That wait for such a troubled hour as this.
    Throw him the blank.

Lys. Melantius, write in that
    Thy choice: My seal is at it.   [*Throws him a paper.*
Mel. It was our honours drew us to this act,
    Not gain; and we will only work our pardons.
Cal. Put my name in too.
Diph. You disclaim'd us all
    But now, Calianax.
Cal. That is all one:
    I'll not be hang'd hereafter by a trick:
    I'll have it in.
Mel. You shall, you shall.—
    Come to the back gate, and we'll call you king,
    And give you up the fort.
Lys. Away, away.   [*Exeunt.*

SCENE IV.—*Antechamber to Evadne's Apartments
in the Palace.*

Enter Aspatia, *in man's apparel.*

Asp. This is my fatal hour.   Heaven may forgive
    My rash attempt, that causelessly hath laid
    Griefs on me that will never let me rest;
    And put a woman's heart into my breast.
    It is more honour for you, that I die;
    For she, that can endure the misery
    That I have on me, and be patient too,
    May live and laugh at all that you can do.

Enter Servant.

    God save you, sir!
Ser. And you, sir.   What's your business?
Asp. With you, sir, now; to do me the fair office
    To help me to your lord.
Ser. What, would you serve him?
Asp. I'll do him any service; but to haste,
    For my affairs are earnest, I desire
    To speak with him.
Ser. Sir, because you're in such haste, I would be loth
    Delay you any longer: You cannot.
Asp. It shall become you, though, to tell your lord.
Ser. Sir, he will speak with nobody; but, in particular,
    I have in charge, about no weighty matters.

Asp. This is most strange.   Art thou gold-proof?
        There's for thee; help me to him.
Ser. Pray be not angry, sir.   I'll do my best.   [*Exit.*
Asp. How stubbornly this fellow answered me!
        There is a vile dishonest trick in man,
        More than in woman: All the men I meet
        Appear thus to me, are all harsh and rude;
        And have a subtilty in everything,
        Which love could never know.   But we fond women
        Harbour the easiest and the smoothest thoughts,
        And think, all shall go so!   It is unjust,
        That men and women should be match'd together.

Enter AMINTOR *and his* Man.

Amin. Where is he?
Ser. There, my lord.
Amin. What would you, sir?
Asp. Please it your lordship to command your man
        Out of the room, I shall deliver things
        Worthy your hearing.
Amin. Leave us.   [*Exit Servant.*
Asp. Oh, that that shape
        Should bury falsehood in it!   [*Aside.*
Amin. Now your will, sir.
Asp. When you know me, my lord, you needs must guess
        My business; and I am not hard to know;
        For till the chance of war mark'd this smooth face
        With these few blemishes, people would call me
        My sister's picture, and her mine.   In short,
        I am the brother to the wrong'd Aspatia.
Amin. The wrong'd Aspatia! 'Would thou wert so too
        Unto the wrong'd Amintor! Let me kiss
        That hand of thine, in honour that I bear
        Unto the wrong'd Aspatia.   Here I stand,
        That did it.   'Would he could not! Gentle youth,
        Leave me; for there is something in thy looks,
        That calls my sins, in a most hideous form,
        Into my mind; and I have grief enough
        Without thy help.
Asp. I would I could with credit.
        Since I was twelve years old, I had not seen
        My sister till this hour; I now arrived:

She sent for me to see her marriage;
A woful one!   But they, that are above,
Have ends in everything.   She used few words,
But yet enough to make me understand
The baseness of the injuries you did her.
That little training I have had, is war:
I may behave myself rudely in peace;
I would not, though.   I shall not need to tell you,
I am but young, and would be loth to lose
Honour, that is not easily gained again.
Fairly I mean to deal: The age is strict
For single combats; and we shall be stopp'd,
If it be publish'd.   If you like your sword,
Use it; if mine appear a better to you,
Change: for the ground is this, and this the time,
To end our difference.

Amin.   Charitable youth,
(If thou be'st such) think not I will maintain
So strange a wrong: And, for thy sister's sake,
Know, that I could not think that desperate thing
I durst not do; yet, to enjoy this world,
I would not see her; for, beholding thee,
I am I know not what.   If I have aught,
That may content thee, take it, and begone;
For death is not so terrible as thou.
Thine eyes shoot guilt into me.

Asp.   Thus, she swore,
Thou wouldst behave thyself; and give me words
That would fetch tears into mine eyes; and so
Thou dost indeed.   But yet she bade me watch,
Lest I were cozen'd; and be sure to fight
Ere I return'd.

Amin.   That must not be with me.
For her I'll die directly; but against her
Will never hazard it.

Asp.   You must be urged.
I do not deal uncivilly with those
That dare to fight; but such a one as you
Must be used thus.   [*She strikes him.*

Amin.   I pr'ythee, youth, take heed.
Thy sister is a thing to me so much
Above mine honour, that I can endure
All this.   Good gods! a blow I can endure!

F 506

But stay not, lest thou draw a timeless death
  Upon thyself.
Asp. Thou art some prating fellow;
  One, that hath studied out a trick to talk,
  And move soft-hearted people; to be kicked
               [She kicks him.
  Thus, to be kick'd!—Why should he be so slow
  In giving me my death?   *[Aside.*
Amin. A man can bear
  No more, and keep his flesh.   Forgive me, then!
  I would endure yet, if I could.   Now show *[Draws.*
  The spirit thou pretend'st, and understand,
  Thou hast no hour to live.——
      [They fight; Aspatia is wounded.
      What dost thou mean?
  Thou canst not fight: the blows thou mak'st at me
  Are quite besides; and those I offer at thee,
  Thou spread'st thine arms, and tak'st upon thy breast,
  Alas, defenceless!
Asp. I have got enough,
  And my desire.   There is no place so fit
  For me to die as here.

   Enter EVADNE, *her Hands bloody, with a Knife.*

Evad. Amintor, I am loaden with events,
  That fly to make thee happy.   I have joys,
  That in a moment can call back thy wrongs,
  And settle thee in thy free state again.
  It is Evadne still that follows thee,
  But not her mischiefs.
Amin. Thou canst not fool me to believe again;
  But thou hast looks and things so full of news,
  That I am stay'd.
Evad. Noble Amintor, put off thy amaze,
  Let thine eyes loose, and speak: Am I not fair?
  Looks not Evadne beauteous, with these rites now
  Were those hours half so lovely in thine eyes,
  When our hands met before the holy man?
  I was too foul within to look fair then:
  Since I knew ill, I was not free till now.
Amin. There is presage of some important thing
  About thee, which, it seems, thy tongue hath lost.
  Thy hands are bloody, and thou hast a knife!

Evad. In this consists thy happiness and mine.
    Joy to Amintor! for the king is dead.
Amin. Those have most power to hurt us, that we love;
    We lay our sleeping lives within their arms!
    Why, thou hast raised up Mischief to his height,
    And found out one, to out-name thy other faults.
    Thou hast no intermission of thy sins,
    But all thy life is a continued ill.
    Black is thy colour now, disease thy nature.
    Joy to Amintor! Thou hast touch'd a life,
    The very name of which had power to chain
    Up all my rage, and calm my wildest wrongs.
Evad. 'Tis done; and since I could not find a way
    To meet thy love so clear as through his life,
    I cannot now repent it.
Amin. Couldst thou procure the gods to speak to me,
    To bid me love this woman, and forgive,
    I think I should fall out with them.   Behold,
    Here lies a youth whose wounds bleed in my breast,
    Sent by his violent fate, to fetch his death
    From my slow hand: And, to augment my woe,
    You now are present, stain'd with a king's blood,
    Violently shed.   This keeps night here,
    And throws an unknown wilderness about me.
Asp. Oh, oh, oh!
Amin. No more; pursue me not.
Evad. Forgive me then,
    And take me to thy bed.   We may not part.   [*Kneels.*
Amin. Forbear!   Be wise, and let my rage go this way.
Evad. 'Tis you that I would stay, not it.
Amin. Take heed;
    It will return with me.
Evad. If it must be,
    I shall not fear to meet it: take me home.
Amin. Thou monster of cruelty, forbear!
Evad. For heaven's sake, look more calm: thine eyes are
        sharper
    Than thou canst make thy sword.
Amin. Away, away!
    Thy knees are more to me than violence.
    I am worse than sick to see knees follow me,
    For that I must not grant.   For Heaven's sake stand.
Evad. Receive me, then.

Amin. I dare not stay thy language;
 In midst of all my anger and my grief,
 Thou dost awake something that troubles me,
 And says, " I loved thee once." I dare not stay;
 There is no end of woman's reasoning. [*Leaves her.*
Evad. Amintor, thou shalt love me now again:
 Go; I am calm. Farewell, and peace for ever!
 Evadne, whom thou hat'st, will die for thee.
          [*Kills herself.*
Amin. I have a little human nature yet,
 That's left for thee, that bids me stay thy hand.
            [*Returns.*
Evad. Thy hand was welcome, but it came too late.
 Oh, I am lost! the heavy sleep makes haste. [*She dies.*
Asp. Oh, oh, oh!
Amin. This earth of mine doth tremble, and I feel
 A stark affrighted motion in my blood:
 My soul grows weary of her house, and I
 All over am a trouble to myself.
 There is some hidden power in these dead things,
 That calls my flesh unto 'em: I am cold!
 Be resolute, and bear 'em company.
 There's something, yet, which I am loth to leave.
 There's man enough in me to meet the fears
 That death can bring; and yet, 'would it were done!
 I can find nothing in the whole discourse
 Of death, I durst not meet the boldest way;
 Yet still, betwixt the reason and the act,
 The wrong I to Aspatia did stands up:
 I have not such another fault to answer.
 Though she may justly arm herself with scorn
 And hate of me, my soul will part less troubled,
 When I have paid to her in tears my sorrow.
 I will not leave this act unsatisfied,
 If all that's left in me can answer it.
Asp. Was it a dream? There stands Amintor still;
 Or I dream still.
Amin. How dost thou? Speak! receive my love and help.
 Thy blood climbs up to his old place again:
 There's hope of thy recovery.
Asp. Did you not name Aspatia?
Amin. I did.
Asp. And talk'd of tears and sorrow unto her?

Amin. 'Tis true; and till these happy signs in thee
Did stay my course, 'twas thither I was going.
Asp. Thou art there already, and these wounds are hers:
Those threats I brought with me sought not revenge;
But came to fetch this blessing from thy hand.
I am Aspatia yet.
Amin. Dare my soul ever look abroad again?
Asp. I shall surely live, Amintor; I am well:
A kind of healthful joy wanders within me.
Amin. The world wants lives to excuse thy loss!
Come, let me bear thee to some place of help.
Asp. Amintor, thou must stay; I must rest here;
My strength begins to disobey my will.
How dost thou, my best soul? I would fain live
Now, if I could: Wouldst thou have loved me then?
Amin. Alas?
All that I am's not worth a hair from thee.
Asp. Give me thy hand; my hands grope up and down,
And cannot find thee: I am wondrous sick:
Have I thy hand, Amintor?
Amin. Thou greatest blessing of the world, thou hast.
Asp. I do believe thee better than my sense.
Oh! I must go. Farewell!   [*Dies*
Amin. She swoons! Aspatia!—Help! for Heaven's sake,
        water!
Such as may chain life ever to this frame.—
Aspatia, speak!—What, no help yet? I fool!
I'll chafe her temples: Yet there's nothing stirs;
Some hidden power tell her, Amintor calls,
And let her answer me!—Aspatia, speak!—
I have heard, if there be any life, but bow
The body thus, and it will show itself.
Oh, she is gone! I will not leave her yet.
Since out of justice we must challenge nothing,
I'll call it mercy, if you'll pity me,
Ye heavenly powers! and lend, for some few years,
The blessed soul to this fair seat again.
No comfort comes; the gods deny me too!
I'll bow the body once again.—Aspatia!—
The soul is fled for ever; and I wrong
Myself, so long to lose her company.
Must I talk now? Here's to be with thee, love!
                                        [*Stabs himself.*

Enter Servant.

Serv. This is a great grace to my lord, to have the new king
come to him: I must tell him he is entering.—Oh, God!
Help! help!

Enter Lysippus, Melantius, Calianax, Cleon, Diphilus,
and Strato.

Lys. Where's Amintor?
Serv. Oh, there, there.
Lys. How strange is this!
Cal. What should we do here?
Mel. These deaths are such acquainted things with me,
That yet my heart dissolves not.   May I stand
Stiff here for ever!   Eyes, call up your tears!
This is Amintor: Heart! he was my friend;
Melt; now it flows.—Amintor, give a word
To call me to thee.
Amin. Oh!
Mel. Melantius calls his friend Amintor.   Oh!
Thy arms are kinder to me than thy tongue!
Speak, speak!
Amin. What?
Mel. That little word was worth all the sounds
That ever I shall hear again.
Diph. Oh, brother!
Here lies your sister slain; you lose yourself
In sorrow there.
Mel. Why, Diphilus, it is
A thing to laugh at, in respect of this:
Here was my sister, father, brother, son;
All that I had!—Speak once again: What youth
Lies slain there by thee?
Amin. 'Tis Aspatia.
My last is said.   Let me give up my soul
Into thy bosom.   [*Dies.*
Cal. What's that? what's that? Aspatia!
Mel. I never did
Repent the greatness of my heart till now;
It will not burst at need.
Cal. My daughter dead here too!   And you have all fine
new tricks to grieve; but I ne'er knew any but direct
crying.

Mel. I am a prattler; but no more.   [*Offers to kill himself.*
Diph. Hold, brother.
Lys. Stop him.
Diph. Fie! how unmanly was this offer in you;
        Does this become our strain?
Cal. I know not what the matter is, but I am grown very
        kind, and am friends with you. You have given me
        that among you will kill me quickly; but I'll go home,
        and live as long as I can.
Mel. His spirit is but poor that can be kept
        From death for want of weapons.
        Is not my hand a weapon sharp enough
        To stop my breath? or, if you tie down those,
        I vow, Amintor, I will never eat,
        Or drink, or sleep, or have to do with that
        That may preserve life! This I swear to keep.
Lys. Look to him though, and bear those bodies in.
        May this a fair example be to me,
        To rule with temper: For, on lustful kings,
        Unlook'd-for, sudden deaths from heaven are sent;
        But curst is he that is their instrument.   [*Exeunt.*

A KING AND NO KING

DRAMATIS PERSONÆ

ARBACES, *King of Iberia.*
TIGRANES, *King of Armenia.*
GOBRIAS, *Lord-Protector, and Father of Arbaces.*
BACURIUS, *a Lord.*
MARDONIUS, } *two Captains.*
BESSUS,
LYGONES, *Father of Spaconia.*
Three Gentlemen.
Two Swordmen.
Three Men.
PHILIP, *a Servant.*

A Messenger.
A Servant to Bacurius.
A Boy.

ARANE, *the Queen-Mother.*
PANTHEA, *her Daughter.*
SPACONIA, *a Lady, Daughter of Lygones.*
MANDANE, *a Waiting-woman; and other* Attendants.
Two Citizens' Wives, *and another* Woman.

SCENE.—DURING THE FIRST ACT, ON THE FRONTIERS OF ARMENIA; AFTERWARDS IN THE METROPOLIS OF IBERIA.

ACT I

SCENE I.—*The Camp of Arbaces, on the Frontiers of Armenia.*

Enter MARDONIUS *and* BESSUS.

Mar. Bessus, the king has made a fair hand on't; he has ended the wars at a blow. 'Would my sword had a close basket hilt, to hold wine, and the blade would make knives; for we shall have nothing but eating and drinking.

Bes. We, that are commanders, shall do well enough.

Mar. 'Faith, Bessus, such commanders as thou may: I had as lieve set thee *perdue* for a pudding i' th' dark, as Alexander the Great.

Bes. I love these jests exceedingly.

Mar. I think thou lov'st 'em better than quarrelling, Bessus; I'll say so much in thy behalf. And yet thou'rt valiant enough upon a retreat: I think thou would'st kill any man that stopp'd thee, an thou couldst.

Bes. But was not this a brave combat, Mardonius?

Mar. Why, didst thou see it?

Bes. You stood with me.

Mar. I did so; but methought thou wink'd'st every blow they strake.

Bes. Well, I believe there are better soldiers than I, that never saw two princes fight in lists.

Mar. By my troth, I think so too, Bessus; many a thousand: But, certainly, all that are worse than thou have seen as much.

Bes. 'Twas bravely done of our king.

Mar. Yes, if he had not ended the wars. I'm glad thou dar'st talk of such dangerous businesses.

Bes. To take a prince prisoner in the heart of his own country, in single combat!

Mar. See how thy blood cruddles at this! I think thou couldst be contented to be beaten i' this passion.

Bes. Shall I tell you truly?

Mar. Ay.

Bes. I could willingly venture for it.

Mar. Hum! no venture neither, good Bessus.

Bes. Let me not live, if I do not think it is a braver piece of service than that I'm so famed for.

Mar. Why, art thou famed for any valour?

Bes. I famed? Ay, I warrant you.

Mar. I am very heartily glad on't; I have been with thee ever since thou cam'st to the wars, and this is the first word that ever I heard on't. Pr'ythee, who fames thee?

Bes. The Christian world.

Mar. 'Tis heathenishly done of 'em; in my conscience, thou deserv'st it not.

Bes. I ha' done good service.

Mar. I do not know how thou may'st wait of a man in's chamber, or thy agility in shifting a trencher; but otherwise no service, good Bessus.

Bes. You saw me do the service yourself.

Mar. Not so hasty, sweet Bessus! Where was it? is the place vanish'd?

Bes. At Bessus' Desperate Redemption.

Mar. At Bessus' Desperate Redemption! where's that?

Bes. There, where I redeem'd the day; the place bears my name.

Mar. Pr'ythee who christen'd it?

Bes. The soldier.

Mar. If I were not a very merrily disposed man, what would become of thee? One that had but a grain of choler in

*F 506

the whole composition of his body, would send thee of an errand to the worms, for putting thy name upon that field: Did not I beat thee there, i' th' head o' th' troops, with a truncheon, because thou wouldst needs run away with thy company, when we should charge the enemy?

Bes. True; but I did not run.

Mar. Right, Bessus: I beat thee out on't.

Bes. But came not I up when the day was gone, and redeem'd all?

Mar. Thou knowest, and so do I, thou meant'st to fly, and thy fear making thee mistake, thou ran'st upon the enemy; and a hot charge thou gavest; as, I'll do thee right, thou art furious in running away; and, I think, we owe thy fear for our victory. If I were the king, and were sure thou wouldst mistake always, and run away upon the enemy, thou shouldst be general, by this light.

Bes. You'll never leave this till I fall foul.

Mar. No more such words, dear Bessus; for though I have ever known thee a coward, and therefore durst never strike thee, yet if thou proceed'st, I will allow thee valiant, and beat thee.

Bes. Come, our king's a brave fellow.

Mar. He is so, Bessus; I wonder how thou com'st to know it. But, if thou wert a man of understanding, I would tell thee, he is vain-glorious and humble, and angry and patient, and merry and dull, and joyful and sorrowful, in extremities, in an hour. Do not think me thy friend, for this; for if I cared who knew it, thou shouldst not hear it, Bessus. Here he is, with the prey in his foot.

Enter ARBACES, TIGRANES, *two* Gentlemen, *and* Attendants.

Arb. Thy sadness, brave Tigranes, takes away
　　From my full victory: Am I become
　　Of so small fame, that any man should grieve
　　When I o'ercome him? They that placed me here,
　　Intended it an honour, large enough
　　For the most valiant living, but to dare
　　Oppose me single, though he lost the day.
　　What should afflict you? You are as free as I.
　　To be my prisoner, is to be more free
　　Than you were formerly. And never think,
　　The man, I held worthy to combat me,

Shall be used servilely.   Thy ransom is,
To take my only sister to thy wife:
A heavy one, Tigranes; for she is
A lady, that the neighbour princes send
Blanks to fetch home.   I have been too unkind
To her, Tigranes: She, but nine years old,
I left her, and ne'er saw her since: Your wars
Have held me long, and taught me, though a youth,
The way to victory.   She was a pretty child;
Then, I was little better; but now fame
Cries loudly on her, and my messengers
Make me believe she is a miracle.
She'll make you shrink, as I did, with a stroke
But of her eye, Tigranes.

Tigr.   Is it the course of
Iberia to use her prisoners thus?
Had fortune thrown my name above Arbaces',
I should not thus have talk'd; for in Armenia,
We hold it base.   You should have kept your temper
Till you saw home again, where 'tis the fashion,
Perhaps, to brag.

Arb.   Be you my witness, earth,
Need I to brag?   Doth not this captive prince
Speak me sufficiently, and all the acts
That I have wrought upon his suffering land?
Should I then boast?   Where lies that foot of ground,
Within his whole realm, that I have not past,
Fighting and conquering: Far then from me
Be ostentation.   I could tell the world,
How I have laid his kingdom desolate,
By this sole arm, propp'd by divinity;
Stript him out of his glories; and have sent
The pride of all his youth to people graves;
And made his virgins languish for their loves;
If I would brag.   Should I, that have the power
To teach the neighbour world humility,
Mix with vain-glory?

Mar.   Indeed, this is none!   [*Aside.*

Arb.   Tigranes, no; did I but take delight
To stretch my deeds as others do, on words,
I could amaze my hearers.

Mar.   So you do.   [*Aside.*

Arb.   But he shall wrong his and my modesty,

That thinks me apt to boast: After an act
Fit for a god to do upon his foe,
A little glory in a soldier's mouth
Is well-becoming; be it far from vain.

Mar. 'Tis pity, that valour should be thus drunk.   [*Aside.*

Arb. I offer you my sister, and you answer,
I do insult: A lady that no suit,
Nor treasure, nor thy crown, could purchase thee,
But that thou fought'st with me.

Tigr.   Though this be worse
Than that you spoke before, it strikes not me;
But, that you think to over-grace me with
The marriage of your sister, troubles me.
I would give worlds for ransoms, were they mine,
Rather than have her.

Arb.   See, if I insult,
That am the conqueror, and for a ransom
Offer rich treasure to the conquered,
Which he refuses, and I bear his scorn!
It cannot be self-flattery to say,
The daughters of your country, set by her,
Would see their shame, run home, and blush to death
At their own foulness.   Yet she is not fair,
Nor beautiful, those words express her not:
They say, her looks have something excellent,
That wants a name yet.   Were she odious,
Her birth deserves the empire of the world:
Sister to such a brother; that hath ta'en
Victory prisoner, and throughout the earth
Carries her bound, and should he let her loose,
She durst not leave him.   Nature did her wrong,
To print continual conquest on her cheeks,
And make no man worthy for her to take,
But me, that am too near her; and as strangely
She did for me: But you will think I brag.

Mar. I do, I'll be sworn. Thy valour and thy passions
severed, would have made two excellent fellows in their
kinds. I know not, whether I should be sorry thou art
so valiant, or so passionate: 'Would one of 'em were
away!   [*Aside.*

Tigr. Do I refuse her, that I doubt her worth?
Were she as virtuous as she would be thought;
So perfect, that no one of her own sex

Could find a want she had; so tempting fair,
That she could wish it off, for damning souls;
I would pay any ransom, twenty lives,
Rather than meet her married in my bed.
Perhaps, I have a love, where I have fix'd
Mine eyes, not to be moved, and she on me;
I am not fickle.

Arb. Is that all the cause?
    Think you, you can so knit yourself in love
To any other, that her searching sight
Cannot dissolve it? So, before you tried,
You thought yourself a match for me in fight.
Trust me, Tigranes, she can do as much
In peace, as I in war; she'll conquer too.
You shall see, if you have the power to stand
The force of her swift looks. If you dislike,
I'll send you home with love, and name your ransom
Some other way; but if she be your choice,
She frees you. To Iberia you must.

Tigr. Sir, I have learn'd a prisoner's sufferance,
And will obey. But give me leave to talk
In private with some friends before I go.

Arb. Some do await him forth, and see him safe;
But let him freely send for whom he please,
And none dare to disturb his conference;
I will not have him know what bondage is,
Till he be free from me. [*Exit Tigranes with Attendants.*
               This, prince, Mardonius,
Is full of wisdom, valour, all the graces
Man can receive.

Mar. And yet you conquer'd him.

Arb. And yet I conquer'd him, and could have done,
Hadst thou joined with him, though thy name in arms
Be great. Must all men, that are virtuous,
Think suddenly to match themselves with me?
I conquer'd him, and bravely; did I not?

Bes. An please your majesty, I was afraid at first——

Mar. When wert thou other?

Arb. Of what?

Bes. That you would not have spied your best advantages;
for your majesty, in my opinion, lay too high; methinks,
under favour, you should have lain thus.

Mar. Like a tailor at a wake.

Bes. And then, if't please your majesty to remember, at
    one time——by my troth, I wish'd myself wi' you.

Mar. By my troth, thou wouldst ha' stunk 'em both out o'
    th' lists.

Arb. What to do?

Bes. To put your majesty in mind of an occasion: you lay
    thus, and Tigranes falsified a blow at your leg, which
    you, by doing thus, avoided; but, if you had whipped
    up your leg thus, and reach'd him on the ear, you had
    made the blood-royal run about his head.

Mar. What country fence-school didst thou learn that at?

Arb. Puff! did not I take him nobly?

Mar. Why, you did, and you have talk'd enough on't.

Arb. Talk enough!
    Will you confine my words? By Heav'n and earth,
    I were much better be a king of beasts
    Than such a people! If I had not patience
    Above a god, I should be call'd a tyrant,
    Throughout the world! They will offend to death
    Each minute: Let me hear thee speak again,
    And thou art earth again. Why, this is like
    Tigranes' speech, that needs would say I bragg'd.
    Bessus, he said I bragg'd.

Bes. Ha, ha, ha!

Arb. Why dost thou laugh?
    By all the world, I'm grown ridiculous
    To my own subjects. Tie me to a chair,
    And jest at me! But I shall make a start,
    And punish some, that others may take heed
    How they are haughty. Who will answer me?
    He said I boasted: speak, Mardonius,
    Did I?—He will not answer. Oh, my temper!
    I give you thanks above, that taught my heart
    Patience; I can endure his silence? What, will none
    Vouchsafe to give me audience? Am I grown
    To such a poor respect? or do you mean
    To break my wind? Speak, speak, some one of you
    Or else, by Heaven——

1 *Gent.* So please your——

Arb. Monstrous!
    I cannot be heard out; they cut me off,
    As if I were too saucy. I will live
    In woods, and talk to trees; they will allow me

To end what I begin.   The meanest subject
Can find a freedom to discharge his soul,
And not I.   Now it is a time to speak;
I hearken.

1 *Gent.* May it please——

Arb. I mean not you;
Did not I stop you once?   But I am grown
To balk!   But I desire let another speak.

2 *Gent.* I hope your majesty——

Arb. Thou draw'st thy words,
That I must wait an hour, where other men
Can hear in instants: Throw your words away
Quick, and to purpose; I have told you this.

Bes. An't please your majesty——

Arb. Wilt thou devour me?   This is such a rudeness
As yet you never show'd me: and I want
Power to command ye; else, Mardonius
Would speak at my request.   Were you my king,
I would have answer'd at your word, Mardonius.
I pray you speak, and truly, did I boast?

Mar. Truth will offend you.

Arb. You take all great care what will offend me,
When you dare to utter such things as these.

Mar. You told Tigranes, you had won his land
With that sole arm, propp'd by divinity:
Was not that bragging, and a wrong to us
That daily ventured lives?

Arb. O, that thy name
Were great as mine! 'would I had paid my wealth
It were as great, as I might combat thee!
I would, through all the regions habitable,
Search thee, and, having found thee, with my sword
Drive thee about the world, 'till I had met
Some place that yet man's curiosity
Hath miss'd of: There, there would I strike thee dead:
Forgotten of mankind, such funeral rites
As beasts would give thee, thou shouldst have.

Bes. The king rages extremely: shall we slink away?
He'll strike us.

2 *Gent.* Content.

Arb. There I would make you know, 'twas this sole arm.
I grant, you were my instruments, and did
As I commanded you; but 'twas this arm

> Moved you like wheels; it moved you as it pleased.
> Whither slip you now? What, are you too good
> To wait on me? I had need have temper,
> That rule such people: I have nothing left
> At my own choice! I would I might be private:
> Mean men enjoy themselves; but 'tis our curse
> To have a tumult, that, out of their loves,
> Will wait on us, whether we will or no.
> Go, get you gone! Why, here they stand like death:
> My words move nothing.

1 Gent. Must we go?

Bes. I know not.

Arb. I pray you, leave me, sirs. I'm proud of this
> That you will be entreated from my sight.

>   *[Exeunt all but Arbaces and Mardonius.*
> Why, now they leave me all. Mardonius!

Mar. Sir.

Arb. Will you leave me quite alone? Methinks,
> Civility should teach you more than this,
> If I were but your friend. Stay here, and wait.

Mar. Sir, shall I speak?

Arb. Why, you would now think much
> To be denied; but I can scarce intreat
> What I would have. Do, speak.

Mar. But will you hear me out?

Arb. With me you article, to talk thus: Well,
> I will hear you out.

Mar. [*Kneels.*] Sir, that I have ever loved you, my sword
> hath spoken for me; that I do, if it be doubted, I dare
> call an oath, a great one, to my witness; and were you
> not my king, from amongst men I should have chose you
> out, to love above the rest: Nor can this challenge thanks;
> for my own sake I should have doted, because I would
> have loved the most deserving man; for so you are.

Arb. Alas, Mardonius, rise! you shall not kneel:
> We all are soldiers, and all venture lives;
> And where there is no difference in men's worths,
> Titles are jests. Who can outvalue thee?
> Mardonius, thou hast loved me, and hast wrong;
> Thy love is not rewarded; but, believe
> It shall be better. More than friend in arms,
> My father, and my tutor, good Mardonius!

Mar. Sir, you did promise you would hear me out.

Arb. And so I will: Speak freely, for from thee
    Nothing can come, but worthy things and true.

Mar. Though you have all this worth, you hold some qualities
    that do eclipse your virtues.

Arb. Eclipse my virtues?

Mar. Yes; your passions; which are so manifold, that they
    appear even in this: When I commend you, you hug
    me for that truth; when I speak your faults, you make
    a start, and fly the hearing: But——

Arb. When you commend me?   Oh, that I should live
    To need such commendations! If my deeds
    Blew not my praise themselves about the earth,
    I were most wretched! Spare your idle praise:
    If thou didst mean to flatter, and shouldst utter
    Words in my praise, that thou thought'st impudence,
    My deeds should make 'em modest.   When you praise,
    I hug you? 'Tis so false, that, wert thou worthy,
    Thou shouldst receive a death, a glorious death,
    From me! But thou shalt understand thy lies;
    For shouldst thou praise me into Heaven, and there
    Leave me enthroned, I would despise thee though
    As much as now, which is as much as dust,
    Because I see thy envy.

Mar. However you will use me after, yet, for your own
    promise sake, hear me the rest.

Arb. I will, and after call unto the winds;
    For they shall lend as large an ear as I
    To what you utter.   Speak!

Mar. Would you but leave these hasty tempers, which I do
    not say take from you all your worths, but darken 'em,
    then you will shine indeed.

Arb. Well.

Mar. Yet I would have you keep some passions, lest men
    should take you for a god, your virtues are such.

Arb. Why, now you flatter.

Mar. I never understood the word.   Were you no king, and
    free from these wild moods, should I chuse a companion
    for wit and pleasure, it should be you; or for honesty
    to interchange my bosom with, it should be you; or
    wisdom to give me counsel, I would pick out you; or
    valour to defend my reputation, still I would find you
    out; for you are fit to fight for all the world, if it could
    come in question. Now I have spoke: Consider to

yourself; find out a use; if so, then what shall fall to
me is not material.

Arb. Is not material? more than ten such lives
    As mine, Mardonius! It was nobly said;
    Thou hast spoke truth, and boldly such a truth
    As might offend another. I have been
    Too passionate and idle; thou shalt see
    A swift amendment. But I want those parts
    You praise me for: I fight for all the world!
    Give thee a sword, and thou wilt go as far
    Beyond me, as thou art beyond in years;
    I know thou dar'st and wilt. It troubles me
    That I should use so rough a phrase to thee:
    Impute it to my folly, what thou wilt,
    So thou wilt pardon me. That thou and I
    Should differ thus!

Mar. Why, 'tis no matter, sir.

Arb. 'Faith, but it is: But thou dost ever take
    All things I do thus patiently; for which
    I never can requite thee, but with love;
    And that thou shalt be sure of. Thou and I
    Have not been merry lately: Pr'ythee tell me,
    Where hadst thou that same jewel in thine ear?

Mar. Why, at the taking of a town.

Arb. A wench, upon my life, a wench, Mardonius,
    Gave thee that jewel.

Mar. Wench! They respect not me; I'm old and rough,
and every limb about me, but that which should, grows
stiffer. I' those businesses, I may swear I am truly
honest; for I pay justly for what I take, and would be
glad to be at a certainty.

Arb. Why, do the wenches encroach upon thee?

Mar. Ay, by this light, do they.

Arb. Didst thou sit at an old rent with 'em?

Mar. Yes, 'faith.

Arb. And do they improve themselves?

Mar. Ay, ten shillings to me, every new young fellow they
come acquainted with.

Arb. How canst live on't?

Mar. Why, I think, I must petition to you.

Arb. Thou shalt take 'em up at my price.

Enter two Gentlemen *and* Bessus.

Mar. Your price?

Arb. Ay, at the king's price.

Mar. That may be more than I'm worth.

2 Gent. Is he not merry now?

1 Gent. I think not.

Bes. He is, he is: We'll show ourselves.

Arb. Bessus! I thought you had been in Iberia by this; I bade you haste; Gobrias will want entertainment for me.

Bes. An't please your majesty, I have a suit.

Arb. Is't not lousy, Bessus? what is't?

Bes. I am to carry a lady with me.

Arb. Then thou hast two suits.

Bes. And if I can prefer her to the lady Panthea, your majesty's sister, to learn fashions, as her friends term it, it will be worth something to me.

Arb. So many nights' lodgings as 'tis thither; will't not?

Bes. I know not that; but gold I shall be sure of.

Arb. Why, thou shalt bid her entertain her from me, so thou wilt resolve me one thing.

Bes. If I can.

Arb. 'Faith, 'tis a very disputable question; and yet, I think, thou canst decide it.

Bes. Your majesty has a good opinion of my understanding.

Arb. I have so good an opinion of it: 'Tis whether thou be valiant.

Bes. Somebody has traduced me to you: Do you see this sword, sir?   [*Draws.*

Arb. Yes.

Bes. If I do not make my back-biters eat it to a knife within this week, say I am not valiant.

Enter a Messenger.

Mes. Health to your majesty!   [*Delivers a letter.*

Arb. From Gobrias?

Mes. Yes, Sir.

Arb. How does he? is he well?

Mes. In perfect health.

Arb. Take that for thy good news.   [*Gives money.*

A trustier servant to his prince there lives not,

Than is good Gobrias.   [*Reads.*

1 Gent. The king starts back.

Mar. His blood goes back as fast.

2 *Gent.* And now it comes again.

Mar. He alters strangely.

Arb. The hand of Heaven is on me: Be it far
    From me to struggle! If my secret sins
    Have pull'd this curse upon me, lend me tears
    Enow to wash me white, that I way feel
    A child-like innocence within my breast!
    Which, once perform'd, oh, give me leave to stand
    As fix'd as constancy herself; my eyes
    Set here unmoved, regardless of the world,
    Though thousand miseries encompass me!

Mar. This is strange!—Sir, how do you?

Arb. Mardonius! my mother——

Mar. Is she dead?

Arb. Alas, she's not so happy! Thou dost know
    How she hath labour'd, since my father died,
    To take by treason hence this loathed life,
    That would but be to serve her. I have pardon'd,
    And pardon'd, and by that have made her fit
    To practise new sins, not repent the old.
    She now had hired a slave to come from thence,
    And strike me here; whom Gobrias, sifting out,
    Took, and condemn'd, and executed there.
    The careful'st servant! Heaven, let me but live
    To pay that man! Nature is poor to me,
    That will not let me have as many deaths
    As are the times that he hath saved my life,
    That I might die 'em over all for him.

Mar. Sir, let her bear her sins on her own head;
    Vex not yourself.

Arb. What will the world,
    Conceive of me? with what unnatural sins
    Will they suppose me laden, when my life
    Is sought by her, that gave it to the world?
    But yet he writes me comfort here: My sister,
    He says, is grown in beauty and in grace;
    In all the innocent virtues that become
    A tender spotless maid: She stains her cheeks
    With mourning tears, to purge her mother's ill;
    And 'mongst that sacred dew she mingles prayers.
    Her pure oblations, for my safe return.—
    If I have lost the duty of a son;

If any pomp or vanity of state
Made me forget my natural offices;
Nay, further, if I have not every night
Expostulated with my wand'r'ing thoughts,
If aught unto my parent they have err'd,
And call'd 'em back; do you direct her arm
Unto this foul dissembling heart of mine.
But if I have been just to her, send out
Your power to compass me, and hold me safe
From searching treason; I will use no means
But prayer: For, rather suffer me to see
From mine own veins issue a deadly flood,
Than wash my dangers off with mother's blood.

Mar. I ne'er saw such sudden extremities.   [*Exeunt.*

SCENE II.—*Another part of the same.*

Enter TIGRANES *and* SPACONIA.

Tigr. Why, wilt thou have me fly, Spaconia?
    What should I do?
Spa. Nay, let me stay alone;
    And when you see Armenia again,
    You shall behold a tomb more worth than I.
    Some friend, that ever loves me or my cause,
    Will build me something to distinguish me
    From other women; many a weeping verse
    He will lay on, and much lament those maids
    That placed their loves unfortunately too high,
    As I have done, where they can never reach.
    But why should you go to Iberia?
Tigr. Alas, that thou wilt ask me!   Ask the man
    That rages in a fever, why he lies
    Distemper'd there, when all the other youths
    Are coursing o'er the meadows with their loves?
    Can I resist it? am I not a slave
    To him that conquer'd me?
Spa. That conquer'd thee,
    Tigranes! He has won but half of thee,
    Thy body; but thy mind may be as free
    As his: His will did never combat thine,
    And take it prisoner.
Tigr. But if he by force
    Convey my body hence, what helps it me,

Or thee, to be unwilling?

Spa. O, Tigranes!
 I know you are to see a lady there;
 To see, and like, I fear: Perhaps, the hope
 Of her makes you forget me, ere we part.
 Be happier than you know to wish! farewell!

Tigr. Spaconia, stay, and hear me what I say
 In short, destruction meet me that I may
 See it, and not avoid it, when I leave
 To be thy faithful lover! Part with me
 Thou shalt not! there are none that know our love;
 And I have given gold unto a captain,
 That goes unto Iberia from the king,
 That he would place a lady of our land
 With the king's sister that is offered me:
 Thither shall you, and, being once got in,
 Persuade her, by what subtle means you can,
 To be as backward in her love as I.

Spa. Can you imagine that a longing maid,
 When she beholds you, can be pull'd away
 With words from loving you?

Tigr. Dispraise my health,
 My honesty, and tell her I am jealous.

Spa. Why, I had rather lose you: Can my heart
 Consent to let my tongue throw out such words?
 And I, that ever yet spoke what I thought,
 Shall find it such a thing at first to lie!

Tigr. Yet, do thy best.

Enter BESSUS.

Bes. What, is your majesty ready?

Tigr. There is the lady, captain.

Bes. Sweet lady, by your leave. I could wish myself more
full of courtship for your fair sake.

Spa. Sir, I shall feel no want of that.

Bes. Lady, you must haste; I have received new letters from
the king, that require more haste than I expected; he
will follow me suddenly himself; and begins to call for
your majesty already.

Tigr. He shall not do so long.

Bes. Sweet lady, shall I call you my charge hereafter?

Spa. I will not take upon me to govern your tongue, sir:
 You shall call me what you please.   [*Exeunt.*

ACT II

SCENE I.—*The Capital of Iberia.   An Apartment in the Palace.*

Enter Gobrias, Bacurius, Arane, Panthea, *and* Mendane, Waiting-women *and* Attendants.

Gob. My Lord Bacurius, you must have regard
 Unto the queen; she is your prisoner;
 'Tis at your peril, if she make escape.
Bac. My Lord, I know't; she is my prisoner,
 From you committed: Yet she is a woman;
 And, so I keep her safe, you will not urge me
 To keep her close.   I shall not shame to say,
 I sorrow for her.
Gob. So do I, my lord:
 I sorrow for her, that so little grace
 Doth govern her, that she should stretch her arm
 Against her king; so little womanhood
 And natural goodness, as to think the death
 Of her own son.
Ara. Thou know'st the reason why,
 Dissembling as thou art, and wilt not speak.
Gob. There is a lady takes not after you;
 Her father is within her; that good man,
 Whose tears paid down his sins.   Mark, how she weeps;
 How well it does become her!   And if you
 Can find no disposition in yourself
 To sorrow, yet, by gracefulness in her,
 Find out the way, and by your reason weep.
 All this she does for you, and more she needs,
 When for yourself you will not lose a tear.
 Think, how this want of grief discredits you;
 And you will weep, because you cannot weep.
Ara. You talk to me, as having got a time
 Fit for your purpose; but you know, I know
 You speak not what you think.
Pan. I would my heart
 Were stone, before my softness should be urged
 Against my mother!   A more troubled thought
 No virgin bears about her!   Should I excuse

My mother's fault, I should set light a life,
In losing which a brother and a king
Were taken from me: If I seek to save
That life so loved, I lose another life,
That gave me being; I should lose a mother;
A word of such a sound in a child's ear,
That it strikes reverence through it.   May the will
Of Heaven be done, and if one needs must fall,
Take a poor virgin's life to answer all!

Ara. But, Gobrias, let us talk.   You know, this fault
Is not in me as in another woman.   [*They walk apart.*

Gob. I know it is not.

Ara. Yet you make it so.

Gob. Why, is not all that's past beyond your help?

Ara. I know it is.

Gob. Nay, should you publish it
Before the world, think you 'twould be believed?

Ara. I know, it would not.

Gob. Nay, should I join with you,
Should we not both be torn, and yet both die
Uncredited?

Ara. I think we should.

Gob. Why, then,
Take you such violent courses?   As for me,
I do but right in saving of the king
From all your plots.

Ara. The king!

Gob. I bade you rest
With patience, and a time would come for me
To reconcile all to your own content:
But, by this way, you take away my power.
And what was done, unknown, was not by me,
But you; your urging.   Being done,
I must preserve mine own; but time may bring
All this to light, and happily for all.

Ara. Accursed be this over-curious brain,
That gave that plot a birth!   Accurs'd this womb,
That after did conceive, to my disgrace!

Bac. My lord-protector, they say, there are divers letters
come from Armenia, that Bessus has done good service,
and brought again a day by his particular valour:
Received you any to that effect?

Gob. Yes; 'tis most certain.

Bac. I'm sorry for't; not that the day was won, but that
  'twas won by him. We held him here a coward: He
  did me wrong once, at which I laughed, and so did all
  the world; for nor I, nor any other, held him worth my
  sword.

Enter Bessus *and* Spaconia.

Bes. Health to my lord-protector? From the king these
  letters; and to your grace, madam, these.
Gob. How does his majesty?
Bes. As well as conquest, by his own means and his valiant
  commanders, can make him: Your letters will tell you
  all.
Pan. I will not open mine, till I do know
  My brother's health: Good captain, is he well?
Bes. As the rest of us that fought are.
Pan. But how's that? is he hurt?
Bes. He's a strange soldier that gets not a knock.
Pan. I do not ask how strange that soldier is
  That gets no hurt, but whether he have one.
Bes. He had divers.
Pan. And is he well again?
Bes. Well again, an't please your grace? Why, I was run
  twice through the body, and shot i' th' head with a
  cross arrow, and yet am well again.
Pan. I do not care how thou do'st: is he well?
Bes. Not care how I do? Let a man, out of the mightiness
  of his spirit, fructify foreign countries with his blood,
  for the good of his own, and thus he shall be answered.
  Why, I may live to relieve, with spear and shield, such
  a lady distressed.
Pan. Why, I will care: I'm glad that thou art well;
  I pr'ythee, is he so?
Gob. The king is well, and will be here to-morrow.
Pan. My prayer is heard. Now will I open mine.   [*Reads.*
Gob. Bacurius, I must ease you of your charge.—
  Madam, the wonted mercy of the king,
  That overtakes your faults, has met with this,
  And struck it out; he has forgiven you freely.
  Your own will is your law; be where you please.
Ara. I thank him.
Gob. You will be ready
  To wait upon his majesty to-morrow?

Ara. I will.

Bac. Madam, be wise, hereafter. I am glad
I have lost this office.   [*Exit Arane.*

Gob. Good captain Bessus, tell us the discourse
Betwixt Tigranes and our king, and how
We got the victory.

Pan. I pr'ythee do;
And if my brother were in any danger,
Let not thy tale make him abide there long,
Before thou bring him off; for all that while
My heart will beat.

Bes. Madam, let what will beat, I must tell truth, and thus
it was: They fought single in lists, but one to one.
As for my own part, I was dangerously hurt but three
days before; else, perhaps, we had been two to two;
I cannot tell, some thought we had. And the occasion
of my hurt was this: the enemy had made trenches——

Gob. Captain, without the manner of your hurt
Be much material to this business,
We'll hear't some other time.

Pan. I pr'ythee, leave it, and go on with my brother.

Bes. I will; but 'twould be worth your hearing. To the
lists they came, and single sword and gauntlet was their
fight.

Pan. Alas!

Bes. Without the lists there stood some dozen captains of
either side mingled, all which were sworn, and one of
those was I; And 'twas my chance to stand next a
captain of the enemies' side, call'd Tiribasus; valiant,
they said, he was. Whilst these two kings were stretching themselves, this Tiribasus cast something a scornful
look on me, and ask'd me, whom I thought would over-
come? I smiled, and told him, if he would fight with
me, he should perceive by the event of that whose king
would win. Something he answer'd, and a scuffle was
like to grow, when one Zipetus offered to help him: I——

Pan. All this of is thyself: I pr'ythee, Bessus,
Tell something of my brother; did he nothing?

Bes. Why, yes; I'll tell your grace. They were not to
fight till the word given; which for my own part, by
my troth, I was not to give.

Pan. See, for his own part!

Bac. I fear, yet, this fellow's abused with a good report.

Bes. Ay, but I——

Pan. Still of himself!

Bes. Cried, "Give the word;" when, as some of them say,
Tigranes was stooping; but the word was not given then:
yet one Cosroes, of the enemies' part, held up his finger
to me, which is as much with us martialists, as, "I will
fight with you:" I said not a word, nor made sign
during the combat; but that once done——

Pan. He slips over all the fight.

Bes. I call'd him to me; "Cosroes," said I——

Pan. I will hear no more.

Bes. No, no, I lie.

Bac. I dare be sworn thou dost.

Bes. "Captain," said I; so 'twas.

Pan. I tell thee, I will hear no further.

Bes. No? Your grace will wish you had.

Pan. I will not wish it. What, is this the lady
My brother writes to me to take?

Bes. An't please your grace this is she.—Charge, will you
come near the princess?

Pan. You are welcome from your country; and this land
Shall show unto you all the kindnesses
That I can make it. What's your name?

Spa. Thalestris.

Pan. You're very welcome: You have got a letter
To put you to me, that has power enough
To place mine enemy here; then much more you,
That are so far from being so to me,
That you ne'er saw me.

Bes. Madam, I dare pass my word for her truth.

Spa. My truth?

Pan. Why, captain, do you think I am afraid she'll steal?

Bes. I cannot tell; servants are slippery; but I dare give
my word for her, and for honesty: she came along with
me, and many favours she did me by the way; but, by
this light, none but what she might do with modesty,
to a man of my rank.

Pan. Why, captain, here's nobody thinks otherwise.

Bes. Nay, if you should, your grace may think your pleasure;
but I am sure I brought her from Armenia, and in all that
way, if ever I touched any bare of her above her knee, I
pray God I may sink where I stand.

Spa. Above my knee?

Bes. No, you know I did not; and if any man will say I
did, this sword shall answer. Nay, I'll defend the
reputation of my charge whilst I live. Your grace
shall understand, I am secret in these businesses, and
know how to defend a lady's honour.

Spa. I hope your grace knows him so well already, I shall not
need to tell you he's vain and foolish.

Bes. Ay, you may call me what you please, but I'll defend
your good name against the world. And so I take my
leave of your grace, and of you, my lord-protector.—
I am likewise glad to see your lordship well.

Bac. Oh, captain Bessus, I thank you. I would speak with
you anon.

Bes. When you please, I will attend your lordship.

[Exit Bessus.

Bac. Madam, I'll take my leave too.

Pan. Good Bacurius!   *[Exit Bacurius.*

Gob. Madam, what writes his majesty to you?

Pan. Oh, my lord,
The kindest words! I'll keep 'em while I live,
Here in my bosom; there's no art in 'em;
They lie disorder'd in this paper, just
As hearty nature speaks 'em.

Gob.   And to me
He writes, what tears of joy he shed, to hear
How you were grown in every virtuous way;
And yields all thanks to me, for that dear care
Which I was bound to have in training you.
There is no princess living that enjoys
A brother of that worth.

Pan.   My lord, no maid
Longs more for anything, and feels more heat
And cold within her breast, than I do now,
In hope to see him.

Gob.   Yet I wonder much
At this: He writes, he brings along with him
A husband for you, that same captive prince;
And if he love you, as he makes a show,
He will allow you freedom in your choice.

Pan. And so he will, my lord, I warrant you;
He will but offer, and give me the power
To take or leave.

Gob. Trust me, were I a lady,

I could not like that man were bargain'd with,
Before I chose him.
Pan. But I am not built
 On such wild humours; if I find him worthy,
 He is not less because he's offered.
Spa. 'Tis true he is not; 'would, he would seem less! [*Apart.*
Gob. I think there is no lady can affect
 Another prince, your brother standing by;
 He doth eclipse men's virtues so with his.
Spa. I know a lady may, and, more I fear,
 Another lady will.   [*Apart.*
Pan. 'Would I might see him!
Gob. Why so you shall. My businesses are great:
 I will attend you when it is his pleasure
 To see you, madam.
Pan. I thank you, good my lord.
Gob. You will be ready, madam?
Pan. Yes.   [*Exit Gobrias.*
Spa. I do beseech you, madam, send away
 Your other women, and receive from me
 A few sad words, which, set against your joys,
 May make 'em shine the more.
Pan. Sirs, leave me all.   [*Exeunt Women.*
Spa. I kneel a stranger here, to beg a thing [*Kneels.*
 Unfit for me to ask, and you to grant.
 'Tis such another strange ill-laid request,
 As if a beggar should entreat a king
 To leave his sceptre and his throne to him,
 And take his rags to wander o'er the world,
 Hungry and cold.
Pan. That were a strange request.
Spa. As ill is mine.
Pan. Then do not utter it.
Spa. Alas, 'tis of that nature, that it must
 Be utter'd, ay, and granted, or I die!
 I am ashamed to speak it; but where life
 Lies at the stake, I cannot think her woman,
 That will not talk something unreasonably
 To hazard saving of it. I shall seem
 A strange petitioner, that wish all ill
 To them I beg of, ere they give me aught;
 Yet so I must: I would you were not fair,
 Nor wise, for in your ill consists my good:

> If you were foolish, you would hear my prayer;
> If foul, you had not power to hinder me;
> He would not love you.

Pan. What's the meaning of it?

Spa. Nay, my request is more without the bounds
> Of reason yet: for 'tis not in the power
> Of you to do, what I would have you grant.

Pan. Why, then, 'tis idle. Pr'ythee speak it out.

Spa. Your brother brings a prince into this land,
> Of such a noble shape, so sweet a grace,
> So full of worth withal, that every maid
> That looks upon him gives away herself
> To him for ever; and for you to have
> He brings him: And so mad is my demand,
> That I desire you not to have this man,
> This excellent man; for whom you needs must die,
> If you should miss him. I do now expect
> You should laugh at me.

Pan. Trust me, I could weep
> Rather; for I have found in all thy words
> A strange disjointed sorrow.

Spa. 'Tis by me
> His own desire so, that you would not love him.

Pan. His own desire! Why, credit me, Thalestris,
> I am no common wooer: If he shall woo me,
> His worth may be such, that I dare not swear
> I will not love him; but if he will stay
> To have me woo him, I will promise thee
> He may keep all his graces to himself,
> And fear no ravishing from me.

Spa. 'Tis yet
> His own desire; but when he sees your face,
> I fear, it will not be: therefore I charge you,
> As you have pity, stop those tender ears
> From his enchanting voice; close up those eyes:
> That you may neither catch a dart from him,
> Nor he from you. I charge you, as you hope
> To live in quiet; for when I am dead,
> For certain I shall walk to visit him,
> If he break promise with me. For as fast
> As oaths, without a formal ceremony,
> Can make me, I am to him.

Pan. Then be fearless;

For if he were a thing 'twixt God and man,
I could gaze on him (if I knew it sin
To love him) without passion.   Dry your eyes:
I swear, you shall enjoy him still for me;
I will not hinder you.   But I perceive,
You are not what you seem: Rise, rise, Thalestris,
If your right name be so.
Spa. Indeed, it is not:
Spaconia is my name; but I desire
Not to be known to others.
Pan. Why, by me
You shall not; I will never do you wrong;
What good I can, I will: Think not my birth
Or education such, that I should injure
A stranger virgin.   You are welcome hither.
In company you wish to be commanded:
But, when we are alone, I shall be ready
To be your servant.   [*Exeunt.*

SCENE II.—*An open Place before the City.   A great
Crowd.*

Enter three Men *and a* Woman.

1 *Man.* Come, come, run, run, run.

2 *Man.* We shall out-go her.

3 *Man.* One were better be hang'd than carry women out
fiddling to these shows.

Wom. Is the king hard by?

1 *Man.* You heard he with the bottles said, he thought we
should come too late.   What abundance of people here
is!

Wom. But what had he in those bottles?

3 *Man.* I know not.

2 *Man.* Why, ink, goodman fool.

3 *Man.* Ink, what to do?

1 *Man.* Why, the king, look you, will many times call for
those bottles, and break his mind to his friends.

Wom. Let's take our places; we shall have no room else.

2 *Man.* The man told us, he would walk o'foot through the
people.

3 *Man.* Ay, marry, did he.

1 *Man.* Our shops are well look'd to now.

2 *Man.* 'Slife, yonder's my master, I think.

1 *Man.* No, 'tis not he.

Enter PHILIP *with two* Citizens' Wives.

1 *Cit. W.* Lord, how fine the fields be! What sweet living 'tis in the country!

2 *Cit. W.* Ay, poor souls, God help 'em, they live as contentedly as one of us.

1 *Cit. W.* My husband's cousin would have had me gone into the country last year. Wert thou ever there?

2 *Cit. W.* Ay, poor souls, I was amongst 'em once.

1 *Cit. W.* And what kind of creatures are they, for love of God?

2 *Cit. W.* Very good people, God help 'em.

1 *Cit. W.* Wilt thou go with me down this summer, when I am brought to bed?

2 *Cit. W.* Alas, 'tis no place for us.

1 *Cit. W.* Why, pr'ythee?

2 *Cit. W.* Why, you can have nothing there; there's nobody cries brooms.

1 *Cit. W.* No?

2 *Cit. W.* No truly, nor milk.

1 *Cit. W.* Nor milk, how do they?

2 *Cit. W.* They are fain to milk themselves i' the country.

1 *Cit. W.* Good lord! But the people there, I think, will be very dutiful to one of us.

2 *Cit. W.* Ay, God knows will they; and yet they do not greatly care for our husbands.

1 *Cit. W.* Do they not? alas! i' good faith, I cannot blame them; For we do not greatly care for them ourselves. Philip, I pray, chuse us a place.

Phil. There's the best, forsooth.

1 *Cit. W.* By your leave, good people, a little.

1 *Man.* What's the matter?

Phil. I pray you, my friends, do not thrust my mistress so; she's with child.

2 *Man.* Let her look to herself then; has she not had thrusting enough yet? If she stay shouldering here, she may hap to go home with a cake in her belly.

3 *Man.* How now, goodman Squitter-breech! why do you lean on me?

Phil. Because I will.

3 *Man.* Will you, Sir Sauce-box?   [*Strikes him.*
1 *Cit. W.* Look, if one ha' not struck Philip.—Come hither,
     Philip; why did he strike thee?
Phil. For leaning on him.
1 *Cit. W.* Why didst thou lean on him?
Phil. I did not think he would have struck me.
1 *Cit. W.* As God save me, la, thou art as wild as a buck;
     there's no quarrel, but thou art at one end or other on't.
3 *Man.* It's at the first end then, for he'll ne'er stay the last.
1 *Cit. W.* Well, stripling, I shall meet with you.
3 *Man.* When you will.
1 *Cit. W.* I'll give a crown to meet with you.
3 *Man.* At a bawdy-house.
1 *Cit. W.* Ay, you're full of your roguery; but if I do meet
     you, it shall cost me a fall.

Flourish.   Enter one running.

4 *Man.* The king, the king, the king, the king! Now, now,
     now, now!

Flourish.   Enter ARBACES, TIGRANES, MARDONIUS,
          and Soldiers.

All. God preserve your majesty!
Arb. I thank you all.   Now are my joys at full,
     When I behold you safe, my loving subjects.
     By you I grow; 'tis your united love
     That lifts me to this height.
     All the account that I can render you
     For all the love you have bestow'd on me,
     All your expenses to maintain my war,
     Is but a little word: You will imagine
     'Tis slender payment; yet 'tis such a word
     As is not to be bought without our bloods:
     'Tis peace!
All. God preserve your majesty!
Arb. Now you may live securely in your towns,
     Your children round about you; you may sit
     Under your vines, and make the miseries
     Of other kingdoms a discourse for you,
     And lend them sorrows.   For yourselves, you may
     Safely forget there are such things as tears;

And you may all, whose good thoughts I have gain'd,
Hold me unworthy, when I think my life
A sacrifice too great to keep you thus
In such a calm estate!

All. God bless your majesty!

Arb. See, all good people, I have brought the man,
Whose very name you fear'd, a captive home.
Behold him; 'tis Tigranes!   In your hearts
Sing songs of gladness and deliverance.

1 *Cit. W.* Out upon him!

2 *Cit. W.* How he looks!

3 *Wom.* Hang him, hang him!

Mar. These are sweet people.

Tigr. Sir, you do me wrong,
To render me a scorned spectacle
To common people.

Arb. It was far from me
To mean it so.   If I have aught deserved,
My loving subjects, let me beg of you
Not to revile this prince, in whom there dwells
All worth, of which the nature of a man
Is capable; valour beyond compare:
The terror of his name has stretch'd itself
Wherever there is sun: And yet for you
I fought with him single, and won him too.
I made his valour stoop, and brought that name,
Soar'd to so unbelieved a height, to fall
Beneath mine.   This, inspired with all your loves,
I did perform; and will, for your content,
Be ever ready for a greater work.

All. The Lord bless your majesty!

Tig. So, he has made me
Amends now with a speech in commendation
Of himself; I would not be so vain-glorious.

Arb. If there be anything in which I may
Do good to any creature here, speak out;
For I must leave you: And it troubles me,
That my occasions, for the good of you,
Are such as call me from you: Else, my joy
Would be to spend my days amongst you all.
You show your loves in these large multitudes
That come to meet me.   I will pray for you.
Heaven prosper you, that you may know old years,

And live to see your children's children
Sit at your boards with plenty! When there is
A want of anything, let it be known
To me, and I will be a father to you.
God keep you all!

                      [Flourish. Exeunt Kings and their Train.

All. God bless your majesty, God bless your majesty!

1 *Man.* Come, shall we go? all's done.

Wom. Ay, for God's sake: I have not made a fire yet.

2 *Man.* Away, away! all's done.

3 *Man.* Content. Farewell, Philip.

1 *Cit. W.* Away, you halter-sack, you!

2 *Man.* Philip will not fight; he's afraid on's face.

Phil. Ay, marry; am I afraid of my face?

3 *Man.* Thou wouldst be, Philip, if thou saw'st it in a glass:
it looks so like a visor.

                  [Exeunt the three Men and Woman.

1 *Cit. W.* You'll be hang'd, sirrah. Come Philip, walk
before us homewards. Did not his majesty say he had
brought us home peas for all our money?

2 *Cit. W.* Yes, marry, did he.

1 *Cit. W.* They're the first I heard on this year, by my troth.
I long'd for some of 'em. Did he not say, we should
have some?

2 *Cit. W.* Yes, and so we shall anon, I warrant you, have
every one a peck brought home to our houses. *[Exeunt.*

ACT III

SCENE I.—*Iberia. A Room in the Palace.*

Enter ARBACES *and* GOBRIAS.

Arb. My sister take it ill?

Gob. Not very ill:
    Something unkindly she does take it, sir,
    To have her husband chosen to her hands.

Arb. Why, Gobrias, let her: I must have her know,
    My will, and not her own, must govern her.
    What, will she marry with some slave at home?

Gob. Oh, she is far from any stubbornness;
    You much mistake her; and, no doubt, will like
    Where you will have her. But, when you behold her,

You will be loth to part with such a jewel.

Arb. To part with her? Why, Gobrias, art thou mad?
She is my sister.

Gob. Sir, I know she is:
But it were a pity to make poor our land,
With such a beauty to enrich another.

Arb. Pish! Will she have him?

Gob. I do hope she will not.——   [*Aside.*
I think she will, sir.

Arb. Were she my father, and my mother too,
And all the names for which we think folks friends,
She should be forced to have him, when I know
'Tis fit. I will not hear her say, she's loth.

Gob. Heaven, bring my purpose luckily to pass!   [*Aside.*
You know 'tis just.—She will not need constraint,
She loves you so.

Arb. How does she love me? Speak.

Gob. She loves you more than people love their health,
That live by labour; more than I could love
A man that died for me, if he could live
Again.

Arb. She is not like her mother, then.

Gob. Oh, no! When you were in Armenia,
I durst not let her know when you were hurt:
For at the first, on every little scratch,
She kept her chamber, wept, and could not eat,
Till you were well; and many times the news
Was so long coming, that, before we heard,
She was as near her death, as you your health.

Arb. Alas, poor soul! But yet she must be ruled.
I know not how I shall requite her well.
I long to see her: Have you sent for her,
To tell her I am ready?

Gob. Sir, I have.

Enter 1 Gentleman *and* TIGRANES.

1 *Gent.* Sir, here is the Armenian king.

Arb. He's welcome.

1 *Gent.* And the queen-mother and the princess wait
Without.

Arb. Good Gobrias, bring 'em in.—   [*Exit Gobrias.*
Tigranes, you will think you are arrived
In a strange land, where mothers cast to poison

Their only sons: Think you, you shall be safe?
Tig. Too safe I am, sir.

Enter GOBRIAS, ARANE, PANTHEA, SPACONIA, BACURIUS,
MARDONIUS, BESSUS, *and two* Gentlemen.

Ara. [*Kneels.*] As low as this I bow to you; and would
As low as is my grave, to show a mind
Thankful for all your mercies.
Arb. Oh, stand up,
And let me kneel! the light will be ashamed
To see observance done to me by you.
Ara. You are my king.
Arb. You are my mother. Rise!
As far be all your faults from your own soul,
As from my memory; then you shall be
As white as Innocence herself.
Ara. I came
Only to show my duty and acknowledge
My sorrows for my sins: Longer to stay,
Were but to draw eyes more attentively
Upon my shame. That power, that kept you safe
From me, preserve you still!
Arb. Your own desires
Shall be your guide.   [*Exit Arane.*
Pan. Now let me die!
Since I have seen my lord the king return
In safety, I have seen all good that life
Can show me. I have ne'er another wish
For Heaven to grant; nor were it fit I should;
For I am bound to spend my age to come,
In giving thanks that this was granted me.
Gob. Why does not your majesty speak?
Arb. To whom?
Gob. To the princess.
Pan. Alas, sir, I am fearful! You do look
On me, as if I were some loathed thing,
That you were finding out a way to shun.
Gob. Sir, you should speak to her.
Arb. Ha?
Pan. I know I am unworthy, yet not ill.
Arm'd with which innocence, here I will kneel
Till I am one with earth, but I will gain
Some words and kindness from you.   [*Kneels.*

Tigr. Will you speak, sir?

Arb. Speak! am I what I was?
    What art thou, that dost creep into my breast,
    And dar'st not see my face? Show forth thyself.
    I feel a pair of fiery wings display'd
    Hither, from thence. You shall not tarry there!
    Up, and begone; if you be'st love, be gone!
    Or I will tear thee from my wounded breast,
    Pull thy lov'd down away, and with a quill,
    By this right arm drawn from thy wanton wing,
    Write to thy laughing mother in thy blood,
    That you are powers belied, and all your darts
    Are to be blown away, by men resolved,
    Like dust. I know thou fear'st my words; away!

Tigr. Oh, misery; why should he be so slow?   [*Apart.*
    There can no falsehood come of loving her.
    Though I have given my faith, she is a thing
    Both to be loved and served beyond my faith.
    I would, he would present me to her quickly.

Pan. Will you not speak at all? Are you so far
    From kind words? Yet, to save my modesty,
    That must talk till you answer, do not stand
    As you were dumb; say something, though it be
    Poison'd with anger that it may strike me dead.

Mar. Have you no life at all? For manhood sake,
    Let her not kneel, and talk neglected thus.
    A tree would find a tongue to answer her,
    Did she but give it such a lov'd respect.

Arb. You mean this lady. Lift her from the earth:
    Why do you let her kneel so long?—Alas!
    Madam, your beauty uses to command,
    And not to beg. What is your suit to me?
    It shall be granted; yet the time is short,
    And my affairs are great. But where's my sister?
    I bade, she should be brought.

Mar. What, is he mad?

Arb. Gobrias, where is she?

Gob. Sir!

Arb. Where is she, man?

Gob. Who, sir?

Arb. Who? hast thou forgot my sister?

Gob. Your sister, sir?

Arb. Your sister, sir! Some one that hath a wit,

Answer, where is she?

Gob. Do you not see her there?

Arb. Where?

Gob. There.

Arb. There? where?

Mar. 'Slight, there! are you blind?

Arb. Which do you mean?   That little one?

Gob. No, sir.

Arb. No, sir?   Why, do you mock me?   I can see
No other here, but that petitioning lady.

Gob. That's she.

Arb. Away!

Gob. Sir, it is she.

Arb. 'Tis false.

Gob. Is it?

Arb. As hell!   By heaven, as false as hell!
My sister!—Is she dead?   If it be so,
Speak boldly to me, for I am a man,
And dare not quarrel with Divinity;
And do not think to cozen me with this.
I see, you all are mute and stand amazed,
Fearful to answer me.   It is too true;
A decreed instant cuts off every life,
For which to mourn is to repine.   She died
A virgin though, more innocent than sleep,
As clear as her own eyes; and blessedness
Eternal waits upon her where she is.
I know she could not make a wish to change
Her state for new; and you shall see me bear
My crosses like a man.   We all must die,
And she has taught us how.

Gob. Do not mistake,
And vex yourself for nothing; for her death
Is a long life off yet, I hope.   'Tis she;
And if my speech deserve not faith, lay death
Upon me, and my latest words shall force
A credit from you.

Arb. Which, good Gobrias?
That lady, dost thou mean?

Gob. That lady, sir:
She is your sister; and she is your sister
That loves you so; 'tis she for whom I weep,
To see you use her thus.

Arb. It cannot be.

Tigr. Pish! this is tedious: [*Apart.*
     I cannot hold; I must present myself.
     And yet the sight of my Spaconia
     Touches me, as a sudden thunder clap
     Does one that is about to sin.

Arb. Away!
     No more of this! Here I pronounce him traitor,
     The direct plotter of my death, that names
     Or thinks her for my sister: 'Tis a lie,
     The most malicious of the world, invented
     To mad your king.   He that will say so next,
     Let him draw out his sword and sheathe it here;
     It is a sin fully as pardonable.
     She is no kin to me, nor shall she be:
     If she were ever, I create her none.
     And which of you can question this?   My power
     Is like the sea, that is to be obey'd,
     And not disputed with.   I have decreed her
     As far from having part of blood with me,
     As the naked Indians.   Come and answer me,
     He that is boldest now: Is that my sister?

Mar. Oh, this is fine!

Bes. No, marry, she is not, an't please your majesty.
     I never thought she was; she's nothing like you.

Arb. No; 'tis true, she is not.

Mar. Thou shouldst be hang'd.   [*To Bessus.*

Pan. Sir, I will speak but once: By the same power
     You make my blood a stranger unto yours,
     You may command me dead; and so much love
     A stranger may importune; pray you, do.
     If this request appear too much to grant,
     Adopt me of some other family,
     By your unquestion'd word; else I shall live
     Like sinful issues, that are left in streets
     By their regardless mothers, and no name
     Will be found for me.

Arb. I will hear no more.—
     Why should there be such music in a voice,
     And sin for me to hear it?   All the world
     May take delight in this; and 'tis damnation
     For me to do so.—You are fair, and wise,
     And virtuous, I think; and he is blessed

That is so near you as a brother is;
But you are naught to me but a disease;
Continual torment without hope of ease.
Such an ungodly sickness I have got,
That he, that undertakes my cure, must first
O'erthrow divinity, all moral laws,
And leave mankind as unconfin'd as beasts;
Allowing 'em to do all actions,
As freely as they drink when they desire.
Let me not hear you speak again; yet so
I shall but languish for the want of that,
The having which would kill me.—No man here
Offer to speak for her; for I consider
As much as you can say; I will not toil
My body and my mind too; rest thou there;
Here's one within will labour for you both.

Pan. I would I were past speaking.

Gob. Fear not, madam;
    The king will alter: 'Tis some sudden rage,
    And you shall see it end some other way.

Pan. Pray Heaven it do!

Tigr. [*Aside.*] Though she to whom I swore be here, I cannot
    Stifle my passion longer; if my father
    Should rise again, disquieted with this,
    And charge me to forbear, yet it would out—
                                    [*Comes forward.*
    Madam, a stranger, and a prisoner begs
    To be bid welcome.

Pan. You are welcome, sir,
    I think; but if you be not, 'tis past me
    To make you so; for I am here a stranger
    Greater than you: We know from whence you come;
    But I appear a lost thing, and by whom
    Is yet uncertain; found here i' the court,
    And only suffer'd to walk up and down,
    As one not worth the owning.

Spa. Oh, I fear
    Tigranes will be caught; he looks, methinks,
    As he would change his eyes with her.   Some help
    There is above for me, I hope!

Tigr. Why do you turn away, and weep so fast,
    And utter things that misbecome your looks?
    Can you want owning?

Spa. Oh, 'tis certain so.

Tigr. Acknowledge yourself mine.

Arb. How now?

Tigr. And then
    See if you want an owner.

Arb. They are talking!

Tigr. Nations shall own you for their queen.

Arb. Tigranes! art not thou my prisoner?

Tigr. I am.

Arb. And who is this?

Tigr. She is your sister.

Arb. She is so.

Mar. Is she so again? that's well.

Arb. And how, then, dare you offer to change words with her?

Tigr. Dare do it? Why, you brought me hither, sir,
    To that intent.

Arb. Perhaps, I told you so:
    If I had sworn it, had you so much folly
    To credit it? The least word that she speaks
    Is worth a life. Rule your disorder'd tongue,
    Or I will temper it!

Spa. Blest be that breath!

Tigr. Temper my tongue! Such incivilities
    As these no barbarous people ever knew:
    You break the laws of nature, and of nations;
    You talk to me as if I were a prisoner
    For theft. My tongue be temper'd! I must speak,
    If thunder check me, and I will.

Arb. You will?

Spa. Alas, my fortune!

Tigr. Do not fear his frown.
    Dear madam, hear me.

Arb. Fear not my frown? But that 'twere base in me
    To fight with one I know I can o'ercome,
    Again thou shouldst be conquered by me.

Mar. He has one ransom with him already; methinks,
    'twere good to fight double or quit.

Arb. Away with him to prison!—Now, sir, see
    If my frown be regardless.—Why delay you?
    Seize him, Bacurius!—You shall know my word
    Sweeps like a wind; and all it grapples with
    Are as the chaff before it.

Tigr. Touch me not.

Arb. Help there!

Tigr. Away!

1 *Gent.* It is in vain to struggle.

2 *Gent.* You must be forced.

Bac. Sir, you must pardon us;
　　We must obey.

Arb. Why do you dally there?
　　Drag him away by anything.

Bac. Come, sir.

Tigr. Justice, thou ought'st to give me strength enough
　　To shake all these off.—This is tyranny,
　　Arbaces, subtler than the burning bull's,
　　Or that famed tyrant's bed.　Thou might'st as well
　　Search i' the deep of winter through the snow
　　For half-starved people, to bring home with thee
　　To show 'em fire and send 'em back again,
　　As use me thus.

Arb. Let him be close, Bacurius.
　　　　　[*Exit Tigranes, led off by Bacurius and Gentlemen.*

Spa. I ne'er rejoiced at any ill to him,
　　But this imprisonment: What shall become
　　Of me forsaken?

Gob. You will not let your sister
　　Depart thus discontented from you, sir?

Arb. By no means, Gobrias: I have done her wrong,
　　And made myself believe much of myself,
　　That is not in me.—You did kneel to me,
　　Whilst I stood stubborn and regardless by,
　　And, like a god incensed, gave no ear
　　To all your prayers.　[*Kneels.*] Behold, I kneel to you:
　　Show a contempt as large as was my own,
　　And I will suffer it; yet, at the last,
　　Forgive me.

Pan. Oh, you wrong me more in this
　　Than in your rage you did: You mock me now.

Arb. Never forgive me, then; which is the worst
　　Can happen to me.

Pan. If you be in earnest,
　　Stand up, and give me but a gentle look,
　　And two kind words, and I shall be in Heaven.

Arb. Rise you then too: Here I acknowledge thee,
　　My hope, the only jewel of my life,
　　The best of sisters, dearer than my breath,

    A happiness as high as I could think,
    And when my actions call thee otherwise,
    Perdition light upon me!

Pan.   This is better
    Than if you had not frowned; it comes to me
    Like mercy at the block; And when I leave
    To serve you with my life, your curse be with me.

Arb.   Then thus I do salute thee; and again,
    To make this knot the stronger. Paradise
    Is there! It may be, you are yet in doubt;
    This third kiss blots it out.—I wade in sin,   [*Aside.*
    And foolishly entice myself along!—
    Take her away; see her a prisoner
    In her own chamber, closely, Gobrias!

Pan.   Alas, sir, why?

Arb.   I must not stay the answer. Do it.

Gob.   Good sir!

Arb.   No more! Do it, I say!

Mar.   This is better and better.

Pan.   Yet, hear me speak.

Arb.   I will not hear you speak.—
    Away with her! Let no man think to speak
    For such a creature; for she is a witch,
    A poisoner, and a traitor!

Gob.   Madam, this office grieves me.

Pan.   Nay, 'tis well;
    The king is pleased with it.

Arb.   Bessus, go you along too with her. I will prove
    All this that I have said, if I may live
    So long. But I am desperately sick;
    For she has given me poison in a kiss:
    She had it 'twixt her lips; and with her eyes
    She witches people. Go, without a word!
       [*Exeunt Gobrias, Panthea, Bessus, and Spaconia.*
    Why should You, that have made me stand in war
    Like Fate itself, cutting what threads I pleased,
    Decree such an unworthy end of me,
    And all my glories? What am I, alas,
    That you oppose me! If my secret thoughts
    Have ever harboured swellings against you,
    They could not hurt you; and it is in you
    To give me sorrow, that will render me
    Apt to receive your mercy: Rather so,

Let it be rather so, than punish me
With such unmanly sins.   Incest is in me
Dwelling already; and it must be holy,
That pulls it thence.—Where art, Mardonius!

Mar. Here, sir.

Arb. I pray thee, bear me, if thou canst.
Am I not grown a strange weight?

Mar. As you were.

Arb. No heavier?

Mar. No, sir.

Arb. Why, my legs
Refuse to bear my body!   Oh, Mardonius,
Thou hast in field beheld me, when thou know'st
I could have gone, though I could never run.

Mar. And so I shall again.

Arb. Oh, no, 'tis past.

Mar. Pray you, go rest yourself.

Arb. Wilt thou, hereafter, when they talk of me,
As thou shalt hear nothing but infamy,
Remember some of those things?

Mar. Yes, I will.

Arb. I pray thee, do; for thou shalt never see
Me so again.   [*Exeunt.*

SCENE II.—*A Room in the House of Bessus.*

Enter BESSUS.

Bes. They talk of fame; I have gotten it in the wars, and
will afford any man a reasonable pennyworth.   Some
will say, they could be content to have it, but that it is
to be atchieved with danger; but my opinion is otherwise: For if I might stand still in cannon-proof, and
have fame fall upon me, I would refuse it.   My reputation came principally by thinking to run away, which
nobody knows but Mardonius; and, I think, he conceals
it to anger me.   Before I went to the wars, I came to
the town a young fellow, without means or parts to
deserve friends; and my empty guts persuaded me to
lie, and abuse people, for my meat; which I did, and they
beat me.   Then would I fast two days, till my hunger
cried out on me, " Rail still: "   Then, methought, I had
a monstrous stomach to abuse 'em again, and did it.

In this state I continued, till they hung me up by the
heels, and beat me with hasle-sticks, as if they would
have baked me, and have cozen'd somebody with me
for venison. After this I rail'd, and eat quietly: For the
whole kingdom took notice of me for a baffled whipp'd
fellow, and what I said was remembered in mirth, but
never in anger, of which I was glad. I would it were at
that pass again! After this, Heaven call'd an aunt of
mine, that left two hundred pounds in a cousin's hand
for me; who, taking me to be a gallant young spirit,
raised a company for me with the money, and sent me
into Armenia with 'em. Away I would have run from
them, but that I could get no company: and alone I
durst not run. I was never at battle but once, and there
I was running, but Mardonius cudgell'd me: Yet I got
loose at last, but was so afraid that I saw no more than
my shoulders do; but fled with my whole company
amongst mine enemies, and overthrew 'em: Now the
report of my valour is come over before me, and they say
I was a raw young fellow, but now I am improved: A
plague on their eloquence! 'twill cost me many a beating;
and Mardonius might help this too, if he would; for now
they think to get honour on me, and all the men I have
abused call me freshly to account (worthily as they call
it) by the way of challenge.

Enter the third Gentleman.

3 *Gent.* Good-morrow, Captain Bessus.
Bes. Good-morrow, sir.
3 *Gent.* I come to speak with you——
Bes. You're very welcome.
3 *Gent.* From one that holds himself wrong'd by you some
three years since. Your worth, he says, is famed, and
he doth nothing doubt but you will do him right, as
beseems a soldier.
Bes. A pox on 'em, so they cry all!
3 *Gent.* And a slight note I have about me for you, for the
delivery of which you must excuse me: It is an office
that friendship calls upon me to do, and no way offensive
to you; since I desire but right on both sides.
                                    [*Gives him a letter.*
Bes. 'Tis a challenge, sir, is it not?

3 Gent. 'Tis an inviting to the field.

Bes. An inviting? Oh, cry you mercy!—What a compliment he delivers it with! he might, as agreeably to my nature, present me poison with such a speech. [*Reads*]. Um, um, um—*Reputation*—um, um, um—*call you to account* —um um, um—*forced to this*—um, um, um—*with my sword*—um, um, um—*like a gentleman*—um, um, um— *dear to me*—um, um, um—*satisfaction.*—'Tis very well, sir; I do accept it; but he must wait an answer this thirteen weeks.

3 Gent. Why, sir, he would be glad to wipe off this stain as soon as he could.

Bes. Sir, upon my credit, I am already engaged to two hundred and twelve; all which must have their stains wiped off, if that be the word, before him.

3 Gent. Sir, if you be truly engaged but to one, he shall stay a competent time.

Bes. Upon my faith, sir, to two hundred and twelve: And I have a spent body, too much bruised in battle; so that I cannot fight, I must be plain, above three combats a-day. All the kindness I can show him, is to set him resolvedly in my roll, the two hundred and thirteenth man, which is something; for, I tell you, I think there will be more after him than before him; I think so. Pray you commend me to him, and tell him this.

3 Gent. I will, sir. Good-morrow to you. [*Exit Gentleman.*

Bes. Good-morrow, good sir.—Certainly, my safest way were to print myself a coward, with a discovery how I came by my credit, and clap it upon every post. I have received above thirty challenges within this two hours: Marry, all but the first I put off with engagement; and, by good fortune, the first is no madder of fighting than I; so that that's referred. The place where it must be ended is four days' journey off, and our arbitrators are these; he has chosen a gentleman in travel, and I have a special friend with a quartain ague, like to hold him this five years, for mine; and when his man comes home, we are to expect my friend's health. If they would send me challenges thus thick, as long as I lived, I would have no other living: I can make seven shillings a-day o' th' paper to the grocers. Yet I learn nothing by all these, but a little skill in comparing of styles: I do find evidently, that there is some one scrivener in this town,

that has a great hand in writing of challenges, for they
are all of a cut, and six of 'em in a hand; and they all
end, " My reputation is dear to me, and I must require
satisfaction."—Who's there? more paper, I hope.   No;
'tis my lord Bacurius.   I fear, all is not well betwixt us.

Enter BACURIUS.

Bac. Now, Captain Bessus! I come about a frivolous matter,
caused by as idle a report: You know, you were a
coward.

Bes. Very right.

Bac. And wrong'd me.

Bes. True, my lord.

Bac. But now, people will call you valiant; desertlessly, I
think; yet, for their satisfaction, I will have you fight
me.

Bes. Oh, my good lord, my deep engagements——

Bac. Tell not me of your engagements, Captain Bessus! It
is not to be put off with an excuse.   For my own part,
I am none of the multitude that believe your conversion
from coward.

Bes. My lord, I seek not quarrels, and this belongs not to me;
I am not to maintain it.

Bac. Who then, pray?

Bes. Bessus the coward wrong'd you.

Bac. Right.

Bes. And shall Bessus the valiant maintain what Bessus the
coward did?

Bac. I pr'ythee leave these cheating tricks! I swear thou
shalt fight with me, or thou shalt be beaten extremely,
and kick'd.

Bes. Since you provoke me thus far, my lord, I will fight
with you; and, by my sword, it shall cost me twenty
pounds, but I will have my leg well a week sooner
purposely.

Bac. Your leg! why, what ail's your leg? I'll do a cure on
you.   Stand up!

Bes. My lord, this is not noble in you.

Bac. What dost thou with such a phrase in thy mouth? I
will kick thee out of all good words before I leave thee.
                                                    [*Kicks him.*

Bes. My lord, I take this as a punishment for the offence I
did when I was a coward.

Bac. When thou wert? confess thyself a coward still, or, by
this light, I'll beat thee into sponge.

Bes. Why, I am one.

Bac. Are you so, sir? and why do you wear a sword then?
Come, unbuckle! quick!

Bes. My lord?

Bac. Unbuckle, I say, and give it me; or, as I live, thy head
will ache extremely.

Bes. It is a pretty hilt; and if your lordship take an affection
to it, with all my heart I present it to you, for a new
year's gift.
         [*Gives him his sword, with a knife in the scabbard.*

Bac. I thank you very heartily, sweet captain! Farewell.

Bes. One word more: I beseech your lordship to render me
my knife again.

Bac. Marry, by all means, captain. [*Gives him back the
knife.*] Cherish yourself with it, and eat hard, good
captain! we cannot tell whether we shall have any more
such.   Adieu, dear captain!   [*Exit Bacurius.*

Bes. I will make better use of this, than of my sword.   A
base spirit has this 'vantage of a brave one; it keeps
always at a stay, nothing brings it down, not beating.
I remember I promised the king, in a great audience,
that I would make my back-biters eat my sword to a
knife: How to get another sword I know not; nor know
any means left for me to maintain my credit, but
impudence: Therefore I will outswear him and all his
followers, that this is all that's left uneaten of my sword.
         [*Exit Bessus.*

SCENE III.—*An Apartment in the Palace.*

Enter Mardonius.

Mar. I'll move the king; he is most strangely alter'd: I
guess the cause, I fear, too right. Heaven has some
secret end in't, and 'tis a scourge, no question, justly
laid upon him. He has follow'd me through twenty
rooms; and ever, when I stay to wait his command, he
blushes like a girl, and looks upon me as if modesty kept
in his business; so turns away from me; but, if I go on,
he follows me again.

Enter ARBACES.

See, here he is. I do not use this, yet, I know not how,
I cannot choose but weep to see him: his very enemies,
I think, whose wounds have bred his fame, if they should
see him now, would find tears i' their eyes.

Arb. I cannot utter it! Why should I keep
A breast to harbour thoughts I dare not speak?
Darkness is in my bosom; and there lie
A thousand thoughts that cannot brook the light.
How wilt thou vex me, when this deed is done,
Conscience, that art afraid to let me name it!

Mar. How do you, sir?

Arb. Why, very well, Mardonius.
How dost thou do?

Mar. Better than you, I fear.

Arb. I hope thou art; for, to be plain with thee,
Thou art in hell else! Secret scorching flames,
That far transcend earthly material fires,
Are crept into me, and there is no cure:
Is it not strange, Mardonius, there's no cure?

Mar. Sir, either I mistake, or there is something hid, that
you would utter to me.

Arb. So there is: but yet I cannot do it.

Mar. Out with it, sir. If it be dangerous, I will not shrink
to do you service: I shall not esteem my life a weightier
matter than indeed it is. I know 'tis subject to more
chances than it has hours; and I were better lose it in
my king's cause, than with an ague, or a fall, or (sleeping)
to a thief; as all these are probable enough. Let me
but know what I shall do for you.

Arb. It will not out! Were you with Gobrias,
And bade him give my sister all content
The place affords, and give her leave to send
And speak to whom she please?

Mar. Yes, sir, I was.

Arb. And did you to Bacurius say as much
About Tigranes?

Mar. Yes.

Arb. That's all my business.

Mar. Oh, say not so; you had an answer of this before:
Besides, I think this business might be utter'd more
carelessly.

Arb. Come, thou shalt have it out.   I do beseech thee,
 By all the love thou hast profess'd to me,
 To see my sister from me.
Mar. Well; and what?
Arb. That's all.
Mar. That's strange!   Shall I say nothing to her?
Arb. Not a word:
 But, if thou lov'st me, find some subtle way
 To make her understand by signs.
Mar. But what shall I make her understand?
Arb. Oh, Mardonius, for that I must be pardon'd.
Mar. You may; but I can only see her then.
Arb. 'Tis true!   [*Gives him a ring.*
 Bear her this ring, then; and, on more advice,
 Thou shalt speak to her: Tell her I do love
 My kindred all; wilt thou?
Mar. Is there no more?
Arb. Oh, yes!   And her the best;
 Better than any brother loves his sister:
 That is all.
Mar. Methinks, this need not have been delivered with such
 a caution.   I'll do it.
Arb. There is more yet: Wilt thou be faithful to me?
Mar. Sir, if I take upon me to deliver it, after I hear it, I'll
 pass through fire to do it.
Arb. I love her better than a brother ought.
 Dost thou conceive me?
Mar. I hope you do not, sir.
Arb. No! thou art dull.   Kneel down before her,
 And never rise again, till she will love me.
Mar. Why, I think she does.
Arb. But, better than she does; another way;
 As wives love husbands.
Mar. Why, I think there are few wives that love their
 husbands better than she does you.
Arb. Thou wilt not understand me! Is it fit
 This should be utter'd plainly?   Take it, then,
 Naked as 'tis; I would desire her love
 Lasciviously, lewdly, incestuously,
 To do a sin that needs must damn us both;
 And thee too.   Dost thou understand me now?
Mar. Yes; there's your ring, again.   What have I done
 Dishonestly, in my whole life, name it,

That you should put so base a business to me?

Arb. Didst thou not tell me, thou wouldst do it?

Mar. Yes, if I undertook it: But if all
My hairs were lives, I would not be engaged
In such a cause to save my last life.

Arb. Oh, guilt, how poor and weak a thing art thou!
This man, that is my servant, whom my breath
Might blow about the world, might beat me here
Having this cause; whilst I, press'd down with sin,
Could not resist him.—Hear, Mardonius!
It was a motion mis-beseeming man,
And I am sorry for it.

Mar. Heaven grant you may be so! You must understand,
nothing that you can utter can remove my love and
service from my prince: but, otherwise, I think, I shall
not love you more: For you are sinful, and, if you do
this crime, you ought to have no laws; for, after this,
it will be great injustice in you to punish any offender,
for any crime. For myself, I find my heart too big;
I feel, I have not patience to look on, whilst you run
these forbidden courses. Means I have none but your
favour; and I am rather glad that I shall lose 'em both
together, than keep 'em with such conditions. I shall
find a dwelling amongst some people, where, though our
garments perhaps be coarser, we shall be richer far
within, and harbour no such vices in 'em. The gods
preserve you, and mend——

Arb. Mardonius! Stay, Mardonius! for, though
My present state requires nothing but knaves
To be about me, such as are prepared
For every wicked act, yet who does know,
But that my loathed fate may turn about,
And I have use for honest men again?
I hope, I may; I pr'ythee leave me not.

Enter BESSUS.

Bes. Where is the king?

Mar. There.

Bes. An't please your majesty, there's the knife.

Arb. What knife?

Bes. The sword is eaten.

Mar. Away, you fool! the king is serious,
And cannot now admit your vanities.

Bes. Vanities! I'm no honest man, if my enemies have not
    brought it to this.   What, do you think I lie?

Arb. No, no; 'tis well, Bessus; tis very well.
    I'm glad on't.

Mar. If your enemies brought it to this, your enemies are
    cutlers.   Come, leave the king.

Bes. Why, may not valour approach him?

Mar. Yes; but he has affairs.   Depart, or I shall be some-
    thing unmannerly with you!

Arb. No; let him stay, Mardonius; let him stay;
    I have occasion with him very weighty,
    And I can spare you now.

Mar. Sir?

Arb. Why, I can spare you now.

Bes. Mardonius, give way to the state affairs.

Mar. Indeed, you are fitter for his present purpose.
                               [Exit Mardonius.

Arb. Bessus, I should employ thee: Wilt thou do't?

Bes. Do't for you?   By this air, I will do anything, without
    exception, be it a good, bad, or indifferent thing.

Arb. Do not swear.

Bes. By this light, but I will; anything whatsoever.

Arb. But I shall name the thing
    Thy conscience will not suffer thee to do.

Bes. I would fain hear that thing.

Arb. Why, I would have thee get my sister for me,—
    Thou understand'st me,—in a wicked manner.

Bes. Oh, you would have a bout with her?   I'll do't, I'll do't,
    i'faith.

Arb. Wilt thou? dost thou make no more on't?

Bes. More?   No.   Why, is there anything else?
    If there be, trust me, it shall be done too.

Arb. Hast thou no greater sense of such a sin?
    Thou art too wicked for my company,
    Though I have hell within me, and may'st yet
    Corrupt me further!   Pr'ythee answer me,
    How do I show to thee after this motion?

Bes. Why, your majesty looks as well, in my opinion, as ever
    you did since you were born.

Arb. But thou appear'st to me, after thy grant,
    The ugliest, loathed, detestable thing,
    That I have ever met with.   Thou hast eyes
    Like flames of sulphur, which, methinks, do dart

      Infection on me; and thou hast a mouth
      Enough to take me in, where there do stand
      Four rows of iron teeth.

Bes. I feel no such thing: But 'tis no matter how I look;
      I'll do your business as well as they that look better.
      And when this is dispatch'd, if you have a mind to your
      mother, tell me, and you shall see I'll set it hard.

Arb. My mother?—Heaven forgive me, to hear this!
      I am inspired with horror.—Now I hate thee
      Worse than my sin; which, if I could come by,
      Should suffer death eternal, ne'er to rise
      In any breast again. Know, I will die
      Languishing mad, as I resolve I shall,
      Ere I will deal by such an instrument:
      Thou art too sinful to employ in this.
      Out of the world, away!   *[Beats him.*

Bes. What do you mean, sir?

Arb. Hung round with curses, take thy fearful flight
      Into the desarts; where, 'mongst all the monsters,
      If thou find'st one so beastly as thyself,
      Thou shalt be held as innocent!

Bes. Good sir——

Arb. If there were no such instruments as thou,
      We kings could never act such wicked deeds!
      Seek out a man that mocks divinity,
      That breaks each precept both of God and man,
      And nature too, and does it without lust,
      Merely because it is a law, and good,
      And live with him; for him thou can'st not spoil.
      Away, I say!—   *[Exit Bessus.*
            I will not do this sin.
      I'll press it here, till it do break my breast:
      It heaves to get out; but thou art a sin,
      And, spite of torture, I will keep thee in.   *[Exit.*

ACT IV

SCENE I.—*The Apartment of the Princess in the Palace.*

Enter GOBRIAS, PANTHEA, *and* SPACONIA.

Gob. Have you written, madam?

Pan. Yes, good Gobrias.

Gob. And with a kindness and such winning words
As may provoke him, at one instant, feel
His double fault, your wrong, and his own rashness?

Pan. I have sent words enough, if words may win him
From his displeasure; and such words, I hope,
As shall gain much upon his goodness, Gobrias.
Yet fearing, since they are many, and a woman's,
A poor belief may follow, I have woven
As many truths within 'em to speak for me,
That if he be but gracious and receive 'em——

Gob. Good lady, be not fearful: Though he should not
Give you your present end in this, believe it,
You shall feel, if your virtue can induce you
To labour out this tempest (which, I know,
Is but a poor proof 'gainst your patience)
All those contents, your spirit will arrive at,
Newer and sweeter to you. Your royal brother,
When he shall once collect himself, and see
How far he has been asunder from himself,
What a mere stranger to his golden temper,
Must, from those roots of virtue, never dying,
Though somewhat stopt with humour, shoot again
Into a thousand glories, bearing his fair branches
High as our hopes can look at, strait as justice,
Loaden with ripe contents. He loves you dearly,
I know it, and, I hope, I need not further
Win you to understand it.

Pan. I believe it;
But, howsoever, I am sure I love him dearly;
So dearly, that if anything I write
For my enlarging should beget his anger,
Heaven be a witness with me, and my faith,
I had rather live entombed here.

Gob. You shall not feel a worse stroke than your grief;
　　I am sorry 'tis so sharp.　I kiss your hand,
　　And this night will deliver this true story,
　　With this hand to your brother.
Pan. Peace go with you!
　　You are a good man.—　　　　　　　　　[*Exit Gobrias.*
　　　　　　　　My Spaconia,
　　Why are you ever sad thus?
Spa. Oh, dear lady!
Pan. Pr'ythee discover not a way to sadness,
　　Nearer than I have in me.　Our two sorrows
　　Work, like two eager hawks, who shall get highest.
　　How shall I lessen thine? for mine, I fear,
　　Is easier known than cured.
Spa. Heaven comfort both,
　　And give yours happy ends, however I
　　Fall in my stubborn fortunes.
Pan. This but teaches
　　How to be more familiar with our sorrows,
　　That are too much our masters.　Good Spaconia,
　　How shall I do you service?
Spa. Noblest lady,
　　You make me more a slave still to your goodness,
　　And only live to purchase thanks to pay you;
　　For that is all the business of my life now.
　　I will be bold, since you will have it so,
　　To ask a noble favour of you.
Pan. Speak it; 'tis yours; for, from so sweet a virtue,
　　No ill demand has issue.
Spa. Then, ever-virtuous, let me beg your will
　　In helping me to see the prince Tigranes;
　　With whom I am equal prisoner, if not more.
Pan. Reserve me to a greater end, Spaconia;
　　Bacurius cannot want so much good manners
　　As to deny your gentle visitation,
　　Though you came only with your own command.
Spa. I know they will deny me, gracious madam,
　　Being a stranger, and so little famed,
　　So utter empty of those excellencies
　　That tame authority: But in you, sweet lady,
　　All these are natural; beside, a power
　　Derived immediate from your royal brother,
　　Whose least word in you may command the kingdom.

Pan. More than my word, Spaconia, you shall carry,
     For fear it fail you.
Spa. Dare you trust a token?
     Madam, I fear I am grown too bold a beggar.
Pan. You are a pretty one; and, trust me, lady,
     It joys me I shall do a good to you,
     Though to myself I never shall be happy.
     Here, take this ring, and from me as a token
     Deliver it: I think they will not stay you.
     So, all your own desires go with you, lady!
Spa. And sweet peace to your grace!
Pan, Pray Heaven, I find it!   [*Exeunt.*

SCENE II.—*A Prison.*

TIGRANES *is discovered.*

Tigr. Fool that I am! I have undone myself,
     And with my own hand turn'd my fortune round,
     That was a fair one. I have childishly
     Play'd with my hope so long, till I have broke it,
     And now too late I mourn for't. Oh, Spaconia!
     Thou hast found an even way to thy revenge now.
     Why didst thou follow me, like a faint shadow,
     To wither my desires? But, wretched fool,
     Why did I plant thee 'twixt the sun and me,
     To make me freeze thus! why did I prefer her
     To the fair princess? Oh, thou fool, thou fool,
     Thou family of fools, live like a slave still!
     And in thee bear thine own hell and thy torment;
     Thou hast deserved it. Couldst thou find no lady,
     But she that has thy hopes, to put her to,
     And hazard all thy peace? none to abuse,
     But she that loved thee ever, poor Spaconia?
     And so much loved thee, that, in honesty
     And honour, thou art bound to meet her virtues!
     She, that forgot the greatness of her grief
     And miseries, that must follow such mad passions,
     Endless and wild in women! she, that for thee,
     And with thee, left her liberty, her name,
     And country! You have paid me equal, heavens,
     And sent my own rod to correct me with,
     A woman! For inconstancy I'll suffer;

Lay it on, justice, till my soul melt in me,
For my unmanly, beastly, sudden doting,
Upon a new face; after all my oaths,
Many, and strange ones.
I feel my old fire flame again and burn
So strong and violent, that, should I see her
Again, the grief, and that, would kill me.

Enter BACURIUS *and* SPACONIA.

Bac. Lady,
Your token I acknowledge; you may pass;
There is the king.
Spa. I thank your lordship for it.   [*Exit Bacurius.*
Tigr. She comes, she comes!   Shame hide me ever from her!
'Would I were buried, or so far removed
Light might not find me out!   I dare not see her.
Spa. Nay, never hide yourself! Or, were you hid
Where earth hides all her riches, near her centre,
My wrongs, without more day, would light me to you:
I must speak ere I die.   Were all your greatness
Doubled upon you, you're a perjured man,
And only mighty in your wickedness
Of wronging women! Thou art false, false, prince.
I live to see it: poor Spaconia lives
To tell thee thou art false; and then no more!
She lives to tell thee, thou art more inconstant
Than all ill women ever were together.
Thy faith is firm as raging overflows,
That no bank can command; as lasting
As boys' gay bubbles, blown i' th' air and broken.
The wind is fix'd to thee; and sooner shall
The beaten mariner, with his shrill whistle,
Calm the loud murmur of the troubled main,
And strike it smooth again, than thy soul fall
To have peace in love with any: Thou art all
That all good men must hate; and if thy story
Shall tell succeeding ages what thou wert,
Oh, let it spare me in it, lest true lovers,
In pity of my wrongs, burn thy black legend,
And with their curses shake thy sleeping ashes.
Tigr. Oh! oh!
Spa. The destinies, I hope, have pointed out
Our ends alike, that thou may'st die for love,

Though not for me; for, this assure thyself,
The princess hates thee deadly, and will sooner
Be won to marry with a bull, and safer,
Than such a beast as thou art.—I have struck,
I fear, too deep; beshrew me for it!—Sir,
This sorrow works me, like a cunning friendship,
Into the same piece with it.—He's ashamed!
Alas, I have been too rugged.—Dear my lord,
I am sorry I have spoken anything,
Indeed I am, that may add more restraint
To that too much you have. Good sir, be pleased
To think it was a fault of love, not malice;
And do as I will do, forgive it, prince.
I do and can forgive the greatest sins
To me you can repent of. Pray believe.
Tig. Oh, my Spaconia! Oh, thou virtuous woman!
Spa. No more; the king, sir.

Enter ARBACES, BACURIUS, *and* MARDONIUS.

Arb. Have you been careful of our noble prisoner,
    That he want nothing fitting for his greatness?
Bac. I hope his grace will quit me for my care, sir.
Arb. 'Tis well.—Royal Tigranes, health!
Tigr. More than the strictness of this place can give, sir,
    I offer back again to great Arbaces.
Arb. We thank you, worthy prince; and pray excuse us,
    We have not seen you since your being here.
    I hope your noble usage has been equal
    With your own person: Your imprisonment,
    If it be any, I dare say, is easy;
    And shall not out-last two days.
Tigr. I thank you.
    My usage here has been the same it was,
    Worthy a royal conqueror. For my restraint,
    It came unkindly, because much unlook'd for;
    But I must bear it.
Arb. What lady's that, Bacurius?
Bac. One of the princess' women, sir.
Arb. I fear'd it.
    Why comes she hither?
Bac. To speak with the prince Tigranes.
Arb. From whom, Bacurius?

Bac. From the princess, sir.

Arb. I knew I had seen her.

Mar. His fit begins to take him now again. 'Tis a strange
 fever, and 'twill shake us all anon, I fear. 'Would he
 were well cured of this raging folly: Give me the wars,
 where men are mad, and may talk what they list, and
 held the bravest fellows; this pelting prating peace is
 good for nothing: Drinking's a virtue to't.

Arb. I see there's truth in no man, nor obedience,
 But for his own ends: Why did you let her in?

Bac. It was your own command to bar none from him:
 Besides, the princess sent her ring, sir, for my warrant.

Arb. A token to Tigranes, did she not?
 Sir, tell truth.

Bac. I do not use to lie, sir.
 'Tis no way I eat, or live by; and I think
 This is no token, sir.

Mar. This combat has undone him: If he had been well
 beaten, he had been temperate. I shall never see him
 handsome again, till he have a horseman's staff yoked
 through his shoulders, or an arm broke with a bullet.

Arb. I am trifled with.

Bac. Sir?

Arb. I know it, as I know thee to be false.

Mar. Now the clap comes.

Bac. You never knew me so, sir, I dare speak it;
 And, durst a worse man tell me, though my better———

Mar. 'Tis well said, by my soul.

Arb. Sirrah, you answer as you had no life.

Bac. That I fear, sir, to lose nobly.

Arb. I say, sir, once again———

Bac. You may say what you please, sir:
 'Would I might do so.

Arb. I will, sir; and say openly,
 This woman carries letters: By my life,
 I know she carries letters; this woman does it.

Mar. 'Would Bessus were here, to take her aside and search
 her; he would quickly tell you what she carried, sir.

Arb. I have found it out, this woman carries letters.

Mar. If this hold, 'twill be an ill world for bawds, chamber-
 maids, and post-boys. I thank Heaven, I have none but
 his letters-patents, things of his own inditing.

Arb. Prince, this cunning cannot do't.

Tigr. Do what, sir? I reach you not.

Arb. It shall not serve your turn, prince.

Tigr. Serve my turn, sir?

Arb. Ay, sir, it shall not serve your turn.

Tigr. Be plainer, good sir.

Arb. This woman shall carry no more letters back to your
love Panthea; by Heaven she shall not; I say she shall
not.

Mar. This would make a saint swear like a soldier, and a
soldier like Termagant.

Tigr. This beats me more, king, than the blows you gave me.

Arb. Take 'em away both, and together let them prisoners
be, strictly and closely kept; or, sirrah, your life shall
answer it; and let nobody speak with 'em hereafter.

Tigr. Well, I am subject to you,
And must endure these passions.

Spa. This is th' imprisonment I have look'd for always,
And the dear place I would choose.

        [Exeunt Tigranes, Spaconia, Bacurius.

Mar. Sir, have you done well now?

Arb. Dare you reprove it?

Mar. No.

Arb. You must be crossing me.

Mar. I have no letters, sir, to anger you,
But a dry sonnet of my corporal's,
To an old sutler's wife; and that I'll burn, sir.
'Tis like to prove a fine age for the ignorant.

Arb. How dar'st thou so often forfeit thy life?
Thou know'st 'tis in my power to take it.

Mar. Yes, and I know you wo' not; or, if you do, you'll miss
it quickly.

Arb. Why?

Mar. Who shall tell you of these childish follies, when I am
dead? who shall put-to his power to draw those virtues
out of a flood of humours, when they are drown'd, and
make 'em shine again? No, cut my head off: Then you
may talk, and be believed, and grow worse, and have
your too self-glorious temper rock'd into a dead sleep,
and the kingdom with you; till foreign swords be in your
throats, and slaughter be everywhere about you, like
your flatterers. Do, kill me!

Arb. Pr'ythee, be tamer, good Mardonius.
Thou know'st I love thee; nay, I honour thee;

Believe it, good old soldier, I am thine:
But I am rack'd clean from myself! Bear with me,
Woo't thou bear with me, my Mardonius?

Enter GOBRIAS.

Mar. There comes a good man; love him too; he's tem
  perate; you may live to have need of such a virtue
  Rage is not still in fashion.
Arb. Welcome, good Gobrias.
Gob. My service, and this letter, to your grace.
Arb. From whom?
Gob. From the rich mine of virtue and beauty,
  Your mournful sister.
Arb. She is in prison, Gobrias, is she not?
Gob. [*Kneels.*] She is, sir, till your pleasure do enlarge her,
  Which on my knees I beg.   Oh, 'tis not fit,
  That all the sweetness of the world in one,
  The youth and virtue that would tame wild tigers,
  And wilder people, that have known no manners,
  Should live thus cloister'd up!   For your love's sake,
  If there be any in that noble heart
  To her, a wretched lady, and forlorn;
  Or for her love to you, which is as much
  As Nature and Obedience ever gave,
  Have pity on her beauties.
Arb. Praythee, stand up: 'Tis true, she is too fair,
  And all these commendations but her own:
  'Would thou hadst never so commended her,
  Or I ne'er lived to have heard it, Gobrias!
  If thou but knew'st the wrong her beauty does her,
  Thou wouldst, in pity of her, be a liar.
  Thy ignorance has drawn me, wretched man,
  Whither myself, nor thou, canst well tell.   Oh, my fate
  I think she loves me, but I fear another
  Is deeper in her heart: How think'st thou, Gobrias?
Gob. I do beseech your grace, believe it not;
  For, let me perish, if it be not false!
  Good sir, read her letter.   [*Arbaces reads.*
Mar. This love, or what a devil it is, I know not, begets
  more mischief than a wake.   I had rather be well beaten
  starved, or lousy, than live within the air on't.   He,
  that had seen this brave fellow charge through a grove
  of pikes but t'other day, and look upon him now, will

ne'er believe his eyes again. If he continue thus but
two days more, a tailor may beat him with one hand
tied behind him.

Arb. Alas, she would be at liberty;
And there be thousand reasons, Gobrias,
Thousands, that will deny it;
Which, if she knew, she would contentedly
Be where she is, and bless her virtues for it,
And me, though she were closer: She would, Gobrias;
Good man, indeed, she would.

Gob. Then, good sir, for her satisfaction,
Send for her, and, with reason, make her know
Why she must live thus from you.

Arb. I will. Go bring her to me.   [*Exeunt.*

SCENE III.—*A Room in the House of Bessus.*

Enter Bessus, *two* Swordmen, *and a* Boy.

Bes. You're very welcome, both! Some stools there, boy;
And reach a table. Gentlemen o' th' sword,
Pray sit, without more compliment. Begone, child!
I have been curious in the searching of you,
Because I understand you wise and valiant persons.

1 *Sw.* We understand ourselves, sir.

Bes. Nay, gentlemen, and dear friends o' the sword,
No compliment, I pray; but to the cause
I hang upon, which, in few, is my honour.

2 *Sw.* You cannot hang too much, sir, for your honour.
But to your cause.

Bes. Be wise, and speak truth.
My first doubt is, my beating by my prince.

1 *Sw.* Stay there a little, sir; Do you doubt a beating?
Or, have you had a beating by your prince?

Bes. Gentlemen o' th' sword, my prince has beaten me.

2 *Sw.* Brother, what think you of this case?

1 *Sw.* If he has beaten him, the case is clear.

2 *Sw.* If he have beaten him, I grant the case.
But how? we cannot be too subtle in this business.
I say, but how?

Bes. Even with his royal hand.

1 *Sw.* Was it a blow of love, or indignation?

Bes. 'Twas twenty blows of indignation, gentlemen;
Besides two blows o' th' face.

2 *Sw.* Those blows o' th' face have made a new cause on't;
    The rest were but an honourable rudeness.
1 *Sw.* Two blows o' th' face, and given by a worse man,
    I must confess, as the swordmen say, had turn'd
    The business: Mark me, brother, by a worse man:
    But, being by his prince, had they been ten,
    And those ten drawn ten teeth, besides the hazard
    Of his nose for ever, all this had been but favours.
    This is my flat opinion, which I'll die in.
2 *Sw.* The king may do much, captain, believe it;
    For had he crack'd your skull through, like a bottle,
    Or broke a rib or two with tossing of you,
    Yet you had lost no honour. This is strange,
    You may imagine, but this is truth now, captain.
Bes. I will be glad to embrace it, gentlemen.
    But how far may he strike me?
1 *Sw.* There's another;
    A new cause rising from the time and distance,
    In which I will deliver my opinion.
    He may strike, beat, or cause to be beaten;
    For these are natural to man:
    Your prince, I say, may beat you so far forth
    As his dominion reaches; that's for the distance;
    The time, ten miles a-day, I take it.
2 *Sw.* Brother, you err, 'tis fifteen miles a-day;
    His stage is ten, his beatings are fifteen.
Bes. 'Tis of the longest, but we subjects must——
1 *Sw.* Be subject to it: You are wise and virtuous.
Bes. Obedience ever makes that noble use on't,
    To which I dedicate my beaten body.
    I must trouble you a little further, gentlemen o' th'
        sword.
2 *Sw.* No trouble at all to us, sir, if we may
    Profit your understanding: We are bound,
    By virtue of our calling, to utter our opinion
    Shortly, and discretely.
Bes. My sorest business is, I have been kick'd.
2 *Sw.* How far, sir?
Bes. Not to flatter myself in it, all over:
    My sword lost, but not forced; for discretely
    I render'd, it, to save that imputation.
1 *Sw.* It show'd discretion, the best part of valour.
2 *Sw.* Brother, this is a pretty cause; pray ponder on't:

Our friend here has been kick'd.

1 *Sw.* He has so, brother.

2 *Sw.* Sorely, he says. Now, had he set down here,
Upon the mere kick, 't had been cowardly.

1 *Sw.* I think, it had been cowardly, indeed.

2 *Sw.* But our friend has redeem'd it, in delivering
His sword without compulsion; and that man
That took it of him, I pronounce a weak one,
And his kicks nullities.
He should have kick'd him after the delivering,
Which is the confirmation of a coward.

1 *Sw.* Brother, I take it you mistake the question;
For, say, that I were kick'd.

2 *Sw.* I must not say so;
Nor I must not hear it spoke by th' tongue of man.
You kick'd, dear brother! You are merry.

1 *Sw.* But put the case, I were kick'd.

2 *Sw.* Let them put it,
That are things weary of their lives, and know
Not honour! Put the case, you were kick'd!

1 *Sw.* I do not say I was kick'd.

2 *Sw.* Nor no silly creature that wears his head
Without a case, his soul in a skin-coat.
You kick'd, dear brother!

Bes. Nay, gentlemen, let us do what we shall do,
Truly and honestly. Good sirs, to the question.

1 *Sw.* Why, then, I say, suppose your boy kick'd, captain.

2 *Sw.* The boy, may be supposed, is liable.
But, kick my brother!

1 *Sw.* A foolish forward zeal, sir, in my friend.
But to the boy: Suppose, the boy were kick'd.

Bes. I do suppose it.

1 *Sw.* Has your boy a sword?

Bes. Surely, no; I pray, suppose a sword too.

1 *Sw.* I do suppose it. You grant, your boy was kick'd then.

2 *Sw.* By no means, captain; let it be supposed still;
The word " grant " makes not for us.

1 *Sw.* I say, this must be granted.

2 *Sw.* This *must* be granted, brother?

1 *Sw.* Ay, this *must* be granted.

2 *Sw.* Still, this *must* ?

1 *Sw.* I say, this *must* be granted.

2 *Sw.* Ay! give me the *must* again! Brother, you palter.

1 *Sw.* I will not hear you, wasp.

2 *Sw.* Brother,
    I say you palter; the *must* three times together!
    I wear as sharp steel as another man,
    And my fox bites as deep.   *Musted,* my dear brother!
    But to the cause again.

Bes. Nay, look you, gentlemen!

2 *Sw.* In a word, I ha' done.

1 *Sw.* A tall man, but intemperate; 'tis great pity.
    Once more, suppose the boy kick'd.

2 *Sw.* Forward.

1 *Sw.* And, being thoroughly kick'd, laughs at the kicker.

2 *Sw.* So much for us.   Proceed.

1 *Sw.* And in this beaten scorn, as I may call it,
    Delivers up his weapon; where lies the error?

Bes. It lies i' the beating, sir: I found it four days since.

2 *Sw.* The error, and a sore one, as I take it,
    Lies in the thing kicking.

Bes. I understand that well; 'tis sore indeed, sir.

1 *Sw.* That is according to the man that did it.

2 *Sw.* There springs a new branch: Whose was the foot?

Bes. A lord's.

1 *Sw.* The cause is mighty; but, had it been two lords,
    And both had kick'd you, if you laugh'd, 'tis clear.

Bes. I did laugh; but how will that help me, gentlemen?

2 *Sw.* Yes, it shall help you, if you laugh'd aloud.

Bes. As loud as a kick'd man could laugh, I laugh'd, sir.

1 *Sw.* My reason now: The valiant man is known
    By suffering and contemning; you have
    Enough of both, and you are valiant.

2 *Sw.* If he be sure he has been kick'd enough:
    For that brave sufferance you speak of, brother,
    Consists not in a beating and away,
    But in a cudgell'd body, from eighteen
    To eight and thirty; in a head rebuked
    With pots of all size, daggers, stools, and bedstaves:
    This shows a valiant man.

Bes. Then I am valiant, as valiant as the proudest;
    For these are all familiar things to me;
    Familiar as my sleep, or want of money;
    All my whole body's but one bruise, with beating.
    I think I have been cudgell'd with all nations,
    And almost all religions.

2 *Sw.* Embrace him, brother! this man is valiant;
    I know it by myself, he's valiant.
1 *Sw.* Captain, thou art a valiant gentleman,
    To bide upon, a very valiant man.
Bes. My equal friends o' th' sword, I must request
    Your hands to this.
2 *Sw.* 'Tis fit it should be.
Bes. Boy,
    Get me some wine, and pen and ink, within.—
    Am I clear, gentlemen?
1 *Sw.* Sir, when the world has taken notice what we have
      done,
    Make much of your body; for I'll pawn my steel,
    Men will be coyer of their legs hereafter.
Bes. I must request you go along, and testify
    To the lord Bacurius, whose foot has struck me,
    How you find my cause.
2 *Sw.* We will; and tell that lord he must be ruled;
    Or there be those abroad, will rule his lordship. [*Exeunt.*

SCENE IV.—*An Apartment in the Palace.*

Enter ARBACES *at one door, and* GOBRIAS *with* PANTHEA
at another.

Gob. Sir, here's the princess.
Arb. Leave us, then, alone;
    For the main cause of her imprisonment
    Must not be heard by any but herself.—   [*Exit Gobrias.*
    You're welcome, sister; and I would to Heaven
    I could so bid you by another name.—
    If you above love not such sins as these,
    Circle my heart with thoughts as cold as snow,
    To quench these rising flames that harbour here.
Pan. Sir, does it please you I shall speak?
Arb. Please me?
    Ay, more than all the art of music can,
    Thy speech doth please me; for it ever sounds
    As thou brought'st joyful unexpected news:
    And yet it is not fit thou shouldst be heard;
    I pray thee, think so.
Pan. Be it so; I will.
    Am I the first that ever had a wrong

So far from being fit to have redress,
That 'twas unfit to hear it? I will back
To prison, rather than disquiet you,
And wait till it be fit.

Arb. No, do not go;
For I will hear thee with a serious thought:
I have collected all that's man about me
Together strongly, and I am resolved
To hear thee largely: But I do beseech thee,
Do not come nearer to me; for there is
Something in that, that will undo us both.

Pan. Alas, sir, am I venom?

Arb. Yes, to me;
Though, of thyself, I think thee to be in
As equal a degree of heat or cold,
As Nature can make: Yet, as unsound men
Convert the sweetness and the nourishing'st meats
Into diseases, so shall I, distemper'd,
Do thee: I pray thee, draw no nearer to me.

Pan. Sir, this is that I would: I am of late
Shut from the world, and why it should be thus
Is all I wish to know.

Arb. Why, credit me,
Panthea, credit me, that am thy brother,
Thy loving brother, that there is a cause
Sufficient, yet unfit for thee to know,
That might undo thee everlastingly,
Only to hear. Wilt thou but credit this?
By heaven, 'tis true; believe it, if thou canst.

Pan. Children and fools are very credulous,
And I am both, I think, for I believe,
If you dissemble, be it on your head!
I'll back unto my prison. Yet, methinks,
I might be kept in some place where you are;
For in myself I find, I know not what
To call it, but it is a great desire
To see you often.

Arb. Fy, you come in a step; what do you mean?
Dear sister, do not so! Alas, Panthea,
Where I am would you be? why, that's the cause
You are imprison'd, that you may not be
Where I am.

Pan. Then I must endure it, sir.

Heaven keep you!

Arb. Nay, you shall hear the cause in short, Panthea;
    And, when thou hear'st it, thou wilt blush for me,
    And hang thy head down like a violet
    Full of the morning's dew. There is a way
    To gain thy freedom; but 'tis such a one
    As puts thee in worse bondage, and I know
    Thou wouldst encounter fire, and make a proof
    Whether the gods have care of innocence,
    Rather than follow it: Know, that I have lost,
    The only difference betwixt man and beast,
    My reason.

Pan. Heaven forbid!

Arb. Nay, it is gone;
    And I am left as far without a bound
    As the wild ocean that obeys the winds;
    Each sudden passion throws me where it lists,
    And overwhelms all that oppose my will.
    I have beheld thee with a lustful eye;
    My heart is set on wickedness, to act
    Such sins with thee, as I have been afraid
    To think of. If thou dar'st consent to this,
    Which, I beseech thee, do not, thou may'st gain
    Thy liberty, and yield me a content;
    If not, thy dwelling must be dark and close,
    Where I may never see thee: For Heaven knows,
    That laid this punishment upon my pride,
    Thy sight at some time will enforce my madness
    To make a start e'en to thy ravishing.
    Now spit upon me, and call all reproaches
    Thou can'st devise together, and at once
    Hurl 'em against me; for I am a sickness
    As killing as the plague, ready to seize thee.

Pan. Far be it from me to revile the king!
    But it is true, that I shall rather choose
    To search out death, that else would search out me,
    And in a grave sleep with my innocence,
    Than welcome such a sin. It is my fate;
    To these cross accidents I was ordain'd,
    And must have patience; and, but that my eyes
    Have more of woman in 'em than my heart,
    I would not weep. Peace enter you again!

Arb. Farewell; and, good Panthea, pray for me,

(Thy prayers are pure) that I may find a death,
However soon, before my passions grow,
That they forget what I desire is sin;
For thither they are tending: If that happen,
Then I shall force thee, though thou wert a virgin
By vow to Heaven, and shall pull a heap
Of strange, yet uninvented, sin upon me.

Pan. Sir, I will pray for you! yet you shall know
It is a sullen fate that governs us:
For I could wish, as heartily as you,
I were no sister to you; I should then
Embrace your lawful love, sooner than health.

Arb. Couldst thou affect me then?

Pan. So perfectly,
That, as it is, I ne'er shall sway my heart
To like another.

Arb. Then I curse my birth!
Must this be added to my miseries,
That thou art willing too? Is there no stop
To our full happiness, but these mere sounds,
Brother and sister?

Pan. There is nothing else:
But these, alas! will separate us more
Than twenty worlds betwixt us.

Arb. I have lived
To conquer men, and now am overthrown
Only by words, brother and sister. Where
Have those words dwelling? I will find 'em out,
And utterly destroy 'em; but they are
Not to be grasp'd: Let them be men or beasts,
And I will cut 'em from the earth; or towns,
And I will raze 'em, and then blow 'em up:
Let 'em be seas, and I will drink 'em off,
And yet have unquench'd fire left in my breast:
Let 'em be anything but merely voice.

Pan. But 'tis not in the power of any force,
Or policy, to conquer them.

Arb. Panthea,
What shall we do? Shall we stand firmly here,
And gaze our eyes out?

Pan. 'Would I could do so!
But I shall weep out mine.

Arb. Accursed man,

Thou bought'st thy reason at too dear a rate;
For thou hast all thy actions bounded in
With curious rules, when every beast is free:
What is there that acknowledges a kindred,
But wretched man? Who ever saw the bull
Fearfully leave the heifer that he liked,
Because they had one dam?

Pan. Sir, I disturb you
And myself too; 'twere better I were gone.

Arb. I will not be so foolish as I was;
Stay, we will love just as becomes our births,
No otherwise: Brothers and sisters may
Walk hand in hand together; so shall we.
Come nearer: Is there any hurt in this?

Pan. I hope not.

Arb. 'Faith, there is none at all:
And tell me truly now, is there not one
You love above me?

Pan. No, by Heaven.

Arb. Why, yet
You sent unto Tigranes, sister.

Pan. True,
But for another: For the truth——

Arb. No more.
I'll credit thee; I know thou canst not lie.
Thou art all truth.

Pan. But is there nothing else
That we may do, but only walk? Methinks,
Brothers and sisters lawfully may kiss.

Arb. And so they may, Panthea; so will we;
And kiss again too; we were too scrupulous
And foolish, but we will be so no more.

Pan. If you have any mercy, let me go
To prison, to my death, to anything;
I feel a sin growing upon my blood,
Worse than all these, hotter, I fear, than yours.

Arb. That is impossible: what should we do?

Pan. Fly, sir, for Heaven's sake.

Arb. So we must; away!
Sin grows upon us more by this delay.

                    [*Exeunt several ways.*

ACT V

SCENE I.—*Before the Palace.*

Enter MARDONIUS *and* LYGONES.

Mar. Sir, the king has seen your commission, and believes it;
and freely by this warrant gives you power to visit
prince Tigranes, your noble master.

Lyg. I thank his grace, and kiss his hand.

Mar. But is the main of all your business ended in this?

Lyg. I have another, but a worse; I am ashamed! It is a
business——

Mar. You serve a worthy person; and a stranger, I am sure
you are: You may employ me, if you please, without
your purse; such offices should ever be their own
rewards.

Lyg. I am bound to your nobleness.

Mar. I may have need of you, and then this courtesy,
If it be any, is not ill bestow'd.
But may I civilly desire the rest?
I shall not be a hurter, if no helper.

Lyg. Sir, you shall know: I have lost a foolish daughter,
And with her all my patience: pilfer'd away
By a mean captain of your king's.

Mar. Stay there, sir:
If he have reach'd the noble worth of captain,
He may well claim a worthy gentlewoman,
Though she were yours, and noble.

Lyg. I grant all that too: But this wretched fellow
Reaches no further than the empty name,
That serves to feed him.   Were he valiant,
Or had but in him any noble nature,
That might hereafter promise him a good man,
My cares were so much lighter, and my grave
A span yet from me.

Mar. I confess, such fellows
Be in all royal camps, and have and must be,
To make the sin of coward more detested
In the mean soldier, that with such a foil
Sets off much valour.   By description,
I should now guess him to you; it was Bessus,
I dare almost with confidence pronounce it.

Lyg. 'Tis such a scurvy name as Bessus;

And, now I think, 'tis he.

Mar. Captain do you call him?
Believe me, sir, you have a misery
Too mighty for your age: A pox upon him!
For that must be an end of all his service.
Your daughter was not mad, sir?

Lyg. No; 'would she had been!
The fault had had more credit. I would do something.

Mar. I would fain counsel you; but to what I know not.
He's so below a beating, that the women
Find him not worthy of their distaves, and
To hang him were to cast away a rope.
He's such an airy, thin, unbodied coward,
That no revenge can catch him.
I'll tell you, sir, and tell you truth; this rascal
Fears neither God nor man; has been so beaten,
Sufferance has made him wainscot; he has had,
Since he was first a slave,
At least three hundred daggers set in's head,
As little boys do new knives in hot meat.
There's not a rib in's body, o' my conscience,
That has not been thrice broken with dry beating!
And now his sides look like two wicker targets,
Every way bended;
Children will shortly take him for a wall,
And set their stone-bows in his forehead.
He is of so base a sense,
I cannot in a week imagine what
Shall be done to him.

Lyg. Sure, I have committed some great sin,
That this base fellow should be made my rod.
I would see him; but I shall have no patience.

Mar. 'Tis no great matter, if you have not: If a laming of
him, or such a toy, may do you pleasure, sir, he has it
for you; and I'll help you to him. 'Tis no news to him
to have a leg broken, or a shoulder out, with being turn'd
o' th' stones like a tansy. Draw not your sword, if you
love it; for, on my conscience, his head will break it;
We use him i' th' wars like a ram, to shake a wall withal.
Here comes the very person of him; do as you shall find
your temper; I must leave you: But if you do not break
him like a biscuit, you're much to blame, sir.

[*Exit Mardonius.*

Enter BESSUS *and the* Swordmen.

Lyg. Is your name Bessus?

Bes. Men call me Captain Bessus.

Lyg. Then, Captain Bessus, you are a rank rascal, without
more exordiums; a dirty frozen slave! and, with the
favour of your friends here, I will beat you.

2 *Sw.* Pray use your pleasure, sir; you seem to be a
gentleman.

Lyg. [*Beats him.*] Thus, Captain Bessus, thus!
Thus twinge your nose, thus kick, thus tread upon you.

Bes. I do beseech you, yield your cause, sir, quickly.

Lyg. Indeed, I should have told you that first.

Bes. I take it so.

1 *Sw.* Captain, he should, indeed; he is mistaken.

Lyg. Sir, you shall have it quickly, and more beating:
You have stolen away a lady, Captain Coward,
And such a one——   [*Beats him.*

Bes. Hold, I beseech you, hold, sir;
I never yet stole any living thing
That had a tooth about it.

Lyg. I know you dare lie.

Bes. With none but summer-whores, upon my life, sir:
My means and manners never could attempt
Above a hedge or haycock.

Lyg. Sirrah, that quits not me: Where is this lady?
Do that you do not use to do, tell truth,
Or, by my hand, I'll beat your captain's brains out,
Wash 'em, and put 'em in again, that will I.

Bes. There was a lady, sir, I must confess,
Once in my charge: The prince Tigranes gave her
To my guard, for her safety. How I used her
She may herself report; she's with the prince now.
I did but wait upon her like a groom,
Which she will testify, I am sure: If not,
My brains are at your service, when you please, sir,
And glad I have 'em for you.

Lyg. This is most likely. Sir, I ask your pardon and am
sorry I was so intemperate.

Bes. Well, I can ask no more. You would think it strange
now, to have me beat you at first sight.

Lyg. Indeed, I would; but, I know, your goodness can forget
twenty beatings: You must forgive me.

Bes. Yes; there's my hand. Go where you will, I shall
think you a valiant fellow for all this.

Lyg. My daughter is a whore. [*Aside.*
I feel it now too sensible; yet I will see her;
Discharge myself from being father to her,
And then back to my country, and there die.—
Farewell, captain.

Bes. Farewell, sir, farewell! Commend me to the gentlewoman, I pray. [*Exit Lygones.*

1 *Sw.* How now, captain? bear up, man.

Bes. Gentlemen o' th' sword, your hands once more; I have
been kick'd again; but the foolish fellow is penitent,
has ask'd me mercy, and my honour's safe.

2 *Sw.* We knew that, or the foolish fellow had better have
kick'd his grandsire.

Bes. Confirm, confirm, I pray.

1 *Sw.* There be our hands again! Now let him come, and
say he was not sorry, and he sleeps for it.

Bes. Alas! good ignorant old man, let him go, let him go;
these courses will undo him. [*Exeunt.*

SCENE II.—*The Prison.*

Enter Lygones *and* Bacurius.

Bac. My lord, your authority is good, and I am glad it is so;
for my consent would never hinder you from seeing
your own king: I am a minister, but not a governor of
this state. Yonder is your king; I'll leave you. [*Exit.*

Enter Tigranes *and* Spaconia.

Lyg. There he is,
Indeed, and with him my disloyal child.

Tigr. I do perceive my fault so much, that yet,
Methinks, thou shouldst not have forgiven me.

Lyg. Health to your majesty!

Tigr. What, good Lygones! welcome!
What business brought thee hither?

Lyg. Several businesses: [*Gives a paper.*
My public business will appear by this;
I have a message to deliver, which,
If it pleases you so to authorise, is
An embassage from the Armenian state

Unto Arbaces for your liberty.
The offer's there set down; please you to read it.

Tigr. There is no alteration happen'd since
　　I came thence?

Lyg. None, sir; all is as it was.

Tigr. And all our friends are well?　　　　　　　*[Reads.*

Lyg. All very well.

Spa. Though I have done nothing but what was good,
　　I dare not see my father: It was fault
　　Enough not to acquaint him with that good.

Lyg. Madam, I should have seen you.

Spa. Oh, good sir, forgive me.

Lyg. Forgive you! why, I am no kin to you, am I?

Spa. Should it be measured by my mean deserts,
　　Indeed you are not.

Lyg. Thou couldst prate unhappily
　　Ere thou couldst go; 'would thou couldst do as well,
　　And how does your custom hold out here?

Spa. Sir?

Lyg. Are you in private still, or how?

Spa. What do you mean?

Lyg. Do you take money? Are you come to sell sin yet?
　　Perhaps, I can help you to liberal clients: Or has not
　　the king cast you off yet? Oh, thou vile creature,
　　whose best commendation is, that thou art a young
　　whore! I would thy mother had lived to see this; or,
　　rather, that I had died ere I had seen it! Why didst
　　not make me acquainted
　　When thou wert first resolved to be a whore?
　　I would have seen thy hot lust satisfied
　　More privately; I would have kept a dancer,
　　And a whole consort of musicians,
　　In my own house, only to fiddle thee.

Spa. Sir, I was never whore.

Lyg. If thou couldst not say so much for thyself thou shouldst
　　be carted.

Tigr. Lygones, I have read it, and I like it;
　　You shall deliver it.

Lyg. Well, sir, I will:
　　But I have private business with you.

Tigr. Speak; what is't?

Lyg. How has my age deserved so ill of you,
　　That you can pick no strumpets i' the land,

But out of my breed?

Tigr. Strumpets, good Lygones?

Lyg. Yes; and I wish to have you know, I scorn
To get a whore for any prince alive:
And yet scorn will not help! Methinks, my daughter
Might have been spared; there were enow besides.

Tigr. May I not prosper but she's innocent
As morning light, for me; and, I dare swear,
For all the world.

Lyg. Why is she with you, then?
Can she wait on you better than your man?
Has she a gift in plucking off your stockings?
Can she make caudles well, or cut your corns?
Why do you keep her with you? For a queen,
I know, you do contemn her; so should I;
And every subject else think much at it.

Tigr. Let 'em think much; but 'tis more firm than earth,
Thou seest thy queen there.

Lyg. Then have I made a fair hand: I call'd her whore. If
I shall speak now as her father, I cannot choose but
greatly rejoice that she shall be a queen: But if I
should speak to you as a statesman, she were more fit
to be your whore.

Tigr. Get you about your business to Arbaces;
Now you talk idly.

Lyg. Yes, sir, I will go.
And shall she be a queen? She had more wit
Than her old father, when she ran away.
Shall she be queen? Now, by my troth, 'tis fine!
I'll dance out of all measure at her wedding:
Shall I not, sir?

Tigr. Yes, marry, shalt thou.

Lyg. I'll make these wither'd kexes bear my body
Two hours together above ground.

Tigr. Nay, go;
My business requires haste.

Lyg. Good Heav'n preserve you!
You are an excellent king.

Spa. Farewell, good father.

Lyg. Farewell, sweet virtuous daughter.
I never was so joyful in my life,
That I remember! Shall she be a queen?
Now I perceive a man may weep for joy;

I had thought they had lied that said so.

[*Exit Lygones.*

Tigr. Come, my dear love.

Spa. But you may see another,
    May alter that again.

Tigr. Urge it no more:
    I have made up a new strong constancy,
    Not to be shook with eyes. I know I have
    The passions of a man; but if I meet
    With any subject that should hold my eyes
    More firmly than is fit, I'll think of thee,
    And run away from it: Let that suffice. [*Exeunt.*

SCENE III.—*The house of Bacurius.*

Enter Bacurius *and a* Servant.

Bac. Three gentlemen without, to speak with me?

Serv. Yes, sir.

Bac. Let them come in.

Enter Bessus, *with the two* Swordmen.

Serv. They are enter'd, sir, already.

Bac. Now, fellows, your business? Are these the gentlemen?

Bes. My lord, I have made bold to bring these gentlemen,
    My friends o' th' sword, along with me.

Bac. I am
    Afraid you'll fight, then.

Bes. My good lord, I will not;
    Your lordship is mistaken; fear not, lord.

Bac. Sir, I am sorry for't.

Bes. I ask no more in honour.—Gentlemen,
    You hear my lord is sorry.

Bac. Not that I have beaten you,
    But beaten one that will be beaten;
    One whose dull body will require a lamming,
    As surfeits do the diet, spring and fall.
    Now, to your swordmen:
    What come they for, good captain Stockfish?

Bes. It seems your lordship has forgot my name.

Bac. No, nor your nature neither; though they are
    Things fitter, I must confess, for anything
    Than my remembrance, or any honest man's:

What shall these billets do? be piled up in my wood-
    yard?

Bes. Your lordship holds your mirth still, heaven continue it!
    But, for these gentlemen, they come——

Bac. To swear you are a coward? Spare your book;
    I do believe it.

Bes. Your lordship still draws wide;
    They come to vouch, under their valiant hands,
    I am no coward.

Bac. That would be a show, indeed, worth seeing. Sirs,
    Be wise and take money for this motion, travel with't;
    And where the name of Bessus has been known,
    Or a good coward stirring, 'twill yield more than
    A tilting. This will prove more beneficial to you,
    If you be thrifty, than your captainship,
    And more natural. Men of most valiant hands,
    Is this true?

2 Sw. It is so, most renowned.

Bac. 'Tis somewhat strange.

1 Sw. Lord, it is strange, yet true.
    We have examined, from your lordship's foot there
    To this man's head, the nature of the beatings;
    And we do find his honour is come off
    Clean and sufficient: This, as our swords shall help us.

Bac. You are much bound to your *bilbo*-men;
    I am glad you're straight again, captain. 'Twere good
    You would think some way how to gratify them;
    They have undergone a labour for you, Bessus,
    Would have puzzled Hercules with all his valour.

2 Sw. Your lordship must understand we are no men
    Of the law, that take pay for our opinions;
    It is sufficient we have cleared our friend.

Bac. Yet there is something due, which I, as touch'd
    In conscience, will discharge.—Captain, I'll pay
    This rent for you.

Bes. Spare yourself, my good lord;
    My brave friends aim at nothing but the virtue.

Bac. That's but a cold discharge, sir, for the pains.

2 Sw. Oh, lord! my good lord!

Bac. Be not so modest; I will give you something.

Bes. They shall dine with your lordship; that's sufficient.

Bac. Something in hand the while. You rogues, you apple-
    squires,

Do you come hither, with your bottled valour,
Your windy froth, to limit out my beatings?
　　　　　　　　　　　　　　　　　　　[Kicks them.

1 *Sw.* I do beseech your lordship.

2 *Sw.* Oh, good lord!

Bac. 'Sfoot, what a bevy of beaten slaves are here!—
Get me a cudgel, sirrah, and a tough one.
　　　　　　　　　　　　　　　　　[Exit Servant.

2 *Sw.* More of your foot, I do beseech your lordship.

Bac. You shall, you shall, dog, and your fellow beagle.

1 *Sw.* O' this side, good my lord.

Bac. Off with your swords;
For if you hurt my foot, I'll have you flead,
You rascals.

1 *Sw.* Mine's off, my lord.　　*[They take off their swords.*

2 *Sw.* I beseech your lordship, stay a little; my strap's
Tied to my cod-piece point: Now, when you please.

Bac. Captain, these are your valiant friends;
You long for a little too?

Bes. I am very well, I humbly thank your lordship.

Bac. What's that in your pocket hurts my toe, you mungrel?
Thy buttocks cannot be so hard; out with't quickly.

2 *Sw.* *[Takes out a pistol.]* Here 'tis, sir; a small piece of
artillery,
That a gentleman, a dear friend of your lordship's,
Sent me with, to get it mended, sir; for, if you mark,
The nose is somewhat loose.

Bac. A friend of mine, you rascal?
I was never wearier of doing nothing,
Than kicking these two foot-balls.

Enter Servant.

Serv. Here's a good cudgel, sir.

Bac. It comes too late; I am weary; pr'ythee,
Do thou beat them.

2 *Sw.* My lord, this is foul play,
I'faith, to put a fresh man upon us:
Men are but men, sir.

Bac. That jest shall save your bones.—Captain, rally up
your rotten regiment, and begone.—I had rather thresh
than be bound to kick these rascals, till they cried,
"ho!" Bessus, you may put your hand to them now,

and then you are quit.—Farewell! as you like this, pray
visit me again; 'twill keep me in good health.   [*Exit.*
2 *Sw.* He has a devilish hard foot; I never felt the like.
1 *Sw.* Nor I; and yet, I am sure, I have felt a hundred.
2 *Sw.* If he kick thus i' the dog-days, he will be dry-foundred.
What cure now, captain, besides oil of bays?
Bes. Why, well enough, I warrant you; you can go?
2 *Sw.* Yes, Heaven be thank'd! but I feel a shrewd ache;
Sure, he's sprang my huckle-bone.
1 *Sw.* I ha' lost a haunch.
Bes. A little butter, friend, a little butter;
Butter and parsley is a sovereign matter:
Probatum est.
2 *Sw.* Captain, we must request
Your hand now to our honours.
Bes. Yes, marry, shall ye;
And then let all the world come, we are valiant
To ourselves, and there's an end.
1 *Sw.* Nay, then, we must be valiant.   Oh, my ribs!
2 *Sw.* Oh, my small guts!
A plague upon these sharp - toed shoes; they are
murderers.   [*Exeunt.*

SCENE IV.—*A Room in the Palace.*

Enter Arbaces *with his sword drawn.*

Arb. It is resolved: I bore it whilst I could;
I can no more.   Hell, open all thy gates,
And I will thorough them: If they be shut,
I'll batter 'em, but I will find the place
Where the most damn'd have dwelling! Ere I end,
Amongst them all they shall not have a sin,
But I may call it mine; I must begin
With murder of my friend, and so go on
To that incestuous ravishing, and end
My life and sins with a forbidden blow
Upon myself!

Enter Mardonius.

Mar. What tragedy is near?
That hand was never wont to draw a sword,
But it cried " dead " to something.

Arb. Mardonius,
    Have you bid Gobrias come?
Mar. How do you, sir?
Arb. Well.   Is he coming?
Mar. Why, sir, are you thus?
    Why do your hands proclaim a lawless war
    Against yourself?
Arb. Thou answer'st me one question with another:
    Is Gobrias coming?
Mar. Sir, he is.
Arb. 'Tis well:
    I can forbear your questions then.   Begone
Mar. Sir, I have mark'd——
Arb. Mark less! it troubles you and me.
Mar. You are more variable than you were.
Arb. It may be so.
Mar. To-day no hermit could be humbler
    Than you were to us all.
Arb. And what of this?
Mar. And now you take new rage into your eyes,
    As you would look us all out of the land.
Arb. I do confess it; will that satisfy?
    I pr'ythee, get thee gone.
Mar. Sir, I will speak.
Arb. Will ye?
Mar. It is my duty.
    I fear you'll kill yourself: I am a subject,
    And you shall do me wrong in't; 'tis my cause,
    And I may speak.
Arb. Thou art not train'd in sin,
    It seems, Mardonius: kill myself! by Heaven,
    I will not do it yet; and, when I will,
    I'll tell thee, then I shall be such a creature
    That thou wilt give me leave without a word.
    There is a method in man's wickedness;
    It grows up by degrees: I am not come
    So high as killing of myself; there are
    A hundred thousand sins 'twixt me and it,
    Which I must do; and I shall come to't at last,
    But, take my oath, not now.   Be satisfied,
    And get thee hence.
Mar. I am sorry 'tis so ill.
Arb. Be sorry, then:

    True sorrow is alone; grieve by thyself.

Mar. I pray you let me see your sword put up
    Before I go: I'll leave you then.

Arb. [*Puts up.*] Why, so.
    What folly is this in thee? is it not
    As apt to mischief as it was before?
    Can I not reach it, think'st thou?   These are toys
    For children to be pleased with, and not men.
    Now I am safe, you think: I would the book
    Of Fate were here: my sword is not so sure
    But I would get it out, and mangle that,
    That all the destinies should quite forget
    Their fix'd decrees, and haste to make us new,
    For other fortunes; mine could not be worse.
    Wilt thou now leave me?

Mar. Heaven put into your bosom temperate thoughts!
    I'll leave you, though I fear.   [*Exit Mardonius.*

Arb. Go; thou art honest.
    Why should the hasty errors of my youth
    Be so unpardonable to draw a sin,
    Helpless, upon me?

Enter GOBRIAS.

Gob. There is the king;
    Now it is ripe.

Arb. Draw near, thou guilty man,
    That art the author of the loathed'st crime
    Five ages have brought forth, and hear me speak.
    Curses incurable, and all the evils
    Man's body or his spirit can receive,
    Be with thee!

Gob. Why, sir, do you curse me thus?

Arb. Why do I curse thee? If there be a man
    Subtle in curses, that exceeds the rest,
    His worst wish on thee! Thou hast broke my heart.

Gob. How, sir! Have I preserved you, from a child,
    From all the arrows malice or ambition
    Could shoot at you, and have I this for pay?

Arb. 'Tis true, thou didst preserve me, and in that
    Wert crueller than hardened murderers
    Of infants and their mothers! Thou didst save me,
    Only till thou hadst studied out a way

How to destroy me cunningly thyself:
This was a curious way of torturing.

Gob. What do you mean?

Arb. Thou know'st the evils thou hast done to me!
Dost thou remember all those witching letters
Thou sent'st unto me to Armenia,
Fill'd with the praise of my beloved sister,
Where thou extol'dst her beauty? What had I
To do with that? what could her beauty be
To me? And thou didst write how well she loved me!
Dost thou remember this? so that I doted
Something before I saw her.

Gob. This is true.

Arb. Is it? and, when I was return'd, thou know'st,
Thou didst pursue it, till thou wound'st me in
To such a strange and unbelieved affection,
As good men cannot think on.

Gob. This I grant;
I think, I was the cause.

Arb. Wert thou? Nay, more.
I think, thou meant'st it.

Gob. Sir, I hate a lie:
As I love Heaven and honesty, I did;
It was my meaning.

Arb. Be thine own sad judge;
A further condemnation will not need:
Prepare thyself to die.

Gob. Why, sir, to die?

Arb. Why shouldst thou live? was ever yet offender
So impudent, that had a thought of mercy,
After confession of a crime like this?
Get out I cannot where thou hurl'st me in;
But I can take revenge; that's all the sweetness
Left for me.

Gob. Now is the time.—Hear me but speak.

Arb. No! Yet I will be far more merciful
Than thou wert to me; thou didst steal into me,
And never gavest me warning: So much time
As I give thee now, had prevented me
For ever.   Notwithstanding all thy sins,
If thou hast hope that there is yet a prayer
To save thee, turn and speak it to thyself.

Gob. Sir, you shall know your sins, before you do 'em:

If you kill me——
Arb. I will not stay then.
Gob. Know—
You kill your father.
Arb. How?
Gob. You kill your father.
Arb. My father? Though I know it for a lie,
Made out of fear, to save thy stained life,
The very reverence of the word comes 'cross me,
And ties mine arm down.
Gob. I will tell you that
Shall heighten you again; I am thy father;
I charge thee hear me.
Arb. If it should be so,
As 'tis most false, and that I should be found
A bastard issue, the despised fruit
Of lawless lust, I should no more admire
All my wild passions! But another truth
Shall be wrung from thee: If I could come by
The spirit of pain, it should be pour'd on thee,
'Till thou allow'st thyself more full of lies
Than he that teaches thee.

Enter ARANE.

Ara. Turn thee about;
I come to speak to thee, thou wicked man!
Hear me, thou tyrant!
Arb. I will turn to thee;
Hear me, thou strumpet! I have blotted out
The name of mother, as thou hast thy shame.
Ara. My shame! Thou hast less shame than anything!
Why dost thou keep my daughter in a prison?
Why dost thou call her sister, and do this?
Arb. Cease, thou strange impudence, and answer quickly!
                                        [*Draws.*
If thou contemn'st me, this will ask an answer,
And have it.
Ara. Help me, gentle Gobrias.
Arb. Guilt dare not help guilt! though they grow together
In doing ill, yet at the punishment
They sever, and each flies the noise of other.
Think not of help; answer!
Ara. I will; to what?

Arb. To such a thing, as, if it be a truth,
    Think what a creature thou hast made thyself,
    That didst not shame to do what I must blush
    Only to ask thee. Tell me who I am,
    Whose son I am, without all circumstance;
    Be thou as hasty as my sword will be,
    If thou refusest.
Ara. Why, you are his son.
Arb. His son? Swear, swear, thou worse than woman
    damn'd!
Ara. By all that s good, you are.
Arb. Then art thou all
    That ever was known bad! Now is the cause
    Of all my strange misfortunes come to light.
    What reverence expect'st thou from a child,
    To bring forth which thou hast offended Heaven,
    Thy husband, and the land? Adulterous witch!
    I know now why thou wouldst have poison'd me:
    I was thy lust, which thou wouldst have forgot!
    Then, wicked mother of my sins, and me,
    Show me the way to the inheritance
    I have by thee, which is a spacious world
    Of impious acts, that I may soon possess it.
    Plagues rot thee, as thou liv'st, and such diseases
    As use to pay lust, recompense thy deed!
Gob. You do not know why you curse thus.
Arb. Too well.
    You are a pair of vipers; and behold
    The serpent you have got! There is no beast,
    But, if he knew it, has a pedigree
    As brave as mine, for they have more descents;
    And I am every way as beastly got,
    As far without the compass of a law,
    As they.
Ara. You spend your rage and words in vain,
    And rail upon a guess; hear us a little.
Arb. No, I will never hear, but talk away
    My breath, and die.
Gob. Why, but you are no bastard.
Arb. How's that?
Ara. Nor child of mine.
Arb. Still you go on
    In wonders to me.

Gob. Pray you, be more patient:
    I may bring comfort to you.
Arb.   I will kneel,   *[Kneels.*
    And hear with the obedience of a child.
    Good father, speak! I do acknowledge you,
    So you bring comfort.
Gob. First know, our last king, your supposed father,
    Was old and feeble when he married her,
    And almost all the land, as she, past hope
    Of issue from him.
Arb.   Therefore she took leave
    To play the whore, because the king was old;
    Is this the comfort?
Ara.   What will you find out
    To give me satisfaction, when you find
    How you have injured me? Let fire consume me
    If ever I were whore!
Gob.   Forbear these starts,
    Or I will leave you wedded to despair,
    As you are now: If you can find a temper,
    My breath shall be a pleasant western wind,
    That cools and blasts not.
Arb.   Bring it out, good father.   *[Lies down.*
    I'll lie, and listen here as reverently
    As to an angel: If I breathe too loud,
    Tell me; for I would be as still as night.
Gob. Our king, I say, was old, and this our queen
    Desired to bring an heir, but her yet husband,
    She thought, was past it; and to be dishonest,
    I think, she would not: If she would have been,
    The truth is, she was watch'd so narrowly,
    And had so slender opportunities,
    She hardly could have been: But yet her cunning
    Found out this way; she feign'd herself with child,
    And posts were sent in haste throughout the land,
    And God was humbly thank'd in every church,
    That so had bless'd the queen; and prayers were made
    For her safe going and delivery.
    She feign'd now to grow bigger; and perceived
    This hope of issue made her fear'd, and brought
    A far more large respect from every man,
    And saw her power increase, and was resolved,
    Since she believed she could not have't indeed,

At least she would be thought to have a child.

Arb. Do I not hear it well? Nay, I will make
No noise at all; but, pray you, to the point,
Quick as you can!

Gob. Now when the time was full
She should be brought to bed, I had a son
Born, which was you: This, the queen hearing of,
Moved me to let her have you; and such reasons
She showed me, as she knew well would tie
My secrecy: She swore you should be king;
And, to be short, I did deliver you
Unto her, and pretended you were dead,
And in mine own house kept a funeral,
And had an empty coffin put in earth.
That night this queen feign'd hastily to labour,
And by a pair of women of her own,
Which she had charm'd, she made the world believe
She was deliver'd of you. You grew up,
As the king's son, till you were six years old;
Then did the king die, and did leave to me
Protection of the realm; and, contrary
To his own expectation, left this queen
Truly with child, indeed, of the fair princess
Panthea. Then she could have torn her hair,
And did alone to me, yet durst not speak
In public, for she knew she should be found
A traitor; and her tale would have been thought
Madness, or anything rather than truth.
This was the only cause why she did seek
To poison you, and I to keep you safe;
And this the reason why I sought to kindle
Some sparks of love in you to fair Panthea,
That she might get part of her right again.

Arb. And have you made an end now? Is this all?
If not, I will be still till I be aged,
Till all my hairs be silver.

Gob. This is all.

Arb. And is it true, say you too, madam?

Ara. Yes.
Heaven knows, it is most true.

Arb. Panthea, then, is not my sister?

Gob. No.

Arb. But can you prove this?

Gob. If you will give consent,
    Else who dares go about it?
Arb. Give consent?
    Why, I will have 'em all that know it rack'd
    To get this from 'em.—All that wait without,
    Come in, whate'er you be, come in, and be
    Partakers of my joy!—Oh, you are welcome!

    Enter BESSUS, Gentlemen, MARDONIUS, *and other*
        Attendants.

    Mardonius, the best news!   Nay, draw no nearer;
    They all shall hear it: I am found No King.
Mar. Is that so good news?
Arb. Yes, the happiest news
    That e'er was heard.
Mar. Indeed, 'twere well for you
    If you might be a little less obey'd.
Arb. One call the queen.
Mar. Why she is there.
Arb. The queen,
    Mardonius? Panthea is the queen,
    And I am plain Arbaces.—Go some one.
    She is in Gobrias' house.—   [*Exit a Gentleman.*
                  Since I saw you,
    There are a thousand things deliver'd to me,
    You little dream of.
Mar. So it should seem.—My lord,
    What fury's this?
Gob. Believe me, 'tis no fury;
    All that he says is truth.
Mar. 'Tis very strange.
Arb. Why do you keep your hats off, gentlemen?
    Is it to me?   I swear, it must not be;
    Nay, trust me, in good faith, it must not be!
    I cannot now command you; but I pray you,
    For the respect you bare me when you took
    Me for your king, each man clap on his hat
    At my desire.
Mar. We will.   You are not found
    So mean a man, but that you may be cover'd
    As well as we; may you not?
Arb. Oh, not here!
    You may, but not I, for here is my father

In presence.

Mar. Where?

Arb. Why, there.   Oh, the whole story
Would be a wilderness, to lose thyself
For ever.—Oh, pardon me, dear father,
For all the idle and unreverend words
That I have spoke in idle moods to you!—
I am Arbaces; we all fellow subjects;
Nor is the queen Panthea now my sister.

Bes. Why, if you remember, fellow-subject Arbaces, I told
you once she was not your sister: Ay, and she look'd
nothing like you.

Arb. I think you did, good captain Bessus.

Bes. Here will arise another question now amongst the swordmen, whether I be to call him to account for beating me,
now he is proved No King.

Enter LYGONES.

Mar. Sir, here's Lygones, the agent for the Armenian state.

Arb. Where is he?—I know your business, good Lygones.

Lyg. We must have our king again, and will.

Arb. I knew that was your business: You shall have
Your king again; and have him so again,
As never king was had.—Go, one of you,
And bid Bacurius bring Tigranes hither;
And bring the lady with him, that Panthea,
The queen Panthea, sent me word this morning
Was brave Tigranes' mistress.   [*Exeunt two Gentlemen.*

Lyg. 'Tis Spaconia.

Arb. Ay, ay, Spaconia.

Lyg. She is my daughter.

Arb. She is so.   I could now tell anything
I never heard.   Your king shall go so home,
As never man went.

Mar. Shall he go on's head?

Arb. He shall have chariots easier than air,
That I will have invented; and ne'er think
He shall pay any ransom!   And thyself,
That art the messenger, shall ride before him
On a horse cut out of an entire diamond,
That shall be made to go with golden wheels,
I know not how yet.

Lyg. Why, I shall be made
    For ever! They belied this king with us,
    And said he was unkind.
Arb. And then thy daughter;
    She shall have some strange thing; we'll have the
        kingdom
    Sold utterly and put into a toy,
    Which she shall wear about her carelessly,
    Somewhere or other.—See, the virtuous queen!—

Enter PANTHEA *and* 1 Gentleman.

    Behold the humblest subject that you have,
    Kneel here before you.   [*Kneels.*
Pan. Why kneel you to me,
    That am your vassal?
Arb. Grant me one request.
Pan. Alas! what can I grant you? what I can I will.
Arb. That you will please to marry me,
    If I can prove it lawful.
Pan. Is that all?
    More willingly than I would draw this air.
Arb. I'll kiss this hand in earnest.
2 Gent. Sir, Tigranes
    Is coming; though he made it strange, at first,
    To see the princess any more.

Enter TIGRANES *and* SPACONIA.

Arb. The queen,
    Thou mean'st.—Oh, my Tigranes, pardon me!
    Tread on my neck: I freely offer it;
    And, if thou be'st so given, take revenge,
    For I have injured thee.
Tigr. No; I forgive,
    And rejoice more that you have found repentance,
    Than I my liberty.
Arb. May'st thou be happy
    In thy fair choice, for thou art temperate!
    You owe no ransom to the state! Know, that
    I have a thousand joys to tell you of,
    Which yet I dare not utter, till I pay
    My thanks to Heaven for 'em. Will you go

    With me, and help me? pray you, do.

Tigr. I will.

Arb. Take then your fair one with you:—And you, queen
    Of goodness and of us, oh, give me leave
    To take your arm in mine!—Come, every one
    That takes delight in goodness, help to sing
    Loud thanks for me, that I am proved No King.

                               [Exeunt.

THE FAITHFUL SHEPHERDESS

TO THAT NOBLE AND TRUE LOVER OF LEARNING
SIR WALTER ASTON
KNIGHT OF THE BATH

SIR, I must ask your patience and be true;
This play was never liked, unless by few
That brought their judgments with 'em; for, of late,
First the infection, then the common prate
Of common people, have such customs got,
Either to silence plays or like them not:
Under the last of which this interlude
Had fallen for ever, pressed down by the rude,
That like a torrent, which the moist south feeds,
Drowns both before him the ripe corn and weeds,
Had not the saving sense of better men
Redeemed it from corruption.   Dear sir, then,
Among the better souls, be you the best,
In whom, as in a centre, I take rest
And proper being; from whose equal eye
And judgment nothing grows but purity.
Nor do I flatter, for, by all those dead,
Great in the Muses, by Apollo's head,
He that adds anything to you, 'tis done
Like his that lights a candle to the sun:
Then be, as you were ever, yourself still,
Moved by your judgment, not by love or will;
And when I sing again (as who can tell
My next devotion to that holy well?)
Your goodness to the Muses shall be all
Able to make a work heroical.

Given to your service,

JOHN FLETCHER.

TO THE INHERITOR OF ALL WORTHINESS
SIR WILLIAM SKIPWITH

ODE

IF, from servile hope or love,
　　　I may prove
But so happy to be thought for
Such a one, whose greatest ease
　　　Is to please,
Worthy sir, I've all I sought for:

For no itch of greater name,
　　　Which some claim
By their verses, do I show it
To the world; nor to protest
　　　'Tis the best;—
These are lean faults in a poet;—

Nor to make it serve to feed
　　　At my need,
Nor to gain acquaintance by it,
Nor to ravish kind attornies
　　　In their journies
Nor to read it after diet.

Far from me are all these aims,
　　　Fittest frames
To build weakness on and pity.
Only to yourself, and such
　　　Whose true touch
Makes all good, let me seem witty.

The admirer of your virtues,

JOHN FLETCHER.

TO THE PERFECT GENTLEMAN
SIR ROBERT TOWNSHEND

IF the greatest faults may crave
Pardon where contrition is,
Noble sir, I needs must have
A long one for a long amiss.
If you ask me, how is this?
   Upon my faith, I'll tell you frankly,
   You love above my means to thank ye.

Yet, according to my talent,
As sour fortune loves to use me,
A poor shepherd I have sent
In home-spun gray for to excuse me;
And may all my hopes refuse me,
   But when better comes ashore,
   You shall have better, newer, more!

Till when, like our desperate debtors,
Or our three-piled sweet protestors,
I must please you in bare letters,
And so pay my debts, like jesters;
Yet I oft have seen good feasters,
   Only for to please the pallet,
   Leave great meat and choose a sallet.

All yours,

JOHN FLETCHER.

TO THE READER

IF you be not reasonably assured of your knowledge in this kind of poem, lay down the book, or read this, which I would wish had been the prologue. It is a pastoral tragi-comedy, which the people seeing when it was played, having ever had a singular gift in defining, concluded to be a play of country hired shepherds in gray cloaks, with curtailed dogs in strings, sometimes laughing together, and sometimes killing one another; and, missing Whitsun-ales, cream, wassail, and morris-dances, began to be angry. In their error I would not have you fall, lest you incur their censure. Understand, therefore, a pastoral to be a representation of shepherds and shepherdesses with their actions and passions, which must be such as may agree with their natures, at least not exceeding former fictions and vulgar traditions; they are not to be adorned with any art, but such improper ones as nature is said to bestow, as singing and poetry; or such as experience may teach them, as the virtues of herbs and fountains, the ordinary course of the sun, moon, and stars, and such like. But you are ever to remember shepherds to be such as all the ancient poets, and modern, of understanding, have received them; that is, the owners of flocks, and not hirelings. A tragi-comedy is not so called in respect of mirth and killing, but in respect it wants deaths, which is enough to make it no tragedy, yet brings some near it, which is enough to make it no comedy, which must be a representation of familiar people, with such kind of trouble as no life be questioned; so that a god is as lawful in this as in a tragedy, and mean people as in a comedy. Thus much I hope will serve to justify my poem, and make you understand it; to teach you more for nothing, I do not know that I am in conscience bound.

JOHN FLETCHER.

THE FAITHFUL SHEPHERDESS

DRAMATIS PERSONÆ

Perigot.	Satyr.
Thenot.	Shepherds.
Daphnis.	
Alexis.	Clorin.
Sullen Shepherd.	Amoret.
Old Shepherd.	Amarillis.
Priest of Pan.	Cloe.
God of the River.	Shepherdesses.

SCENE.—Thessaly.

ACT I

SCENE I.—*The Wood before Clorin's Bower.*

Enter Clorin.

Clorin. Hail, holy earth, whose cold arms do embrace
    The truest man that ever fed his flocks
    By the fat plains of fruitful Thessaly!
    Thus I salute thy grave; thus do I pay
    My early vows and tribute of mine eyes
    To thy still-lovèd ashes; thus I free
    Myself from all ensuing heats and fires
    Of love; all sports, delights, and jolly games,
    That shepherds hold full dear, thus put I off:
    Now no more shall these smooth brows be begirt
    With youthful coronals, and lead the dance;
    No more the company of fresh fair maids
    And wanton shepherds be to me delightful,
    Nor the shrill pleasing sound of merry pipes
    Under some shady dell, when the cool wind
    Plays on the leaves: all be far away,
    Since thou art far away, by whose dear side
    How often have I sat crowned with fresh flowers
    For summer's queen, whilst every shepherd's boy
    Puts on his lusty green, with gaudy hook,
    And hanging scrip of finest cordevan.

But thou art gone, and these are gone with thee,
And all are dead but thy dear memory;
That shall outlive thee, and shall ever spring,
Whilst there are pipes or jolly shepherds sing.
And here will I, in honour of thy love,
Dwell by thy grave, forgetting all those joys
That former times made precious to mine eyes;
Only remembering what my youth did gain
In the dark, hidden virtuous use of herbs:
That will I practise, and as freely give
All my endeavours as I gained them free.
Of all green wounds I know the remedies
In men or cattle, be they stung with snakes,
Or charmed with powerful words of wicked art,
Or be they love-sick, or through too much heat
Grown wild or lunatic, their eyes or ears
Thickened with misty film of dulling rheum;
These I can cure, such secret virtue lies
In herbs applièd by a virgin's hand.
My meat shall be what these wild woods afford,
Berries and chestnuts, plantains, on whose cheeks
The sun sits smiling, and the lofty fruit
Pulled from the fair head of the straight-grown pine;
On these I'll feed with free content, and rest,
When night shall blind the world, by thy side blest.

Enter Satyr *with a Basket of Fruit.*

Sat. Through yon same bending plain,
That flings his arms down to the main,
And through these thick woods, have I run,
Whose bottom never kissed the sun
Since the lusty spring began;
All to please my master Pan,
Have I trotted without rest
To get him fruit; for at a feast
He entertains, this coming night,
His paramour, the Syrinx bright.—
But, behold, a fairer sight!
           [*Seeing Clorin he stands amazed.*
By that heavenly form of thine,
Brightest fair, thou art divine,
Sprung from great immortal race
Of the gods; for in thy face

Shines more awful majesty
Than dull weak mortality
Dare with misty eyes behold,
And live: therefore on this mould
Lowly do I bend my knee
In worship of thy deity.
Deign it, goddess, from my hand
To receive whate'er this land
From her fertile womb doth send
Of her choice fruits; and but lend
Belief to that the Satyr tells:
Fairer by the famous wells
To this present day ne'er grew,
Never better nor more true.
Here be grapes, whose lusty blood
Is the learnèd poets' good,
Sweeter yet did never crown
The head of Bacchus; nuts more brown
Than the squirrel's teeth that crack them;
Deign, O fairest fair, to take them!
For these black-eyèd Dryope
Hath oftentimes commanded me
With my claspèd knee to climb:
See how well the lusty time
Hath decked their rising cheeks in red
Such as on your lips is spread!
Here be berries for a queen,
Some be red, some be green;
These are of that luscious meat,
The great god Pan himself doth eat:
All these, and what the woods can yield,
The hanging mountain or the field,
I freely offer, and ere long
Will bring you more, more sweet and strong;
Till when, humbly leave I take,
Lest the great Pan do awake,
That sleeping lies in a deep glade,
Under a broad beech's shade.
I must go, I must run
Swifter than the fiery sun.   [*Exit.*

Clo.   And all my fears go with thee!
What greatness, or what private hidden power,
Is there in me, to draw submission

From this rude man and beast?   Sure I am mortal,
The daughter of a shepherd; he was mortal,
And she that bore me mortal: prick my hand,
And it will bleed; a fever shakes me, and
The self-same wind that makes the young lambs shrink
Makes me a-cold: my fear says I am mortal,
Yet I have heard (my mother told it me,
And now I do believe it), if I keep
My virgin-flower uncropt, pure, chaste, and fair,
No goblin, wood-god, fairy, elf, or fiend,
Satyr, or other power that haunts the groves,
Shall hurt my body, or by vain illusion
Draw me to wander after idle fires;
Or voices calling me in dead of night,
To make me follow, and so tole me on,
Through mire and standing pools, to find my ruin.
Else why should this rough thing, who never knew
Manners nor smooth humanity, whose heats
Are rougher than himself and more mis-shapen,
Thus mildly kneel to me?   Sure there is a power
In that great name of virgin, that binds fast
All rude uncivil bloods, all appetites
That break their confines: then, strong chastity,
Be thou my strongest guard, for here I'll dwell
In opposition against fate and hell!

        [Retires into the bower.

SCENE II.—*In the Neighbourhood of a Village.*

Enter Old Shepherd, *with four couples of* Shepherds *and* Shepherdesses, *among whom are* PERIGOT *and* AMORET.

Old Shep. Now we have done this holy festival
  In honour of our great god, and his rites
  Performed, prepare yourselves for chaste
  And uncorrupted fires; that as the priest
  With powerful hand shall sprinkle on your brows
  His pure and holy water, ye may be
  From all hot flames of lust and loose thoughts free.
  Kneel, shepherds, kneel; here comes the priest of Pan.

Enter Priest of Pan.

Priest. Shepherds, thus I purge away
       [Sprinkling them with water.

Whatsoever this great day,
Or the past hours, gave not good,
To corrupt your maiden blood.
From the high rebellious heat
Of the grapes, and strength of meat,
From the wanton quick desires
They do kindle by their fires
I do wash you with this water;
Be you pure and fair hereafter!
From your livers and your veins
Thus I take away the stains;
All your thoughts be smooth and fair:
Be ye fresh and free as air!
Never more let lustful heat
Through your purgèd conduits beat,
Or a plighted troth be broken,
Or a wanton verse be spoken
In a shepherdess's ear:
Go your ways, ye are all clear.   [*They rise and sing.*

> Sing his praises that doth keep
>   Our flocks from harm,
> Pan, the father of our sheep;
>   And arm in arm
> Tread we softly in a round,
>   Whilst the hollow neighbouring ground
> Fills the music with her sound.
>
> Pan, O great god Pan, to thee
>   Thus do we sing!
> Thou that keep'st us chaste and free
>   As the young spring;
> Ever be thy honour spoke,
>   From that place the Morn is broke
> To that place Day doth unyoke!
>   [*Exeunt all except Perigot and Amoret.*

Peri. [*Detaining her.*] Stay, gentle Amoret, thou fair-browed
      maid;
   Thy shepherd prays thee stay, that holds thee dear,
   Equal with his soul's good.
Amo.   Speak; I give
   Thee freedom, shepherd; and thy tongue be still
   The same it ever was, as free from ill
   As he whose conversation never knew
   The court or city; be thou ever true!
Peri. When I fall off from my affection,
   Or mingle my clean thoughts with foul desires,

First, let our great god cease to keep my flocks,
That, being left alone without a guard,
The wolf, or winter's rage, summer's great heat
And want of water, rots, or what to us
Of ill is yet unknown, fall speedily,
And in their general ruin let me go!

Amo. I pray thee, gentle shepherd, wish not so:
I do believe thee; 'tis as hard for me
To think thee false, and harder, than for thee
To hold me foul.

Peri.   Oh, you are fairer far
Than the chaste blushing morn, or that fair star
That guides the wandering seaman through the deep;
Straighter than straightest pine upon the steep
Head of an agèd mountain; and more white
Than the new milk we strip before day-light
From the full-freighted bags of our fair flocks;
Your hair more beauteous than those hanging locks
Of young Apollo!

Amo.   Shepherd, be not lost;
You are sailed too far already from the coast
Of your discourse.

Peri.   Did you not tell me once
I should not love alone, I should not lose
Those many passions, vows, and holy oaths,
I have sent to heaven? did you not give your hand,
Even that fair hand, in hostage? Do not, then,
Give back again those sweets to other men,
You yourself vowed were mine.

Amo. Shepherd, so far as maiden's modesty
May give assurance, I am once more thine,
Once more I give my hand: be ever free
From that great foe to faith, foul jealousy!

Peri. I take it as my best good; and desire,
For stronger confirmation of our love,
To meet this happy night in that fair grove,
Where all true shepherds have rewarded been
For their long service: say, sweet, shall it hold?

Amo. Dear friend, you must not blame me, if I make
A doubt of what the silent night may do,
Coupled with this day's heat, to move your blood:
Maids must be fearful. Sure you have not been
Washed white enough, for yet I see a stain

    Stick in your liver: go and purge again.
Peri. Oh, do not wrong my honest simple truth!
    Myself and my affections are as pure
    As those chaste flames that burn before the shrine
    Of the great Dian: only my intent
    To draw you thither was to plight our troths,
    With interchange of mutual chaste embraces,
    And ceremonious tying of our souls.
    For to that holy wood is consecrate
    A virtuous well, about whose flowery banks
    The nimble-footed fairies dance their rounds
    By the pale moonshine, dipping oftentimes
    Their stolen children, so to make them free
    From dying flesh and dull mortality:
    By this fair fount hath many a shepherd sworn,
    And given away his freedom, many a troth
    Been plight, which neither envy nor old time
    Could ever break, with many a chaste kiss given,
    In hope of coming happiness;
    By this fresh fountain many a blushing maid
    Hath crowned the head of her long-lovèd shepherd
    With gaudy flowers, whilst he happy sung
    Lays of his love and dear captivity;
    There grow all herbs fit to cool looser flames
    Our sensual parts provoke, chiding our bloods,
    And quenching by their power those hidden sparks
    That else would break out, and provoke our sense
    To open fires; so virtuous is that place.
    Then, gentle shepherdess, believe, and grant:
    In troth, it fits not with that face to scant
    Your faithful shepherd of those chaste desires
    He ever aimed at, and——
Amo. Thou hast prevailed: farewell. This coming night
    Shall crown thy chaste hopes with long-wished delight.
Peri. Our great god Pan reward thee for that good
    Thou hast given thy poor shepherd! Fairest bud
    Of maiden virtues, when I leave to be
    The true admirer of thy chastity,
    Let me deserve the hot polluted name
    Of a wild woodman, or affect some dame
    Whose often prostitution hath begot
    More foul diseases than e'er yet the hot
    Sun bred thorough his burnings, whilst the Dog

Pursues the raging Lion, throwing fog
And deadly vapour from his angry breath,
Filling the lower world with plague and death!

[*Exit Amoret.*

Enter AMARILLIS.

Amar. Shepherd, may I desire to be believed,
    What I shall blushing tell?
Peri.   Fair maid, you may.
Amar. Then, softly thus: I love thee, Perigot;
    And would be gladder to be loved again
    Than the cold earth is in his frozen arms
    To clip the wanton spring. Nay, do not start,
    Nor wonder that I woo thee; thou that art
    The prime of our young grooms, even the top
    Of all our lusty shepherds. What dull eye,
    That never was acquainted with desire,
    Hath seen thee wrestle, run, or cast the stone
    With nimble strength and fair delivery,
    And hath not sparkled fire, and speedily
    Sent secret heat to all the neighbouring veins?
    Who ever heard thee sing, that brought again
    That freedom back was lent unto thy voice?
    Then, do not blame me, shepherd, if I be
    One to be numbered in this company,
    Since none that ever saw thee yet were free.
Peri. Fair shepherdess, much pity I can lend
    To your complaints; but sure I shall not love:
    All that is mine, myself and my best hopes,
    Are given already. Do not love him, then,
    That cannot love again; on other men
    Bestow those heats, more free, that may return
    You fire for fire, and in one flame equal burn.
Amar. Shall I rewarded be so slenderly
    For my affection, most unkind of men?
    If I were old, or had agreed with art
    To give another nature to my cheeks,
    Or were I common Mistress to the love
    Of every swain, or could I with such ease
    Call back my love as many a wanton doth,
    Thou mightst refuse me, shepherd; but to **thee**
    I am only fixed and set; let it not be
    A sport, thou gentle shepherd, to abuse

The love of silly maid.
Peri.   Fair soul, you use
These words to little end: for, know, I may
Better call back that time was yesterday,
Or stay the coming night, than bring my love
Home to myself again, or recreant prove.
I will no longer hold you with delays:
This present night I have appointed been
To meet that chaste fair that enjoys my soul,
In yonder grove, there to make up our loves.
Be not deceived no longer, choose again:
These neighbouring plains have many a comely swain,
Fresher and freer far than I e'er was;
Bestow that love on them, and let me pass.
Farewell: be happy in a better choice!   [*Exit.*
Amar. Cruel, thou hast struck me deader with thy voice
Than if the angry heavens with their quick flames
Had shot me through.   I must not leave to love,
I cannot; no, I must enjoy thee, boy,
Though the great dangers 'twixt my hopes and that
Be infinite.   There is a shepherd dwells
Down by the moor, whose life hath ever shown
More sullen discontent than Saturn's brow
When he sits frowning on the births of men;
One that doth wear himself away in loneness,
And never joys, unless it be in breaking
The holy plighted troths of mutual souls;
One that lusts after every several beauty,
But never yet was known to love or like,
Were the face fairer or more full of truth
Than Phœbe in her fulness, or the youth
Of smooth Lyæus; whose nigh-starvèd flocks
Are always scabby, and infect all sheep
They feed withal; whose lambs are ever last,
And die before their weaning; and whose dog
Looks, like his master, lean and full of scurf,
Not caring for the pipe or whistle.   This man may,
If he be well wrought, do a need of wonder,
Forcing me passage to my long desires:
And here he comes, as fitly to my purpose
As my quick thoughts could wish for.

Enter Sullen Shepherd.

Sull. Shep. Fresh beauty, let me not be thought uncivil,
    Thus to be partner of your loneness: 'twas
    My love (that ever-working passion) drew
    Me to this place, to seek some remedy
    For my sick soul.   Be not unkind and fair,
    For such the mighty Cupid in his doom
    Hath sworn to be avenged on; then, give room
    To my consuming fires, that so I may
    Enjoy my long desires, and so allay
    Those flames that else would burn my life away.
Amar. Shepherd, were I but sure thy heart were sound
    As thy words seem to be, means might be found
    To cure thee of thy long pains; for to me
    That heavy youth-consuming misery
    The love-sick soul endures never was pleasing:
    I could be well content with the quick easing
    Of thee and thy hot fires, might it procure
    Thy faith and farther service to be sure.
Sull. Shep. Name but that work, danger, or what can
    Be compassed by the wit or art of man.
    And, if I fail in my performance, may
    I never more kneel to the rising day!
Amar. Then, thus I try thee, shepherd.   This same night
    That now comes stealing on, a gentle pair
    Have promised equal love, and do appoint
    To make yon wood the place where hands and hearts
    Are to be tied for ever: break their meeting
    And their strong faith, and I am ever thine.
Sull. Shep. Tell me their names, and if I do not move
    By my great power, the centre of their love
    From his fixed being, let me never more
    Warm me by those fair eyes I thus adore.
Amar. Come; as we go, I'll tell thee what they are,
    And give thee fit directions for thy work.   [*Exeunt.*

SCENE III.—*Another part of the Wood.*

Enter CLOE.

Cloe. How have I wronged the times or men, that thus,
    After this holy feast, I pass unknown
    And unsaluted?   'Twas not wont to be

Thus frozen with the younger company
Of jolly shepherds; 'twas not then held good
For lusty grooms to mix their quicker blood
With that dull humour, most unfit to be
The friend of man, cold and dull chastity.
Sure I am held not fair, or am too old,
Or else not free enough, or from my fold
Drive not a flock sufficient great to gain
The greedy eyes of wealth-alluring swain.
Yet, if I may believe what others say,
My face has foil enough; nor can they lay
Justly too strict a coyness to my charge;
My flocks are many, and the downs as large
They feed upon: then, let it ever be
Their coldness, not my virgin-modesty
Makes me complain.

Enter THENOT.

The.   Was ever man but I
Thus truly taken with uncertainty;
Where shall that man be found that loves a mind
Made up in constancy, and dares not find
His love rewarded? Here, let all men know,
A wretch that lives to love his mistress so.

Cloe. Shepherd, I pray thee stay. Where hast thou been?
Or whither goest thou? Here be woods as green
As any; air likewise as fresh and sweet
As where smooth Zephyrus plays on the fleet
Face of the curlèd streams; with flowers as many
As the young spring gives, and as choice as any;
Here be all new delights, cool streams and wells,
Arbours o'ergrown with woodbines, caves, and dells;
Choose where thou wilt, whilst I sit by and sing,
Or gather rushes, to make many a ring
For thy long fingers; tell thee tales of love,—
How the pale Phœbe, hunting in a grove,
First saw the boy Endymion, from whose eyes
She took eternal fire that never dies;
How she conveyed him softly in a sleep,
His temples bound with poppy, to the steep
Head of old Latmus, where she stoops each night,
Gilding the mountain with her brother's light,
To kiss her sweetest.

The.   Far from me are these
     Hot flashes, bred from wanton heat and ease;
     I have forgot what love and loving meant;
     Rhymes, songs, and merry rounds, that oft are sent
     To the soft ear of maid, are strange to me:
     Only I live to admire a chastity,
     That neither pleasing age, smooth tongue, nor gold,
     Could ever break upor., so sure the mould
     Is that her mind was cast in; 'tis to her
     I only am reserved; she is my form I stir
     By, breathe and move; 'tis she, and only she,
     Can make me happy, or give misery.
Cloe. Good Shepherd, may a stranger crave to know
     To whom this dear observance you do owe?
The. You may, and by her virtue learn to square
     And level out your life; for to be fair,
     And nothing virtuous, only fits the eye
     Of gaudy youth and swelling vanity.
     Then, know, she's called the Virgin of the Grove,
     She that hath long since buried her chaste love,
     And now lives by his grave, for whose dear soul
     She hath vowed herself into the holy roll
     Of strict virginity: 'tis her I so admire,
     Not any looser blood or new desire.   *[Exit.*
Cloe. Farewell, poor swain! thou art not for my bend;
     I must have quicker souls, whose words may tend
     To some free action: give me him dare love
     At first encounter, and as soon dare prove!

            Sings. Come, shepherds, come!
                   Come away
                   Without delay,
                   Whilst the gentle time doth stay.
                   Green woods are dumb,
                   And will never tell to any
                   Those dear kisses, and those many
                   Sweet embraces that are given;
                   Dainty pleasures, that would even
                   Raise in coldest age a fire,
                   And give virgin-blood desire.
                   Then, if ever,
                   Now or never,
                   Come and have it:
                   Think not I
                   Dare deny,
                   If you crave it.

Enter DAPHNIS.

Here comes another.　Better be my speed,
Thou god of blood!　But certain, if I read
Not false, this is that modest shepherd, he
That only dare salute, but ne'er could be
Brought to kiss any, hold discourse, or sing,
Whisper, or boldly ask that wishèd thing
We all are born for;　one that makes loving faces,
And could be well content to covet graces,
Were they not got by boldness.　In this thing
My hopes are frozen;　and, but fate doth bring
Him hither, I would sooner choose
A man made out of snow, and freer use
An eunuch to my ends;　but since he's here,
Thus I attempt him.—[*Aside.*] Thou, of men most dear;
Welcome to her that only for thy sake
Hath been content to live!　Here, boldly take
My hand in pledge, this hand, that never yet
Was given away to any;　and but sit
Down on this rushy bank, whilst I go pull
Fresh blossoms from the boughs, or quickly cull
The choicest delicates from yonder mead,
To make thee chains or chaplets, or to spread
Under our fainting bodies, when delight
Shall lock up all our senses.　How the sight
Of those smooth rising cheeks renew the story
Of young Adonis, when in pride and glory
He lay infolded 'twixt the beating arms
Of willing Venus!　Methinks stronger charms
Dwell in those speaking eyes, and on that brow
More sweetness than the painters can allow
To their best pieces.　Not Narcissus, he
That wept himself away in memory
Of his own beauty, nor Silvanus' boy,
Nor the twice-ravished maid, for whom old Troy
Fell by the hand of Pyrrhus, may to thee
Be otherwise compared, than some dead tree
To a young fruitful olive.

Daph.　　　　　　　　I can love,
But I am loath to say so, lest I prove
Too soon unhappy.

Cloe.　　　　　　　Happy, thou wouldst say.

My dearest Daphnis, blush not; if the day
To thee and thy soft heats be enemy,
Then take the coming night; fair youth, 'tis free
To all the world.   Shepherd, I'll meet thee then
When darkness hath shut up the eyes of men,
In yonder grove: speak, shall our meeting hold?
Indeed you are too bashful; be more bold,
And tell me ay.

Daph.   I am content to say so,
And would be glad to meet, might I but pray so
Much from your fairness, that you would be true.

Cloe. Shepherd, thou hast thy wish.

Daph.   Fresh maid, adieu.
Yet one word more: since you have drawn me on
To come this night, fear not to meet alone
That man that will not offer to be ill,
Though your bright self would ask it, for his fill
Of this world's goodness; do not fear him, then,
But keep your 'pointed time.   Let other men
Set up their bloods to sale, mine shall be ever
Fair as the soul it carries, and unchaste never.   [*Exit.*

Cloe. Yet am I poorer than I was before.
Is it not strange, among so many a score
Of lusty bloods, I should pick out these things,
Whose veins, like a dull river far from springs,
Is still the same, slow, heavy, and unfit
For stream or motion, though the strong winds hit
With their continual power upon his sides?
Oh, happy be your names that have been brides,
And tasted those rare sweets for which I pine!
And far more heavy be thy grief and tine,
Thou lazy swain, that mayst relieve my needs,
Than his, upon whose liver always feeds
A hungry vulture!

Enter ALEXIS.

Alex.   Can such beauty be
Safe in his own guard, and not draw the eye
Of him that passeth on, to greedy gaze
Or covetous desire, whilst in a maze
The better part contemplates, giving rein,
And wishèd freedom to the labouring vein?
Fairest and whitest, may I crave to know

The cause of your retirement, why you go
Thus all alone? Methinks the downs are sweeter,
And the young company of swains more meeter,
Than these forsaken and untrodden places.
Give not yourself to loneness, and those graces
Hide from the eyes of men, that were intended
To live amongst us swains.

Cloe.   Thou art befriended,
Shepherd: in all my life I have not seen
A man, in whom greater contents have been,
Than thou thyself art. I could tell thee more,
Were there but any hope left to restore
My freedom lost. Oh, lend me all thy red,
Thou shame-faced Morning, when from Tithon's bed
Thou risest ever-maiden!

Alex.   If for me,
Thou sweetest of all sweets, these flashes be,
Speak, and be satisfied. Oh, guide her tongue,
My better angel; force my name among
Her modest thoughts, that the first word may be——

Cloe. Alexis, when the sun shall kiss the sea,
Taking his rest by the white Thetis' side,
Meet me in the holy wood, where I'll abide
Thy coming, shepherd.

Alex.   If I stay behind,
An everlasting dulness, and the wind,
That as he passeth by shuts up the stream
Of Rhine or Volga, whilst the sun's hot beam
Beats back again, seize me, and let me turn
To coldness more than ice! Oh, how I burn
And rise in youth and fire! I dare not stay.

Cloe. My name shall be your word.

Alex. Fly, fly, thou day!   *[Exit.*

Cloe. My grief is great, if both these boys should fail:
He that will use all winds must shift his sail.   *[Exit.*

ACT II

SCENE I.—*A Pasture.*

Enter Old Shepherd *ringing a bell, and* Priest of Pan
following.

Priest. Shepherds all, and maidens fair,
Fold your flocks up, for the air
'Gins to thicken, and the sun
Already his great course hath run.
See the dew-drops how they kiss
Every little flower that is;
Hanging on their velvet heads,
Like a rope of crystal beads;
See the heavy clouds low falling,
And bright Hesperus down calling
The dead Night from under ground;
At whose rising mists unsound,
Damps and vapours fly apace,
Hovering o'er the wanton face
Of these pastures, where they come,
Striking dead both bud and bloom:
Therefore, from such danger lock
Every one his lovèd flock;
And let your dogs lie loose without,
Lest the wolf come as a scout
From the mountain, and, ere day,
Bear a lamb or kid away;
Or the crafty thievish fox
Break upon your simple flocks.
To secure yourselves from these,
Be not too secure in ease;
Let one eye his watches keep,
Whilst the other eye doth sleep;
So you shall good shepherds prove,
And for ever hold the love
Of our great god.   Sweetest slumbers,
And soft silence, fall in numbers
On your eyelids!   So, farewell:
Thus I end my evening's knell   [*Exeunt.*

SCENE II.—*The Wood before Clorin's bower.*

Enter CLORIN, *sorting herbs.*

Clo. Now let me know what my best art hath done,
　　Helped by the great power of the virtuous moon
　　In her full light. Oh, you sons of earth,
　　You only brood, unto whose happy birth
　　Virtue was given, holding more of nature
　　Than man, her first-born and most perfect creature,
　　Let me adore you! you, that only can
　　Help or kill nature, drawing out that span
　　Of life and breath even to the end of time;
　　You, that these hands did crop long before prime
　　Of day, give me your names, and, next, your hidden
　　　　power.
　　This is the clote, bearing a yellow flower;
　　And this, black horehound; both are very good
　　For sheep or shepherd bitten by a wood
　　Dog's venomed tooth: these rhamnus' branches are,
　　Which, stuck in entries, or about the bar
　　That holds the door, kill all enchantments, charms
　　(Were they Medea's verses), that do harms
　　To men or cattle: these for frenzy be
　　A speedy and a sovereign remedy,
　　The bitter wormwood, sage, and marigold;
　　Such sympathy with man's good they do hold:
　　This tormentil, whose virtue is to part
　　All deadly killing poison from the heart:
　　And, here, narcissus root, for swellings best:
　　Yellow lysimachus, to give sweet rest
　　To the faint shepherd, killing, where it comes,
　　All busy gnats, and every fly that hums:
　　For leprosy, darnel and celandine,
　　With calamint, whose virtues do refine
　　The blood of man, making it free and fair
　　As the first hour it breathed, or the best air:
　　Here, other two; but your rebellious use
　　Is not for me, whose goodness is abuse;
　　Therefore, foul standergrass, from me and mine
　　I banish thee, with lustful turpentine;
　　You that entice the veins and stir the heat
　　To civil mutiny, scaling the seat

Our reason moves in, and deluding it
With dreams and wanton fancies, till the fit
Of burning lust be quenched, by appetite
Robbing the soul of blessedness and light:
And thou, light vervain, too, thou must go after,
Provoking easy souls to mirth and laughter;
No more shall I dip thee in water now,
And sprinkle every post and every bough
With thy well-pleasing juice, to make the grooms
Swell with high mirth, and with joy all the rooms.

Enter THENOT.

The. This is the cabin where the best of all
  Her sex that ever breathed, or ever shall
  Give heat or happiness to the shepherd's side,
  Doth only to her worthy self abide.
  Thou blessèd star, I thank thee for thy light,
  Thou by whose power the darkness of sad night
  Is banished from the earth, in whose dull place
  Thy chaster beams play on the heavy face
  Of all the world, making the blue sea smile,
  To see how cunningly thou dost beguile
  Thy brother of his brightness, giving day
  Again from chaos; whiter than the way
  That leads to Jove's high court, and chaster far
  Than chastity itself, you blessèd star
  That nightly shines! thou, all the constancy
  That in all women was or e'er shall be;
  From whose fair eye-balls flies that holy fire
  That poets style the mother of desire,
  Infusing into every gentle breast
  A soul of greater price, and far more blest,
  Than that quick power which gives a difference
  'Twixt man and creatures of a lower sense!
Clo. Shepherd, how cam'st thou hither to this place?
  No way is trodden; all the verdant grass
  The spring shot up stands yet unbruisèd here
  Of any foot; only the dappled deer,
  Far from the fearèd sound of crookèd horn,
  Dwells in this fastness.
The.   Chaster than the morn,
  I have not wandered, or by strong illusion
  Into this virtuous place have made intrusion:

But hither am I come (believe me, fair),
To seek you out, of whose great good the air
Is full, and strongly labours, whilst the sound
Breaks against heaven, and drives into a stound
Th'amazèd shepherd, that such virtue can
Be resident in lesser than a man.

Clo. If any art I have, or hidden skill,
May cure thee of disease or festered ill
Whose grief or greenness to another's eye
May seem unpossible of remedy,
I dare yet undertake it.

The.   'Tis no pain
I suffer through disease, no beating vein
Conveys infection dangerous to the heart,
No part imposthumed, to be cured by art,
This body holds; and yet a fuller grief
Than ever skilful hand did give relief
Dwells on my soul, and may be healed by you,
Fair, beauteous virgin.

Clo.   ·   Then, shepherd, let me sue
To know thy grief: that man yet never knew
The way to health that durst not show his sore.

The. Then, fairest, know, I love you.

Clo.   Swain, no more!
Thou hast abused the strictness of this place,
And offered sacrilegious foul disgrace
To the sweet rest of these interrèd bones;
For fear of whose ascending, fly at once,
Thou and thy idle passions, that the sight
Of death and speedy vengeance may not fright
Thy very soul with horror.

The.   Let me not,
Thou all perfection, merit such a blot
For my true zealous faith.

Clo.   Dar'st thou abide
To see this holy earth at once divide,
And give her body up? for sure it will,
If thou pursu'st with wanton flames to fill
This hallowed place: therefore repent and go,
Whilst I with prayers appease his ghost below,
That else would tell thee what it were to be
A rival in that virtuous love that he
Embraces yet.

The.　　　　　　　　　　　　　'Tis not the white or red
　　　Inhabits in your cheek that thus can wed
　　　My mind to adoration; nor your eye,
　　　Though it be full and fair, your forehead high
　　　And smooth as Pelops' shoulder; not the smile
　　　Lies watching in those dimples to beguile
　　　The easy soul; your hands and fingers long,
　　　With veins enamelled richly; nor your tongue,
　　　Though it spoke sweeter than Arion's harp;
　　　Your hair woven into many a curious warp,
　　　Able in endless error to enfold
　　　The wandering soul; not the true perfect mould
　　　Of all your body, which as pure doth show
　　　In maiden-whiteness as the Alpen-snow:
　　　All these, were but your constancy away,
　　　Would please me less than a black stormy day
　　　The wretched seaman toiling through the deep.
　　　But, whilst this honoured strictness you dare keep,
　　　Though all the plagues that e'er begotten were
　　　In the great womb of air were settled here,
　　　In opposition, I would, like the tree,
　　　Shake off those drops of weakness, and be free
　　　Even in the arm of danger.

Clo.　　　　　　　　　　Wouldst thou have
　　　Me raise again, fond man, from silent grave
　　　Those sparks, that long ago were buried here
　　　With my dear friend's cold ashes?

The.　　　　　　　　　　　　Dearest dear,
　　　I dare not ask it, nor you must not grant:
　　　Stand strongly to your vow, and do not faint.
　　　Remember how he loved you, and be still
　　　The same opinion speaks you: let not will,
　　　And that great god of women, appetite,
　　　Set up your blood again; do not invite
　　　Desire and fancy from their long exile,
　　　To seat them once more in a pleasing smile:
　　　Be, like a rock, made firmly up 'gainst all
　　　The power of angry heaven, or the strong fall
　　　Of Neptune's battery.　If you yield, I die
　　　To all affection; 'tis that loyalty
　　　You tie unto this grave I so admire:
　　　And yet there's something else I would desire,
　　　If you would hear me, but withal deny.

Oh, Pan, what an uncertain destiny
Hangs over all my hopes!   I will retire;
For, if I longer stay, this double fire
Will lick my life up.

Clo.   Do; and let time wear out
What art and nature cannot bring about.

The.   Farewell, thou soul of virtue, and be blest
For ever, whilst that here I wretched rest
Thus to myself!   Yet grant me leave to dwell
In kenning of this arbour: yon same dell,
O'ertopped with mourning cypress and sad yew,
Shall be my cabin, where I'll early rue,
Before the sun hath kissed this dew away,
The hard uncertain chance which faith doth lay
Upon this head.

Clo.   The gods give quick release
And happy cure unto thy hard disease!

        [*Exit Thenot, Clorin retiring into the Bower.*

SCENE III.—*Another part of the Wood.*

Enter Sullen Shepherd.

Sull. Shep.   I do not love this wench that I should meet;
For ne'er did my unconstant eye yet greet
That beauty, were it sweeter or more fair
Than the new blossoms when the morning-air
Blows gently on them, or the breaking light,
When many maiden-blushes to our sight
Shoot from his early face: were all these set
In some neat form before me, 'twould not get
The least love from me; some desire it might,
Or present burning.   All to me in sight
Are equal; be they fair, or black, or brown,
Virgin, or careless wanton, I can crown
My appetite with any; swear as oft,
And weep, as any; melt my words as soft
Into a maiden's ears, and tell how long
My heart has been her servant, and how strong
My passions are; call her unkind and cruel;
Offer her all I have to gain the jewel
Maidens so highly prize; then loathe, and fly:
This do I hold a blessèd destiny.

Enter AMARILLIS.

Amar. Hail, shepherd!   Pan bless both thy flock and thee,
 For being mindful of thy word to me!
Sull. Shep. Welcome, fair shepherdess!   Thy loving swain
 Gives thee the self-same wishes back again;
 Who till this present hour ne'er knew that eye
 Could make me cross mine arms, or daily die
 With fresh consumings.   Boldly tell me, then,
 How shall we part their faithful loves, and when?
 Shall I belie him to her? shall I swear
 His faith is false and he loves every where?
 I'll say he mocked her th' other day to you;
 Which will by your confirming show as true,
 For she is of so pure an honesty,
 To think, because she will not, none will lie.
 Or else to him I'll slander Amoret,
 And say, she but seems chaste; I'll swear she met
 Me 'mongst the shady sycamores last night,
 And loosely offered up her flame and sprite
 Into my bosom; made a wanton bed
 Of leaves and many flowers, where she spread
 Her willing body to be pressed by me;
 There have I carved her name on many a tree,
 Together with mine own.   To make this show
 More full of seeming,—Hobinal, you know,
 Son to the agèd shepherd of the glen,
 Him I have sorted out of many men,
 To say he found us at our private sport,
 And roused us 'fore our time by his resort:
 This to confirm, I've promised to the boy
 Many a pretty knack and many a toy;
 As gins to catch him birds, with bow and bolt
 To shoot at nimble squirrels in the holt;
 A pair of painted buskins, and a lamb
 Soft as his own locks or the down of swan.
 This I have done to win you; which doth give
 Me double pleasure: discord makes me live.
Amar. Loved swain, I thank you. These tricks might
  prevail
 With other rustic shepherds, but will fail
 Even once to stir, much more to overthrow,
 His fixèd love from judgment, who doth know

Your nature, my end, and his chosen's merit;
Therefore some stronger way must force his spirit,
Which I have found: give second, and my love
Is everlasting thine.
Sull. Shep.   Try me, and prove.
Amar. These happy pair of lovers meet straightway
    Soon as they fold their flocks up with the day,
    In the thick grove bordering upon yon hill,
    In whose hard side nature hath carved a well,
    And, but that matchless spring which poets know,
    Was ne'er the like to this: by it doth grow,
    About the sides, all herbs which witches use,
    All simples good for medicine or abuse,
    All sweets that crown the happy nuptial day,
    With all their colours; there the month of May
    Is ever dwelling, all is young and green;
    There's not a grass on which was ever seen
    The falling autumn or cold winter's hand;
    So full of heat and virtue is the land
    About this fountain, which doth slowly break,
    Below yon mountain's foot, into a creek
    That waters all the valley, giving fish
    Of many sorts to fill the shepherd's dish.
    This holy well, my grandame that is dead,
    Right wise in charms, hath often to me said,
    Hath power to change the form of any creature,
    Being thrice dipped o'er the head, into what feature
    Or shape 'twould please the letter-down to crave,
    Who must pronounce this charm too, which she gave
                              [*Showing a scroll.*
    Me on her death-bed; told me what, and how,
    I should apply unto the patient's brow
    That would be changed, casting them thrice asleep,
    Before I trusted them into this deep:
    All this she showed me, and did charge me prove
    This secret of her art, if crost in love.
    I'll this attempt now, shepherd; I have here
    All her prescriptions, and I will not fear
    To be myself dipped.   Come, my temples bind
    With these sad herbs, and when I sleep you find,
    As you do speak your charm, thrice down me let,
    And bid the water raise me Amoret;
    Which being done, leave me to my affair,

And ere the day shall quite itself outwear,
I will return unto my shepherd's arm;
Dip me again, and then repeat this charm,
And pluck me up myself, whom freely take,
And the hott'st fire of thine affection slake.
Sull. Shep. And if I fit thee not, then fit not me.
    I long the truth of this well's power to see.   [*Exeunt.*

SCENE IV.—*Another part of the Wood.*

Enter DAPHNIS.

Daph. Here will I stay, for this the covert is
    Where I appointed Cloe.   Do not miss,
    Thou bright-eyed virgin; come, oh come, my fair!
    Be not abused with fear, nor let cold care
    Of honour stay thee from thy shepherd's arm,
    Who would as hard be won to offer harm
    To thy chaste thoughts, as whiteness from the day,
    Or yon great round to move another way:
    My language shall be honest, full of truth,
    My flames as smooth and spotless as my youth;
    I will not entertain that wandering thought,
    Whose easy current may at length be brought
    To a loose vastness.
Alexis. [*Within.*]   Cloe!
Daph.   'Tis her voice,
    And I must answer.—Cloe!—Oh, the choice
    Of dear embraces, chaste and holy strains
    Our hands shall give!   I charge you, all my veins,
    Through which the blood and spirit take their way,
    Lock up your disobedient heats, and stay
    Those mutinous desires that else would grow
    To strong rebellion; do not wilder show
    That blushing modesty may entertain.
Alexis. [*Within.*] Cloe!
Daph. There sounds that blessèd name again,
    And I will meet it.   Let me not mistake;

Enter ALEXIS.

This is some shepherd.   Sure, I am awake:
What may this riddle mean?   I will retire,
To give myself more knowledge.   [*Retires.*
Alexis.   Oh, my fire,

How thou consum'st me!—Cloe, answer me!
Alexis, strong Alexis, high and free,
Calls upon Cloe.   See, mine arms are full
Of entertainment, ready for to pull
That golden fruit which too, too long hath hung
Tempting the greedy eye.   Thou stay'st too long;
I am impatient of these mad delays:
I must not leave unsought those many ways
That lead into this centre, till I find
Quench for my burning lust.   I come, unkind!   [*Exit.*

Daph. [*Coming forward.*] Can my imagination work me so
        much ill,
    That I may credit this for truth, and still
    Believe mine eyes? or shall I firmly hold
    Her yet untainted, and these sights but bold
    Illusion?   Sure, such fancies oft have been
    Sent to abuse true love, and yet are seen
    Daring to blind the virtuous thought with error;
    But be they far from me with their fond terror!
    I am resolved my Cloe yet is true.

Cloe. [*Within.*]   Cloe!
Daph. Hark! Cloe! Sure, this voice is new,
    Whose shrillness, like the sounding of a bell,
    Tells me it is a woman.—Cloe, tell
    Thy blessèd name again.
Cloe. [*Within.*]   Cloe! here!
Daph. Oh, what a grief is this, to be so near,
    And not encounter!

                    Enter Cloe.

Cloe.   Shepherd, we are met:
    Draw close into the covert, lest the wet,
    Which falls like the lazy mist upon the ground,
    Soak through your startups.
Daph.   Fairest, are you found?
    How have we wandered, that the better part
    Of this good night is perished?   Oh, my heart!
    How have I longed to meet you, how to kiss
    Those lily hands, how to receive the bliss
    That charming tongue gives to the happy ear
    Of him that drinks your language!   But I fear
    I am too much unmannered, far too rude,
    And almost grown lascivious, to intrude

These hot behaviours; where regard of fame,
Honour and modesty, a virtuous name,
And such discourse as one fair sister may
Without offence unto the brother say,
Should rather have been tendered.   But, believe,
Here dwells a better temper: do not grieve,
Then, ever-kindest, that my first salute
Seasons so much of fancy; I am mute
Henceforth to all discourses but shall be
Suiting to your sweet thoughts and modesty.
Indeed, I will not ask a kiss of you,
No, not to wring your fingers, nor to sue
To those blest pair of fixèd stars for smiles;
All a young lover's cunning, all his wiles,
And pretty wanton dyings, shall to me
Be strangers; only to your chastity
I am devoted ever.

Cloe.   Honest swain,
First let me thank you, then return again
As much of my love.—No, thou art too cold,
Unhappy boy, not tempered to my mould;
Thy blood falls heavy downward. 'Tis not fear
To offend in boldness wins; they never wear
Deservèd favours that deny to take
When they are offered freely.   Do I wake,
To see a man of his youth, years, and feature,
And such a one as we call goodly creature,
Thus backward?   What a world of precious art
Were merely lost, to make him do his part!
But I will shake him off, that dares not hold:
Let men that hope to be beloved be bold.   [*Aside.*
Daphnis, I do desire, since we are met
So happily, our lives and fortunes set
Upon one stake, to give assurance now,
By interchange of hands and holy vow,
Never to break again.   Walk you that way,
Whilst I in zealous meditation stray
A little this way: when we both have ended
These rites and duties, by the woods befriended
And secrecy of night, retire and find
An agèd oak, whose hollowness may bind
Us both within his body; thither go;
It stands within yon bottom.

Daph.   Be it so.   [*Exit.*
Cloe. And I will meet there never more with thee,
    Thou idle shamefacedness!
Alexis. [*Within.*]   Cloe!
Cloe.   'Tis he!
    That dare, I hope, be bolder.
Alexis. [*Within.*]   Cloe!
Cloe.   Now,
    Great Pan, for Syrinx' sake, bid speed our plough!
                                          [*Exit.*

ACT III

SCENE I.—*Part of the Wood with the holy Well.*

Enter Sullen Shepherd, *carrying* AMARILLIS *asleep.*

Sull. Shep. From thy forehead thus I take
    These herbs, and charge thee not awake
    Till in yonder holy well
    Thrice, with powerful magic spell
    Filled with many a baleful word
    Thou hast been dipped. Thus, with my cord
    Of blasted hemp, by moonlight twined
    I do thy sleepy body bind.
    I turn thy head unto the east,
    And thy feet unto the west,
    Thy left arm to the south put forth,
    And thy right unto the north.
    I take thy body from the ground,
    In this deep and deadly swound,
    And into this holy spring
    I let thee slide down by my string.—
                          [*Lets her down into the Well.*
    Take this maid, thou holy pit
    To thy bottom; nearer yet;
    In thy water pure and sweet
    By thy leave I dip her feet;
    Thus I let her lower yet,
    That her ankles may be wet;
    Yet down lower, let her knee
    In thy waters washèd be;
    There stop.—Fly away,
    Everything that loves the day!

Truth, that hath but one face,
Thus I charm thee from this place.
Snakes that cast your coats for new,
Chameleons that alter hue,
Hares that yearly sexes change,
Proteus altering oft and strange,
Hecatè with shapes three,
Let this maiden changèd be,
With this holy water wet,
To the shape of Amoret!
Cynthia, work thou with my charm!—
Thus I draw thee, free from harm,
     [*Draws her out of the well, in the shape of Amoret.*
Up out of this blessèd lake:
Rise both like her and awake!

Amar. Speak, shepherd, am I Amoret to sight?
  Or hast thou missed in any magic rite,
  For want of which any defect in me
  May make our practices discovered be?

Sull. Shep. By yonder moon, but that I here do stand,
  Whose breath hath thus transformed thee, and whose hand
  Let thee down dry, and plucked thee up thus wet,
  I should myself take thee for Amoret!
  Thou art, in clothes, in feature, voice and hue,
  So like, that sense can not distinguish you.

Amar. Then, this deceit, which cannot crossèd be,
  At once shall lose her him, and gain thee me.
  Hither she needs must come, by promise made;
  And, sure, his nature never was so bad,
  To bid a virgin meet him in the wood,
  When night and fear are up, but understood
  'Twas his part to come first.   Being come, I'll say,
  My constant love made me come first and stay;
  Then will I lead him further to the grove:
  But stay you here, and, if his own true love
  Shall seek him here, set her in some wrong path,
  Which say her lover lately trodden hath;
  I'll not be far from hence.   If need there be,
  Here is another charm, whose power will free
                       [*Gives a scroll.*
  The dazzled sense, read by the moonbeams clear,
  And in my own true shape make me appear.

Enter PERIGOT.

Sull. Shep. Stand close: here's Perigot; whose constant
heart
  Longs to behold her in whose shape thou art.
  [Retires with Amarillis.
Peri. This is the place.—Fair Amoret!—The hour
  Is yet scarce come. Here every sylvan power
  Delights to be, about yon sacred well,
  Which they have blessed with many a powerful spell;
  For never traveller in dead of night,
  Nor strayèd beasts have fall'n in; but when sight
  Hath failed them, then their right way they have found
  By help of them, so holy is the ground.
  But I will farther seek, lest Amoret
  Should be first come, and so stray long unmet.—
  My Amoret, Amoret! *[Exit.*
Amar. [*Coming forward.*] Perigot!
Peri. [*Within.*] My love!
Amar. I come, my love! *[Exit.*
Sull. Shep. Now she hath got
  Her own desires, and I shall gainer be
  Of my long-looked-for hopes, as well as she.
  How bright the moon shines here, as if she strove
  To show her glory in this little grove

Enter AMORET

  To some new-lovèd shepherd! Yonder is
  Another Amoret. Where differs this
  From that? but that she Perigot hath met,
  I should have ta'en this for the counterfeit.
  Herbs, woods, and springs, the power that in you lies,
  If mortal men could know your properties! *[Aside.*
Amo. Methinks it is not night; I have no fear,
  Walking this wood, of lion or of bear,
  Whose names at other times have made me quake,
  When any shepherdess in her tale spake
  Of some of them, that underneath a wood
  Have torn true lovers that together stood;
  Methinks there are no goblins, and men's talk,
  That in these woods the nimble fairies walk,
  Are fables: such a strong heart I have got,

Because I come to meet with Perigot.—
My Perigot! Who's that? my Perigot?

Sull. Shep. [*Coming forward.*]   Fair maid!

Amo.   Aye me, thou art not Perigot?

Sull. Shep. But I can tell you news of Perigot:
    An hour together under yonder tree
    He sat with wreathèd arms, and called on thee,
    And said, " Why, Amoret, stay'st thou so long? "
    Then starting up, down yonder path he flung,
    Lest thou hadst missed thy way. Were it daylight,
    He could not yet have borne him out of sight.

Amo. Thanks, gentle shepherd; and beshrew my stay,
    That made me fearful I had lost my way
    As fast as my weak legs (that cannot be
    Weary with seeking him) will carry me,
    I'll follow; and, for this thy care of me,
    Pray Pan thy love may ever follow thee!   [*Exit.*

Sull. Shep. How bright she was, how lovely did she show!
    Was it not pity to deceive her so?
    She plucked her garments up, and tripped away,
    And with a virgin-innocence did pray
    For me that perjured her. Whilst she was here,
    Methought the beams of light that did appear
    Were shot from her; methought the moon gave none
    But what it had from her. She was alone
    With me; if then her presence did so move,
    Why did I not assay to win her love?
    She would not sure have yielded unto me;
    Women love only opportunity,
    And not the man; or if she had denied,
    Alone, I might have forced her to have tried
    Who had been stronger: oh, vain fool, to let
    Such blessed occasion pass! I'll follow yet;
    My blood is up; I cannot now forbear.

Enter ALEXIS *and* CLOE.

I come, sweet Amoret!—Soft, who is here?
    A pair of lovers? He shall yield her me:
    Now lust is up, alike all women be.   [*Aside and retires.*

Alexis. Where shall we rest? But for the love of me,
    Cloe, I know, ere this would weary be.

Cloe. Alexis, let us rest here, if the place
    Be private, and out of the common trace

Of every shepherd; for, I understood,
This night a number are about the wood:
Then, let us choose some place, where, out of sight,
We freely may enjoy our stol'n delight.

Alexis. Then, boldly here, where we shall ne'er be found:
No shepherd's way lies here, 'tis hallowed ground;
No maid seeks here her strayèd cow or sheep;
Fairies and fawns and satyrs do it keep.
Then, carelessly rest here, and clip and kiss,
And let no fear make us our pleasures miss.

Cloe. Then, lie by me: the sooner we begin,
The longer ere the day descry our sin. [*They lie down.*

Sull. Shep. [*Coming forward.*] Forbear to touch my love;
or, by yon flame,
The greatest power that shepherds dare to name,
Here where thou sit'st, under this holy tree,
Her to dishonour, thou shalt buried be!

Alexis. If Pan himself should come out of the lawns,
With all his troops of satyrs and of fawns,
And bid me leave, I swear by her two eyes
(A greater oath than thine), I would not rise!

Sull. Shep. Then, from the cold earth never thou shalt move,
But lose at one stroke both thy life and love.
[*Wounds him with his spear.*

Cloe. Hold, gentle shepherd!
Sull. Shep.   Fairest shepherdess,
Come you with me; I do not love you less
Than that fond man, that would have kept you there
From me of more desert.

Alexis.   Oh, yet forbear
To take her from me! Give me leave to die
By her!

Enter Satyr; Sullen Shepherd *runs one way, and*
Cloe *another*.

Sat.   Now, whilst the moon doth rule the sky,
And the stars, whose feeble light
Gives a pale shadow to the night,
Are up, great Pan commanded me
To walk this grove about, whilst he,
In a corner of the wood,
Where never mortal foot hath stood,
Keeps dancing, music, and a feast,

To entertain a lovely guest;
Where he gives her many a rose,
Sweeter than the breath that blows
The leaves, grapes, berries of the best;
I never saw so great a feast.
But, to my charge.   Here must I stay,
To see what mortals lose their way,
And by a false fire, seeming bright,
Train them in and leave them right,
Then must I watch if any be
Forcing of a chastity;
If I find it, then in haste
Give my wreathèd horn a blast,
And the fairies all will run,
Wildly dancing by the moon,
And will pinch him to the bone,
Till his lustful thoughts be gone.

Alexis. Oh, death!

Sat. Back again about this ground;
Sure, I hear a mortal sound.—
I bind thee by this powerful spell,
By the waters of this well,
By the glimmering moonbeams bright,
Speak again, thou mortal wight!

Alexis. Oh!

Sat. Here the foolish mortal lies,
Sleeping on the ground.—Arise!—
The poor wight is almost dead;
On the ground his wounds have bled,
And his clothes fouled with his blood:
To my goddess in the wood
Will I lead him, whose hands pure
Will help this mortal wight to cure.

[*Exit carrying Alexis*

Re-enter CLOE.

Cloe. Since I beheld yon shaggy man, my breast
Doth pant; each bush, methinks, should hide a beast.
Yet my desire keeps still above my fear:
I would fain meet some shepherd, knew I where;
For from one cause of fear I am most free,
It is impossible to ravish me,
I am so willing.   Here upon this ground

I left my love, all bloody with his wounds;
Yet, till that fearful shape made me begone,
Though he were hurt, I furnished was of one;
But now both lost.—Alexis, speak or move,
If thou hast any life; thou art yet my love!—
He's dead, or else is with his little might
Crept from the bank for fear of that ill sprite.—
Then, where art thou that struck'st my love?   Oh, stay!
Bring me thyself in change, and then I'll say
Thou hast some justice: I will make thee trim
With flowers and garlands that were meant for him;
I'll clip thee round with both mine arms, as fast
As I did mean he should have been embraced.
But thou art fled.—What hope is left for me?
I'll run to Daphnis in the hollow tree,
Whom I did mean to mock; though hope be small
To make him bold, rather than none at all,
I'll try him; his heart, and my behaviour too,
Perhaps may teach him what he ought to do.   [*Exit.*

Re-enter Sullen Shepherd.

Sull. Shep. This was the place.   'Twas but my feeble sight,
Mixed with the horror of my deed, and night,
That shaped these fears, and made me run away,
And lose my beauteous hardly-gotten prey.—
Speak, gentle shepherdess! I am alone,
And tender love for love.—But she is gone
From me, that, having struck her lover dead,
For silly fear left her alone, and fled.
And see, the wounded body is removed
By her of whom it was so well beloved.
But all these fancies must be quite forgot.
I must lie close; here comes young Perigot,
With subtle Amarillis in the shape
Of Amoret.   Pray, love, he may not 'scape! [*Retires.*

Enter PERIGOT, *and* AMARILLIS *in the shape of*
AMORET.

Amar. Belovèd Perigot, show me some place,
Where I may rest my limbs, weak with the chase
Of thee, an hour before thou cam'st at least.
Peri. Beshrew my tardy steps!   Here shalt thou rest
Upon this holy bank: no deadly snake

K 506

Upon this turf herself in folds doth make;
Here is no poison for the toad to feed;
Here boldly spread thy hands; no venomed weed
Dares blister them; no slimy snail dare creep
Over thy face when thou art fast asleep;
Here never durst the dabbling cuckoo spit;
No slough of falling star did ever hit
Upon this bank: let this thy cabin be;
This other, set with violets, for me.   *[They lie down.*

Amar. Thou dost not love me, Perigot.
Peri.   Fair maid,
You only love to hear it often said;
You do not doubt.
Amar.   Believe me, but I do.
Peri. What, shall we now begin again to woo?
'Tis the best way to make your lover last,
To play with him when you have caught him fast.
Amar. By Pan I swear, belovèd Perigot,
And by yon moon, I think thou lov'st me not.
Peri. By Pan I swear,—and, if I falsely swear,
Let him not guard my flock; let foxes tear
My earliest lambs, and wolves, whilst I do sleep,
Fall on the rest; a rot among my sheep,—
I love thee better than the careful ewe
The new-yeaned lamb that is of her own hue;
I dote upon thee more than that young lamb
Doth on the bag that feeds him from his dam!
Were there a sort of wolves got in my fold,
And one ran after thee, both young and old
Should be devoured, and it should be my strife
To save thee, whom I love above my life.
Amar. How should I trust thee, when I see thee choose
Another bed, and dost my side refuse?
Peri. 'Twas only that the chaste thoughts might be shown
'Twixt thee and me, although we were alone.
Amar. Come, Perigot will show his power, that he
Can make his Amoret, though she weary be,
Rise nimbly from her couch, and come to his.
Here, take thy Amoret; embrace and kiss.
                                        [Lies down beside him.

Peri. What means my love?
Amar.   To do as lovers should,
That are to be enjoyed, not to be wooed.

> There's ne'er a shepherdess in all the plain
> Can kiss thee with more art; there's none can feign
> More wanton tricks.

Peri.   Forbear, dear soul, to try
> Whether my heart be pure; I'll rather die
> Than nourish one thought to dishonour thee.

Amar. Still think'st thou such a thing as chastity
> Is amongst women? Perigot, there's none
> That with her love is in a wood alone,
> And would come home a maid: be not abused
> With thy fond first belief; let time be used.

> > > > > > *[Perigot rises.*

> Why dost thou rise?

Peri.   My true heart thou hast slain!

Amar. Faith, Perigot, I'll pluck thee down again.

Peri. Let go, thou serpent, that into my breast
> Hast with thy cunning dived!—Art not in jest?

Amar. Sweet love, lie down.

Peri.   Since this I live to see,
> Some bitter north wind blast my flocks and me!

Amar. You swore you loved, yet will not do my will.

Peri. Oh, be as thou wert once, I'll love thee still!

Amar. I am as still I was, and all my kind;
> Though other shows we have, poor men to blind.

Peri. Then, here I end all love; and, lest my vain
> Belief should ever draw me in again,
> Before thy face, that hast my youth misled,
> I end my life! my blood be on thy head!

> > > > *[Offers to kill himself with his spear*

Amar. [*Rising.*] Oh, hold thy hands, thy Amoret doth cry!

Peri. Thou counsel'st well; first, Amoret shall die,
> That is the cause of my eternal smart!

Amar. Oh, hold!   *[Exit.*

Peri.   This steel shall pierce thy lustful heart!

> > > > *[Exit, running after her.*

Sull. Shep. [*Coming forward.*] Up and down, every where,
> I strew the herbs, to purge the air:
> Let your odour drive hence
> All mists that dazzle sense.
> Herbs and springs, whose hidden might
> Alters shapes, and mocks the sight,
> Thus I charge ye to undo
> All before I brought ye to!

Let her fly, let her 'scape;
Give again her own shape!   [*Retires.*

Re-enter AMARILLIS *in her own shape, and* PERIGOT
following with his spear.

Amar. Forbear, thou gentle swain! thou dost mistake;
　　　She whom thou follow'dst fled into the brake,
　　　And as I crossed thy way, I met thy wrath;
　　　The only fear of which near slain me hath.
Peri. Pardon, fair shepherdess: my rage and night
　　　Were both upon me, and beguiled my sight:
　　　But far be it from me to spill the blood
　　　Of harmless maids that wander in the wood!
　　　　　　　　　　　　　　　　[*Exit Amarillis.*

Enter AMORET.

Amo. Many a weary step, in yonder path,
　　　Poor hopeless Amoret twice trodden hath,
　　　To seek her Perigot; yet cannot hear
　　　His voice.—My Perigot! She loves thee dear
　　　That calls.
Peri. 　　　　See yonder where she is! how fair
　　　She shows! and yet her breath infects the air.
Amo. My Perigot!
Peri. 　　　　Here.
Amo. 　　　　　　　　Happy!
Peri. 　　　　　　　　　　　Hapless! first
　　　It lights on thee: the next blow is the worst.
　　　　　　　　　　　　　　　　[*Wounds her.*
Amo. Stay, Perigot! my love, thou art unjust.   [*Falls.*
Peri. Death is the best reward that's due to lust.   [*Exit.*
Sull. Shep. Now shall their love be crossed; for, being struck,
　　　I'll throw her in the fount, lest being took
　　　By some night-traveller, whose honest care
　　　May help to cure her.   [*Aside, and then comes forward.*
　　　　　　　　　　　　　Shepherdess, prepare
　　　Yourself to die!
Amo. 　　　　　　No mercy do I crave;
　　　Thou canst not give a worse blow than I have.
　　　Tell him that gave me this; who loved him too,
　　　He struck my soul, and not my body through;
　　　Tell him, when I am dead, my soul shall be
　　　At peace, if he but think he injured me.

Sull. Shep. In this fount be thy grave. Thou wert not meant
    Sure for a woman, thou art so innocent.—
                                [Flings her into the well.
    She cannot 'scape, for, underneath the ground,
    In a long hollow the clear spring is bound,
    Till on yon side, where the morn's sun doth look,
    The struggling water breaks out in a brook.   *[Exit.*

    The God of the River *rises with* Amoret *in his arms.*

God of the R. What powerful charms my streams do bring
    Back again unto their spring,
    With such force that I their god,
    Three times striking with my rod,
    Could not keep them in their ranks?
    My fishes shoot into the banks;
    There's not one that stays and feeds,
    All have hid them in the weeds.
    Here's a mortal almost dead,
    Fall'n into my river-head,
    Hallowed so with many a spell,
    That till now none ever fell.
    'Tis a female young and clear,
    Cast in by some ravisher:
    See, upon her breast a wound,
    On which there is no plaster bound.
    Yet, she's warm, her pulses beat,
    'Tis a sign of life and heat.—
    If thou be'st a virgin pure,
    I can give a present cure:
    Take a drop into thy wound,
    From my watery locks, more round
    Than orient pearl, and far more pure
    Than unchaste flesh may endure.—
    See, she pants, and from her flesh
    The warm blood gusheth out afresh.
    She is an unpolluted maid;
    I must have this bleeding stayed.
    From my banks I pluck this flower
    With holy hand, whose virtuous power
    Is at once to heal and draw.
    The blood returns.   I never saw
    A fairer mortal.   Now doth break
    Her deadly slumber.—Virgin, speak.

Amo. Who hath restored my sense, given me new breath,
 And brought me back out of the arms of death?
God of the R. I have healed thy wounds.
Amo.   Aye, me!
God of the R. Fear-not him that succoured thee.
 I am this fountain's god: below,
 My waters to a river grow,
 And 'twixt two banks with osiers set,
 That only prosper in the wet,
 Through the meadows do they glide,
 Wheeling still on every side,
 Sometimes winding round about,
 To find the evenest channel out.
 And if thou wilt go with me,
 Leaving mortal company,
 In the cool streams shalt thou lie,
 Free from harm as well as I:
 I will give thee for thy food
 No fish that useth in the mud;
 But trout and pike, that love to swim
 Where the gravel from the brim
 Through the pure streams may be seen;
 Orient pearl fit for a queen,
 Will I give, thy love to win,
 And a shell to keep them in;
 Not a fish in all my brook
 That shall disobey thy look,
 But, when thou wilt, come sliding by,
 And from thy white hand take a fly:
 And, to make thee understand
 How I can my waves command,
 They shall bubble, whilst I sing,
 Sweeter than the silver string.   [*Sings.*

     Do not fear to put thy feet
     Naked in the river sweet;
     Think not leech, or newt, or toad,
     Will bite thy foot, when thou hast trod;
     Nor let the water rising high,
     As thou wad'st in, make thee cry
     And sob; but ever live with me,
     And not a wave shall trouble thee.

Amo. Immortal power, that rul'st this holy flood,
 I know myself unworthy to be wooed

By thee, a god; for ere this, but for thee,
I should have shown my weak mortality:
Besides, by holy oath betwixt us twain,
I am betrothed unto a shepherd-swain,
Whose comely face, I know, the gods above
May make me leave to see, but not to love.
God of the R. May he prove to thee as true!
Fairest virgin, now adieu:
I must make my waters fly,
Lest they leave their channels dry,
And beasts that come unto the spring
Miss their morning's watering;
Which I would not; for of late
All the neighbour-people sate
On my banks, and from the fold
Two white lambs of three weeks old
Offered to my deity;
For which this year they shall be free
From raging floods, that as they pass
Leave their gravel in the grass;
Nor shall their meads be overflown
When their grass is newly mown.
Amo. For thy kindness to me shown,
Never from thy banks be blown
Any tree, with windy force,
Cross thy streams, to stop thy course;
May no beast that comes to drink,
With his horns cast down thy brink;
May none that for thy fish do look,
Cut thy banks to dam thy brook;
Barefoot may no neighbour wade
In thy cool streams, wife nor maid,
When the spawns on stones do lie,
To wash their hemp, and spoil the fry!
God of the R. Thanks, virgin.   I must down again.
Thy wound will put thee to no pain:
Wonder not so soon 'tis gone;
A holy hand was laid upon.   [*Descends.*
Amo. And I, unhappy born to be,
Must follow him that flies from me.   [*Exit.*

ACT IV

SCENE I.—*Part of the Wood.*

Enter PERIGOT.

Peri. She is untrue, unconstant, and unkind;
　　She's gone, she's gone! Blow high, thou north-west wind,
　　And raise the sea to mountains; let the trees
　　That dare oppose thy raging fury leese
　　Their firm foundation; creep into the earth,
　　And shake the world, as at the monstrous birth
　　Of some new prodigy; whilst I constant stand,
　　Holding this trusty boar-spear in my hand,
　　And falling thus upon it.　　　*[Offers to fall on his spear.*

Enter AMARILLIS *running.*

Amar. Stay thy dead-doing hand! thou art too hot
　　Against thyself.　Believe me, comely swain,
　　If that thou diest, not all the showers of rain
　　The heavy clouds send down can wash away
　　That foul unmanly guilt the world will lay
　　Upon thee.　Yet thy love untainted stands:
　　Believe me, she is constant; not the sands
　　Can be so hardly numbered as she won.
　　I do not trifle, shepherd; by the moon,
　　And all those lesser lights our eyes do view,
　　All that I told thee, Perigot, is true:
　　Then, be a free man; put away despair
　　And will to die; smooth gently up that fair,
　　Dejected forehead; be as when those eyes
　　Took the first heat.

Peri.　　　　　　　Alas, he double dies
　　That would believe, but cannot! 'Tis not well
　　You keep me thus from dying, here to dwell
　　With many worse companions.　But, oh, death!
　　I am not yet enamoured of this breath
　　So much but I dare leave it; 'tis not pain
　　In forcing of a wound, nor after-gain
　　Of many days, can hold me from my will:
　　'Tis not myself but Amoret, bids kill.

Amar. Stay but a little, little; but one hour;
    And if I do not show thee, through the power
    Of herbs and words I have, as dark as night,
    Myself turned to thy Amoret, in sight,
    Her very figure, and the robe she wears,
    With tawny buskins, and the hook she bears
    Of thine own carving, where your names are set,
    Wrought underneath with many a curious fret,
    The primrose-chaplet, tawdry-lace, and ring,
    Thou gav'st her for her singing, with each thing
    Else that she wears about her, let me feel
    The first fell stroke of that revenging steel!
Peri. I am contented, if there be a hope,
    To give it entertainment for the scope
    Of one poor hour.   Go; you shall find me next
    Under yon shady beech, even thus perplext,
    And thus believing.
Amar.   Bind, before I go,
    Thy soul by Pan unto me, not to do
    Harm or outrageous wrong upon thy life,
    Till my return.
Peri.   By Pan, and by the strife
    He had with Phœbus for the mastery,
    When golden Midas judged their minstrelsy,
    I will not!   [*Exeunt severally.*

SCENE II.—*The Wood before Clorin's Bower.*

Clorin *discovered in the Bower.*

Enter Satyr *carrying* Alexis.

Sat. Softly gliding as I go,
    With this burthen full of woe,
    Through still silence of the night,
    Guided by the glow-worm's light,
    Hither am I come at last.
    Many a thicket have I past;
    Not a twig that durst deny me,
    Not a bush that durst descry me
    To the little bird that sleeps
    On the tender spray; nor creeps
    That hardy worm with pointed tail,
    But if I be under sail,

Flying faster than the wind,
Leaving all the clouds behind,
But doth hide her tender head
In some hollow tree, or bed
Of seeded nettles; not a hare
Can be started from his fare
By my footing; nor a wish
Is more sudden, nor a fish
Can be found with greater ease
Cut the vast unbounded seas,
Leaving neither print nor sound,
Than I, when nimbly on the ground
I measure many a league an hour.
But, behold, the happy power
That must ease me of my charge,
And by holy hand enlarge
The soul of this sad man, that yet
Lies fast bound in deadly fit:
Heaven and great Pan succour it!—
Hail, thou beauty of the bower,
Whiter than the paramour
Of my master! Let me crave
Thy virtuous help, to keep from grave
This poor mortal, that here lies,
Waiting when the Destinies
Will undo his thread of life:
View the wound, by cruel knife
Trenched into him.

Clo. [*Coming from the bower.*] What art thou call'st me from
      my holy rites,
And with the fearèd name of death affrights
My tender ears? speak me thy name and will.

Sat. I am the Satyr that did fill
Your lap with early fruit; and will,
When I hap to gather more,
Bring you better and more store.
Yet I come not empty now:
See, a blossom from the bough;
But beshrew his heart that pulled it,
And his perfect sight that culled it
From the other springing blooms!
For a sweeter youth the grooms
Cannot show me, nor the downs,

Nor the many neighbouring towns.
Low in yonder glade I found him;
Softly in mine arms I bound him;
Hither have I brought him sleeping
In a trance, his wounds fresh weeping,
In remembrance such youth may
Spring and perish in a day.

Clo. Satyr, they wrong thee that do term thee rude;
Though thou be'st outward-rough and tawny-hued,
Thy manners are as gentle and as fair
As his who brags himself born only heir
To all humanity.   Let me see the wound:
This herb will stay the current, being bound
Fast to the orifice, and this restrain
Ulcers and swellings, and such inward pain
As the cold air hath forced into the sore;
This to draw out such putrefying gore
As inward falls.

Sat. Heaven grant it may do good!

Clo. Fairly wipe away the blood:
Hold him gently, till I fling
Water of a virtuous spring
On his temples; turn him twice
To the moonbeams; pinch him thrice;
That the labouring soul may draw
From his great eclipse.

Sat.   I saw
His eyelids moving.

Clo.   Give him breath;
All the danger of cold death
Now is vanished! with this plaster,
And this unction do I master
All the festered ill that may
Give him grief another day.

Sat. See, he gathers up his sprite,
And begins to hunt for light;
Now he gapes and breathes again:
How the blood runs to the vein
That erst was empty!

Alexis.   O my heart!
My dearest, dearest Cloe!   Oh, the smart
Runs through my side!   I feel some pointed thing
Pass through my bowels, sharper than the sting

Of scorpion.—
Pan, preserve me!—What are you?
Do not hurt me: I am true
To my Cloe, though she fly,
And leave me to this destiny:
There she stands, and will not lend
Her smooth white hand to help her friend.
But I am much mistaken, for that face
Bears more austerity and modest grace,
More reproving and more awe,
Than these eyes yet ever saw
In my Cloe.   Oh, my pain
Eagerly renews again!
Give me your help for his sake you love best.

Clo. Shepherd, thou canst not possibly take rest,
Till thou hast laid aside all heats, desires,
Provoking thoughts that stir up lusty fires,
Commerce with wanton eyes, strong blood, and will
To execute; these must be purged until
The vein grow whiter; then repent, and pray
Great Pan to keep you from the like decay,
And I shall undertake your care with ease;
Till when, this virtuous plaster will displease
Your tender sides.   Give me your hand, and rise!
Help him a little, Satyr; for his thighs
Yet are feeble.

Alexis. [*Rising.*]   Sure, I have lost much blood.

Sat. 'Tis no matter; 'twas not good.
Mortal, you must leave your wooing:
Though there be a joy in doing,
Yet it brings much grief behind it;
They best feel it, that do find it.

Clo. Come, bring him in; I will attend his sore.—
When you are well, take heed you lust no more.
                        [*Alexis is led into the bower.*

Sat. Shepherd, see, what comes of kissing;
By my head, 'twere better missing.
Brightest, if there be remaining
Any service, without feigning
I will do it; were I set
To catch the nimble wind, or get
Shadows gliding on the green,
Or to steal from the great queen

Of fairies all her beauty;
I would do it, so much duty
Do I owe those precious eyes.

Clo. I thank thee, honest Satyr. If the cries
Of any other, that be hurt or ill,
Draw thee unto them, prithee, do thy will
To bring them hither.

Sat. I will; and when the weather
Serves to angle in the brook,
I will bring a silver hook,
With a line of finest silk,
And a rod as white as milk,
To deceive the little fish:
So I take my leave, and wish
On this bower may ever dwell
Spring and summer!

Clo.   Friend, farewell. [*Exit Satyr.   Scene closes.*

SCENE III.—*Part of the Wood with the Holy Well.*

Enter AMORET.

Amo. This place is ominous; for here I lost
My love and almost life, and since have crost
All these woods over; ne'er a nook or dell,
Where any little bird or beast doth dwell,
But I have sought it; ne'er a bending brow
Of any hill, or glade the wind sings through,
Nor a green bank, nor shade where shepherds use
To sit and riddle, sweetly pipe, or choose
Their valentines, that I have missed, to find
My love in.   Perigot!   Oh, too unkind,
Why hast thou fled me? whither art thou gone?
How have I wronged thee? was my love alone
To thee worthy this scorned recompense?   'Tis well;
I am content to feel it.   But I tell
Thee, shepherd, and these lusty woods shall hear,
Forsaken Amoret is yet as clear
Of any stranger fire, as heaven is
From foul corruption, or the deep abyss
From light and happiness; and thou mayst know
All this for truth, and how that fatal blow
Thou gav'st me, never from desert of mine
Fell on my life, but from suspect of thine,

Or fury more than madness: therefore here,
Since I have lost my life, my love, my dear,
Upon this cursèd place, and on this green
That first divorced us, shortly shall be seen
A sight of so great pity, that each eye
Shall daily spend his spring in memory
Of my untimely fall.

Enter AMARILLIS.

Amar.   I am not blind,
Nor is it through the working of my mind
That this shows Amoret. Forsake me, all
That dwell upon the soul, but what men call
Wonder, or, more than wonder, miracle!
For, sure, so strange as this, the oracle
Never gave answer of; it passeth dreams,
Or madmen's fancy, when the many streams
Of new imaginations rise and fall:
'Tis but an hour since these ears heard her call
For pity to young Perigot; whilst he
Directed by his fury, bloodily
Lanched up her breast, which bloodless fell and cold;
And, if belief may credit what was told,
After all this, the Melancholy Swain
Took her into his arms, being almost slain,
And to the bottom of the holy well
Flung her, for ever with the waves to dwell.
'Tis she, the very same; 'tis Amoret,
And living yet; the great powers will not let
Their virtuous love be crossed. [*Aside.*]—Maid, wipe
    away
Those heavy drops of sorrow, and allay
The storm that yet goes high, which, not deprest,
Breaks heart and life and all before it rest.
Thy Perigot——
Amo.   Where, which is Perigot?
Amar. Sits there below, lamenting much, God wot,
Thee and thy fortune. Go, and comfort him;
And thou shalt find him underneath a brim
Of sailing pines, that edge yon mountain in.
Amo. I go, I run. Heaven grant me I may win
His soul again!   [*Exit.*

Enter Sullen Shepherd.

Sull. Shep. Stay, Amarillis, stay!
　You are too fleet; 'tis two hours yet to day.
　I have performed my promise; let us sit
　And warm our bloods together, till the fit
　Come lively on us.
Amar. Friend, you are too keen;
　The morning riseth, and we shall be seen;
　Forbear a little.
Sull. Shep. I can stay no longer.
Amar. Hold, shepherd, hold! learn not to be a wronger
　Of your word. Was not your promise laid,
　To break their loves first?
Sull. Shep. I have done it, maid.
Amar. No; they are yet unbroken, met again,
　And are as hard to part yet as the stain
　Is from the finest lawn.
Sull. Shep. I say, they are
　Now at this present parted, and so far
　That they shall never meet.
Amar. Swain, 'tis not so;
　For do but to yon hanging mountain go,
　And there believe your eyes.
Sull. Shep. You do but hold
　Off with delays and trifles.—Farewell, cold
　And frozen bashfulness, unfit for men!—
　Thus I salute thee, virgin! 　　*[Attempts to seize her.*
Amar. And thus, then,
　I bid you follow: catch me if you can! *[Exit running.*
Sull. Shep. And, if I stay behind, I am no man!
　　　　　　　　　　　　[Exit, running after her.

SCENE IV.—*A Dale in the Wood.*

Enter PERIGOT.

Peri. Night, do not steal away; I woo thee yet
　To hold a hard hand o'er the rusty bit
　That guides thy lazy team. Go back again,
　Boötes, thou that driv'st thy frozen wain
　Round as a ring, and bring a second night,
　To hide my sorrows from the coming light;
　Let not the eyes of men stare on my face,

And read my falling; give me some black place,
Where never sunbeam shot his wholesome light,
That Ì may sit and pour out my sad sprite
Like running water, never to be known
After the forcèd fall and sound is gone.

Enter AMORET.

Amo. This is the bottom.—Speak, if thou be here,
    My Perigot! Thy Amoret, thy dear,
    Calls on thy lovèd name.
Peri.   What art thou dare
    Tread these forbidden paths, where death and care
    Dwell on the face of darkness?
Amo.   'Tis thy friend,
    Thy Amoret, come hither, to give end
    To these consumings. Look up, gentle boy:
    I have forgot those pains and dear annoy
    I suffered for thy sake, and am content
    To be thy love again. Why hast thou rent
    Those curlèd locks, where I have often hung
    Ribbons and damask-roses, and have flung
    Waters distilled, to make thee fresh and gay,
    Sweeter than nosegays on a bridal day?
    Why dost thou cross thine arms, and hang thy face
    Down to thy bosom, letting fall apace
    From those two little heavens, upon the ground,
    Showers of more price, more orient, and more round,
    Than those that hang upon the moon's pale brow?
    Cease these complainings, shepherd: I am now
    The same I ever was, as kind and free,
    And can forgive before you ask of me;
    Indeed, I can and will.
Peri.   So spoke my fair!
    Oh, you great working powers of earth and air,
    Water and forming fire, why have you lent
    Your hidden virtues of so ill intent?
    Even such a face, so fair, so bright of hue,
    Had Amoret; such words, so smooth and new,
    Came flowing from her tongue; such was her eye,
    And such the pointed sparkle that did fly
    Forth like a bleeding shaft; all is the same,
    The robe and buskins, painted hook, and frame
    Of all her body. Oh me, Amoret!

Amo. Shepherd, what means this riddle? who hath set
    So strong a difference 'twixt myself and me,
    That I am grown another? Look, and see
    The ring thou gav'st me, and about my wrist
    That curious bracelet thou thyself didst twist
    From those fair tresses. Know'st thou Amoret?
    Hath not some newer love forced thee forget
    Thy ancient faith?
Peri.   Still nearer to my love!
    These be the very words she oft did prove
    Upon my temper; so she still would take
    Wonder into her face, and silent make
    Signs with her head and hand, as who would say,
    " Shepherd, remember this another day."
Amo. Am I not Amoret? where was I lost?
    Can there be heaven, and time, and men, and most
    Of these inconstant? Faith, where art thou fled?
    Are all the vows and protestations dead,
    The hands held up, the wishes and the heart?
    Is there not one remaining, not a part
    Of all these to be found? Why, then, I see
    Men never knew that virtue, constancy.
Peri. Men ever were most blessèd, till cross fate
    Brought love and woman forth, unfortunate
    To all that ever tasted of their smiles;
    Whose actions are all double, full of wiles;
    Like to the subtle hare, that 'fore the hounds
    Makes many turnings, leaps and many rounds,
    This way and that way, to deceive the scent
    Of her pursuers.
Amo.   'Tis but to prevent
    Their speedy coming on, that seek her fall;
    The hands of cruel men, more bestial,
    And of a nature more refusing good
    Than beasts themselves or fishes of the flood.
Peri. Thou art all these, and more than nature meant
    When she created all; frowns, joys, content;
    Extreme fire for an hour, and presently
    Colder than sleepy poison, or the sea
    Upon whose face sits a continual frost;
    Your actions ever driven to the most,
    Then down again as low, that none can find
    The rise or falling of a woman's mind.

Amo. Can there be any age, or days, or time,
    Or tongues of men, guilty so great a crime
    As wronging simple maid? Oh, Perigot,
    Thou that wast yesterday without a blot;
    Thou that wast every good and everything
    That men call blessèd; thou that wast the spring
    From whence our looser grooms drew all their best;
    Thou that wast always just and always blest
    In faith and promise; thou that hadst the name
    Of virtuous given thee, and made good the same
    Even from thy cradle; thou that wast that all
    That men delighted in! Oh, what a fall
    Is this, to have been so, and now to be
    The only best in wrong and infamy!
    And I to live to know this! and by me,
    That loved thee dearer than mine eyes, or that
    Which we esteemed our honour, virgin-state!
    Dearer than swallows love the early morn,
    Or dogs of chase the sound of merry horn;
    Dearer than thou canst love thy new love, if thou hast
    Another, and far dearer than the last;
    Dearer than thou canst love thyself, though all
    The self-love were within thee that did fall
    With that coy swain that now is made a flower,
    For whose dear sake Echo weeps many a shower!
    And am I thus rewarded for my flame?
    Loved worthily to get a wanton's name?
    Come, thou forsaken willow, wind my head,
    And noise it to the world, my love is dead!
    I am forsaken, I am cast away,
    And left for every lazy groom to say
    I was unconstant, light, and sooner lost
    Than the quick clouds we see, or the chill frost
    When the hot sun beats on it! Tell me yet,
    Canst thou not love again thy Amoret?
Peri. Thou art not worthy of that blessed name:
    I must not know thee: fling thy wanton flame
    Upon some lighter blood that may be hot
    With words and feignèd passions; Perigot
    Was ever yet unstained, and shall not now
    Stoop to the meltings of a borrowed brow.
Amo. Then hear me, Heaven, to whom I call for right,
    And you, fair twinkling stars, that crown the night;

And hear me, woods, and silence of this place,
And ye, sad hours, that move a sullen pace;
Hear me, ye shadows, that delight to dwell
In horrid darkness, and ye powers of hell,
Whilst I breathe out my last!   I am that maid,
That yet-untainted Amoret, that played
The careless prodigal, and gave away
My soul to this young man that now dares say
I am a stranger, not the same, more vild;
And thus with much belief I was beguiled:
I am that maid, that have delayed, denied,
And almost scorned the loves of all that tried
To win me, but this swain; and yet confess
I have been wooed by many with no less
Soul of affection; and have often had
Rings, belts, and cracknels, sent me from the lad
That feeds his flocks down westward; lambs and doves
By young Alexis; Daphnis sent me gloves;
All which I gave to thee: nor these nor they
That sent them did I smile on, or e'er lay
Up to my after-memory.   But why
Do I resolve to grieve, and not to die?
Happy had been the stroke thou gav'st, if home;
By this time had I found a quiet room,
Where every slave is free, and every breast,
That living bred new care, now lies at rest;
And thither will poor Amoret.

Peri.   Thou must.
Was ever any man so loath to trust
His eyes as I? or was there ever yet
Any so like as this to Amoret?
For whose dear sake I promise, if there be
A living soul within thee, thus to free
Thy body from it!   [*Wounds her with his spear.*

Amo. [*Falling.*]   So, this work hath end.
Farewell, and live; be constant to thy friend
That loves thee next.

Enter Satyr; Perigot *runs off.*

Sat. See, the day begins to break,
And the light shoots like a streak
Of subtle fire; the wind blows cold,

Whilst the morning doth unfold;
Now the birds begin to rouse,
And the squirrel from the boughs
Leaps, to get him nuts and fruit:
The early lark, that erst was mute,
Carols to the rising day
Many a note and many a lay:
Therefore here I end my watch,
Lest the wandering swain should catch
Harm, or lose himself.

Amo.   Ah me!

Sat. Speak again, whate'er thou be;
I am ready; speak, I say;
By the dawning of the day,
By the power of night and Pan,
I enforce thee speak again!

Amo. Oh, I am most unhappy!

Sat. Yet more blood!
Sure, these wanton swains are wood.
Can there be a hand or heart
Dare commit so vild a part
As this murder? By the moon,
That hid herself when this was done,
Never was a sweeter face:
I will bear her to the place
Where my goddess keeps, and crave
Her to give her life or grave.   [*Exit, carrying Amoret.*

SCENE V.—*The Wood before* Clorin's *Bower.*

Enter Clorin.

Clo. Here whilst one patient takes his rest secure,
I steal abroad to do another cure.—
Pardon, thou buried body of my love,
That from thy side I dare so soon remove;
I will not prove unconstant, nor will leave
Thee for an hour alone: when I deceive
My first-made vow, the wildest of the wood
Tear me, and o'er thy grave let out my blood!
I go by wit to cure a lover's pain,
Which no herb can; being done, I'll come again. [*Exit.*

Enter THENOT.

The. Poor shepherd, in this shade for ever lie,
    And seeing thy fair Clorin's cabin, die!   [*Lying down.*
    Oh, hapless love, which being answered, ends!
    And, as a little infant cries and bends
    His tender brows, when, rolling of his eye,
    He hath espied something that glisters nigh,
    Which he would have, yet, give it him, away
    He throws it straight, and cries afresh to play
    With something else; such my affection, set
    On that which I should loathe, if I could get.

Re-enter CLORIN.

Clo. See, where he lies!   Did ever man but he
    Love any woman for her constancy
    To her dead lover, which she needs must end
    Before she can allow him for her friend,
    And he himself must needs the cause destroy
    For which he loves, before he can enjoy?
    Poor shepherd, Heaven grant I at once may free
    Thee from thy pain, and keep my loyalty!—   [*Aside.*
    Shepherd, look up.
The.   Thy brightness doth amaze;
    So Phœbus may at noon bid mortals gaze;
    Thy glorious constancy appears so bright,
    I dare not meet the beams with my weak sight.
Clo. Why dost thou pine away thyself for me?
The. Why dost thou keep such spotless constancy?
Clo. Thou holy shepherd, see what for thy sake
    Clorin, thy Clorin, now dare undertake.
The. [*Starting up.*] Stay there, thou constant Clorin! if
      there be
    Yet any part of woman left in thee,
    To make thee light, think yet before thou speak.
Clo. See, what a holy vow for thee I break;
    I, that already have my fame far spread
    For being constant to my lover dead.
The. Think yet, dear Clorin, of your love; how true,
    If you had died, he would have been to you.
Clo. Yet, all I'll lose for thee——
The.   Think but how blest

A constant woman is above the rest!

Clo. And offer up myself, here on this ground,
To be disposed by thee.

The.   Why dost thou wound
His heart with malice against women more,
That hated all the sex but thee before?
How much more pleasant had it been to me
To die than to behold this change in thee!
Yet, yet return; let not the woman sway!

Clo. Insult not on her now, nor use delay,
Who for thy sake hath ventured all her fame.

The. Thou hast not ventured, but bought certain shame:
Your sex's curse, foul falsehood, must and shall,
I see, once in your lives, light on you all.
I hate thee now.   Yet turn!

Clo.   Be just to me:
Shall I at once lose both my fame and thee?

The. Thou hadst no fame; that which thou didst like good
Was but thy appetite that swayed thy blood
For that time to the best: for as a blast
That through a house comes, usually doth cast
Things out of order, yet by chance may come,
And blow some one thing to his proper room,
So did thy appetite, and not thy zeal,
Sway thee by chance to do some one thing well.
Yet turn!

Clo.   Thou dost but try me, if I would
Forsake thy dear embraces for my old
Love's, though he were alive: but do not fear.

The. I do contemn thee now, and dare come near,
And gaze upon thee; for methinks that grace,
Austerity, which sate upon that face,
Is gone, and thou like others.   False maid, see,
This is the gain of foul inconstancy!   [*Exit.*

Clo. 'Tis done:—great Pan, I give thee thanks for it!—
What art could not have cured is healed by wit.

Re-enter THENOT.

The. Will you be constant yet? will you remove
Into the cabin to your buried love?

Clo. No, let me die, but by thy side remain.

The. There's none shall know but thou didst ever stain

Thy worthy strictness, but shalt honoured be,
And I will lie again under this tree,
And pine and die for thee with more delight
Than I have sorrow now to know thee light.
Clo. Let me have thee, and I'll be where thou wilt.
The. Thou art of women's race, and full of guilt.
Farewell all hope of that sex! Whilst I thought
There was one good, I feared to find one naught:
But since their minds I all alike espy,
Henceforth I'll choose, as others, by mine eye.   [*Exit.*
Clo. Blest be ye powers that gave such quick redress,
And for my labours sent so good success!
I rather choose, though I a woman be,
He should speak ill of all than die for me.
    [*Exit into the bower.*

ACT V

SCENE I.—*A Village.*

Enter Priest of Pan *and* Old Shepherd.

Priest. Shepherds, rise, and shake off sleep!
See, the blushing morn doth peep
Through the windows, whilst the sun
To the mountain-tops is run,
Gilding all the vales below
With his rising flames, which grow
Greater by his climbing still.
Up, ye lazy grooms, and fill
Bag and bottle for the field!
Clasp your cloaks fast, lest they yield
To the bitter north-east wind.
Call the maidens up, and find
Who lay longest, that she may
Go without a friend all day;
Then reward your dogs, and pray
Pan to keep you from decay:
So unfold, and then away!
What, not a shepherd stirring? Sure, the grooms
Have found their beds too easy, or the rooms
Filled with such new delight and heat, that they
Have both forgot their hungry sheep and day.

Knock, that they may remember what a shame
Sloth and neglect lays on a shepherd's name.

Old Shep. [*After knocking at several doors.*] It is to little
purpose; not a swain
This night hath known his lodging here, or lain
Within these cotes; the woods, or some near town
That is a neighbour to the bordering down,
Hath drawn them thither, 'bout some lusty sport,
Or spicèd wassail bowl, to which resort
All the young men and maids of many a cote,
Whilst the trim minstrel strikes his merry note.

Priest. God pardon sin!—Show me the way that leads
To any of their haunts.

Old Shep.   This to the meads,
And that down to the woods.

Priest.   Then, this for me.
Come, shepherd, let me crave your company.   [*Exeunt.*

SCENE II.—*The Wood before* Clorin's *Bower.*

CLORIN *and* ALEXIS *discovered in the bower; at the side
of the stage, a hollow tree, in which are* CLOE *and* DAPHNIS.

Clo. Now your thoughts are almost pure,
And your wound begins to cure;
Strive to banish all that's vain,
Lest it should break out again.

Alex. Eternal thanks to thee, thou holy maid!
I find my former wandering thoughts well staid
Through thy wise precepts; and my outward pain
By thy choice herbs is almost gone again:
Thy sex's vice and virtue are revealed
At once; for what one hurt another healed.

Clo. May thy grief more appease!
Relapses are the worst disease.
Take heed how you in thought offend;
So mind and body both will mend.

Enter Satyr, *carrying* AMORET.

Amo. Be'st thou the wildest creature of the wood,
That bear'st me thus away, drowned in my blood,
And dying, know I cannot injured be;
I am a maid; let that name fight for me.

Sat. Fairest virgin, do not fear
　　Me, that doth thy body bear,
　　Not to hurt, but healed to be;
　　Men are ruder far than we.—
　　See, fair goddess, in the wood
　　They have let out yet more blood:
　　Some savage man hath struck her breast,
　　So soft and white, that no wild beast
　　Durst have touched, asleep or 'wake;
　　So sweet, that adder, newt, or snake,
　　Would have lain, from arm to arm,
　　On her bosom to be warm
　　All a night, and, being hot,
　　Gone away, and stung her not.
　　Quickly clap herbs to her breast.
　　A man, sure, is a kind of beast.
Clo. With spotless hand on spotless breast
　　I put these herbs, to give thee rest:
　　Which till I heal thee, there will bide,
　　If both be pure; if not, off slide.—
　　See, it falls off from the wound!
　　Shepherdess, thou art not sound,
　　Full of lust.
Sat. 　　　　　　Who would have thought it?
　　So fair a face!
Clo. 　　　　　　Why, that hath brought it.
Amo. For aught I know or think, these words my last,
　　Yet, Pan so help me as my thoughts are chaste!
Clo. And so may Pan bless this my cure,
　　As all my thoughts are just and pure!
　　Some uncleanness nigh doth lurk,
　　That will not let my medicines work.—
　　Satyr, search if thou canst find it.
Sat. Here away methinks I wind it:
　　Stronger yet.—Oh, here they be;
　　Here, here, in a hollow tree,
　　Two fond mortals have I found.
Clo. Bring them out; they are unsound.
Sat. [*Bringing out Cloe and Daphnis.*] By the fingers thus I
　　　　wring ye,
　　To my goddess thus I bring ye;
　　Strife is vain, come gently in.—
　　I scented them; they're full of sin.

Clo. Hold, Satyr; take this glass,
  Sprinkle over all the place,
  Purge the air from lustful breath,
  To save this shepherdess from death:
  And stand you still whilst I do dress
  Her wound, for fear the pain increase.
Sat. From this glass I throw a drop
  Of crystal water on the top
  Of every grass, on flowers a pair:
  Send a fume, and keep the air
  Pure and wholesome, sweet and blest,
  Till this virgin's wound be drest.
Clo. Satyr, help to bring her in.
Sat. By Pan, I think she hath no sin,
      [Carrying Amoret into the bower.
  She is so light.—Lie on these leaves.
  Sleep, that mortal sense deceives,
  Crown thine eyes and ease thy pain;
  May'st thou soon be well again!
Clo. Satyr, bring the shepherd near;
  Try him, if his mind be clear.
Sat. Shepherd, come.
Daph.   My thoughts are pure.
Sat. The better trial to endure.
Clo. In this flame his finger thrust,
  Which will burn him if he lust;
  But if not, away will turn,
  As loath unspotted flesh to burn.—
    [Satyr applies Daphnis's finger to the taper.
  See, it gives back; let him go.
Sat. Farewell, mortal: keep thee so. *[Exit Daphnis.*
  Stay, fair nymph; fly not so fast;
  We must try if you be chaste.—
  Here's a hand that quakes for fear;
  Sure, she will not prove so clear.
Clo. Hold her finger to the flame;
  That will yield her praise or shame.
Sat. To her doom she dares not stand,
      [Applies Cloe's finger to the taper.
  But plucks away her tender hand;
  And the taper darting sends
  His hot beams at her fingers' ends.—
  Oh, thou art foul within, and hast

A mind, if nothing else, unchaste!
Alex. Is not that Cloe? 'Tis my love, 'tis she!
    Cloe, fair Cloe!
Cloe. My Alexis!
Alex.   He.
Cloe.   Let me embrace thee.
Clo. Take her hence,
    Lest her sight disturb his sense.
Alex. Take not her; take my life first!
Clo. See, his wound again is burst:
    Keep her near, here in the wood,
    Till I have stopt these streams of blood.
                    [Satyr leads off Cloe.
    Soon again he ease shall find,
    If I can but still his mind.
    This curtain thus I do display,
    To keep the piercing air away.
        [Draws a curtain before the bower. Scene closes.

SCENE III.—*A Pasture.*

Enter Old Shepherd *and* Priest of Pan.

Priest. Sure, they are lost for ever: 'tis in vain
    To find them out with trouble and much pain,
    That have a ripe desire and forward will
    To fly the company of all but ill.
    What shall be counselled now? shall we retire,
    Or constant follow still that first desire
    We had to find them?
Old Shep.   Stay a little while;
    For, if the morning's mist do not beguile
    My sight with shadows, sure I see a swain;
    One of this jolly troop's come back again.

Enter THENOT.

Priest. Dost thou not blush, young shepherd, to be known
    Thus without care leaving thy flocks alone,
    And following what desire and present blood
    Shapes out before thy burning sense for good;
    Having forgot what tongue hereafter may
    Tell to the world thy falling off, and say
    Thou art regardless both of good and shame.

Spurning at virtue and a virtuous name?
And like a glorious desperate man, that buys
A poison of much price, by which he dies,
Dost thou lay out for lust, whose only gain
Is foul disease, with present age and pain,
And then a grave? These be the fruits that grow
In such hot veins, that only beat to know
Where they may take most ease, and grow ambitious
Through their own wanton fire and pride delicious.

The. Right holy sir, I have not known this night
What the smooth face of mirth was, or the sight
Of any looseness; music, joy, and ease,
Have been to me as bitter drugs to please
A stomach lost with weakness, not a game
That I am skilled at thoroughly: nor a dame,
Went her tongue smoother than the feet of time,
Her beauty ever-living like the rhyme
Our blessèd Tityrus did sing of yore;
No, were she more enticing than the store
Of fruitful summer, when the loaden tree
Bids the faint traveller be bold and free;
'Twere but to me like thunder 'gainst the bay,
Whose lightning may enclose, but never stay
Upon his charmèd branches; such am I
Against the catching flames of woman's eye.

Priest. Then, wherefore hast thou wandered?
The.   'Twas a vow
That drew me out last night, which I have now
Strictly performed, and homewards go to give
Fresh pasture to my sheep, that they may live.

Priest. 'Tis good to hear you, shepherd, if the heart
In this well-sounding music bear his part.
Where have you left the rest?
The.   I have not seen,
Since yesternight we met upon this green
To fold our flocks up, any of that train;
Yet have I walked those woods round, and have lain
All this long night under an agèd tree;
Yet neither wandering shepherd did I see,
Or shepherdess; or drew into mine ear
The sound of living thing, unless it were
The nightingale, among the thick-leaved spring
That sits alone in sorrow, and doth sing

Whole nights away in mourning; or the owl,
Or our great enemy, that still doth howl
Against the moon's cold beams.
Priest.   Go, and beware
Of after-falling.
The.   Father, 'tis my care.   [*Exit.*

Enter Daphnis.

Old Shep. Here comes another straggler; sure I see
A shame in this young shepherd.—Daphnis?
Daph.   He.
Priest. Where hast thou left the rest, that should have been
Long before this grazing upon the green
Their yet-imprisoned flocks?
Daph.   Thou holy man,
Give me a little breathing, till I can
Be able to unfold what I have seen;
Such horror, that the like hath never been
Known to the ear of shepherd.   Oh, my heart
Labours a double motion to impart
So heavy tidings!   You all know the bower
Where the chaste Clorin lives, by whose great power
Sick men and cattle have been often cured;
There lovely Amoret, that was assured
To lusty Perigot, bleeds out her life,
Forced by some iron hand and fatal knife;
And, by her, young Alexis.

Enter Amarillis, *running.*

Amar.   If there be
Ever a neighbour-brook or hollow tree,
Receive my body, close me up from lust
That follows at my heels!   Be ever just,
Thou god of shepherds, Pan, for her dear sake
That loves the rivers' brinks, and still doth shake
In cold remembrance of thy quick pursuit;
Let me be made a reed, and, ever mute,
Nod to the waters' fall, whilst every blast
Sings through my slender leaves that I was chaste!
Priest. This is a night of wonder.—Amarill,
Be comforted: the holy gods are still
Revengers of these wrongs.

Amar.　　　　　　　　　　　　　Thou blessèd man,
　　Honoured upon these plains, and loved of Pan,
　　Hear me, and save from endless infamy
　　My yet-unblasted flower, virginity!
　　By all the garlands that have crowned that head,
　　By thy chaste office, and the marriage-bed
　　That still is blessed by thee; by all the rites
　　Due to our god, and by those virgin-lights
　　That burn before his altar; let me not
　　Fall from my former state, to gain the blot
　　That never shall be purged! I am not now
　　That wanton Amarillis: here I vow
　　To Heaven, and thee, grave father, if I may
　　Scape this unhappy night, to know the day
　　A virgin, never after to endure
　　The tongues or company of men unpure!
　　I hear him come; save me!
Priest.　　　　　　　　　　　　Retire a while
　　Behind this bush, till we have known that vile
　　Abuser of young maidens.　　　　　　*[They retire.*

　　　　　　　　Enter Sullen Shepherd.

Sull. Shep.　　　　　　　　　　Stay thy pace,
　　Most lovèd Amarillis; let the chase
　　Grow calm and milder; fly me not so fast:
　　I fear the pointed brambles have unlaced
　　Thy golden buskins. Turn again, and see
　　Thy shepherd follow, that is strong and free,
　　Able to give thee all content and ease:
　　I am not bashful, virgin; I can please
　　At first encounter, hug thee in mine arm,
　　And give thee many kisses, soft and warm
　　As those the sun prints on the smiling cheek
　　Of plums or mellow peaches; I am sleek
　　And smooth as Neptune when stern Æolus
　　Locks up his surly winds, and nimbly thus
　　Can show my active youth. Why dost thou fly?
　　Remember, Amarillis, it was I
　　That killed Alexis for thy sake, and set
　　An everlasting hate 'twixt Amoret
　　And her belovèd Perigot; 'twas I
　　That drowned her in the well, where she must lie

Till time shall leave to be. Then, turn again,
Turn with thy open arms, and clip the swain
That hath performed all this; turn, turn, I say;
I must not be deluded.
Priest. [*Coming forward.*] Monster, stay!
    Thou that art like a canker to the state
    Thou liv'st and breath'st in, eating with debate
    Through every honest bosom, forcing still
    The veins of any that may serve thy will;
    Thou that hast offered with a sinful hand
    To seize upon this virgin, that doth stand
    Yet trembling here!
Sull. Shep.   Good holiness, declare
    What had the danger been, if being bare
    I had embraced her; tell me, by your art,
    What coming wonders would that sight impart.
Priest. Lust and a branded soul.
Sull. Shep.   Yet, tell me more;
    Hath not our mother Nature, for her store
    And great encrease, said it is good and just,
    And willed that every living creature must
    Beget his like?
Priest.   You're better read than I,
    I must confess, in blood and lechery.—
    Now to the bower, and bring this beast along,
    Where he may suffer penance for his wrong. [*Exeunt.*

SCENE IV.—*Part of the Wood.*

Enter Perigot, *with his hand bloody.*

Peri. Here will I wash it in the morning's dew,
    Which she on every little grass doth strew
    In silver drops against the sun's appear:
    'Tis holy water, and will make me clear.
    My hand will not be cleansed.—My wrongèd love,
    If thy chaste spirit in the air yet move,
    Look mildly down on him that yet doth stand
    All full of guilt, thy blood upon his hand;
    And though I struck thee undeservedly,
    Let my revenge on her that injured thee
    Make less a fault which I intended not,
    And let these dew-drops wash away my spot!—

It will not cleanse. Oh, to what sacred flood
Shall I resort, to wash away this blood?
Amidst these trees the holy Clorin dwells,
In a low cabin of cut boughs, and heals
All wounds: to her I will myself address,
And my rash faults repentantly confess;
Perhaps she'll find a means, by art or prayer,
To make my hand, with chaste blood stainèd, fair.
That done, not far hence, underneath some tree
I'll have a little cabin built, since she
Whom I adored is dead; there will I give
Myself to strictness, and, like Clorin, live.   [*Exit.*

SCENE V.—*The Wood before Clorin's Bower.*

CLORIN *discovered sitting in the Bower,* AMORET *sitting on one
side of her,* ALEXIS *and* CLOE *on the other; the* Satyr
standing by.

Clo. Shepherd, once more your blood is staid:
　　Take example by this maid,
　　Who is healed ere you be pure;
　　So hard it is lewd lust to cure.
　　Take heed, then, how you turn your eye
　　On this other lustfully.—
　　And, shepherdess, take heed lest you
　　Move his willing eye thereto:
　　Let no wring, nor pinch, nor smile,
　　Of yours, his weaker sense beguile.—
　　Is your love yet true and chaste,
　　And for ever so to last?
Alex. I have forgot all vain desires,
　　All looser thoughts, ill-tempered fires:
　　True love I find a pleasant fume,
　　Whose moderate heat can ne'er consume.
Cloe. And I a new fire feel in me,
　　Whose chaste flame is not quenched to be.
Clo. Join your hands with modest touch,
　　And for ever keep you such.

Enter PERIGOT.

Peri. Yon is her cabin: thus far off I'll stand,
　　And call her forth; for my unhallowed hand

I dare not bring so near yon sacred place.—   [*Aside.*
Clorin, come forth, and do a timely grace
To a poor swain.

Clo. What art thou that dost call?
Clorin is ready to do good to all:
Come near.

Peri.   I dare not.

Clo.   Satyr, see
Who it is that calls on me.

Sat. [*Coming from the bower.*] There, at hand, some swain
    doth stand,
Stretching out a bloody hand.

Peri. Come, Clorin, bring thy holy waters clear,
To wash my hand.

Clo. [*Coming out.*] What wonders have been here
To-night! Stretch forth thy hand, young swain;
Wash and rub it, whilst I rain
Holy water.

Peri.   Still you pour,
But my hand will never scour.

Clo. Satyr, bring him to the bower:
We will try the sovereign power
Of other waters.

Sat.   Mortal, sure,
'Tis the blood of maiden pure
That stains thee so.

The Satyr *leads him to the Bower, where, seeing* AMORET,
he kneels down before her.

Peri.   Whate'er thou be,
Be'st thou her sprite, or some divinity,
That in her shape thinks good to walk this grove,
Pardon poor Perigot!

Amo.   I am thy love,
Thy Amoret, for evermore thy love:
Strike once more on my naked breast, I'll prove
As constant still. Oh, couldst thou love me yet,
How soon could I my former griefs forget!

Peri. So over-great with joy that you live, now
I am, that no desire of knowing how
Doth seize me. Hast thou still power to forgive?

Amo. Whilst thou hast power to love, or I to live:

More welcome now than hadst thou never gone
Astray from me!

Peri.   And when thou lov'st alone,
And not I thee, death, or some lingering pain
That's worse, light on me!

Clo.   Now your stain
Perhaps will cleanse thee; once again.
See, the blood that erst did stay,
With the water drops away.
All the powers again are pleased,
And with this new knot are appeased.
Join your hands, and rise together:
Pan be blessed that brought you hither!

      Enter Priest of Pan *and* Old Shepherd.

Go back again, whate'er thou art; unless
Smooth maiden-thoughts possess thee, do not press
This hallowed ground.—Go, Satyr, take his hand,
And give him present trial.

Sat.   Mortal, stand,
Till by fire I have made known
Whether thou be such a one
That mayst freely tread this place.
Hold thy hand up.—Never was
       [Applying the Priest's hand to the taper.
More untainted flesh than this.
Fairest, he is full of bliss.

Clo. Then boldly speak, why dost thou seek this place?

Priest. First, honoured virgin, to behold thy face,
Where all good dwells that is; next, for to try
The truth of late report was given to me,—
Those shepherds that have met with foul mischance
Through much neglect and more ill governance,
Whether the wounds they have may yet endure
The open air, or stay a longer cure;
And lastly, what the doom may be shall light
Upon those guilty wretches, through whose spite
All this confusion fell; for to this place,
Thou holy maiden, have I brought the race
Of these offenders, who have freely told
Both why and by what means they gave this bold
Attempt upon their lives.

Clo.   Fume all the ground,

And sprinkle holy water, for unsound
And foul infection 'gins to fill the air:
It gathers yet more strongly; take a pair
                        [*The Satyr fumes the ground, etc.*
Of censers filled with frankincense and myrrh,
Together with cold camphire: quickly stir
Thee, gentle Satyr, for the place begins
To sweat and labour with th' abhorrèd sins
Of those offenders: let them not come nigh,
For full of itching flame and leprosy
Their very souls are, that the ground goes back,
And shrinks to feel the sullen weight of black
And so unheard-of venom.—Hie thee fast,
Thou holy man, and banish from the chaste
These manlike monsters; let them never more
Be known upon these downs, but, long before
The next sun's rising, put them from the sight
And memory of every honest wight:
Be quick in expedition, lest the sores
Of these weak patients break into new gores.
                           [*Exit Priest of Pan.*

Peri. My dear, dear Amoret, how happy are
Those blessèd pairs, in whom a little jar
Hath bred an everlasting love, too strong
For time, or steel, or envy to do wrong!
How do you feel your hurts? Alas, poor heart,
How much I was abused! Give me the smart,
For it is justly mine.

Amo.   I do believe:
It is enough, dear friend; leave off to grieve,
And let us once more, in despite of ill,
Give hands and hearts again.

Peri.   With better will
Than e'er I went to find in hottest day
Cool crystal of the fountain, to allay
My eager thirst. May this band never break!
Hear us, oh, Heaven!

Amo.   Be constant.

Peri.   Else Pan wreak
With double vengeance my disloyalty!
Let me not dare to know the company
Of men, or any more behold those eyes!

Amo. Thus, shepherd, with a kiss all envy dies.

Re-enter Priest of Pan.

Priest. Bright maid, I have performed your will. The swain
    In whom such heat and black rebellions reign
    Hath undergone your sentence and disgrace:
    Only the maid I have reserved, whose face
    Shows much amendment; many a tear doth fall
    In sorrow of her fault: great fair, recall
    Your heavy doom, in hope of better days,
    Which I dare promise; once again upraise
    Her heavy spirit, that near drownèd lies
    In self-consuming care that never dies.
Clo. I am content to pardon; call her in.—
                  [Priest of Pan brings in Amarillis.
    The air grows cool again, and doth begin
    To purge itself: how bright the day doth show
    After this stormy cloud!—Go, Satyr, go,
    And with this taper boldly try her hand:
    If she be pure and good, and firmly stand
    To be so still, we have performed a work
    Worthy the gods themselves.
Sat. Come forward, maiden; do not lurk,
    Nor hide your face with grief and shame;
    Now or never get a name
    That may raise thee, and re-cure
    All thy life that was impure.
    Hold your hand unto the flame;
    If thou be'st a perfect dame,
    Or hast truly vowed to mend,
    This pale fire will be thy friend.—
                [Applies her hand to the taper.
    See, the taper hurts her not!
    Go thy ways; let never spot
    Henceforth seize upon thy blood:
    Thank the gods, and still be good.
Clo. Young shepherdess, now you are brought again
    To virgin-state, be so, and so remain
    To thy last day, unless the faithful love
    Of some good shepherd force thee to remove;
    Then labour to be true to him, and live
    As such a one that ever strives to give
    A blessèd memory to after-time;
    Be famous for your good, not for your crime.—

Now, holy man, I offer up again
These patients, full of health and free from pain:
Keep them from after-ills; be ever near
Unto their actions; teach them how to clear
The tedious way they pass through from suspect;
Keep them from wronging others, or neglect
Of duty in themselves; correct the blood
With thrifty bits and labour: let the flood,
Or the next neighbouring spring, give remedy
To greedy thirst and travail, not the tree
That hangs with wanton clusters; let not wine,
Unless in sacrifice or rites divine,
Be ever known of shepherds; have a care,
Thou man of holy life!   Now do not spare
Their faults through much remissness, nor forget
To cherish him whose many pains and sweat
Hath given increase and added to the downs;
Sort all your shepherds from the lazy clowns
That feed their heifers in the budded brooms;
Teach the young maidens strictness, that the grooms
May ever fear to tempt their blowing youth;
Banish all compliment, but single truth,
From every tongue and every shepherd's heart;
Let them still use persuading, but no art.
Thus, holy priest, I wish to thee and these
All the best goods and comforts that may please.

All. And all those blessings Heaven did ever give,
We pray upon this bower may ever live.

Priest. Kneel, every shepherd, while with powerful hand
I bless your after-labours, and the land
You feed your flocks upon.   Great Pan defend you
From misfortune, and amend you;
Keep you from those dangers still
That are followed by your will;
Give ye means to know at length,
All your riches, all your strength,
Cannot keep your foot from falling
To lewd lust, that still is calling
At your cottage, till his power
Bring again that golden hour
Of peace and rest to every soul;
May his care of you controul
All diseases, sores, or pain,

That in after-time may reign
Either in your flocks or you;
Give ye all affections new,
New desires, and tempers new,
That ye may be ever true!
Now rise, and go; and, as ye pass away,
Sing to the God of Sheep that happy lay
That honest Dorus taught ye,—Dorus, he
That was the soul and god of melody.

[*They sing and strew the ground with flowers*

All ye woods, and trees, and bowers,
All ye virtues and ye powers
That inhabit in the lakes,
In the pleasant springs or brakes,
    Move your feet
      To our sound,
    Whilst we greet
      All this ground
With his honour and his name
That defends our flocks from blame.

He is great, and he is just,
He is ever good, and must
Thus be honoured.   Daffadillies,
Roses, pinks, and lovèd lilies,
    Let us fling,
    Whilst we sing,
    Ever holy,
    Ever holy,
Ever honoured, ever young!
Thus great Pan is ever sung!

[*Exeunt all except Clorin and Satyr*

Sat. Thou divinest, fairest, brightest,
Thou most powerful maid and whitest,
Thou most virtuous and most blessèd,
Eyes of stars, and golden-tressèd
Like Apollo; tell me, sweetest,
What new service now is meetest
For the Satyr?   Shall I stray
In the middle air, and stay
The sailing rack, or nimbly take
Hold by the moon, and gently make
Suit to the pale queen of night
For a beam to give thee light?
Shall I dive into the sea,
And bring thee coral, making way
Through the rising waves that fall
In snowy fleeces?   Dearest, shall

I catch thee wanton fawns, or flies
Whose woven wings the summer dyes
Of many colours? get thee fruit,
Or steal from Heaven old Orpheus' lute?
All these I'll venture for, and more,
To do her service all these woods adore.

Clo. No other service, Satyr, but thy watch
About these thicks, lest harmless people catch
Mischief or sad mischance.

Sat. Holy virgin, I will dance
Round about these woods as quick
As the breaking light, and prick
Down the lawns and down the vales
Faster than the windmill-sails.
So I take my leave, and pray
All the comforts of the day,
Such as Phœbus' heat doth send
On the earth, may still befriend
Thee and this arbour!

Clo.   And to thee
All my master's love be free!   *[Exeunt.*

THE WILD-GOOSE CHASE

DRAMATIS PERSONÆ

DE GARD, *a noble stayed Gentle-man, that, being newly lighted from his Travels, assists his Sister Oriana, in her Chase of Mirabel the Wild-Goose.*

LA CASTRE, *the indulgent Father to Mirabel.*

MIRABEL, *the Wild-Goose, a travelled Monsieur, and great defier of all Ladies in the way of Marriage, otherwise their much loose Servant, at last caught by the despised Oriana.*

PINAC, *his Fellow-Traveller, of a lively spirit, and Servant to the no less sprightly Lillia-Bianca.*

BELLEUR, *Companion to both, of a stout blunt humour, in Love with Rosalura.*

NANTOLET, *Father to Rosalura and Lillia-Bianca.*

LUGIER, *the rough and confident Tutor to the Ladies, and chief engine to entrap the Wild-Goose.*

ORIANA, *the fair betrothed of Mirabel, and witty follower of the Chase.*

ROSALURA,
LILLIA-BIANCA, } *the airy Daughters of Nantolet.*

PETELLA, *their Waiting-Woman.*
MARIANA, *an English Courtesan.*
A Young Man *disguised as a Factor.*
Page, Servants, Singing-Boy, *Two* Merchants, Priest, *Four* Women.

SCENE.—PARIS.

ACT I

SCENE I.—*A Room in La Castre's House.*

Enter DE GARD, *and a* Footboy.

De Ga. Sirrah, you know I have rid hard; stir my horse well,
And let him want no litter.

Boy. I am sure I have run hard;
'Would somebody would walk me, and see me litter'd,
For I think my fellow horse cannot in reason
Desire more rest, nor take up his chamber before me:
But we are the beasts now, and the beasts are our masters.

De Ga. When you have done, step to the ten-crown ordinary——

Boy. With all my heart, sir; for I have a twenty-crown stomach.

De Ga. And there bespeak a dinner.

314

Boy. [*Going.*] Yes, sir, presently.
De Ga. For whom, I beseech you, sir?
Boy. For myself, I take it, sir.
De Ga. In truth, you shall not take it; 'tis not meant for
you;
There's for your provender.   Bespeak a dinner
For Monsieur Mirabel, and his companions;
They'll be in town within this hour.   When you have
done, sirrah,
Make ready all things at my lodgings, for me,
And wait me there.
Boy. The ten-crown ordinary?
De Ga. Yes, sir, if you have not forgot it.
Boy. I'll forget my feet first:
'Tis the best part of a footman's faith.   [*Exit Boy.*
De Ga. These youths,
For all they have been in Italy to learn thrift,
And seem to wonder at men's lavish ways,
Yet they cannot rub off old friends, their French itches;
They must meet sometimes to disport their bodies
With good wine, and good women; and good store too.
Let 'em be what they will, they are arm'd at all points,
And then hang saving, let the sea grow high!
This ordinary can fit 'em of all sizes.
They must salute their country with old customs.

Enter La Castre *and* Oriana.

Ori. Brother!
De Ga. My dearest sister!
Ori. Welcome, welcome!
Indeed, you are welcome home, most welcome!
De Ga. Thank ye!
You're grown a handsome woman, Oriana:
Blush at your faults.   I am wond'rous glad to see you!—
Monsieur La Castre, let not my affection
To my fair sister make me held unmannerly:
I am glad to see you well, to see you lusty,
Good health about you, and in fair company;
Believe me, I am proud——
La Ca. Fair sir, I thank you.
Monsieur De Gard, you are welcome from your journey!
Good men have still good welcome: Give me your hand,
sir.
*L 506

Once more, you are welcome home! You look still
    younger.

De Ga. Time has no leisure to look after us;
    We wander everywhere; age cannot find us.

La Ca. And how does all?

De Ga. All well, sir, and all lusty.

La Ca. I hope my son be so: I doubt not, sir,
    But you have often seen him in your journeys,
    And bring me some fair news.

De Ga. Your son is well, sir,
    And grown a proper gentleman; he's well, and lusty.
    Within this eight hours I took leave of him,
    And over-hied him, having some slight business
    That forced me out o' th' way: I can assure you,
    He will be here to-night.

La Ca. You make me glad, sir,
    For, o' my faith, I almost long to see him!
    Methinks he has been away——

De Ga. 'Tis but your tenderness;
    What are three years? a love-sick wench will allow it.
    His friends, that went out with him, are come back
      too,
    Belleur, and young Pinac: He bid me say little,
    Because he means to be his own glad messenger.

La Ca. I thank you for this news, sir.   He shall be welcome,
    And his friends too: Indeed, I thank you heartily!
    And how (for I dare say you will not flatter him)
    Has Italy wrought on him? has he mew'd yet
    His wild fantastic toys? They say, that climate
    Is a great purger of those humorous fluxes.
    How is he improved, I pray you?

De Ga. No doubt, sir, well.
    He has borne himself a full and noble gentleman;
    To speak him further is beyond my charter.

La Ca. I am glad to hear so much good.   Come, I see
    You long to enjoy your sister; yet I must entreat you,
    Before I go, to sup with me to-night,
    And must not be denied.

De Ga. I am your servant.

La Ca. Where you shall meet fair, merry, and noble company;
    My neighbour Nantolet; and his two fair daughters.

De Ga. Your supper's season'd well, sir: I shall wait upon
    you.

La Ca. Till then I'll leave ye: And you are once more
　　　welcome!　　　　　　　　　　　　　　　　　*[Exit.*
De Ga. I thank you, noble sir!—Now, Oriana,
　　　How have ye done since I went? have ye had your
　　　　health well?
　　　And your mind free?
Ori. You see, I am not bated;
　　　Merry, and eat my meat.
De Ga. A good preservative.
　　　And how have you been used? You know, Oriana,
　　　Upon my going out, at your request,
　　　I left your portion in La Castre's hands,
　　　The main means you must stick to: For that reason,
　　　And 'tis no little one, I ask you, sister,
　　　With what humanity he entertains you,
　　　And how you find his courtesy?
Ori. Most ready:
　　　I can assure you, sir, I am used most nobly.
De Ga. I am glad to hear it: But, I pr'ythee tell me,
　　　And tell me true, what end had you, Oriana,
　　　In trusting your money here? He is no kinsman,
　　　Nor any tie upon him of a guardian;
　　　Nor dare I think you doubt my prodigality.
Ori. No, certain, sir; none of all this provoked me;
　　　Another private reason.
De Ga. 'Tis not private,
　　　Nor carried so; 'tis common, my fair sister;
　　　Your love to Mirabel: Your blushes tell it.
　　　'Tis too much known, and spoken of too largely;
　　　And with no little shame I wonder at it.
Ori. Is it a shame to love?
De Ga. To love undiscreetly:
　　　A virgin should be tender of her honour,
　　　Close, and secure.
Ori. I am as close as can be,
　　　And stand upon as strong and honest guards too;
　　　Unless this warlike age need a portcullis.
　　　Yet, I confess, I love him.
De Ga. Hear the people.
Ori. Now I say, hang the people! he that dares
　　　Believe what they say, dares be mad, and give
　　　His mother, nay, his own wife, up to rumour.
　　　All grounds of truth, they build on, is a tavern;

And their best censure's sack, sack in abundance;
For as they drink, they think: They ne'er speak modestly,
Unless the wine be poor, or they want money.
Believe them? Believe Amadis de Gaul,
The Knight o' th' Sun, or Palmerin of England;
For these, to them, are modest and true stories!
Pray understand me; if their tongues be truth,
As if *in vino veritas* be an oracle,
What woman is, or has been ever, honest?
Give 'em but ten round cups, they'll swear Lucretia
Died not for want of power to resist Tarquin,
But want of pleasure that he stay'd no longer:
And Portia, that was famous for her piety
To her loved lord, they'll face ye out, died o' th' pox.

De Ga. Well, there is something, sister.

Ori. If there be, brother,
    'Tis none of their things; 'tis not yet so monstrous:
    My thing is marriage; and, at his return,
    I hope to put their squint eyes right again.

De Ga. Marriage? 'Tis true, his father is a rich man,
    Rich both in land and money; he his heir,
    A young and handsome man, I must confess too;
    But of such qualities, and such wild flings,
    Such admirable imperfections, sister,
    (For all his travel, and bought experience)
    I should be loth to own him for my brother.
    Methinks, a rich mind in a state indifferent
    Would prove the better fortune.

Ori. If he be wild.
    The reclaiming him to good and honest, brother,
    Will make much for my honour; which, if I prosper,
    Shall be the study of my love, and life too.

De Ga. You say well; 'would he thought as well, and loved too!
    He marry? he'll be hang'd first; he knows no more
    What the conditions and the ties of love are,
    The honest purposes and grounds of marriage,
    Nor will know, nor be ever brought to endeavour,
    Than I do how to build a church: He was ever
    A loose and strong defier of all order;
    His loves are wanderers, they knock at each door,
    And taste each dish, but are no residents.

Or say, he may be brought to think of marriage,
(As 'twill be no small labour) thy hopes are strangers:
I know, there is a labour'd match now follow'd,
Now at this time, for which he was sent for home too:
Be not abused; Nantolet has two fair daughters,
And he must take his choice.
Ori. Let him take freely:
    For all this I despair not; my mind tells me
    That I, and only I, must make him perfect;
    And in that hope I rest.
De Ga. Since you're so confident,
    Prosper your hope! I'll be no adversary;
    Keep yourself fair and right, he shall not wrong you.
Ori. When I forget my virtue, no man know me! [*Exeunt.*

SCENE II.—*A Street before the same House.*

Enter MIRABEL, PINAC, BELLEUR, *and* Servants.

Mir. Welcome to Paris, once more, gentlemen!
    We have had a merry and a lusty ordinary,
    And wine, and good meat, and a bouncing reckoning!
    And let it go for once; 'tis a good physic:
    Only the wenches are not for my diet;
    They are too lean and thin, their embraces brawn
        fallen.
    Give me the plump Venetian, fat, and lusty,
    That meets me soft and supple; smiles upon me,
    As if a cup of full wine leap'd to kiss me;
    These slight things I affect not.
Pinac. They are ill-built;
    Pin-buttock'd, like your dainty Barbaries,
    And weak i' th' pasterns; they'll endure no hardness.
Mir. There's nothing good or handsome bred amongst us:
    Till we are travell'd, and live abroad, we are coxcombs.
    You talk of France; a slight unseason'd country,
    Abundance of gross food, which makes us blockheads!
    We are fair set out indeed, and so are fore-horses:
    Men say, we are great courtiers; men abuse us!
    We are wise, and valiant too; *non credo, signor!*
    Our women the best linguists; they are parrots;
    O' this side the Alps they're nothing but mere drolleries.
    Ha! *Roma la Santa*, Italy for my money!
    Their policies, their customs, their frugalities,

Their courtesies so open, yet so reserved too,
As, when you think you are known best, you're a
    stranger;
Their very pick-teeth speak more man than we do,
And season of more salt!

Pinac. 'Tis a brave country;
Not pester'd with your stubborn precise puppies,
That turn all useful and allow'd contentments
To scabs and scruples: Hang 'em, capon-worshippers!

Bel. I like that freedom well, and like their women too,
And would fain do as others do; but I'm so bashful,
So naturally an ass——Look ye, I can look upon 'em,
And very willingly I go to see 'em,
(There's no man willinger) and I can kiss 'em,
And make a shift——

Mir. But if they chance to flout you,
Or say, " You are too bold! fy, sir, remember!
I pray, sit further off——"

Bel. 'Tis true—I am humbled,
I am gone; I confess ingenuously, I am silenced;
The spirit of amber cannot force me answer.

Pinac. Then would I sing and dance——

Bel. You have wherewithal, sir.

Pinac. And charge her up again.

Bel. I can be hang'd first;
Yet, where I fasten well, I am a tyrant.

Mir. Why, thou dar'st fight?

Bel. Yes, certainly I dare fight,
And fight with any man at any weapon;
'Would the other were no more! but a pox on't!
When I am sometimes in my height of hope,
And reasonable valiant that way, my heart harden'd,
Some scornful jest or other chops between me
And my desire: What would you have me to do then,
    gentlemen?

Mir. Belleur, you must be bolder: Travel three years,
And bring home such a baby to betray you
As bashfulness? a great fellow, and a soldier?

Bel. You have the gift of impudence; be thankful;
Every man has not the like talent. I will study,
And if it may be reveal'd to me——

Mir. Learn of me,
And of Pinac: No doubt, you'll find employment;

Ladies will look for courtship.

Pinac. 'Tis but fleshing,

But standing one good brunt or two. Hast thou any
mind to marriage?

We'll provide thee some soft-natur'd wench, that's
dumb too.

Mir. Or an old woman that cannot refuse thee in charity.

Bel. A dumb woman, or an old woman, that were eager,

And cared not for discourse, I were excellent at.

Mir. You must now put on boldness (there's no avoiding it)

And stand all hazards, fly at all games bravely;

They'll say, you went out like an ox, and return'd like
an ass else.

Bel. I shall make danger, sure.

Mir. I am sent for home now,

I know it is to marry; but my father shall pardon me:

Although it be a weighty ceremony,

And may concern me hereafter in my gravity,

I will not lose the freedom of a traveller;

A new strong lusty bark cannot ride at one anchor.

Shall I make divers suits to show to the same eyes?

'Tis dull and home-spun! study several pleasures,

And want employments for 'em? I'll be hang'd first!

Tie me to one smock? make my travels fruitless?

I'll none of that; for every fresh behaviour,

By your leave, father, I must have a fresh mistress,

And a fresh favour too.

Bel. I like that passingly;

As many as you will, so they be willing,

Willing, and gentle, gentle.

Pinac. There's no reason

A gentleman, and a traveller, should be clapt up,

(For 'tis a kind of bilboes to be married)

Before he manifest to the world his good parts:

Tug ever, like a rascal, at one oar?

Give me the Italian liberty!

Mir. That I study,

And that I will enjoy. Come, go in, gentlemen;

There mark how I behave myself, and follow.

[Exeunt.

SCENE III.—*A Room in La Castre's House.*

Enter La Castre, Nantolet, Lugier, Rosalura,
and Lillia Bianca.

La Ca. You and your beauteous daughters are most welcome!
  Beshrew my blood they are fair ones!—Welcome,
    beauties,
  Welcome, sweet birds!
Nant. They are bound much to your courtesies.
La Ca. I hope we shall be nearer acquainted.
Nant. That's my hope too;
  For, certain, sir, I much desire your alliance.
  You see 'em; they are no gypsies; for their breeding,
  It has not been so coarse, but they are able
  To rank themselves with women of fair fashion.
  Indeed, they have been trained well.
Lug. Thank me!
Nant. Fit for the heirs of that state I shall leave 'em;
  To say more, is to sell 'em.   They say, your son,
  Now he has travell'd, must be wond'rous curious
  And choice in what he takes; these are no coarse ones.
  Sir, here's a merry wench—let him look to himself;
  All heart, i'faith!—may chance to startle him;
  For all his care and travell'd caution,
  May creep into his eye: If he love gravity,
  Affect a solemn face, there's one will fit him.
La Ca. So young and so demure?
Nant. She is my daughter,
  Else I would tell you, sir, she is a mistress
  Both of those manners, and that modesty,
  You would wonder at: She is no often-speaker,
  But, when she does, she speaks well; nor no reveller,
  Yet she can dance, and has studied the court elements,
  And sings, as some say, handsomely; if a woman,
  With the decency of her sex, may be a scholar,
  I can assure you, sir, she understands too.
La Ca. These are fit garments, sir.
Lug. Thank them that cut 'em!
  Yes, they are handsome women, they have handsome
    parts too,
  Pretty becoming parts.
La Ca. 'Tis like they have, sir.

Lug. Yes, yes, and handsome education they have had too,
    Had it abundantly; they need not blush at it:
    I taught it, I'll avouch it.
La Ca. You say well, sir.
Lug. I know what I say, sir, and I say but right, sir:
    I am no trumpet of their commendations
    Before their father; else I should say farther.
La Ca. 'Pray you, what's this gentleman?
Nant. One that lives with me, sir;
    A man well bred and learn'd, but blunt and bitter;
    Yet it offends no wise man; I take pleasure in't:
    Many fair gifts he has, in some of which,
    That lie most easy to their understandings,
    He has handsomely bred up my girls, I thank him.
Lug. I have put it to 'em, that's my part, I have urged it;
    It seems, they are of years now to take hold on't.
Nant. He's wond'rous blunt.
La Ca. By my faith, I was afraid of him;
    Does he not fall out with the gentlewomen sometimes?
Nant. No, no; he's that way moderate and discreet, sir.
Ros. If he did, we should be too hard for him.
Lug. Well said, sulphur!
    Too hard for thy husband's head, if he wear not armour.
Nant. Many of these bickerings, sir.
La Ca. I am glad, they are no oracles!
    Sure as I live, he beats them, he's so puissant.

Enter Mirabel, Pinac, Belleur, De Gard, *and* Oriana.

Ori. Well, if you do forget——
Mir. Pr'ythee, hold thy peace!
    I know thou art a pretty wench; I know thou lov'st me;
    Preserve it till we have a fit time to discourse on't,
    And a fit place; I'll ease my heart, I warrant thee;
    Thou seest, I have much to do now.
Ori. I am answer'd, sir:
    With me you shall have nothing on these conditions.
De Ga. Your father and your friends.
La Ca. You are welcome home, sir!
    'Bless you, you are very welcome! 'Pray know this
      gentleman,
    And these fair ladies.

Nant. Monsieur Mirabel,
> I am much affected with your fair return, sir;
> You bring a general joy.

Mir. I bring you service,
> And these bright beauties, sir.

Nant. Welcome home, gentlemen!
> Welcome with all my heart!

Bel. Pinac. We thank you, sir.

La Ca. Your friends will have their share too.

Bel. Sir, we hope
> They'll look upon us, though we show like strangers.

Nant. Monsieur De Gard, I must salute you also,
> And this fair gentlewoman: you are welcome from your
>> travel too!
> All welcome, all! [*La Castre and Mirabel speak apart.*

De Ga. We render you our loves, sir,
> The best wealth we bring home. By your favours,
>> beauties!—
> One of these two. You know my meaning.

Ori. Well, sir;
> They are fair and handsome, I must needs confess it,
> And, let it prove the worst, I shall live after it:
> Whilst I have meat and drink, love cannot starve me;
> For, if I die o' th' first fit, I am unhappy,
> And worthy to be buried with my heels upward.

Mir. To marry, sir?

La Ca. You know, I am an old man,
> And every hour declining to my grave,
> One foot already in; more sons I have not,
> Nor more I dare not seek whilst you are worthy;
> In you lies all my hope, and all my name,
> The making good or wretched of my memory;
> The safety of my state.

Mir. And you have provided,
> Out of this tenderness, these handsome gentlewomen,
> Daughters to this rich man, to take my choice of?

La Ca. I have, dear son.

Mir. 'Tis true, you are old, and feebled;
> 'Would you were young again, and in full vigour!
> I love a bounteous father's life, a long one;
> I am none of those, that, when they shoot to ripeness,
> Do what they can to break the boughs they grew on;
> I wish you many years, and many riches,

And pleasures to enjoy 'em: But for marriage,
    I neither yet believe in't, nor affect it,
    Nor think it fit.
La Ca. You'll render me your reasons?
Mir. Yes, sir, both short and pithy, and these they are:
    You would have me marry a maid?
La Ca. A maid? what else?
Mir. Yes, there be things called widows, dead men's wills,
    I never loved to prove those; nor never long'd yet
    To be buried alive in another man's cold monument.
    And there be maids appearing, and maids being:
    The appearing are fantastic things, mere shadows;
    And, if you mark 'em well, they want their heads too;
    Only the world, to cozen misty eyes,
    Has clapt 'em on new faces.   The maids being
    A man may venture on, if he be so mad to marry,
    If he have neither fear before his eyes, nor fortune;
    And let him take heed how he gather these too;
    For look you, father, they are just like melons,
    Musk-melons are the emblems of these maids;
    Now they are ripe, now cut 'em they taste pleasantly,
    And are a dainty fruit, digested easily;
    Neglect this present time, and come to-morrow,
    They are so ripe, they are rotten—gone! their sweetness
    Run into humour, and their taste to surfeit!
La Ca. Why, these are now ripe, son.
Mir. I'll try them presently,
    And, if I like their taste——
La Ca. 'Pray you please yourself, sir.
Mir. That liberty is my due, and I'll maintain it.—
    Lady, what think you of a handsome man now?
Ros. A wholesome too, sir?
Mir. That's as you make your bargain.
    A handsome, wholesome man then, and a kind man,
    To cheer your heart up, to rejoice you, lady?
Ros. Yes, sir, I love rejoicing.
Mir. To lie close to you?
    Close as a cockle? keep the cold nights from you?
Ros. That will be look'd for too; our bodies ask it.
Mir. And get two boys at every birth?
Ros. That's nothing;
    I have known a cobler do it, a poor thin cobler,
    A cobler out of mouldy cheese perform it,

Cabbage, and coarse black thread; methinks, a gentleman

Should take foul scorn to have an awl out-name him.
Two at a birth? Why, every house-dove has it:
That man that feeds well, promises as well too,
I should expect indeed something of worth from.
You talk of two?

Mir. She would have me get two dozen,
Like buttons at a birth.

Ros. You love to brag, sir;
If you proclaim these offers at your marriage,
(You are a pretty-timber'd man; take heed!)
They may be taken hold of, and expected,
Yes, if not hoped for at a higher rate too.

Mir. I will take heed, and thank you for your counsel.—
Father, what think you?

La Ca. 'Tis a merry gentlewoman;
Will make, no doubt, a good wife.

Mir. Not for me:
I marry her, and, happily, get nothing;
In what a state am I then, father? I shall suffer,
For anything I hear to th' contrary, *more majorum ;*
I were as sure to be a cuckold, father,
A gentleman of antler——

La Ca. Away, away, fool!

Mir. As I am sure to fail her expectation.
I had rather get the pox than get her babies!

La Ca. You are much to blame! If this do not affect you,
Pray try the other; she's of a more demure way.

Bel. That I had but the audacity to talk thus!   [*Aside.*
I love that plain-spoken gentlewoman admirably;
And, certain, I could go as near to please her,
If down-right doing——She has a perilous countenance!
If I could meet one that would believe me,
And take my honest meaning without circumstance——

Mir. You shall have your will, sir; I will try the other;
But 'twill be to small use.—I hope, fair lady
(For, methinks, in your eyes, I see more mercy),
You will enjoin your lover a less penance;
And though I'll promise much, as men are liberal,
And vow an ample sacrifice of service,
Yet your discretion, and your tenderness,
And thriftiness in love, good huswife's carefulness

To keep the stock entire——

Lil. Good sir, speak louder,
That these may witness too, you talk of nothing:
I should be loth to bear the burthen
Of so much indiscretion.

Mir. Hark ye, hark ye!
Ods-bobs, you are angry, lady!

Lil. Angry? no, sir;
I never own'd an anger to lose poorly.

Mir. But you can love, for all this; and delight too,
For all your set austerity, to hear
Of a good husband, lady?

Lil. You say true, sir;
For, by my troth, I have heard of none these ten years,
They are so rare; and there are so many, sir,
So many longing women on their knees too,
That pray the dropping-down of these good husbands—
The dropping-down from Heaven; for they are not bred
    here—
That you may guess at all my hope, but hearing——

Mir. Why may not I be one?

Lil. You were near 'em once, sir,
When ye came o'er the Alps; those are near Heaven:
But since you miss'd that happiness, there's no hope of
    you.

Mir. Can ye love a man?

Lil. Yes, if the man be lovely;
That is, be honest, modest. I would have him valiant,
His anger slow, but certain for his honour;
Travell'd he should be, but through himself exactly,
For 'tis fairer to know manners well than countries;
He must be no vain talker, nor no lover
To hear himself talk; they are brags of a wanderer,
Of one finds no retreat for fair behaviour.
Would you learn more?

Mir. Yes.

Lil. Learn to hold your peace, then:
Fond girls are got with tongues, women with tempers.

Mir. Women, with I know what; but let that vanish:
Go thy way, good wife Bias! Sure thy husband
Must have a strong philosopher's stone, he will ne'er
    please thee else.
Here's a starcht piece of austerity!—Do you hear, father?

Do you hear this moral lecture?

La Ca. Yes, and like it.

Mir. Why, there's your judgment now; there's an old bolt
    shot!
    This thing must have the strangest observation
    (Do you mark me, father?) when she is married once,
    The strangest custom, too, of admiration
    On all she does and speaks, 'twill be past sufferance;
    I must not lie with her in common language,
    Nor cry, " Have at thee, Kate!" I shall be hiss'd then;
    Nor eat my meat without the sauce of sentences,
    Your powder'd beef and problems, a rare diet!
    My first son monsieur Aristotle, I know it,
    Great master of the metaphysicks, or so;
    The second, Solon, and the best law-setter;
    And I must look Egyptian god-fathers,
    Which will be no small trouble: My eldest daughter
    Sappho, or such a fiddling kind of poetess,
    And brought up, *invitâ Minerva*, at her needle;
    My dogs must look their names too, and all Spartan,
    Lelaps, Melampus; no more Fox and Baudiface.
    I married to a sullen set of sentences?
    To one that weighs her words and her behaviours
    In the gold weights of discretion! I'll be hang'd first.

La Ca. Pr'ythee reclaim thyself.

Mir. Pray ye, give me time then:
    If they can set me anything to play at,
    That seems fit for a gamester, have at the fairest!
    Till then, see more and try more!

La Ca. Take your time then;
    I'll bar you no fair liberty.—Come, gentlemen;
    And, ladies, come; to all, once more, a welcome!
    And now let's in to supper.   *[Exit.*

Mir. How dost like 'em?

Pinac. They are fair enough, but of so strange behaviours——

Mir. Too strange for me: I must have those have mettle,
    And mettle to my mind. Come, let's be merry.

Bel. Bless me from this woman! I would stand the cannon,
    Before ten words of hers.

De Ga. Do you find him now?
    Do you think he will be ever firm?

Ori. I fear not.   *[Exeunt.*

ACT II

SCENE I.—*A Street.*

Enter MIRABEL, PINAC, *and* BELLEUR.

Mir. Ne'er tell me of this happiness; 'tis nothing;
    The state they bring with being sought-to, scurvy!
    I had rather make mine own play, and I will do.
    My happiness is in mine own content,
    And the despising of such glorious trifles,
    As I have done a thousand more. For my humour,
    Give me a good free fellow, that sticks to me,
    A jovial fair companion; there's a beauty!
    For women, I can have too many of them;
    Good women too, as the age reckons 'em,
    More than I have employment for.
Pinac. You're happy.
Mir. My only fear is that I must be forced,
    Against my nature, to conceal myself:
    Health and an able body are two jewels.
Pinac. If either of these two women were offer'd to me now,
    I would think otherwise, and do accordingly;
    Yes, and recant my heresies, I would, sir,
    And be more tender of opinion,
    And put a little of my travell'd liberty
    Out of the way, and look upon 'em seriously.
    Methinks, this grave-carried wench——
Bel. Methinks, the other,
    The home-spoken gentlewoman, that desires to be
        fruitful,
    That treats of the full manage of the matter
    (For there lies all my aim), that wench, methinks,
    If I were but well set on, for she is affable,
    If I were but hounded right, and one to teach me:
    She speaks to th' matter, and comes home to th' point!
    Now do I know I have such a body to please her,
    As all the kingdom cannot fit her with, I am sure on't,
    If I could but talk myself into her favour.
Mir. That's easily done.
Bel. That's easily said; 'would 'twere done!
    You should see then how I would lay about me.
    If I were virtuous, it would never grieve me,

Or anything that might justify my modesty;
But when my nature is prone to do a charity,
And my calf's tongue will not help me——

Mir. Will you go to 'em?
They cannot but take it courteously.

Pinac. I'll do my part,
Though I am sure 'twill be the hardest I e'er play'd yet;
A way I never tried too, which will stagger me;
And, if it do not shame me, I am happy.

Mir. Win 'em, and wear 'em; I give up my interest.

Pinac. What say you, monsieur Belleur?

Bel. 'Would I could say,
Or sing, or anything that were but handsome!
I would be with her presently!

Pinac. Yours is no venture;
A merry, ready wench.

Bel. A vengeance squibber!
She'll fleer me out of faith too.

Mir. I'll be near thee;
Pluck up thy heart; I'll second thee at all brunts.
Be angry, if she abuse thee, and beat her a little;
Some women are won that way.

Bel. Pray be quiet,
And let me think: I am resolved to go on;
But how I shall get off again——

Mir. I am persuaded
Thou wilt so please her, she'll go near to ravish thee.

Bel. I would 'twere come to that once! Let me pray a little.

Mir. Now for thine honour, Pinac! Board me this modesty,
Warm but this frozen snow-ball, 'twill be a conquest
(Although I know thou art a fortunate wencher,
And hast done rarely in thy days) above all thy ventures.

Bel. You will be ever near?

Mir. At all necessities;
And take thee off, and set thee on again, boy,
And cherish thee, and stroke thee.

Bel. Help me out too;
For I know I shall stick i' th' mire. If ye see us close
once,
Be gone, and leave me to my fortune, suddenly,
For I am then determined to do wonders.
Farewell, and fling an old shoe. How my heart throbs!
Would I were drunk! Farewell, Pinac! Heaven send us

A joyful and a merry meeting, man!

Pinac. Farewell,
And cheer thy heart up! and remember, Belleur,
They are but women.

Bel. I had rather they were lions.

Mir. About it; I'll be with you instantly.—

[Exeunt Belleur and Pinac.

Enter ORIANA.

Shall I ne'er be at rest? no peace of conscience?
No quiet for these creatures? am I ordain'd
To be devour'd quick by these she-cannibals?
Here's another they call handsome; I care not for her,
I ne'er look after her: When I am half tippled,
It may be I should turn her, and peruse her;
Or, in my want of women, I might call for her;
But to be haunted when I have no fancy,
No maw to th' matter——Now! why do you follow me?

Ori. I hope, sir, 'tis no blemish to my virtue:
Nor need you, out of scruple, ask that question,
If you remember you, before you travel,
The contract you tied to me: 'Tis my love, sir,
That makes me seek you, to confirm your memory;
And that being fair and good, I cannot suffer.
I come to give you thanks too.

Mir. For what, pr'ythee?

Ori. For that fair piece of honesty you show'd, sir,
That constant nobleness.

Mir. How? for I am short-headed.

Ori. I'll tell ye then; for refusing that free offer
Of monsieur Nantolet's, those handsome beauties,
Those two prime ladies, that might well have prest ye
If not to have broken, yet to have bow'd your promise.
I know it was for my sake, for your faith sake,
You slipt 'em off; your honesty compell'd ye;
And let me tell ye, sir, it show'd most handsomely.

Mir. And let me tell thee, there was no such matter;
Nothing intended that way, of that nature:
I have more to do with my honesty than to fool it,
Or venture it in such leak barks as women.
I put 'em off because I loved 'em not,
Because they are too queasy for my temper,
And not for thy sake, nor the contract sake,

Nor vows nor oaths; I have made a thousand of 'em;
They are things indifferent, whether kept or broken;
Mere venial slips, that grows not near the conscience;
Nothing concerns those tender parts; they are trifles:
For, as I think, there was never man yet hoped for
Either constancy or secrecy from a woman,
Unless it were an ass ordain'd for sufferance;
Nor to contract with such can be a tial!
So let them know again; for 'tis a justice,
And a main point of civil policy,
Whate'er we say or swear, they being reprobates,
Out of the state of faith, we are clear of all sides,
And 'tis a curious blindness to believe us.

Ori. You do not mean this, sure?

Mir. Yes, sure, and certain;
 And hold it positively, as a principle,
 As ye are strange things, and made of strange fires and
  fluxes,
 So we are allow'd as strange ways to obtain ye,
 But not to hold; we are all created errant.

Ori. You told me other tales.

Mir. I not deny it;
 I have tales of all sorts for all sorts of women,
 And protestations likewise of all sizes,
 As they have vanities to make us coxcombs:
 If I obtain a good turn, so it is,
 I am thankful for it; if I be made an ass,
 The 'mends are in mine own hands, or the surgeon's,
 And there's an end on't.

Ori. Do not you love me then?

Mir. As I love others; heartily I love thee;
 When I am high and lusty, I love thee cruelly:
 After I have made a plenteous meal, and satisfied
 My senses with all delicates, come to me,
 And thou shalt see how I love thee.

Ori. Will not you marry me?

Mir. No, certain, no, for anything I know yet:
 I must not lose my liberty, dear lady,
 And, like a wanton slave, cry for more shackles.
 What should I marry for? do I want anything?
 Am I an inch the farther from my pleasure?
 Why should I be at charge to keep a wife of mine own,
 When other honest married men's will ease me,

And thank me too, and be beholding to me?
Thou think'st I am mad for a maidenhead; thou art
  cozen'd:
Or, if I were addicted to that diet,
Can you tell me where I should have one? Thou art
  eighteen now,
And if thou hast thy maidenhead yet extant,
Sure, 'tis as big as cods-head; and those grave dishes
I never love to deal withal. Dost thou see this book
  here?
Look over all these ranks; all these are women,
Maids, and pretenders to maidenheads; these are my
  conquests;
All these I swore to marry, as I swore to thee,
With the same reservation, and most righteously:
Which I need not have done neither; for, alas, they
  made no scruple,
And I enjoyed 'em at my will, and left 'em:
Some of 'em are married since, and were as pure maids
  again,
Nay, o' my conscience, better than they were bred for;
The rest, fine sober women.
Ori. Are you not ashamed, sir?
Mir. No, by my troth, sir; there's no shame belongs to it;
I hold it as commendable to be wealthy in pleasure,
As others do in rotten sheep and pasture.

Enter De Gard.

Ori. Are all my hopes come to this? Is there no faith,
No troth, nor modesty, in men?   [*Weeps.*
De Ga. How now, sister?
Why weeping thus? Did I not prophesy?
Come, tell me why——
Ori. I am not well; pray ye pardon me.   [*Exit.*
De Ga. Now, monsieur Mirabel, what ails my sister?
You have been playing the wag with her.
Mir. As I take it,
She is crying for a cod-piece. Is she gone?
Lord, what an age is this! I was calling for ye;
For, as I live, I thought she would have ravish'd me.
De Ga. You are merry, sir.
Mir. Thou know'st this book, De Gard, this inventory?
De Ga. The debt-book of your mistresses; I remember it.

Mir. Why, this was it that anger'd her; she was stark mad
     She found not her name here; and cried down-right,
     Because I would not pity her immediately,
     And put her in my list.
De Ga. Sure she had more modesty.
Mir. Their modesty is anger to be over-done;
     They'll quarrel sooner for precedence here,
     And take it in more dudgeon to be slighted,
     Than they will in public meetings; 'tis their natures:
     And, alas, I have so many to dispatch yet,
     And to provide myself for my affairs too,
     That, in good faith——
De Ga. Be not too glorious foolish;
     Sum not your travels up with vanities;
     It ill becomes your expectation!
     Temper your speech, sir! Whether your loose story
     Be true or false (for you are so free, I fear it)
     Name not my sister in't, I must not hear it;
     Upon your danger, name her not! I hold her
     A gentlewoman of those happy parts and carriage,
     A good man's tongue may be right proud to speak her.
Mir. Your sister, sir? do ye blench at that? do ye cavil?
     Do ye hold her such a piece she may not be play'd
         withal?
     I have had an hundred handsomer and nobler,
     Have sued to me too, for such a courtesy;
     Your sister comes i' th' rear. Since ye are so angry,
     And hold your sister such a strong Recusant,
     I tell ye, I may do it; and, it may be, will too;
     It may be, have too; there's my free confession:
     Work upon that now!
De Ga. If I thought ye had, I would work,
     And work such stubborn work should make your heart
         ache!
     But I believe ye, as I ever knew ye,
     A glorious talker, and a legend-maker
     Of idle tales, and trifles; a depraver
     Of your own truth: their honours fly about ye!
     And so I take my leave; but with this caution,
     Your sword be surer than your tongue; you'll smart else.
Mir. I laugh at thee, so little I respect thee!
     And I'll talk louder, and despise thy sister;
     Set up a chamber-maid that shall out-shine her,

And carry her in my coach too, and that will kill her.
Go, get thy rents up, go!
De Ga. You are a fine gentleman!   [*Exit.*
Mir. Now, have at my two youths! I'll see how they do;
How they behave themselves; and then I'll study
What wench shall love me next, and when I'll lose her.
                                        [*Exit.*

SCENE II.—*A Hall in La Castre's House.*

Enter Pinac *and a* Servant.

Pinac. Art thou her servant, say'st thou?
Serv. Her poor creature;
    But servant to her horse, sir.
Pinac. Canst thou show me
    The way to her chamber, or where I may conveniently
    See her, or come to talk to her?
Serv. That I can, sir;
    But the question is, whether I will or no.
Pinac. Why, I'll content thee.
Serv. Why, I'll content thee then; now you come to me.
Pinac. There's for your diligence.   [*Gives money.*
Serv. There's her chamber, sir,
    And this way she comes out; stand you but here, sir,
    You have her at your prospect, or your pleasure.
Pinac. Is she not very angry?
Serv. You'll find that quickly
    May be she'll call you saucy, scurvy fellow,
    Or some such familiar name; may be she knows you,
    And will fling a piss-pot at you, or a pantofle,
    According as you are in acquaintance: If she like you,
    May be she'll look upon you; may be no;
    And two months hence call for you.
Pinac. This is fine.
    She is monstrous proud then?
Serv. She is a little haughty;
    Of a small body, she has a mind well mounted.
    Can you speak Greek?
Pinac. No, certain.
Serv. Get you gone then!—
    And talk of stars, and firmaments, and fire-drakes?
    Do you remember who was Adam's schoolmaster,

And who taught Eve to spin? She knows all these,
And will run you over the beginning o' th' world
As familiar as a fiddler.
Can you sit seven hours together, and say nothing?
Which she will do, and, when she speaks, speak oracles,
Speak things that no man understands, nor herself
    neither.

Pinac. Thou mak'st me wonder!

Serv. Can you smile?

Pinac. Yes, willingly;
For naturally I bear a mirth about me.

Serv. She'll ne'er endure you then; she's never merry;
If she see one laugh, she'll swoon past *aquæ vitæ*.
Never come near her, sir; if you chance to venture,
And talk not like a doctor, you are damn'd too.
I have told you enough for your crown, and so good
    speed you!   *[Exit.*

Pinac. I have a pretty task if she be thus curious,
As, sure, it seems she is! If I fall off now,
I shall be laugh'd at fearfully; if I go forward,
I can but be abused, and that I look for;
And yet I may hit right, but 'tis unlikely.
Stay! in what mood and figure shall I attempt her?
A careless way?   No, no, that will not waken her;
Besides, her gravity will give me line still,
And let me lose myself; yet this way often
Has hit, and handsomely.   A wanton method?
Ay, if she give it leave to sink into her consideration:
But there's the doubt: If it but stir her blood once,
And creep into the crannies of her fancy,
Set her a-gog——But if she chance to slight it,
And by the power of her modesty fling it back,
I shall appear the arrant'st rascal to her,
The most licentious knave—for I shall talk lewdly.
To bear myself austerely? rate my words?
And fling a general gravity about me,
As if I meant to give laws?   But this I cannot do,
This is a way above my understanding:
Or, if I could, 'tis odds she'll think I mock her;
For serious and sad things are ever still
Suspicious.   Well, I'll say something:
But learning I have none, and less good manners,
Especially for ladies.   Well; I'll set my best face.

I hear some coming. This is the first woman
I ever fear'd yet, the first face that shakes me.

[Stands apart.

Enter LILLIA *and* PETELLA.

Lit. Give me my hat, Petella; take this veil off,
This sullen cloud; it darkens my delights.
Come, wench, be free, and let the music warble;
Play me some lusty measure. *[Music.*
Pinac. This is she, sure,
The very same I saw, the very woman,
The gravity I wonder'd at. Stay, stay;
Let me be sure. Ne'er trust me, but she danceth!
Summer is in her face now, and she skippeth.
I'll go a little nearer.
Lil. Quicker time, fellows!
I cannot find my legs yet. Now, Petella!

Enter MIRABEL.

Pinac. I am amazed! I am founder'd in my fancy!
Mir. Ha! say you so? Is this your gravity?
This the austerity you put upon you?
I'll see more o' this sport. *[Stands apart.*
Lil. A song now!
Call in for a merry, and a light song;
And sing it with a liberal spirit.

Enter a Singing Boy.

Boy. Yes, madam.
Lil. And be not amazed, sirrah, but take us for your own
company.
Let's walk ourselves: Come, wench. 'Would we had a
man or two!
Pinac. Sure, she has spied me, and will abuse me dreadfully;
She has put on this for the purpose; yet I will try her.—
Madam, I would be loth my rude intrusion,
Which I must crave a pardon for——
Lil. Oh, you are welcome,
You are very welcome, sir! we want such a one.
Strike up again. I dare presume you dance well.
Quick, quick, sir, quick! the time steals on.
Pinac. I would talk with you.

Lil. Talk as you dance.   [*They dance.*

Mir. She'll beat him off his legs first.

This is the finest masque!

Lil. Now, how do you, sir?

Pinac. You have given me a shrewd heat.

Lil. I'll give you a hundred.

Come, sing now, sing; for I know you sing well;

I see you have a singing face.

Pinac. A fine modesty!

If I could, she'd never give me breath.—Madam, 'would

I might sit and recover.

Lil. Sit here, and sing now;

Let's do things quickly, sir, and handsomely.—

Sit close, wench, close.—Begin, begin!

Pinac. I am lesson'd.   [*Song.*

Lil. 'Tis very pretty, i' faith. Give me some wine now.

Pinac. I would fain speak to you.

Lil. You shall drink first, believe me.

Here's to you a lusty health.

Pinac. I thank you, lady.—

'Would I were off again! I smell my misery;

I was never put to this rack! I shall be drunk too.

Mir. If thou be'st not a right one, I have lost mine aim much:

I thank Heaven, that I have 'scaped thee! To her,

Pinac;

For thou art as sure to have her, and to groan for her—

I'll see how my other youth does; this speeds trimly.

A fine grave gentlewoman, and worth much honour!

                                      [*Exit.*

Lil. How do you like me, sir?

Pinac. I like you rarely.

Lil. You see, sir, though sometimes we are grave and silent,

And put on sadder dispositions,

Yet we're compounded of free parts, and sometimes too

Our lighter, airy, and our fiery metals

Break out, and show themselves: And what think you of

that, sir?

Pinac. Good lady, sit (for I am very weary)

And then I'll tell you.

Lil. Fy! a young man idle?

Up, and walk; be still in action;

The motions of the body are fair beauties:

Besides, 'tis cold. Odds-me, sir, let's walk faster!

What think you now of the lady Felicia?
And Bella-Fronte, the duke's fair daughter? ha?
Are they not handsome things?   There is Duarta,
And brown Olivia——

Pinac. I know none of 'em.

Lil. But brown must not be cast away, sir.   If young Lelia
Had kept herself till this day from a husband,
Why, what a beauty, sir!   You know Ismena,
The fair gem of Saint-Germains?

Pinac. By my troth, I do not.

Lil. And then, I know, you must hear of Brisac,
How unlike a gentleman——

Pinac. As I live, I heard nothing.

Lil. Strike me another galliard!

Pinac. By this light, I cannot!
In troth, I have sprain'd my leg, madam.

Lil. Now sit you down, sir,
And tell me why you came hither? why you chose me
    out?
What is your business? your errand? Dispatch,
    dispatch!
May be you are some gentleman's man (and I mistook
    you)
That have brought me a letter, or a haunch of venison,
Sent me from some friend of mine.

Pinac. Do I look like a carrier?
You might allow me, what I am, a gentleman.

Lil. 'Cry you mercy, sir!   I saw you yesterday:
You are new come out of travel; I mistook you.
And how do all our impudent friends in Italy?

Pinac. Madam, I came with duty, and fair courtesy,
Service, and honour to you.

Lil. You came to jeer me!
You see I am merry, sir; I have changed my copy:
None of the sages now, and pray you proclaim it;
Fling on me what aspersion you shall please, sir,
Of wantonness, or wildness; I look for it;
And tell the world, I am an hypocrite,
Mask in a forc'd and borrow'd shape, I expect it;
But not to have you believed: For, mark you, sir,
I have won a nobler estimation,
A stronger tie by my discretion
Upon opinion (howe'er you think I forc'd it)

Than either tongue or art of yours can slubber,
And, when I please, I will be what I please, sir,
So I exceed not mean; and none shall brand it,
Either with scorn or shame, but shall be slighted.

Pinac. Lady, I come to love you.

Lil. Love yourself, sir;
And when I want observers, I'll send for you.
Heigh-ho! my fit's almost off; for we do all by fits, sir.
If you be weary, sit till I come again to you.

[*Exit with Petella.*

Pinac. This is a wench of a dainty spirit; but
Hang me if I know yet either what to think
Or make of her; she had her will of me,
And baited me abundantly, I thank her;
And, I confess, I never was so blurted,
Nor ever so abused: I must bear mine own sins.
You talk of travels; here's a curious country!
Yet I will find her out, or forswear my faculty.   [*Exit.*

SCENE III.—*Another Room in the same.*

Enter ROSALURA *and* ORIANA.

Ros. Ne'er vex yourself, nor grieve; you are a fool then.

Ori. I am sure I am made so: Yet, before I suffer
Thus like a girl, and give him leave to triumph——

Ros. You say right; for as long as he perceives you
Sink under his proud scornings, he'll laugh at you:
For me, secure yourself; and for my sister,
I partly know her mind too: Howsoever,
To obey my father, we have made a tender
Of our poor beauties to the travell'd monsieur,
Yet two words to a bargain! He slights us
As skittish things, and we shun him as curious.
May be, my free behaviour turns his stomach,
And makes him seem to doubt a loose opinion:
I must be so sometimes, though all the world saw it.

Ori. Why should not you? Are not minds only measured?
As long as here you stand secure——

Ros. You say true;
As long as mine own conscience makes no question,
What care I for report? that woman's miserable,
That's good or bad for their tongue's sake. Come, let's
retire,

And get my veil, wench; by my troth, your sorrow,
And the consideration of men's humorous maddings,
Have put me into a serious contemplation.

Enter Mirabel *and* Belleur, *and stand apart.*

Ori. Come, 'faith, let's sit and think.
Ros. That's all my business.
Mir. Why stand'st thou peeping here? Thou great slug
    forward!
Bel. She is there; peace!
Mir. Why stand'st thou here then,
    Sneaking, and peaking, as thou wouldst steal linen?
    Hast thou not place and time?
Bel. I had a rare speech
    Studied, and almost ready; and your violence
    Has beat it out of my brains.
Mir. Hang your rare speeches!
    Go me on like a man.
Bel. Let me set my beard up.
    How has Pinac perform'd?
Mir. He has won already:
    He stands not thrumming of caps thus.
Bel. Lord, what should I ail!
    What a cold I have over my stomach; 'would I had
      some hum!
    Certain I have a great mind to be at her,
    A mighty mind.
Mir. On, fool!
Bel. Good words, I beseech you;
    For I will not be abused by both.
Mir. Adieu, then
    (I will not trouble you; I see you are valiant),
    And work your own way.
Bel. Hist, hist! I will be ruled;
    I will, i' faith; I will go presently:
    Will you forsake me now, and leave me i' th' suds?
    You know, I am false-hearted this way; I beseech you,
    Good sweet Mirabel (I'll cut your throat if you leave me,
    Indeed I will!) sweet-heart!
Mir. I will be ready,
    Still at thine elbow; take a man's heart to thee,
    And speak thy mind; the plainer still the better.
    She is a woman of that free behaviour,

Indeed, that common courtesy, she cannot deny thee:
Go bravely on.

Bel. Madam—keep close about me.
Still at my back.—Madam, sweet madam——

Ros. Ha!
What noise is that? what saucy sound to trouble me?

Mir. What said she?

Bel. I am saucy.

Mir. 'Tis the better.

Bel. She comes; must I be saucy still?

Mir. More saucy.

Ros. Still troubled with these vanities? Heaven bless us!
What are we born to?—Would you speak with any of
   my people?
Go in, sir; I am busy.

Bel. This is not she, sure:
Is this two children at a birth? I'll be hang'd then
Mine was a merry gentlewoman, talk'd daintily,
Talk'd of those matters that befitted women;
This is a parcel-prayer-book; I'm served sweetly!
And now I am to look too; I was prepared for th' other
   way.

Ros. Do you know that man?

Ori. Sure, I have seen him, lady.

Ros. Methinks 'tis pity such a lusty fellow
Should wander up and down, and want employment.

Bel. She takes me for a rogue!—You may do well, madam,
To stay this wanderer, and set him at work, forsooth;
He can do something that may please your ladyship;
I have heard of women that desire good breedings,
Two at a birth, or so.

Ros. The fellow's impudent.

Ori. Sure, he is crazed.

Ros. I have heard of men too that have had good manners;
Sure, this is want of grace; Indeed, 'tis great pity
The young man has been bred so ill; but this lewd age
Is full of such examples.

Bel. I am founder'd,
And some shall rue the setting of me on!

Mir. Ha! so bookish, lady? is it possible?
Turn'd holy at the heart too? I'll be hang'd then.
Why, this is such a feat, such an activity.
Such fast and loose——

Enter Servant, *with a veil.*

                              A veil too for your knavery?
        O Dio, Dio !
Ros. What do you take me for, sir?
Mir. An hypocrite, a wanton, a dissembler,
        Howe'er you seem, and thus you are to be handled;
        (Mark me, Belleur) and this you love, I know it.
Ros. Stand off, bold sir!
Mir. You wear good clothes to this end,
        Jewels; love feasts, and masques.
Ros. Ye are monstrous saucy!
Mir. All this to draw on fools; and thus, thus, lady,
                                    [*Takes hold of her.*
        Ye are to be lull'd.
Bel. Let her alone, I'll swinge ye else,
        I will, i' faith! for though I cannot skill o' this matter
        Myself, I will not see another do it before me,
        And do it worse.
Ros. Away! you are a vain thing!
        You have travell'd far, sir, to return again
        A windy and poor bladder!   You talk of women,
        That are not worth the favour of a common one,
        The grace of her grew in an hospital!
        Against a thousand such blown fooleries,
        I am able to maintain good women's honours,
        Their freedoms, and their fames, and I will do it——
Mir. She has almost struck me dumb too.
Ros. And declaim
        Against your base malicious tongues, your noises,
        For they are nothing else.   You teach behaviours?
        Or touch us for our freedoms? Teach yourselves
            manners,
        Truth and sobriety, and live so clearly
        That our lives may shine in ye; and then task us.
        It seems, ye are hot; the suburbs will supply ye:
        Good women scorn such gamesters; so I'll leave ye!
        I am sorry to see this: 'Faith, sir, live fairly.   [*Exit.*
Mir. This woman, if she hold on, may be virtuous;
        'Tis almost possible: We'll have a new day.
Bel. Ye brought me on, ye forced me to this foolery;
        I am shamed, I am scorn'd, I am flurted! yes, I am so!
        Though I cannot talk to a woman like your worship,

And use my phrases, and my learned figures,
Yet I can fight with any man.

Mir. Fy!

Bel. I can, sir;
And I will fight.

Mir. With whom?

Bel. With you; with any man;
For all men now will laugh at me.

Mir. Pr'thee be moderate.

Bel. And I'll beat all men. Come!

Mir. I love thee dearly.

Bel. I will beat all that love; love has undone me!
Never tell me! I will not be a history.

Mir. Thou art not.

Bel. 'Sfoot, I will not! Give me room,
And let me see the proudest of ye jeer me;
And I'll begin with you first.

Mir. Pr'ythee, Belleur!
If I do not satisfy thee——

Bel. Well, look you do.
But, now I think on't better, 'tis impossible!
I must beat somebody; I am maul'd myself,
And I ought in justice——

Mir. No, no, no, ye are cozen'd:
But walk, and let me talk to thee.

Bel. Talk wisely,
And see that no man laugh, upon no occasion;
For I shall think then 'tis at me.

Mir. I warrant thee.

Bel. Nor no more talk of this.

Mir. Dost think I am maddish?

Bel. I must needs fight yet; for I find it concerns me:
A pox on't: I must fight.

Mir. I' faith, thou shalt not.   [*Exeunt.*

ACT III

SCENE I.—*The Garden of the same House.*

Enter De Gard *and* Lugier.

De Ga. I know you are a scholar, and can do wonders.
Lug. There's no great scholarship belongs to this, sir;
　　What I am, I am: I pity your poor sister,
　　And heartily I hate these travellers,
　　These gim-cracks, made of mops and motions:
　　There's nothing in their houses here but hummings;
　　A bee has more brains.　I grieve and vex too
　　The insolent licentious carriage
　　Of this out-facing fellow Mirabel;
　　And I am mad to see him prick his plumes up.
De Ga. His wrongs you partly know.
Lug. Do not you stir, sir;
　　Since he has begun with wit, let wit revenge it:
　　Keep your sword close; we'll cut his throat a new way.
　　I am ashamed the gentlewoman should suffer
　　Such base, lewd wrongs.
De Ga. I will be ruled; he shall live,
　　And left to your revenge.
Lug. Ay, ay, I'll fit him:
　　He makes a common scorn of handsome women;
　　Modesty and good manners are his may-games;
　　He takes up maidenheads with a new commission;
　　The church-warrant's out of date.　Follow my counsel,
　　For I am zealous in the cause.
De Ga. I will, sir,
　　And will be still directed; for the truth is,
　　My sword will make my sister seem more monstrous:
　　Besides, there is no honour won on reprobates.
Lug. You are i' th' right.　The slight he has show'd my
　　　　pupils
　　Sets me a-fire too.　Go; I'll prepare your sister,
　　And, as I told you——
De Ga. Yes; all shall be fit, sir.
Lug. And seriously and handsomely.
De Ga. I warrant you.
Lug. A little counsel more.　　　　　　　　　[*Whispers.*
De Ga. 'Tis well.

Lug. Most stately!
   See that observed; and then!
De Ga. I have you every way.
Lug. Away then, and be ready.
De Ga. With all speed, sir.   [*Exit.*
Lug. We'll learn to travel too, may be, beyond him.

Enter LILLIA, ROSALURA, *and* ORIANA.

   Good day, fair beauties!
Lil. You have beautified us,
   We thank you, sir; you have set us off most gallantly
   With your grave precepts.
Ros. We expected husbands
   Out of your documents and taught behaviours,
   Excellent husbands; thought men would run stark mad
      on us,
   Men of all ages, and all states; we expected
   An inundation of desires and offers,
   A torrent of trim suitors; all we did,
   Or said, or purposed, to be spells about us,
   Spells to provoke.
Lil. You have provoked us finely!
   We follow'd your directions, we did rarely,
   We were stately, coy, demure, careless, light, giddy,
   And play'd at all points: This, you swore, would carry.
Ros. We made love, and contemn'd love; now seem'd holy,
   With such a reverend put-on reservation
   Which could not miss, according to your principles;
   Now gave more hope again; now close, now public,
   Still up and down we beat it like a billow;
   And ever those behaviours you read to us,
   Subtle, and new: But all this will not help us!
Lil. They help to hinder us of all acquaintance,
   They have frighted off all friends! What am I better
   For all my learning, if I love a dunce,
   A handsome dunce? to what use serves my reading?
   You should have taught me what belongs to horses,
   Dogs, dice, hawks, banquets, masques, free and fair
      meetings,
   To have studied gowns and dressings.
Lug. Ye are not mad, sure!
Ros. We shall be, if we follow your encouragements:
   I'll take mine own way now!

Lil. And I my fortune;
    We may live maids else till the moon drop millstones.
    I see, your modest women are taken for monsters;
    A dowry of good breeding is worth nothing.
Lug. Since ye take it so to th' heart, pray ye give me leave
        yet,
    And you shall see how I'll convert this heretic:
    Mark how this Mirabel——
Lil. Name him no more;
    For, though I long for a husband, I hate him,
    And would be married sooner to a monkey,
    Or to a Jack of Straw, than such a juggler.
Ros. I am of that mind too; he is too nimble,
    And plays at fast and loose too learnedly,
    For a plain-meaning woman; that's the truth on't.
    Here's one too, that we love well, would be angry;
                          [Pointing to Oriana.
    And reason why.   No, no, we will not trouble you
    Nor him at this time: May he make you happy!
    We'll turn ourselves loose now, to our fair fortunes;
    And the down-right way——
Lil. The winning way we'll follow;
    We'll bait that men may bite fair, and not be frighted;
    Yet we'll not be carried so cheap neither; we'll have
        some sport,
    Some mad-morris or other for our money, tutor.
Lug. 'Tis like enough: Prosper your own devices!
    Ye are old enough to chuse: But, for this gentlewoman,
    So please her give me leave——
Ori. I shall be glad, sir,
    To find a friend whose pity may direct me.
Lug. I'll do my best, and faithfully deal for ye;
    But then ye must be ruled.
Ori. In all, I vow to you.
Ros. Do, do: He has a lucky hand sometimes, I'll assure
        you;
    And hunts the recovery of a lost lover deadly.
Lug. You must away straight.
Ori. Yes.
Lug. And I'll instruct you:
    Here you can know no more.
Ori. By your leave, sweet ladies;
    And all our fortunes arrive at our own wishes!
*M 506

Lil. Amen, amen!

Lug. I must borrow your man.

Lil. Pray take him;
    He is within: To do her good, take anything,
    Take us and all.

Lug. No doubt, ye may find takers;
    And so we'll leave ye to your own disposes.

                        [*Exeunt Lugier and Oriana.*

Lil. Now, which way, wench?

Ros. We'll go a brave way, fear not;
    A safe and sure way too; and yet a bye-way.
    I must confess, I have a great mind to be married.

Lil. So have I too a grudging of good-will that way;
    And would as fain be dispatch'd. But this monsieur
        Quicksilver——

Ros. No, no; we'll bar him, bye and main: Let him trample:
    There is no safety in his surquedry:
    An army-royal of women are too few for him;
    He keeps a journal of his gentleness,
    And will go near to print his fair dispatches,
    And call it his triumph over time and women:
    Let him pass out of memory! What think you
    Of his two companions?

Lil. Pinac, methinks, is reasonable;
    A little modesty he has brought home with him,
    And might be taught, in time, some handsome duty.

Ros. They say, he is a wencher too.

Lil. I like him better;
    A free light touch or two becomes a gentleman,
    And sets him seemly off: So he exceed not,
    But keep his compass clear, he may be look'd at.
    I would not marry a man that must be taught,
    And conjured up with kisses; the best game
    Is play'd still by the best gamesters.

Ros. Fy upon thee!
    What talk hast thou?

Lil. Are not we alone, and merry?
    Why should we be ashamed to speak what we think?
        Thy gentleman,
    The tall fat fellow, he that came to see thee——

Ros. Is't not a goodly man?

Lil. A wondrous goodly!
    He has weight enough, I warrant thee: Mercy upon me,

What a serpent wilt thou seem under such a St. George!

Ros. Thou art a fool! Give me a man brings mettle,
Brings substance with him, needs no broths to lare him.
These little fellows show like fleas in boxes,
Hop up and down, and keep a stir to vex us:
Give me the puissant pike; take you the small shot.

Lil. Of a great thing, I have not seen a duller:
Therefore, methinks, sweet sister——

Ros. Peace, he's modest;
A bashfulness; which is a point of grace, wench:
But, when these fellows come to moulding, sister,
To heat, and handling.—As I live, I like him;
And, methinks, I could form him.

Enter Mirabel.

Lil. Peace! the fire-drake.

Mir. Bless ye, sweet beauties, sweet incomparable ladies,
Sweet wits, sweet humours! Bless you, learned lady!
And you, most holy nun! Bless your devotions!

Lil. And bless your brains, sir, your most pregnant brains,
sir!
They are in travail; may they be deliver'd
Of a most hopeful Wild-Goose!

Ros. Bless your manhood!
They say you are a gentleman of action,
A fair accomplish'd man, and a rare engineer;
You have a trick to blow up maidenheads,
A subtle trick, they say abroad.

Mir. I have, lady.

Ros. And often glory in their ruins.

Mir. Yes, forsooth;
I have a speedy trick, please you to try it:
My engine will dispatch you instantly.

Ros. I would I were a woman, sir, fit for you,
As there be such, no doubt, may engine you too;
May, with a counter-mine, blow up your valour.
But, in good faith, sir, we are both too honest;
And, the plague is, we cannot be persuaded:
For, look you, if we thought it were a glory
To be the last of all your lovely ladies——

Mir. Come, come; leave prating: This has spoil'd your
market!
This pride and puft-up heart will make ye fast, ladies,

Fast, when ye are hungry too.

Ros. The more our pain, sir.

Lil. The more our health, I hope too.

Mir. Your behaviours
Have made men stand amazed; those men that loved ye;
Men of fair states and parts.   Your strange conversions
Into I know not what, nor how, nor wherefore;
Your scorns of those that came to visit ye;
Your studied whim-whams, and your fine set faces:
What have these got ye?   Proud and harsh opinions!
A travell'd monsieur was the strangest creature,
The wildest monster to be wonder'd at;
His person made a public scoff, his knowledge
(As if he had been bred 'mongst bears or bandogs)
Shunn'd and avoided; his conversation snuff'd at:
What harvest brings all this?

Ros. I pray you proceed, sir.

Mir. Now ye shall see in what esteem a traveller,
An understanding gentleman, and a monsieur,
Is to be held; and to your griefs confess it,
Both to your griefs and galls!

Lil. In what, I pray ye, sir?
We would be glad to understand your excellence.

Mir. Go on, sweet ladies; it becomes ye rarely!
For me, I have blest me from ye; scoff on seriously
And note the man ye mock'd.   You, lady Learning,
Note the poor traveller that came to visit ye,
That flat unfurnish'd fellow; note him throughly!
You may chance to see him anon.

Lil. 'Tis very likely.

Mir. And see him courted by a travell'd lady,
Held dear, and honour'd by a virtuous virgin;
May be a beauty not far short of yours neither;
It may be, clearer.

Lil. Not unlikely.

Mir. Younger:
As killing eyes as yours, a wit as poignant;
May be, a state too that may top your fortune:
Inquire how she thinks of him, how she holds him;
His good parts, in what precious price already;
Being a stranger to him, how she courts him;
A stranger to his nation too, how she dotes on him;
Inquire of this; be sick to know: Curse, lady,

And keep your chamber; cry, and curse!   A sweet one,
A thousand in yearly land, well bred, well friended,
Travell'd, and highly follow'd for her fashions!

Lil. Bless his good fortune, sir.

Mir. This scurvy fellow,
I think they call his name Pinac, this serving-man
That brought you venison, as I take it, madam,
Note but this scab! 'Tis strange, that this coarse
   creature,
That has no more set-off but his jugglings,
His travell'd tricks——

Lil. Good sir, I grieve not at him,
Nor envy not his fortune: Yet I wonder!
He's handsome, yet I see no such perfection.

Mir. 'Would I had his fortune! for it is a woman
Of that sweet-temper'd nature, and that judgment,
Besides her state, that care, clear understanding,
And such a wife to bless him——

Ros. Pray you whence is she?

Mir. Of England, and a most accomplish'd lady;
So modest that men's eyes are frighted at her,
And such a noble carriage—How now, sirrah?

Enter a Boy.

Boy. Sir, the great English lady——

Mir. What of her, sir?

Boy. Has newly left her coach, and coming this way,
Where you may see her plain: Monsieur Pinac
The only man that leads her.

Enter PINAC, MARIANA, *and* Attendants.

Mir. He is much honour'd;
'Would I had such a favour!—Now vex, ladies,
Envy, and vex, and rail!

Ros. You are short of us, sir.

Mir. Bless your fair fortune, sir!

Pinac. I nobly thank you.

Mir. Is she married, friend?

Pinac. No, no.

Mir. A goodly lady;
A sweet and delicate aspéct!—Mark, mark, and wonder!
Hast thou any hope of her?

Pinac. A little.

Mir. Follow close then;
  Lose not that hope.

Pinac. To you, sir.   [*Mariana courtesies to him.*

Mir. Gentle lady!

Ros. She is fair, indeed.

Lil. I have seen a fairer; yet
  She is well.

Ros. Her clothes sit handsome too.

Lil. She dresses prettily.

Ros. And, by my faith, she's rich; she looks still sweeter.
  A well-bred woman, I warrant her.

Lil. Do you hear, sir?
  May I crave this gentlewoman's name?

Pinac. Mariana, lady.

Lil. I will not say I owe you a quarrel, monsieur,
  For making me your stale! A noble gentleman
  Would have had more courtesy, at least more faith,
  Than to turn off his mistress at first trial:
  You know not what respect I might have show'd you;
  I find you have worth.

Pinac. I cannot stay to answer you;
  You see my charge. I am beholding to you
  For all your merry tricks you put upon me,
  Your bobbs, and base accounts: I came to love you,
  To woo you, and to serve you; I am much indebted to
      you
  For dancing me off my legs, and then for walking me,
  For telling me strange tales I never heard of,
  More to abuse me; for mistaking me,
  When you both knew I was a gentleman,
  And one deserved as rich a match as you are!

Lil. Be not so bitter, sir.

Pinac. You see this lady:
  She is young enough, and fair enough, to please me;
  A woman of a loving mind, a quiet,
  And one that weighs the worth of him that loves her;
  I am content with this, and bless my fortune:
  Your curious wits, and beauties——

Lil. 'Faith, see me once more.

Pinac. I dare not trouble you.

Lil. May I speak to your lady?

Pinac. I pray you content yourself: I know you are bitter,

And, in your bitterness, you may abuse her;
Which, if she comes to know (for she understands you
    not)
It may breed such a quarrel to your kindred,
And such an indiscretion fling on you too
(For she is nobly friended)——

Lil. I could eat her!   *[Aside.*

Pinac. Rest as ye are, a modest noble gentlewoman,
And afford your honest neighbours some of your prayers.
          [Exeunt Pinac, Mariana, and Attendants.

Mir. What think you now?

Lil. 'Faith, she's a pretty whiting;
She has got a pretty catch too!

Mir. You are angry,
Monstrous angry now, grievously angry;
And the pretty heart does swell now!

Lil. No, in troth, sir.

Mir. And it will cry anon, " A pox upon it! "
And it will curse itself, and eat no meat, lady;
And it will sigh!

Lil. Indeed you are mistaken;
It will be very merry.

Ros. Why, sir, do you think
There are no more men living, nor no handsomer,
Than he, or you?   By this light, there be ten thousand,
Ten   thousand   thousand! Comfort yourself, dear
    monsieur!
Faces, and bodies, wits, and all abiliments:
There are so many we regard 'em not.

Mir. That such a noble lady—I could burst now!
So far above such trifles——

Enter BELLEUR, *and two* Gentlemen.

Bel. You did laugh at me;
And I know why ye laugh'd!

1 *Gent.* I pray ye be satisfied
If we did laugh, we had some private reason,
And not at you.

2 *Gent.* Alas, we know you not, sir.

Bel. I'll make you know me!   Set your faces soberly;
Stand this way, and look sad; I'll be no may-game!
Sadder, demurer yet!

Ros. What is the matter?
   What ails this gentleman?
Bel. Go off now backward, that I may behold ye;
   And not a simper, on your lives!   [*Exeunt Gentlemen.*
Lil. He's mad, sure.
Bel. Do you observe me too?
Mir. I may look on you.
Bel. Why do you grin?   I know your mind.
Mir. You do not.
   You are strangely humorous: Is there no mirth nor
      pleasure
   But you must be the object?
Bel. Mark, and observe me: Wherever I am named,
   The very word shall raise a general sadness,
   For the disgrace this scurvy woman did me,
   This proud pert thing!   Take heed you laugh not at me:
   Provoke me not; take heed!
Ros. I would fain please you;
   Do anything to keep you quiet.
Bel. Hear me:
   Till I receive a satisfaction
   Equal to the disgrace and scorn you gave me,
   You are a wretched woman; till thou woo'st me,
   And I scorn thee as much, as seriously
   Jeer and abuse thee; ask, what Gill thou art,
   Or any baser name; I will proclaim thee,
   I will so sing thy virtue, so be-paint thee——
Ros. Nay, good sir, be more modest.
Bel. Do you laugh again?
   Because you are a woman, you are lawless,
   And out of compass of an honest anger.
Ros. Good sir, have a better belief of me.
Lil. Away, dear sister.   [*Exeunt Rosalura and Lillia.*
Mir. Is not this better now, this seeming madness,
   Than falling out with your friends?
Bel. Have I not frighted her?
Mir. Into her right wits, I warrant thee: Follow this
      humour,
   And thou shalt see how prosperously 'twill guide thee.
Bel. I am glad I have found a way to woo yet; I was afraid
      once
   I never should have made a civil suitor.
   Well, I'll about it still.

Mir. Do, do, and prosper.—   [*Exit Belleur.*
    What sport do I make with these fools! what pleasure
    Feeds me, and fats my sides at their poor innocence!
    Wooing and wiving! hang it! give me mirth,
    Witty and dainty mirth! I shall grow in love, sure,
    With mine own happy head.

Enter LUGIER.

                  Who's this?—To me, sir?
    What youth is this?
Lug. Yes, sir, I would speak with you,
    If your name be monsieur Mirabel.
Mir. You have hit it:
    Your business, I beseech you?
Lug. This it is, sir;
    There is a gentlewoman hath long time affected you,
    And loved you dearly.
Mir. Turn over, and end that story;
    'Tis long enough: I have no faith in women, sir.
Lug. It seems so, sir: I do not come to woo for her,
    Or sing her praises, though she well deserve 'em;
    I come to tell you, you have been cruel to her,
    Unkind and cruel, false of faith, and careless;
    Taking more pleasure in abusing her,
    Wresting her honour to your wild disposes,
    Than noble in requiting her affection:
    Which, as you are a man, I must desire you
    (A gentleman of rank) not to persist in,
    No more to load her fair name with your injuries.
Mir. Why, I beseech you, sir?
Lug. Good sir, I'll tell you.
    And I'll be short; I'll tell you, because I love you;
    Because I would have you shun the shame may follow.
    There is a nobleman, new come to town, sir,
    A noble and a great man, that affects her,
    (A countryman of mine, a brave Savoyan,
    Nephew to th' duke) and so much honours her,
    That 'twill be dangerous to pursue your old way,
    To touch at anything concerns her honour,
    Believe, most dangerous: Her name is Oriana,
    And this great man will marry her. Take heed, sir;
    For howsoe'er her brother, a staid gentleman,

Lets things pass upon better hopes, this lord, sir,
Is of that fiery and that poignant metal
(Especially provoked on by affection)
That 'twill be hard—But you are wise.

Mir. A lord, sir?

Lug. Yes, and a noble lord.

Mir. 'Send her good fortune!
This will not stir her lord?—A baroness?
Say you so? say you so? By'r lady, a brave title!
Top, and top-gallant now! Save her great ladyship!
I was a poor servant of hers, I must confess, sir,
And in those days I thought I might be jovy,
And make a little bold to call in to her;
But, *basta!* now, I know my rules and distance;
Yet, if she want an usher, such an implement,
One that is throughly paced, a clean-made gentleman,
Can hold a hanging up with approbation,
Plant his hat formally, and wait with patience,
I do beseech you, sir——

Lug. Sir, leave your scoffing,
And, as you are a gentleman, deal fairly:
I have given you a friend's counsel; so I'll leave you.

Mir. But, hark ye, hark ye, sir! Is't possible
I may believe what you say?

Lug. You may choose, sir.

Mir. No baits? no fish-hooks, sir? no gins? no nooses?
No pitfalls to catch puppies?

Lug. I tell you certain:
You may believe; if not, stand to the danger! [*Exit.*

Mir. A lord of Savoy, says he? the duke's nephew?
A man so mighty? By'r lady, a fair marriage!
By my faith a handsome fortune! I must leave prating:
For, to confess the truth, I have abused her,
For which I should be sorry, but that will seem scurvy.
I must confess she was, ever since I knew her,
As modest as she was fair; I am sure she loved me;
Her means good, and her breeding excellent;
And for my sake she has refused fair matches:
I may play the fool finely.—Stay! who are these?

Enter DE GARD *disguised,* ORIANA, *and* Attendants.

'Tis she, I am sure; and that the lord, it should seem;
He carries a fair port, is a handsome man too.

I do begin to feel I am a coxcomb.

Ori. Good my lord, chuse a nobler; for I know
I am so far below your rank and honour,
That what you can say this way, I must credit
But spoken to beget yourself sport.   Alas, sir,
I am so far off from deserving you,
My beauty so unfit for your affection,
That I am grown the scorn of common railers,
Of such injurious things, that, when they cannot
Reach at my person, lie with my reputation.
I am poor, besides.

De Ga. You are all wealth and goodness;
And none but such as are the scum of men,
The ulcers of an honest state, spite-weavers,
That live on poison only, like swoln spiders,
Dare once profane such excellence, such sweetness.

Mir. This man speaks loud indeed.

De Ga. Name but the men, lady;
Let me but know these poor and base depravers,
Lay but to my revenge their persons open,
And you shall see how suddenly, how fully,
For your most beauteous sake, how direfully,
I'll handle their despites.   Is this thing one?
Be what he will——

Mir. Sir!

De Ga. Dare your malicious tongue, sir——

Mir. I know you not, nor what you mean.

Ori. Good my lord!

De Ga. If he, or any he——

Ori. I beseech your honour!
This gentleman's a stranger to my knowledge;
And, no doubt, sir, a worthy man.

De Ga. Your mercy!
But, had he been a tainter of your honour,
A blaster of those beauties reign within you——
But we shall find a fitter time.   Dear lady,
As soon as I have freed you from your guardian,
And done some honour'd offices unto you,
I'll take you, with those faults the world flings on you,
And dearer than the whole world I'll esteem you!

                                        [*Exeunt.*

Mir. This is a thundering lord: I am glad I 'scaped him.
How lovingly the wench disclaim'd my villainy!

I am vex'd now heartily that he shall have her;
Not that I care to marry, or to lose her,
But that this bilbo-lord shall reap that maidenhead
That was my due; that he shall rig and top her!
I'd give a thousand crowns now, he might miss her.

Enter a Servant.

Serv. Nay, if I bear your blows, and keep your counsel,
    You have good luck, sir: I'll teach you to strike lighter.
Mir. Come hither, honest fellow: Canst thou tell me
    Where this great lord lies? this Savoy lord? Thou
      met'st him;
    He now went by thee, certain.
Serv. Yes, he did, sir;
    I know him, and I know you are fool'd.
Mir. Come hither;   [*Gives money.*
    Here's all this, give me truth.
Serv. Not for your money
    (And yet that may do much), but I have been beaten,
    And by the worshipful contrivers beaten, and I'll tell you.
    This is no lord, no Savoy lord.
Mir. Go forward.
Serv. This is a trick, and put upon you grossly
    By one Lugier: The lord is monsieur De Gard, sir,
    An honest gentleman, and a neighbour here:
    Their ends you understand better than I, sure.
Mir. Now I know him;
    Know him now plain!
Serv. I have discharged my choler; so God be wi' you, sir!
                                   [*Exit.*
Mir. What a purblind puppy was I! Now I remember him;
    All the whole cast on's face, though it were umber'd,
    And mask'd with patches. What a dunder-whelp,
    To let him domineer thus! How he strutted,
    And what a load of lord he clapt upon him!
    'Would I had him here again! I would so bounce him,
    I would so thank his lordship for his lewd plot——
    Do they think to carry it away, with a great band made
      of bird-pots,
    And a pair of pin-buttock'd breeches?—Ha!

Enter De Gard, Oriana, *and* Attendants.

'Tis he again; he comes, he comes, he comes! have at
    him.—   *[Sings.*
My Savoy lord, why dost thou frown on me?
And will that favour never sweeter be?
Wilt thou, I say, for ever play the fool?
De Gard, be wise, and, Savoy, go to school!
My lord De Gard, I thank you for your antick;
My lady bright, that will be sometimes frantic;
You worthy train that wait upon this pair,
—'Send you more wit, and them a bouncing bair!
And so I take my humble leave of your honours! [*Exit.*

De Ga. We are discover'd, there's no remedy.
Lillia Bianca's man, upon my life.
In stubbornness, because Lugier corrected him—
A shameless slave! plague on him for a rascal!

Ori. I was in perfect hope. The bane on't is now,
He will make mirth on mirth, to persecute us.

De Ga. We must be patient; I am vex'd to th' proof too.
I'll try once more; then if I fail, here's one speaks.
                          [Puts his hand on his sword.

Ori. Let me be lost, and scorn'd first!

De Ga. Well, we'll consider.
Away, and let me shift; I shall be hooted else. [*Exeunt.*

ACT IV

SCENE I.—*A Street before the House of Pinac.*

Enter Lugier, Lillia, *and* Servant, *with a willow
garland.*

Lug. Faint not, but do as I direct ye; trust me.
Believe me too, for what I have told you, lady,
As true as you are Lillia, is authentic;
I know it, I have found it: 'Tis a poor courage
Flies off for one repulse. These travellers
Shall find, before we have done, a home-spun wit,
A plain French understanding, may cope with 'em.
They have had the better yet, thank your sweet squire
    here!
And let 'em brag. You would be revenged?

Lil. Yes, surely.

Lug. And married too?

Lil. I think so.

Lug. Then be counsell'd;
You know how to proceed.   I have other irons
Heating as well as yours, and I will strike
Three blows with one stone home.   Be ruled, and happy;
And so I leave you.   Now's the time.   [*Exit.*

Lil. I am ready,
If he do come to do me.

Serv. Will you stand here,
And let the people think you are God knows what,
        mistress?
Let boys and prentices presume upon you?

Lil. Pr'ythee hold thy peace.

Serv. Stand at his door that hates you?

Lil. Pr'ythee leave prating.

Serv. Pray you go to th' tavern: I'll give you a pint of
        wine there.
If any of the mad-cap gentlemen should come by,
That take up women upon special warrant,
You were in a wise case now.

Lil. Give me the garland;
And wait you here.

Enter MIRABEL, PINAC, MARIANA, Priest, *and*
Attendants.

Mir. She is here to seek thee, sirrah:
I told thee what would follow; she is mad for thee!
Show, and advance.   So early stirring, lady?
It shows a busy mind, a fancy troubled.
A willow garland too?   Is't possible?
'Tis pity so much beauty should lie musty;
But 'tis not to be help'd now.

Lil. The more's my misery.
Good fortune to you, lady, you deserve it;
To me, too-late repentance, I have sought it.
I do not envy, though I grieve a little,
You are mistress of that happiness, those joys,
That might have been, had I been wise.—But fortune——

Pinac. She understands you not; pray you do not trouble
        her!
And do not cross me like a hare thus; 'tis as ominous.

Lil. I come not to upbraid your levity,
(Though you made show of love, and though I liked you)
To claim an interest (we are yet both strangers;
But what we might have been, had you persévered, sir!)
To be an eye-sore to your loving lady:
This garland shows, I give myself forsaken,
(Yet, she must pardon me, 'tis most unwillingly!)
And all the power and interest I had in you
(As I persuade myself, somewhat you loved me!)
Thus patiently I render up, I offer
To her that must enjoy you, and so bless you!
Only, I heartily desire this courtesy,
And would not be denied, to wait upon you
This day, to see you tied, then no more trouble you.
Pinac. It needs not, lady.
Lil. Good sir, grant me so much.
Pinac. 'Tis private, and we make no invitation.
Lil. My presence, sir, shall not proclaim it public.
Pinac. May be, 'tis not in town.
Lil. I have a coach, sir,
And a most ready will to do you service.
Mir. Strike, now or never! make it sure! I tell thee,
                                 [*Aside to Pinac.*
She will hang herself, if she have thee not.
Pinac. Pray you, sir,
Entertain my noble mistress: Only a word or two
With this importunate woman, and I'll relieve you.—
Now you see what your flings are, and your fancies,
Your states, and your wild stubbornness; now you find
What 'tis to gird and kick at men's fair services,
To raise your pride to such a pitch and glory,
That goodness shows like gnats, scorn'd under you,
'Tis ugly, naught; a self-will in a woman,
Chain'd to an overweening thought, is pestilent,
Murders fair Fortune first, then fair Opinion:
There stands a pattern, a true patient pattern,
Humble, and sweet.
Lil. I can but grieve my ignorance.
Repentance, some say too, is the best sacrifice;
For sure, sir, if my chance had been so happy
(As I confess I was mine own destroyer)
As to have arrived at you (I will not prophesy,
But certain, as I think), I should have pleased you;

Have made you as much wonder at my courtesy,
My love, and duty, as I have dishearten'd you.
Some hours we have of youth, and some of folly;
And being free-born maids, we take a liberty,
And to maintain that, sometimes we strain highly.

Pinac. Now you talk reason.

Lil. But being yoak'd and govern'd,
Married, and those light vanities purged from us,
How fair we grow! how gentle, and how tender,
We twine about those loves that shoot up with us!
A sullen woman fear, that talks not to you;
She has a sad and darken'd soul, loves dully:
A merry and a free wench, give her liberty,
Believe her, in the lightest form she appears to you,
Believe her excellent, though she despise you;
Let but these fits and flashes pass, she'll show to you
As jewels rubb'd from dust, or gold new burnish'd:
Such had I been, had you believed!

Pinac. Is't possible?

Lil. And to your happiness I dare assure you,
If true love be accounted so.   Your pleasure,
Your will, and your command, had tied my motions:
But that hope's gone.   I know you are young and
giddy,
And, till you have a wife can govern with you,
You sail upon this world's sea, light and empty;
Your bark in danger daily.   'Tis not the name neither
Of wife can steer you, but the noble nature,
The diligence, the care, the love, the patience;
She makes the pilot, and preserves the husband,
That knows and reckons every rib he is built on.
But this I tell you to my shame.

Pinac. I admire you;
And now am sorry that I aim beyond you.—

Mir. So, so, so! fair and softly! She is thine own, boy;
She comes now without lure.—   [*Apart to him.*

Pinac. But that it must needs
Be reckon'd to me as a wantonness,
Or worse, a madness, to forsake a blessing,
A blessing of that hope——

Lil. I dare not urge you:
And yet, dear sir——

Pinac. 'Tis most certain, I had rather,

If 'twere in my own choice—for you're my country-
    woman,
A neighbour, here born by me; she a stranger,
And who knows how her friends——

Lil. Do as you please, sir;
    If you be fast, not all the world—I love you.
    It is most true, and clear, I would persuade you;
    And I shall love you still.

Pinac. Go, get before me:
    So much you have won upon me—do it presently:
    Here's a priest ready—I'll have you.

Lil. Not now, sir;
    No, you shall pardon me!—Advance your lady;
    I dare not hinder your most high preferment:
    'Tis honour enough for me I have unmask'd you.

Pinac. How's that?

Lil. I have caught you, sir! Alas, I am no stateswoman,
    Nor no great traveller, yet I have found you:
    I have found your lady too, your beauteous lady;
    I have found her birth and breeding too, her discipline,
    Who brought her over, and who kept your lady,
    And, when he laid her by, what virtuous nunnery
    Received her in; I have found all these! Are you blank
        now?
    Methinks, such travell'd wisdoms should not fool thus;
    Such excellent indiscretions——

Mir. How could she know this?

Lil. 'Tis true, she is English born, but most part French now,
    And so I hope you will find her to your comfort.
    Alas, I am ignorant of what she cost you!
    The price of these hired clothes I do not know, gentlemen!
    Those jewels are the broker's, how you stand bound
        for 'em!

Pinac. Will you make this good?

Lil. Yes, yes; and to her face, sir,
    That she's an English whore! a kind of fling-dust,
    One of your London light o' loves, a right one!
    Came over in thin pumps, and half a petticoat,
    One faith, and one smock, with a broken haberdasher:
    I know all this without a conjurer.
    Her name is Jumping-Joan, an ancient sin-weaver:
    She was first a lady's chambermaid, there slipp'd,
    And broke her leg above the knee; departed,

And set up shop herself; stood the fierce conflicts
Of many a furious term; there lost her colours,
And last shipp'd over hither.

Mir. We are betray'd!

Lil. Do you come to fright me with this mystery?
To stir me with a stink none can endure, sir?
I pray you proceed; the wedding will become you!
Who gives the lady? you? An excellent father!
A careful man, and one that knows a beauty!
Send you fair shipping, sir! and so I'll leave you.
Be wise and manly, then I may chance to love you!

[*Exit.*

Mir. As I live, I am ashamed this wench has reach'd me,
Monstrous ashamed; but there's no remedy.
This skew'd-eyed carrion——

Pinac. This I suspected ever.
Come, come, uncase; we have no more use of you;
Your clothes must back again.

Mariana. Sir, you shall pardon me;
'Tis not our English use to be degraded.
If you will visit me, and take your venture,
You shall have pleasure for your properties;
And so, sweetheart——   [*Exit.*

Mir. Let her go, and the devil go with her!
We have never better luck with these preludiums.
Come, be not daunted; think she's but a woman,
And let her have the devil's wit, we'll reach her!

[*Exeunt.*

SCENE II.—*A Grove near Nantolet's House.*

Enter ROSALURA *and* LUGIER.

Ros. You have now redeem'd my good opinion, tutor,
And you stand fair again.

Lug. I can but labour,
And sweat in your affairs. I am sure Belleur
Will be here instantly, and use his anger,
His wonted harshness.

Ros. I hope he will not beat me.

Lug. No, sure, he has more manners. Be you ready!

Ros. Yes, yes, I am; and am resolved to fit him,
With patience to out-do all he can offer.
But how does Oriana?

Lug. Worse, and worse still;
      There is a sad house for her; she is now,
      Poor lady, utterly distracted.
Ros. Pity!
      Infinite pity! 'Tis a handsome lady.
      That Mirabel's a beast, worse than a monster,
      If this affliction work not.

Enter Lillia Bianca.

Lil. Are you ready?
      Belleur is coming on, here, hard behind me:
      I have no leisure to relate my fortune;
      Only I wish you may come off as handsomely.
      Upon the sign you know what.   [*Exit.*
Ros. Well, well; leave me!

Enter Belleur.

Bel. How now?
Ros. You are welcome, sir.
Bel. 'Tis well ye have manners!
      That court'sy again, and hold your countenance staidly!
      That look's too light; take heed! so, sit ye down now;
      And to confirm me that your gall is gone,
      Your bitterness dispersed (for so I'll have it)
      Look on me steadfastly, and, whatsoe'er I say to you,
      Move not, nor alter in your face; you are gone then!
      For if you do express the least distaste,
      Or show an angry wrinkle (mark me, woman!
      We are now alone) I will so conjure thee,
      The third part of my execution
      Cannot be spoke.
Ros. I am at your dispose, sir.
Bel. Now rise, and woo me a little; let me hear that faculty:
      But touch me not; nor do not lie, I charge you!
      Begin now.
Ros. If so mean and poor a beauty
      May ever hope the grace——
Bel. You cog, you flatter!
      Like a lewd thing, you lie! " May hope that grace? "
      Why, what grace canst thou hope for? Answer not;
      For if thou dost, and liest again, I'll swinge thee!
      Do not I know thee for a pestilent woman?
      A proud at both ends? Be not angry,

      Nor stir not o' your life!

Ros. I am counsell'd, sir.

Bel. Art thou not now (confess, for I'll have the truth out)
    As much unworthy of a man of merit,
    Or any of ye all, nay, of mere man,
    Though he were crooked, cold, all wants upon him,
    Nay, of any dishonest thing that bears that figure,
    As devils are of mercy?

Ros. We are unworthy.

Bel. Stick to that truth, and it may chance to save thee.
    And is it not our bounty that we take ye?
    That we are troubled, vex'd, or tortured with ye,
    Our mere and special bounty?

Ros. Yes.

Bel. Our pity,
    That for your wickedness we swinge ye soundly;
    Your stubbornness, and your stout hearts, we belabour
      ye?
    Answer to that!

Ros. I do confess your pity.

Bel. And dost not thou deserve in thine own person,
    Thou impudent, thou pert—Do not change countenance!

Ros. I dare not, sir.

Bel. For if you do——

Ros. I am settled.

Bel. Thou wagtail, peacock, puppy, look on me:
    I am a gentleman.

Ros. It seems no less, sir.

Bel. And darest thou in thy surquedry——

Ros. I beseech you!
    It was my weakness, sir, I did not view you,
    I took not notice of your noble parts,
    Nor culled your person, nor your proper fashion.

Bel. This is some amends yet.

Ros. I shall mend, sir, daily,
    And study to deserve.

Bel. Come a little nearer!
    Canst thou repent thy villainy?

Ros. Most seriously.

Bel. And be ashamed!

Ros. I am ashamed.

Bel. Cry!

Ros. It will be hard to do, sir.

Bel. Cry now instantly;
    Cry monstrously, that all the town may hear thee;
    Cry seriously, as if thou hadst lost thy monkey;
    And, as I like thy tears——
Ros. Now!

Enter Lillia, *and four* Women *laughing.*

Bel. How! how! do you jeer me?
    Have you broke your bounds again, dame?
Ros. Yes, and laugh at you,
    And laugh most heartily.
Bel. What are these? whirlwinds?
    Is hell broke loose, and all the furies flutter'd?
    Am I greased once again?
Ros. Yes, indeed are you;
    And once again you shall be, if you quarrel!
    Do you come to vent your fury on a virgin?
    Is this your manhood, sir?
1 *Wom.* Let him do his best;
    Let's see the utmost of his indignation;
    I long to see him angry.   Come; proceed, sir.
    Hang him, he dares not stir; a man of timber!
2 *Wom.* Come hither to fright maids with thy bull-faces?
    To threaten gentlewomen!   Thou a man? a maypole!
    A great dry pudding!
3 *Wom.* Come, come, do your worst, sir;
    Be angry if thou darest.
Bel. The Lord deliver me!
4 *Wom.* Do but look scurvily upon this lady,
    Or give us one foul word—We are all mistaken;
    This is some mighty dairy-maid in man's clothes.
Lil. I am of that mind too.
Bel. What will they do to me?
Lil. And hired to come and abuse us: A man has manners;
    A gentleman, civility and breeding.
    Some tinker's trull, with a beard glew'd on.
1 *Wom.* Let's search him,
    And as we find him——
Bel. Let me but depart from ye,
    Sweet Christian women!
Lil. Hear the thing speak, neighbours.
Bel. 'Tis but a small request: If e'er I trouble ye,
    If e'er I talk again of beating women,

　　　　Or beating anything that can but turn to me,
　　　　Of ever thinking of a handsome lady
　　　　But virtuously and well, of ever speaking
　　　　But to her honour—This I'll promise ye,
　　　　I will take rhubarb, and purge choler mainly.
　　　　Abundantly I'll purge.
Lil. I'll send you broths, sir.
Bel. I will be laugh'd at, and endure it patiently;
　　　　I will do anything!
Ros. I'll be your bail then.
　　　　When you come next to woo, pray you come not
　　　　　　boisterously,
　　　　And furnish'd like a bear-ward.
Bel. No, in truth, forsooth.
Ros. I scented you long since.
Bel. I was to blame, sure;
　　　　I will appear a gentleman.
Ros. 'Tis the best for you,
　　　　For a true noble gentleman's a brave thing.
　　　　Upon that hope, we quit you.　You fear seriously?
Bel. Yes, truly do I; I confess I fear you,
　　　　And honour you, and anything!
Ros. Farewell then!
Wom. And when you come to woo next, bring more mercy!
　　　　　　　　　　　　[*Exeunt Rosalura and Women.*

　　　　　　　　Enter two Gentlemen.

Bel. A dairy-maid! a tinker's trull! Heaven bless me!
　　　　Sure, if I had provoked 'em, they had quarter'd me.
　　　　I am a most ridiculous ass, now I perceive it;
　　　　A coward, and a knave too.
1 *Gent.* 'Tis the mad gentleman;
　　　　Let's set our faces right.
Bel. No, no; laugh at me,
　　　　And laugh aloud.
2 *Gent.* We are better manner'd, sir.
Bel. I do deserve it; call me patch, and puppy,
　　　　And beat me, if you please.
1 *Gent.* No, indeed; we know you.
Bel. 'Death, do as I would have ye!
2 *Gent.* You are an ass then,
　　　　A coxcomb, and a calf!
Bel. I am a great calf.

Kick me a little now: Why, when? Sufficient.

> [*They kick him.*

Now laugh aloud, and scorn me; so God b' wi' ye!
And ever when ye meet me, laugh.

1 *Gent.* We will, sir.   [*Exeunt.*

SCENE III.—*A Room in La Castre's House.*

Enter NANTOLET, LA CASTRE, DE GARD, LUGIER, *and*
MIRABEL.

Mir. Your patience, gentlemen! Why do ye bait me?
Nant. Is't not a shame you are so stubborn-hearted,
  So stony and so dull, to such a lady,
  Of her perfections and her misery?
Lug. Does she not love you? Does not her distraction
  For your sake only, her most pitied lunacy
  Of all but you, show ye? Does it not compel ye?
Mir. Soft and fair, gentlemen; pray ye proceed temperately.
Lug. If you have any feeling, any sense in you,
  The least touch of a noble heart——
La Ca. Let him alone:
  It is his glory that he can kill beauty.
  You bear my stamp, but not my tenderness;
  Your wild unsavoury courses set that in you!
  For shame, be sorry, though you cannot cure her;
  Show something of a man, of a fair nature.
Mir. You make me mad!
De Ga. Let me pronounce this to you;
  You take a strange felicity in slighting
  And wronging women, which my poor sister feels now;
  Heaven's hand be gentle on her! Mark me, sir,
  That very hour she dies (there's small hope otherwise)
  That minute, you and I must grapple for it;
  Either your life or mine!
Mir. Be not so hot, sir;
  I am not to be wrought on by these policies,
  In truth, I am not! nor do I fear the tricks,
  Or the high-sounding threats, of a Savoyan.
  I glory not in cruelty (ye wrong me)
  Nor grow up water'd with the tears of women.
  This let me tell ye, howso'er I show to ye,
  Wild, as ye please to call it, or self-will'd,

When I see cause I can both do and suffer,
Freely, and feelingly, as a true gentleman.

Enter Rosalura *and* Lillia.

Ros. Oh, pity, pity! thousand, thousand pities!
Lil. Alas, poor soul! she will die! she is grown senseless;
  She will not know, nor speak now.
Ros. Die for love?
  And love of such a youth? I would die for a dog first!
  He that kills me, I'll give him leave to eat me!
  I'll know men better, ere I sigh for any of 'em.
Lil. Ye have done a worthy act, sir, a most famous;
  You have kill'd a maid the wrong way; ye're a conqueror!
Ros. A conqueror? a cobler! Hang him, sowter!
  Go hide thyself, for shame! go lose thy memory!
  Live not 'mongst men; thou art a beast, a monster,
  A blatant beast!
Lil. If you have yet any honesty,
  Or ever heard of any, take my counsel;
  Off with your garters, and seek out a bough,
  A handsome bough; for I would have you hang like a
    gentleman;
  And write some doleful matter to the world,
  A warning to hard-hearted men.
Mir. Out, kittlings!
  What catterwauling's here! what gibing!
  Do you think my heart is soften'd with a black santis?
  Show me some reason.

ORIANA *is brought in, lying on a bed.*

Ros. Here then, here is a reason.
Nant. Now, if ye be a man, let this sight shake ye!
La Ca. Alas, poor gentlewoman! Do you know me, lady?
Lug. How she looks up, and stares!
Ori. I know you very well;
  You are my godfather: and that's the monsieur.
De Ga. And who am I?
Ori. You are Amadis de Gaul, sir.
  Oh, oh, my heart! Were ye never in love, sweet lady?
  And do you never dream of flowers and gardens?
  I dream of walking fires: Take heed! It comes now.
  Who's that? Pray stand away. I have seen that face
    sure.

How light my head is!
Ros. Take some rest.
Ori. I cannot;
    For I must be up to-morrow to go to church,
    And I must dress me, put my new gown on,
    And be as fine to meet my love!   Heigh-ho!
    Will not you tell we where my love lies buried?
Mir. He is not dead.—Beshrew my heart, she stirs me!

                                                    [Aside.

Ori. He is dead to me.
Mir. Is't possible my nature
    Should be so damnable, to let her suffer?—
    Give me your hand.
Ori. How soft you feel, how gentle!
    I'll tell you your fortune, friend.
Mir. How she stares on me!
Ori. You have a flattering face, but 'tis a fine one;
    I warrant you may have a hundred sweethearts.
    Will ye pray for me?   I shall die to-morrow;
    And will ye ring the bells?
Mir. I am most unworthy,
    I do confess, unhappy.   Do you know me?
Ori. I would I did!
Mir. Oh, fair tears, how ye take me!
Ori. Do ye weep too?   You have not lost your lover?
    You mock me; I'll go home and pray.
Mir. Pray you pardon me;
    Or, if it please you to consider justly,
    Scorn me, for I deserve it; scorn and shame me,
    Sweet Oriana!
Lil. Let her alone; she trembles:
    Her fits will grow more strong, if ye provoke her.
La Ca. Certain she knows you not, yet loves to see you.
    How she smiles now!

Enter Belleur.

Bel. Where are ye?   Oh, why do not you laugh?   Come,
      laugh at me!
    Why 'a devil art thou sad, and such a subject,
    Such a ridiculous subject, as I am,
    Before thy face?
Mir. Pr'ythee put off this lightness;
N 306

This is no time for mirth, nor place; I have used too
   much on't:
I have undone myself, and a sweet lady,
By being too indulgent to my foolery,
Which truly I repent.   Look here!

Bel. What ails she?

Mir. Alas, she is mad.

Bel. Mad?

Mir. Yes, too sure; for me too.

Bel. Dost thou wonder at that?   By this good light, they are
   all so;
They are cozening mad, they are brawling mad, they are
   proud mad;
They are all, all mad. I came from a world of mad
   women,
Mad as March hares: Get 'em in chains, then deal with
   'em.
There's one that's mad; she seems well, but she is dog-
   mad.
Is she dead, dost think?

Mir. Dead?   Heaven forbid!

Bel. Heaven further it!
For, till they be key-cold dead, there's no trusting of 'em.
Whate'er they seem, or howsoe'er they carry it,
Till they be chap-fall'n, and their tongues at peace,
Nail'd in their coffins sure, I'll ne'er believe 'em.
Shall I talk with her?

Mir. No, dear friend, be quiet,
And be at peace a while.

Bel. I'll walk aside,
And come again anon.   But take heed to her:
You say she is a woman?

Mir. Yes.

Bel. Take great heed;
For if she do not cozen thee, then hang me.
Let her be mad, or what she will, she'll cheat thee!
                              [*Exit.*

Mir. Away, wild fool!—How vile this shows in him now!
Now take my faith (before ye all I speak it)
And with it my repentant love.

La Ca. This seems well.

Mir. Were but this lady clear again, whose sorrows
My very heart melts for, were she but perfect

(For thus to marry her would be two miseries)
Before the richest and the noblest beauty,
France, or the world could show me, I would take her:
As she now is, my tears and prayers shall wed her.
De Ga. This makes some small amends.
Ros. She beckons to you:
　To us too, to go off.
Nant. Let's draw aside all.

[Exeunt all but Oriana and Mirabel.
Ori. Oh, my best friend! I would fain——
Mir. What! She speaks well,
　And with another voice.
Ori. But I am fearful,
　And shame a little stops my tongue——
Mir. Speak boldly.
Ori. Tell you, I am well, I am perfect well (pray you mock
　　not);
　And that I did this to provoke your nature;
　Out of my infinite and restless love,
　To win your pity.　Pardon me!
Mir. Go forward:
　Who set you on?
Ori. None, as I live, no creature;
　Not any knew, or ever dream'd what I meant.
　Will you be mine?
Mir. 'Tis true, I pity you;
　But when I marry you, you must be wiser.
　Nothing but tricks? devices?
Ori. Will you shame me?
Mir. Yes, marry, will I.—Come near, come near! a miracle!
　The woman's well; she was only mad for marriage,
　Stark mad to be stoned to death; give her good counsel.—
　Will this world never mend?—Are you caught, damsel?

Enter Belleur, La Castre, Lugier, Nantolet, De Gard,
　　　Rosalura, *and* Lillia.

Bel. How goes it now?
Mir. Thou art a kind of prophet;
　The woman's well again, and would have gull'd me;
　Well, excellent well, and not a taint upon her.
Bel. Did not I tell you?　Let 'em be what can be,
　Saints, devils, anything, they will abuse us.

Thou wert an ass to believe her so long, a coxcomb;
Give 'em a minute, they'll abuse whole millions.

Mir. And am not I a rare physician, gentlemen,
That can cure desperate mad minds?

De Ga. Be not insolent.

Mir. Well, go thy ways: From this hour I disclaim thee,
Unless thou hast a trick above this; then I'll love thee.
You owe me for your cure.—Pray have a care of her,
For fear she fall into a relapse.—Come, Belleur;
We'll set up bills to cure diseased virgins.

Bel. Shall we be merry?

Mir. Yes.

Bel. But I'll no more projects:
If we could make 'em mad, it were some mastery!

[*Exeunt.*

Lil. I am glad she is well again.

Ros. So am I, certain.—
Be not ashamed.

Ori. I shall never see a man more.

De Ga. Come, you're a fool! had you but told me this trick,
He should not have gloried thus.

Lug. He shall not long, neither.

La Ca. Be ruled, and be at peace: You have my consent,
And what power I can work with.

Nant. Come, leave blushing;
We are your friends: An honest way compell'd you.
Heaven will not see so true a love unrecompensed.
Come in, and slight him too.

Lug. The next shall hit him. [*Exeunt.*

ACT V

SCENE I.—*A Street.*

Enter De Gard *and* Lugier.

De Ga. 'Twill be discover'd.

Lug. That's the worst can happen:
If there be any way to reach, and work upon him,
Upon his nature suddenly, and catch him—That he loves,
Though he dissemble it and would show contrary,
And will at length relent, I'll lay my fortune;
Nay, more, my life.

De Ga. Is she won?

Lug.   Yes, and ready,
  And my designments set.

De Ga. They are now for travel;
  All for that game again; they have forgot wooing.

Lug. Let 'em; we'll travel with 'em.

De Ga.   Where's his father?

Lug. Within; he knows my mind too, and allows it,
  Pities your sister's fortune most sincerely;
  And has appointed, for our more assistance,
  Some of his secret friends.

De Ga.   'Speed the plough!

Lug.   Well said:
  And be you serious too.

De Ga.   I shall be diligent.

Lug. Let's break the ice for one, the rest will drink too
  (Believe me, sir) of the same cup: My young gentlewomen
  Wait but who sets the game a-foot; though they seem
      stubborn,
  Reserv'd, and proud now, yet I know their hearts,
  Their pulses how they beat, and for what cause, sir,
  And how they long to venture their abilities
  In a true quarrel.   Husbands they must and will have,
  Or nunneries, and thin collations
  To cool their bloods.   Let's all about our business;
  And, if this fail, let Nature work!

De Ga. You have armed me.   [*Exeunt.*

SCENE II.—*Before La Castre's House.*

Enter MIRABEL, NANTOLET, *and* LA CASTRE.

La Ca. Will you be wilful then?

Mir.   Pray, sir, your pardon;
  For I must travel.   Lie lazy here,
  Bound to a wife? chain'd to her subtleties,
  Her humours, and her wills, which are mere fetters?
  To have her to-day pleased, to-morrow peevish,
  The third day mad, the fourth rebellious?
  You see, before they are married, what moriscoes,
  What masques and mummeries they put upon us:
  To be tied here, and suffer their lavoltas!

Nant. 'Tis your own seeking.

Mir. Yes, to get my freedom.
    Were they as I could wish 'em——
La Ca. Fools and meacocks,
    To endure what you think fit to put upon 'em!
    Come, change your mind.
Mir. Not before I have changed air, father.
    When I know women worthy of my company,
    I will return again and wait upon 'em;
    Till then, dear sir, I'll amble all the world over,
    And run all hazards, misery, and poverty,
    So I escape the dangerous bay of matrimony!

Enter BELLEUR *and* PINAC.

Pinac. Are you resolved?
Mir. Yes, certain; I will out again.
Pinac. We are for you, sir; we are your servants once more:
    Once more we'll seek our fortune in strange countries:
    Ours is too scornful for us.
Bel. Is there ne'er a land
    That you have read, or heard of (for I care not how far it
      be,
    Nor under what pestiferous star it lies),
    A happy kingdom, where there are no women?
    Nor have been ever? nor no mention
    Of any such lewd things, with lewder qualities?
    For thither would I travel; where 'tis felony
    To confess he had a mother; a mistress, treason.
La Ca. Are you for travel too?
Bel. For anything,
    For living in the moon, and stopping hedges,
    Ere I stay here to be abused, and baffled.
Nant. Why did you not break your minds to me? they are
      my daughters;
    And sure I think I should have that command over 'em,
    To see 'em well bestow'd. I know ye are gentlemen,
    Men of fair parts and states; I know your parents;
    And had ye told me of your fair affections——
    Make but one trial more, and let me second ye.
Bel. No; I'll make hob-nails first, and mend old kettles!
    Can you lend me an armour of high proof, to appear in,
    And two or three field-pieces to defend me?
    The king's guard are mere pigmies.
Nant. They'll not eat you.

Bel. Yes, and you too, and twenty fatter monsieurs,
　　If their high stomachs hold: They came with chopping-
　　　　knives,
　　To cut me into rands and sirloins, and so powder me.—
　　Come, shall we go?
Nant. You cannot be so discourteous,
　　If ye intend to go, as not to visit 'em,
　　And take your leaves.
Mir. That we dare do, and civilly,
　　And thank 'em too.
Pinac. Yes, sir, we know that honesty.
Bel. I'll come i' th' rear, forty foot off, I'll assure you,
　　With a good gun in my hand; I'll no more Amazons,
　　I mean no more of their frights: I'll make my three legs,
　　Kiss my hand twice, and if I smell no danger,
　　If the interview be clear, may be I'll speak to her;
　　I'll wear a privy coat too, and behind me,
　　To make those parts secure, a bandog.
La Ca. You are a merry gentleman.
Bel. A wary gentleman, I do assure you;
　　I have been warn'd, and must be arm'd.
La Ca. Well, son,
　　These are your hasty thoughts; when I see you are bent
　　　　to it,
　　Then I'll believe, and join with you; so we'll leave ye.
　　There is a trick will make ye stay.　　　　　[*Exit.*
Nant. I hope so.　　　　　　　　　　　　　　[*Exit.*
Mir. We have won immortal fame now, if we leave 'em.
Pinac. You have, but we have lost.
Mir. Pinac, thou art cozen'd;
　　I know they love you; and to gain you handsomely,
　　Not to be thought to yield, they would give millions:
　　Their father's willingness, that must needs show you.
Pinac. If I thought so——
Mir. You shall be hang'd, you recreant!
　　Would you turn renegado now?
Bel. No; let's away, boys,
　　Out of the air and tumult of their villainies.
　　Though I were married to that grasshopper,
　　And had her fast by th' legs, I should think she would
　　　　cozen me.

Enter a young Man, disguised as a Factor.

Fac. Monsieur Mirabel, I take it?

Mir. You are i' th' right, sir.

Fac. I am come to seek you, sir; I have been at your father's,
　　And understanding you were here——

Mir. You are welcome.
　　May I crave your name?

Fac. Fosse, sir, and your servant.
　　That you may know me better, I am factor
　　To your old merchant, Leverdure.

Mir. How does he?

Fac. Well, sir, I hope; he is now at Orleans,
　　About some business.

Mir. You are once more welcome.
　　Your master's a right honest man, and one
　　I am much beholding to, and must very shortly
　　Trouble his love again.

Fac. You may be bold, sir.

Mir. Your business, if you please now?

Fac. This it is, sir.
　　I know you well remember, in your travel,
　　A Genoa merchant——

Mir. I remember many.

Fac. But this man, sir, particularly; your own benefit
　　Must needs imprint him in you; one Alberto,
　　A gentleman you saved from being murder'd
　　A little from Bologna:
　　I was then myself in Italy, and supplied you;
　　Though happily you have forgot me now.

Mir. No, I remember you,
　　And that Alberto too; a noble gentleman.
　　More to remember were to thank myself, sir.
　　What of that gentleman?

Fac. He's dead.

Mir. I am sorry.

Fac. But on his death-bed, leaving to his sister
　　All that he had, beside some certain jewels
　　(Which, with a ceremony, he bequeathed to you,
　　In grateful memory), he commanded strictly
　　His sister, as she loved him and his peace,
　　To see those jewels safe and true deliver'd,
　　And, with them, his last love.　She, as tender to

Observe this will, not trusting friend nor servant
With such a weight, is come herself to Paris,
And at my master's house.

Mir. You tell me a wonder.

Fac. I tell you a truth, sir.   She is young and handsome,
And well attended; of much state and riches;
So loving and obedient to her brother,
That, on my conscience, if he had given her also,
She would most willingly have made her tender.

Mir. May not I see her?

Fac. She desires it heartily.

Mir. And presently?

Fac. She is now about some business,
Passing accounts of some few debts here owing,
And buying jewels of a merchant.

Mir. Is she wealthy?

Fac. I would you had her, sir, at all adventure:
Her brother had a main state.

Mir. And fair too?

Fac. The prime of all those parts of Italy,
For beauty and for courtesy.

Mir. I must needs see her.

Fac. 'Tis all her business, sir.   You may now see her;
But to-morrow will be fitter for your visitation,
For she's not yet prepared.

Mir. Only her sight, sir:
And, when you shall think fit, for further visit.

Fac. Sir, you may see her, and I'll wait your coming.

Mir. And I'll be with ye instantly.   I know the house;
Meantime, my love, and thanks, sir!

Fac. Your poor servant.   [*Exit.*

Pinac. Thou hast the strangest luck!   What was that
Alberto?

Mir. An honest noble merchant, 'twas my chance
To rescue from some rogues had almost slain him;
And he in kindness to remember this!

Bel. Now we shall have you
(For all your protestations, and your forwardness)
Find out strange fortunes in this lady's eyes,
And new enticements to put off your journey;
And who shall have honour then?

Mir. No, no, never fear it:
I must needs see her, to receive my legacy.

*N 506

Bel. If it be tied up in her smock, Heaven help thee!
    May not we see too?
Mir. Yes, afore we go:
    I must be known myself ere I be able
    To make thee welcome.   Wouldst thou see more women?
    I thought you had been out of love with all.
Bel. I may be,
    (I find that) with the least encouragement;
    Yet I desire to see whether all countries
    Are naturally possess'd with the same spirits,
    For if they be, I'll take a monastery,
    And never travel; for I had rather be a friar,
    And live mewed up, than be a fool, and flouted.
Mir. Well, well, I'll meet you anon, then tell you more, boys:
    However, stand prepared, prest for our journey;
    For certain, we shall go, I think, when I have seen her,
    And viewed her well.
Pinac. Go, go, and we'll wait for ye;
    Your fortune directs ours.
Bel. You shall find us i' th' tavern,
    Lamenting in sack and sugar for our losses,
    If she be right Italian, and want servants,
    You may prefer the properest man: How I could
    Worry a woman now!
Pinac. Come, come, leave prating:
    You may have enough to do, without this boasting.
                                                [*Exeunt.*

SCENE III.—*A Room in La Castre's House.*

Enter LUGIER, DE GARD, ROSALURA, *and* LILLIA BIANCA.

Lug. This is the last adventure.
De Ga. And the happiest,
    As we hope, too.
Ros. We should be glad to find it.
Lil. Who shall conduct us thither?
Lug. Your man is ready,
    For I must not be seen; no, nor this gentleman;
    That may beget suspicion; all the rest
    Are people of no doubt.   I would have ye, ladies,
    Keep your old liberties, and do as we instruct ye.
    Come, look not pale, ye shall not lose your wishes,
    Nor beg 'em neither, but be yourselves and happy.

Ros. I tell you true, I cannot hold off longer,
    Nor give no more hard language.
De Ga. You shall not need.
Ros. I love the gentleman, and must now show it:
    Shall I beat a proper man out of heart?
Lug. There's none advises you.
Lil. 'Faith, I repent me too.
Lug. Repent and spoil all;
    Tell what you know, you had best!
Lil. I'll tell what I think;
    For if he ask me now, if I can love him,
    I'll tell him, yes, I can.   The man's a kind man,
    And out of his true honesty affects me.
    Although he play'd the fool, which I requited,
    Must I still hold him at the stave's end?
Lug. You are two strange women.
Ros. We may be, if we fool still.
Lug. Dare ye believe me?
    Follow but this advice I have set you in now,
    And if ye lose—Would ye yield now so basely?
    Give up without your honours saved?
De Ga. Fy, ladies!
    Preserve your freedom still.
Lil. Well, well, for this time.
Lug. And carry that full state——
Ros. That's as the wind stands;
    If it begin to chop about, and scant us,
    Hang me, but I know what I'll do!   Come, direct us;
    I make no doubt, we shall do handsomely.
De Ga. Some part o' th' way, we'll wait upon you, ladies;
    The rest your man supplies.
Lug. Do well, I'll honour ye.   [*Exeunt.*

SCENE IV.—*A Room in a neighbouring House with a
            Gallery.*

Enter the young Man *disguised as a* Factor *and* MIRABEL
    above ; ORIANA *disguised, and two disguised as* Mer-
    chants.

Fac. Look you, sir, there she is; you see how busy.
    Methinks you are infinitely bound to her, for her journey.
Mir. How gloriously she shows!   She's a tall woman.

Fac. Of a fair size, sir. My master not being at home,
    I have been so out of my wits to get her company!
    I mean, sir, of her own fair sex and fashion——
Mir. Afar off, she's most fair too.
Fac. Near, most excellent.—
    At length, I have entreated two fair ladies
    (And happily you know 'em), the young daughters
    Of monsieur Nantolet——
Mir. I know 'em well, sir.
    What are those? jewels?
Fac. All.
Mir. They make a rich show.
Fac. There is a matter of ten thousand pounds too
    Was owing here: You see those merchants with her;
    They have brought it in now.
Mir. How handsomely her shape shows!
Fac. Those are still neat; your Italians are most curious.
    Now she looks this way.
Mir. She has a goodly presence!
    How full of courtesy! Well, sir, I'll leave you;
    And if I may be bold to bring a friend or two,
    Good noble gentlemen——
Fac. No doubt, you may, sir;
    For you have most command.
Mir. I have seen a wonder!   *[Exit.*
Ori. Is he gone?
Fac. Yes.
Ori. How?
Fac. Taken to the utmost:
    A wonder dwells about him.
Ori. He did not guess at me?
Fac. No; be secure, you show another woman.
    He is gone to fetch his friends.
Ori. Where are the gentlewomen?

       Enter below ROSALURA, LILLIA, *and* Servant.

Fac. Here, here; now they are come,
    Sit still, and let them see you.
Ros. Pray you, where's my friend, sir?
Fac. She is within, ladies; but here's another gentlewoman,
    A stranger to this town: So please you visit her,
    'Twill be well taken.

Lil. Where is she?

Fac. There, above, ladies.

Enter ROSALURA, LILLIA, *and* Servant.

Serv. Bless me! what thing is this? Two pinnacles
Upon her pate! Is't not a glade to catch woodcocks?

Ros. Peace, you rude knave!

Serv. What a bouncing bum she has too!
There's sail enough for a carrack.

Ros. What is this lady?
For, as I live, she is a goodly woman.

Fac. Guess, guess.

Lil. I have not seen a nobler presence.

Serv. 'Tis a lusty wench! Now could I spend my forty-
pence,
With all my heart, to have but one fling at her,
To give her but a swashing blow.

Lil. You rascal!

Serv. Ay, that's all a man has for's good will: 'Twill be long
enough
Before you cry, " Come, Anthony, and kiss me."

Lil. I'll have you whipt.

Ros. Has my friend seen this lady?

Fac. Yes, yes, and is well known to her.

Ros. I much admire her presence.

Lil. So do I too;
For, I protest, she is the handsomest,
The rarest, and the newest to mine eye,
That ever I saw yet.

Ros. I long to know her;
My friend shall do that kindness.

Ori. So she shall, ladies:
Come, pray you come up.

Ros. Oh me!

Lil. Hang me, if I knew her!
Were I a man myself, I should now love you;
Nay, I should dote.

Ros. I dare not trust mine eyes;
For, as I live, you are the strangest alter'd——
I must come up to know the truth.

Serv. So must I, lady;
For I'm a kind of unbeliever too.

Lil. Get you gone, sirrah;
 And what you have seen be secret in; you are paid else!
 No more of your long tongue.
Fac. Will ye go in, ladies,
 And talk with her? These ventures will come straight.
 Away with this fellow.
Lil. There, sirrah; go, disport you.
Serv. I would the trunk-hosed woman would go with me.
            [Exit.

SCENE V.—*The Street before the same House.*

Enter MIRABEL, PINAC, *and* BELLEUR.

Pinac. Is she so glorious handsome?
Mir. You would wonder;
 Our women look like gipsies, like Gills to her;
 Their clothes and fashions beggerly, and bankrupt,
 Base, old, and scurvy.
Bel. How looks her face?
Mir. Most heavenly;
 And the becoming motion of her body
 So sets her off!
Bel. Why, then we shall stay.
Mir. Pardon me,
 That's more than I know; if she be that woman
 She appears to be——
Bel. As 'tis impossible.
Mir. I shall then tell you more.
Pinac. Did you speak to her?
Mir. No, no, I only saw her, she was busy:
 Now I go for that end; and mark her, gentlemen,
 If she appear not to you one of the sweetest,
 The handsomest, the fairest, in behaviour——
 We shall meet the two wenches there too; they come to
  visit her,
 To wonder, as we do.
Pinac. Then we shall meet 'em.
Bel. I had rather meet two bears.
Mir. There you may take your leaves, dispatch that business,
 And, as ye find their humours——
Pinac. Is your love there too?
Mir. No, certain; she has no great heart to set out again.
 This is the house; I'll usher you.

Bel. I'll bless me,
> And take a good heart, if I can.
Mir. Come, nobly.   [*Exeunt*

SCENE VI.—*A Room in the same House.*

Enter Factor, Rosalura, Lillia, *and* Oriana.

Fac. They are come in.   Sit you two off, as strangers.

Enter Boy.

> There, lady.—Where's the boy?   Be ready, sirrah,
> And clear your pipes; the music now; they enter.
> > [*Music.*

Enter Mirabel, Pinac, *and* Belleur.

Pinac. What a state she keeps!   How far off they sit from
>   her!
> How rich she is!   Ay, marry, this shows bravely!
Bel. She is a lusty wench, and may allure a good man;
> But if she have a tongue, I'll not give two-pence for her.
> There sits my fury; how I shake to see her!
Fac. Madam, this is the gentleman.
Mir. How sweet she kisses!
> She has a spring dwells on her lips, a Paradise!
> This is the legacy.

SONG.

> From the honour'd dead I bring
> Thus his love and last off'ring.
> Take it nobly, 'tis your due,
> From a friendship ever true.
> From a faith, etc.

Ori. Most noble sir,
> This from my now-dead brother, as his love,
> And grateful memory of your great benefit;
> From me my thanks, my wishes, and my service.
> Till I am more acquainted, I am silent;
> Only I dare say this, you are truly noble.
Mir. What should I think?
Pinac. Think you've a handsome fortune:
> 'Would I had such another!
Ros. Ye are well met, gentlemen;

We hear ye are for travel?

Pinac. You hear true, lady;
And come to take our leaves.

Lil. We'll along with ye:
We see you're grown so witty by your journey,
We cannot chuse but step out too.   This lady
We mean to wait upon as far as Italy.

Bel. I'll travel into Wales, amongst the mountains,
In hope they cannot find me.

Ros. If you go further,
So good and free society we hold ye,
We'll jog along too.

Pinac. Are you so valiant, lady?

Lil. And we'll be merry, sir, and laugh.

Pinac. It may be
We'll go by sea.

Lil. Why, 'tis the only voyage;
I love a sea-voyage, and a blustering tempest;
And let all split!

Pinac. This is a dainty damosel!
I think 'twill tame you.—Can you ride post?

Lil. Oh, excellently! I am never weary that way:
A hundred mile a-day is nothing with me.

Bel. I'll travel under ground.   Do you hear, sweet lady?
I find it will be dangerous for a woman.

Ros. No danger, sir; I warrant; I love to be under.

Bel. I see she will abuse me all the world over!—
But say we pass through Germany, and drink hard?

Ros. We'll learn to drink and swagger too.

Bel. She'll beat me!—
Lady, I'll live at home.

Ros. And I'll live with thee;
And we'll keep house together.

Bel. I'll keep hounds first;
And those I hate right heartily.

Pinac. I go for Turkey!
And so it may be up into Persia.

Lil. We cannot know too much; I'll travel with you.

Pinac. And you'll abuse me?

Lil. Like enough.

Pinac. 'Tis dainty!

Bel. I will live in a bawdy-house.

Ros. I dare come to you.

Bel. Say I'm disposed to hang myself?
Ros. There I'll leave you.
Bel. I am glad I know how to avoid you.—
Mir. May I speak yet?
Fac. She beckons to you.
Mir. Lady, I could wish I knew to recompense,
    Even with the service of my life, those pains,
    And those high favours you have thrown upon me:
    Till I be more desertful in your eye,
    And till my duty shall make known I honour you,
    Noblest of women, do me but this favour,
    To accept this back again, as a poor testimony.
Ori. I must have you too with 'em; else the will,
    That says they must rest with you, is infringed, sir;
    Which, pardon me, I dare not do.
Mir. Take me then,
    And take me with the truest love.
Ori. 'Tis certain,
    My brother loved you dearly, and I ought
    As dearly to preserve that love: But, sir,
    Though I were willing, these are but your ceremonies.
Mir. As I have life, I speak my soul!
Ori. I like you:
    But how you can like me, without I have testimony,
    A stranger to you ——
Mir. I'll marry you immediately;
    A fair state I dare promise you.
Bel. Yet she'll cozen thee.
Ori. 'Would some fair gentleman durst promise for you!
Mir. By all that's good——

Enter La Castre, Nantolet, Lugier, *and* De Gard.

All. And we'll make up the rest, lady.
Ori. Then, Oriana takes you.   Nay she has caught you!
    If you start now, let all the world cry shame on you!
    I have out-travell'd you.
Bel. Did not I say she would cheat thee?
Mir. I thank you! I am pleased you have deceived me,
    And willingly I swallow it, and joy in't:
    And yet, perhaps, I knew you.   Whose plot was this?
Lug. He's not ashamed that cast it: He that executed,
    Follow'd your father's will.

Mir. What a world's this!

Nothing but craft and cozenage?

Ori. Who begun, sir?

Mir. Well; I do take thee upon mere compassion;

And I do think I shall love thee. As a testimony,

I'll burn my book, and turn a new leaf over.

But these fine clothes you shall wear still.

Ori. I obey you, sir, in all.

Nant. And how, how, daughters? What say you to these gentlemen?

What say ye, gentlemen, to the girls?

Pinac. By my troth—if she can love me—

Lil. How long?

Pinac. Nay, if once you love——

Lil. Then take me,

And take your chance.

Pinac. Most willingly! You are mine, lady;

And if I use you not, that you may love me——

Lil. A match, i' faith.

Pinac. Why, now you travel with me.

Ros. How that thing stands!

Bel. It will, if you urge it.

Bless your five wits!

Ros. Nay, pr'ythee, stay; I'll have thee.

Bel. You must ask me leave first.

Ros. Wilt thou use me kindly,

And beat me but once a week?

Bel. If you deserve no more.

Ros. And wilt thou get me with child?

Bel. Dost thou ask me seriously?

Ros. Yes, indeed do I.

Bel. Yes, I will get thee with child. Come presently,

An't be but in revenge, I'll do thee that courtesy.

Well, if thou wilt fear God, and me, have at thee!

Ros. I'll love you, and I'll honour you.

Bel. I am pleased then.

Mir. This Wild-Goose Chase is done; we have won o' both sides.

Brother, your love, and now to church of all hands;

Let's lose no time.

Pinac. Our travelling lay by.

Bel. No more for Italy; for the Low Countries, I. [*Exeunt.*

BONDUCA

DRAMATIS PERSONÆ

CARATACH, *General of the Britons,*
  Cousin to Bonduca.
NENNIUS, *a great Soldier, a British*
  Commander.
HENGO, *a brave Boy, Nephew to*
  Caratach and Bonduca.
SUETONIUS, *General to the Roman*
  Army in Britain.
PENIUS, *a brave Roman Com-*
  mander, but stubborn to the
  General.
JUNIUS, *a Roman Captain, in*
  Love with Bonduca's Daughter.
PETILLIUS, *a merry Roman Cap-*
  tain, but somewhat wanton.

DEMETRIUS, } *Roman Com-*
DECIUS, } *manders.*
REGULUS,
DRUSIUS,
MACER, } *Roman Officers.*
CURIUS,
JUDAS, *a Corporal, a cowardly*
  hungry Knave.
Herald.
Druids.
Soldiers.
Guides.

BONDUCA, *Queen of the Iceni, a*
  brave virago.
Her two Daughters, *by Prasutagus.*

SCENE.—BRITAIN.

ACT I

SCENE I.—*The British Camp.*

Enter BONDUCA, Daughters, HENGO, NENNIUS, *and*
Soldiers.

Bond. The hardy Romans? Oh, ye gods of Britain,
The rust of arms, the blushing shame of soldiers!

Enter CARATACH.

Are these the men that conquer by inheritance?
The fortune-makers? these the Julians,
That with the sun measure the end of nature,
Making the world but one Rome, and one Cæsar?
Shame, how they flee! Cæsar's soft soul dwells in 'em,
Their mothers got 'em sleeping, Pleasure nursed 'em;
Their bodies sweat with sweet oils, love's allurements,
Not lusty arms. Dare they send these to seek us,
These Roman girls? Is Britain grown so wanton?
Twice we have beat 'em, Nennius, scatter'd 'em:
And through their big-boned Germans, on whose pikes

The honour of their actions sits in triumph,
Made themes for songs to shame 'em: And a woman,
A woman beat 'em, Nennius; a weak woman,
A woman, beat these Romans!

Car. So it seems;
A man would shame to talk so.

Bond. Who's that?

Car. I.

Bond. Cousin, do you grieve my fortunes?

Car. No, Bonduca;
If I grieve, 'tis the bearing of your fortunes:
You put too much wind to your sail; discretion
And hardy valour are the twins of honour,
And, nursed together, make a conqueror;
Divided, but a talker. 'Tis a truth,
That Rome has fled before us twice, and routed;
A truth we ought to crown the gods for, lady,
And not our tongues; a truth is none of ours,
Nor in our ends, more than the noble bearing;
For then it leaves to be a virtue, lady,
And we, that have been victors, beat ourselves,
When we insult upon our honour's subject.

Bond. My valiant cousin, is it foul to say
What liberty and honour bid us do,
And what the gods allow us?

Car. No, Bonduca;
So what we say exceed not what we do.
You call the Romans " fearful, fleeing Romans,
And Roman girls, the lees of tainted pleasures: "
Does this become a doer? are they such?

Bond. They are no more.

Car. Where is your conquest then?
Why are your altars crown'd with wreaths of flowers?
The beasts with gilt horns waiting for the fire?
The holy Druides composing songs
Of everlasting life to victory?
Why are these triumphs, lady? for a May-game?
For hunting a poor herd of wretched Romans?
Is it no more? Shut up your temples, Britons,
And let the husbandman redeem his heifers,
Put out your holy fires, no timbrel ring,
Let's home and sleep; for such great overthrows,
A candle burns too bright a sacrifice,

A glow-worm's tail too full of flame.—Oh, Nennius,
Thou hadst a noble uncle knew a Roman,
And how to speak him, how to give him weight
In both his fortunes.

Bond. By the gods, I think
You dote upon these Romans, Caratach!

Car. Witness these wounds, I do; they were fairly given:
I love an enemy; I was born a soldier;
And he that in the head on's troop defies me,
Bending my manly body with his sword,
I make a mistress. Yellow-tressed Hymen
Ne'er tied a longing virgin with more joy,
Than I am married to that man that wounds me:
And are not all these Roman? Ten struck battles
I suck'd these honour'd scars from, and all Roman;
Ten years of bitter nights and heavy marches,
(When many a frozen storm sung through my cuirass,
And made it doubtful whether that or I
Were the more stubborn metal) have I wrought through,
And all to try these Romans. Ten times a-night
I have swam the rivers, when the stars of Rome
Shot at me as I floated, and the billows
Tumbled their watry ruins on my shoulders,
Charging my batter'd sides with troops of agues;
And still to try these Romans, whom I found
(And, if I lie, my wounds be henceforth backward,
And be you witness, gods, and all my dangers)
As ready, and as full of that I brought,
(Which was not fear, nor flight) as valiant,
As vigilant, as wise, to do and suffer,
Ever advanced as forward as the Britons,
Their sleeps as short, their hopes as high as ours,
Ay, and as subtle, lady. 'Tis dishonour,
And, follow'd, will be impudence, Bonduca,
And grow to no belief, to taint these Romans.
Have not I seen the Britons——

Bond. What?

Car. Dishearten'd,
Run, run, Bonduca! not the quick rack swifter!
The virgin from the hated ravisher
Not half so fearful; not a flight drawn home.
A round stone from a sling, a lover's wish,
E'er made that haste that they have. By the gods,

I have seen these Britons, that you magnify,
Run as they would have out-run time, and roaring,
Basely for mercy roaring; the light shadows,
That in a thought scur o'er the fields of corn,
Halted on crutches to 'em.

Bond. Oh, ye powers,
What scandals do I suffer!

Car. Yes, Bonduca,
I have seen thee run too; and thee, Nennius;
Yea, run apace, both; then, when Penius
(The Roman girl!) cut through your armed carts,
And drove 'em headlong on ye, down the hill;
Then, when he hunted ye like Britain foxes,
More by the scent than sight; then did I see
These valiant and approved men of Britain,
Like boding owls, creep into tods of ivy,
And hoot their fears to one another nightly.

Nen. And what did you then, Caratach?

Car. I fled too,
But not so fast; your jewel had been lost then,
Young Hengo there; he trasht me, Nennius:
For, when your fears out-run him, then stept I,
And in the head of all the Roman fury
Took him, and, with my tough belt, to my back
I buckled him; behind him my sure shield;
And then I follow'd. If I say I fought
Five times in bringing off this bud of Britain,
I lie not, Nennius. Neither had you heard
Me speak this, or ever seen the child more,
But that the sun of virtue, Penius,
Seeing me steer through all these storms of danger,
My helm still in my hand (my sword), my prow
Turn'd to my foe (my face), he cried out nobly,
" Go, Briton, bear thy lion's whelp off safely;
Thy manly sword has ransom'd thee; grow strong,
And let me meet thee once again in arms;
Then, if thou stand'st, thou'rt mine." I took his offer,
And here I am to honour him.

Bond. Oh, cousin,
From what a flight of honour hast thou check'd me!
What wouldst thou make me, Caratach?

Car. See, lady,
The noble use of others in our losses.

Does this afflict you?   Had the Romans cried this,
And, as we have done theirs, sung out these fortunes,
Rail'd on our base condition, hooted at us,
Made marks as far as th' earth was ours, to show us
Nothing but sea could stop our flights, despised us,
And held it equal whether banqueting
Or beating of the Britons were more business,
It would have gall'd you.

Bond. Let me think we conquer'd.

Car. Do; but so think, as we may be conquer'd;
And where we have found virtue, though in those
That came to make us slaves, let's cherish it.
There's not a blow we gave since Julius landed,
That was of strength and worth, but, like records,
They file to after-ages.   Our registers
The Romans are, for noble deeds of honour;
And shall we burn their mentions with upbraidings?

Bond. No more; I see myself.   Thou hast made me, cousin,
More than my fortunes durst, for they abused me,
And wound me up so high, I swell'd with glory:
Thy temperance has cured that tympany,
And given me health again, nay, more, discretion,
Shall we have peace? for now I love these Romans.

Car. Thy love and hate are both unwise ones, lady.

Bond. Your reason?

Nen. Is not peace the end of arms?

Car. Not where the cause implies a general conquest:
Had we a difference with some petty isle,
Or with our neighbours, lady, for our land-marks,
The taking in of some rebellious lord,
Or making head against commotions,
After a day of blood, peace might be argued;
But where we grapple for the ground we live on,
The liberty we hold as dear as life,
The gods we worship, and, next those, our honours,
And with those swords that know no end of battle:
Those men, beside themselves, allow no neighbour;
Those minds that where the day is, claim inheritance,
And where the sun makes ripe the fruits, their harvest,   •
And where they march, but measure out more ground
To add to Rome, and here i' th' bowels on us;
It must not be.   No, as they are our foes,
And those that must be so until we tire 'em,

Let's use the peace of honour, that's fair dealing,
But in our hands our swords. That hardy Roman
That hopes to graft himself into my stock,
Must first begin his kindred under-ground,
And be allied in ashes.

Bond. Caratach,
As thou hast nobly spoken, shall be done;
And Hengo to thy charge I here deliver:
The Romans shall have worthy wars.

Car. They shall:
And, little sir, when your young bones grow stiffer,
And when I see you able in a morning
To beat a dozen boys, and then to breakfast,
I'll tie you to a sword.

Hengo. And what then, uncle?

Car. Then you must kill, sir, the next valiant Roman
That calls you knave.

Hengo. And must I kill but one?

Car. An hundred, boy, I hope.

Hengo. I hope five hundred.

Car. That is a noble boy!—Come, worthy lady,
Let's to our several charges, and henceforth
Allow an enemy both weight and worth.   [*Exeunt.*

SCENE II.—*The Roman Camp.*

Enter JUNIUS *and* PETILLIUS.

Pet. What ail'st thou, man? dost thou want meat?

Jun. No.

Pet. Clothes?

Jun. Neither. For Heaven's love, leave me!

Pet. Drink?

Jun. You tire me.

Pet. Come, it is drink; I know 'tis drink.

Jun. 'Tis no drink.

Pet. I say 'tis drink; for what affliction
Can light so heavy on a soldier,
To dry him up as thou art, but no drink?
Thou shalt have drink.

Jun. Pr'ythee, Petillius——

Pet. And, by mine honour, much drink, valiant drink:
Never tell me, thou shalt have drink. I see,

    Like a true friend, into thy wants; 'tis drink;
    And when I leave thee to a desolation,
    Especially of that dry nature, hang me.
Jun. Why do you do this to me?
Pet. For I see,
    Although your modesty would fain conceal it,
    Which sits as sweetly on a soldier
    As an old side-saddle——
Jun. What do you see?
Pet. I see as fair as day, that thou want'st drink.
    Did I not find thee gaping like an oyster
    For a new tide? Thy very thoughts lie bare,
    Like a low ebb; thy soul, that rid in sack,
    Lies moor'd for want of liquor. Do but see
    Into thyself; for, by the gods, I do;
    For all thy body's chapt and crack'd like timber,
    For want of moisture: What is't thou want'st there,
        Junius,
    An if it be not drink?
Jun. You have too much on't.
Pet. It may be a whore too; say it be; come, meecher,
    Thou shalt have both; a pretty valiant fellow,
    Die for a little lap and lechery?
    No, it shall ne'er be said in our country,
    Thou diedst o' th' chin-cough. Hear, thou noble Roman,
    The son of her that loves a soldier,
    Hear what I promised for thee! thus I said:
    " Lady, I take thy son to my companion;
    Lady, I love thy son, thy son loves war,
    The war loves danger, danger drink, drink discipline,
    Which is society and lechery;
    These two beget commanders: Fear not, lady;
    Thy son shall lead."
Jun. 'Tis a strange thing, Petillius,
    That so ridiculous and loose a mirth
    Can master your affections.
Pet. Any mirth,
    And any way, of any subject, Junius,
    Is better than unmanly mustiness.
    What harm's in drink? in a good wholesome wench?
    I do beseech you, sir, what error? Yet
    It cannot out of my head handsomely,
    But thou wouldst fain be drunk; come, no more fooling;

The general has new wine, new come over.

Jun. He must have new acquaintance for it too,
For I will none, I thank ye.

Pet. " None, I thank you? "
A short and touchy answer! " None, I thank you? "
You do not scorn it, do you?

Jun. Gods defend, sir!
I owe him still more honour.

Pet. " None, I thank you? "
No company, no drink, no wench, " I thank you? "
You shall be worse entreated, sir.

Jun. Petillius,
As thou art honest, leave me!

Pet. " None, I thank you? "
A modest and a decent resolution,
And well put on. Yes; I will leave you, Junius,
And leave you to the boys, that very shortly
Shall all salute you, by your new sirname
Of " Junius None-I-thank-you." I would starve now,
Hang, drown, despair, deserve the forks, lie open
To all the dangerous passes of a wench,
Bound to believe her tears, and wed her aches,
Ere I would own thy follies. I have found you,
Your lays, and out-leaps, Junius, haunts, and lodges:
I have viewed you, and I have found you by my skill
To be a fool o' th' first head, Junius,
And I will hunt you: You are in love, I know it;
You are an ass, and all the camp shall know it;
A peevish idle boy, your dame shall know it;
A wronger of my care, yourself shall know it.

Enter JUDAS *and four* Soldiers.

Judas. A bean? a princely diet, a full banquet,
To what we compass.

1 *Sold.* Fight like hogs for acorns?

2 *Sold.* Venture our lives for pig-nuts?

Pet. What ail these rascals?

3 *Sold.* If this hold we are starved.

Judas. For my part, friends,
Which is but twenty beans a-day (a hard world
For officers, and men of action!)
And those so clipt by Master Mouse, and rotten—
(For understand 'em French beans, where the fruits

    Are ripen'd like the people, in old tubs)
For mine own part, I say, I am starved already,
Not worth another bean, consumed to nothing,
Nothing but flesh and bones left, miserable:
Now if this musty provender can prick me
To honourable matters of atchievement, gentlemen,
Why, there's the point.

4 Sold. I'll fight no more.

Pet. You'll hang then!
    A sovereign help for hunger. Ye eating rascals,
Whose gods are beef and brewis! whose brave angers
Do execution upon these, and chibbals!
Ye dog's head in the porridge-pot! ye fight no more?
Does Rome depend upon your resolution
For eating mouldy pie-crust?

3 Sold. 'Would we had it!

Judas. I may do service, captain.

Pet. In a fish-market.
    You, corporal Curry-comb, what will your fighting
Profit the commonwealth? Do you hope to triumph?
Or dare your vamping valour, goodman Cobler,
Clap a new sole to th' kingdom? 'Sdeath, ye dog-
      whelps,
You fight, or not fight!

Judas. Captain!

Pet. Out, ye flesh-flies!
    Nothing but noise and nastiness!

Judas. Give us meat,
    Whereby we may do.

Pet. Whereby hangs your valour?

Judas. Good bits afford good blows.

Pet. A good position:
    How long is't since thou eat'st last? Wipe thy mouth,
And then tell truth.

Judas. I have not eat to th' purpose——

Pet. " To th' purpose? " what's that? half a cow and garlick?
    Ye rogues, my company eat turf, and talk not;
Timber they can digest, and fight upon't;
Old mats, and mud with spoons, rare meats. Your
      shoes, slaves;
Dare ye cry out for hunger, and those extant?
Suck your sword-hilts, ye slaves; if ye be valiant,
Honour will make 'em marchpane. " To the purpose? "

A grievous penance! Dost thou see that gentleman,
That melancholy monsieur?

Jun. Pray you, Petillius!

Pet. He has not eat these three weeks.

2 *Sold.* He has drunk the more then.

3 *Sold.* And that's all one.

Pet. Nor drunk nor slept these two months.

Judas. Captain, we do beseech you, as poor soldiers,
Men that have seen good days, whose mortal stomachs
May sometimes feel afflictions——   [*To Junius.*

Jun. This, Petillius,
Is not so nobly done.

Pet. 'Tis common profit;
Urge him to th' point, he'll find you out a food
That needs no teeth nor stomach; a strange furmity
Will feed you up as fat as hens i' th' forehead,
And make ye fight like fichoks; to him.

Judas. Captain——

Jun. Do you long to have your throats cut?

Pet. See what mettle
It makes in him: Two meals more of this melancholy,
And there lies Caratach.

Judas. We do beseech you——

2 *Sold.* Humbly beseech your valour——

Jun. Am I only
Become your sport, Petillius?

Judas. But to render
In way of general good, in preservation——

Jun. Out of my thoughts, ye slaves!

4 *Sold.* Or rather pity——

3 *Sold.* Your warlike remedy against the maw-worms.

Judas. Or notable receipt to live by nothing.

Pet. Out with your table-books!

Jun. Is this true friendship?
And must my killing griefs make others' May-games?
                     [*Draws.*
Stand from my sword's point, slaves! your poor starved
    spirits
Can make me no oblations; else, oh, Love,
Thou proudly-blind destruction, I would send thee
Whole hecatombs of hearts, to bleed my sorrows.
                    [*Exit Junius.*

Judas. Alas, he lives by love, sir.

Pet. So he does, sir;
    And cannot you do so too? All my company
    Are now in love; ne'er think of meat, nor talk
    Of what provant is: *Ay-mes*, and hearty *hey-hoes*
    Are sallads fit for soldiers. Live by meat?
    By larding up your bodies? 'tis lewd, and lazy,
    And shows ye merely mortal, dull, and drives ye
    To fight, like camels, with baskets at your noses.
    Get ye in love! Ye can whore well enough,
    That all the world knows; fast ye into famine,
    Yet ye can crawl like crabs to wenches; handsomely
    Fall but in love now, as ye see example,
    And follow it but with all your thoughts, *probatum*,
    There's so much charge saved, and your hunger's ended.
                        [Drum afar off.
    Away! I hear the general. Get ye in love all,
    Up to the ears in love, that I may hear
    No more of these rude murmurings; and discretely
    Carry your stomachs, or I prophesy
    A pickled rope will choke ye. Jog, and talk not!
                           [Exeunt.

Enter Suetonius, Demetrius, Decius, *Drum and Colours.*

Suet. Demetrius, is the messenger dispatch'd
    To Penius, to command him to bring up
    The Volans regiment!
Dem. He's there by this time.
Suet. And are the horse well view'd we brought from Mona?
Dec. The troops are full and lusty.
Suet. Good Petillius,
    Look to those eating rogues, that bawl for victuals,
    And stop their throats a day or two: Provision
    Waits but the wind to reach us.
Pet. Sir, already
    I have been tampering with their stomachs, which I find
    As deaf as adders to delays: Your clemency
    Hath made their murmurs, mutinies; nay, rebellions;
    Now, an they want but mustard, they are in uproars!
    No oil but Candy, Lusitanian figs,
    And wine from Lesbos, now can satisfy 'em;
    The British waters are grown dull and muddy,
    The fruit disgustful; Orontes must be sought for,

And apples from the Happy Isles; the truth is,
They are more curious now in having nothing,
Than if the sea and land turned up their treasures.
This lost the colonies, and gave Bonduca
(With shame we must record it) time and strength
To look into our fortunes; great discretion
To follow offer'd victory; and last, full pride
To brave us to our teeth, and scorn our ruins.

Suet. Nay, chide not, good Petillius! I confess
My will to conquer Mona, and long stay
To execute that will, let in these losses;
All shall be right again, and, as a pine,
Rent from Oëta by a sweeping tempest,
Jointed again, and made a mast, defies
Those angry winds that split him; so will I,
Pieced to my never-failing strength and fortune,
Steer through these swelling dangers, plough their prides
        up,
And bear like thunder through their loudest tempests.
They keep the field still?

Dem. Confident and full.

Pet. In such a number, one would swear they grew:
The hills are wooded with their partizans,
And all the vallies overgrown with darts,
As moors are with rank rushes; no ground left us
To charge upon, no room to strike. Say fortune
And our endeavours bring us into 'em,
They are so infinite, so ever-springing,
We shall be kill'd with killing; of desperate women,
That neither fear or shame e'er found, the devil
Has rank'd amongst 'em multitudes; say the men fail,
They'll poison us with their petticoats; say they fail,
They have priests enough to pray us into nothing

Suet. These are imaginations, dreams of nothings;
The man that doubts or fears——

Dec. I am free of both.

Dem. The self-same I.

Pet. And I as free as any;
As careless of my flesh, of that we call life,
So I may lose it nobly, as indifferent
As if it were my diet. Yet, noble general,
It was a wisdom learn'd from you, I learn'd it,
And worthy of a soldier's care, most worthy,

To weigh with most deliberate circumstance
The ends of accidents, above their offers;
How to go on, and yet to save a Roman,
Whose one life is more worth in way of doing,
Than millions of these painted wasps; how, viewing,
To find advantage out; how, found, to follow it
With counsel and discretion, lest mere fortune
Should claim the victory.

Suet.   'Tis true, Petillius,
And worthily remember'd: The rule is certain,
The uses no less excellent; but where time
Cuts off occasions, danger, time and all
Tend to a present peril, 'tis required
Our swords and manhoods be best counsellors,
Our expeditions, precedents.   To win is nothing,
Where Reason, Time, and Counsel are our camp-masters:
But there to bear the field, then to be conquerors,
Where pale Destruction takes us, takes us beaten,
In wants and mutinies, ourselves but handfuls,
And to ourselves our own fears, needs a new way,
A sudden and a desperate execution:
Here, how to save, is loss; to be wise, dangerous;
Only a present well-united strength,
And minds made up for all attempts, dispatch it:
Disputing and delay here cool the courage;
Necessity gives [no] time for doubts; things infinite,
According to the spirit they are preach'd to;
Rewards like them, and names for after-ages,
Must steel the soldier, his own shame help to arm
      him:
And having forced his spirit, ere he cools,
Fling him upon his enemies; sudden and swift,
Like tigers amongst foxes, we must fight for't:
Fury must be our fortune; shame we have lost,
Spurs ever in our sides to prick us forward:
There is no other wisdom nor discretion
Due to this day of ruin, but destruction;
The soldier's order first, and then his anger.

Dem.   No doubt they dare redeem all.

Suet.   Then no doubt
The day must needs be ours.   That the proud woman
Is infinite in number better likes me,
Than if we dealt with squadrons; half her army

Shall choke themselves, their own swords dig their
　　graves.
I'll tell ye all my fears; one single valour,
The virtues of the valiant Caratach,
More doubts me than all Britain.　He's a soldier
So forged out, and so temper'd for great fortunes,
So much man thrust into him, so old in dangers,
So fortunate in all attempts, that his mere name
Fights in a thousand men, himself in millions,
To make him Roman: But no more.—Petillius,
How stands your charge?

Pet.　Ready for all employments,
To be commanded too, sir.

Suet.　'Tis well govern'd;
To-morrow we'll draw out, and view the cohorts:
I' th' mean time, all apply their offices.
Where's Junius?

Pet.　In's cabin, sick o' th' mumps, sir.

Suet.　How?

Pet.　In love, indeed in love, most lamentably loving,
To the tune of Queen Dido.

Dec.　Alas poor gentleman!

Suet.　'Twill make him fight the nobler.　With what lady?
I'll be a spokesman for him.

Pet.　You'll scant speed, sir.

Suet.　Who is't?

Pet.　The devil's dam, Bonduca's daughter,
Her youngest, crack'd i' th' ring.

Suet.　I am sorry for him:
But sure his own discretion will reclaim him;
He must deserve our anger else.　Good captains,
Apply yourselves in all the pleasing forms
Ye can, unto the soldiers; fire their spirits,
And set 'em fit to run this action;
Mine own provisions shall be shared amongst 'em,
Till more come in; tell 'em, if now they conquer,
The fat of all the kingdom lies before 'em.
Their shames forgot, their honours infinite,
And want for ever banish'd.　Two days hence,
Our fortunes, and our swords, and gods be for us!

　　　　　　　　　　　　　　　　　　　[Exeunt.

ACT II

SCENE I.—*The same.   The Tent of Penius.*

Enter PENIUS, REGULUS, MACER, *and* DRUSIUS.

Pen. I *must* come?

Macer. So the general commands, sir.

Pen. I *must* bring up my regiment?

Macer. Believe, sir,
     I bring no lie.

Pen. But did he say, I *must* come?

Macer. So delivered.

Pen. How long is't, Regulus, since I commanded
     In Britain here?

Reg. About five years, great Penius.

Pen. The general some five months.   Are all my actions
     So poor and lost, my services so barren,
     That I am remember'd in no nobler language
     But *must* come up?

Macer. I do beseech you, sir,
     Weigh but the time's estate.

Pen. Yes, good lieutenant,
     I do, and his that sways it.   *Must* come up?
     Am I turn'd bare centurion?   *Must* and *shall*,
     Fit embassies to court my honour?

Macer. Sir——

Pen. Set me to lead a handful of my men
     Against an hundred thousand barbarous slaves,
     That have march'd name by name with Rome's best
         doers?
     Serve 'em up some other meat; I'll bring no food
     To stop the jaws of all those hungry wolves:
     My regiment's mine own.   I *must*, my language?

Enter CURIUS.

Cur. Penius, where lies the host?

Pen. Where Fate may find 'em.

Cur. Are they ingirt?

Pen. The battle's lost.

Cur. So soon?

Pen. No; but 'tis lost, because it must be won;
     The Britons must be victors.   Whoe'er saw

A troop of bloody vultures hovering
About a few corrupted carcasses,
Let him behold the silly Roman host,
Girded with millions of fierce Britain swains,
With deaths as many as they have had hopes;
And then go thither, he that loves his shame!
I scorn my life, yet dare not lose my name.

Cur. Do not you hold it a most famous end,
When both our names and lives are sacrificed
For Rome's increase?

Pen. Yes, Curius; but mark this too:
What glory is there, or what lasting fame
Can be to Rome or us, what full example,
When one is smother'd with a multitude,
And crowded in amongst a nameless press?
Honour got out of flint, and on their heads
Whose virtues, like the sun, exhaled all valours,
Must not be lost in mists and fogs of people,
Noteless and not of name, but rude and naked:
Nor can Rome task us with impossibilities,
Or bid us fight against a flood; we serve her,
That she may proudly say she has good soldiers,
Not slaves, to choke all hazards.   Who but fools,
That make no difference betwixt certain dying,
And dying well, would fling their fames and fortunes
Into this Britain gulf, this quicksand ruin,
That, sinking, swallows us? what noble hand
Can find a subject fit for blood there? or what sword
Room for his execution? what air to cool us,
But poison'd with their blasting breaths and curses,
Where we lie buried quick above the ground,
And are with labouring sweat, and breathless pain,
Kill'd like to slaves, and cannot kill again?

Drus. Penius, mark ancient wars, and know that then
A captain weigh'd an hundred thousand men.

Pen. Drusius, mark ancient wisdom, and you'll find then,
He gave the overthrow that saved his men.
I must not go.

Reg. The soldiers are desirous,
Their eagles all drawn out, sir.

Pen. Who drew up, Regulus?
Ha? speak! did you? whose bold will durst attempt
this?

    Drawn out? why, who commands, sir? on whose warrant
    Durst they advance?

Reg. I keep mine own obedience.

Drus. 'Tis like the general cause, their love of honour,
    Relieving of their wants——

Pen. Without my knowledge?
    Am I no more? my place but at their pleasures?
    Come, who did this?

Drus. By Heaven, sir, I am ignorant.

        [Drum softly within, then enter Soldiers, *with drum
        and colours.*

Pen. What! am I grown a shadow?—Hark! they march.
    I'll know, and will be myself.—Stand! Disobedience?
    He that advances one foot higher, dies for't.
    Run through the regiment, upon your duties,
    And charge 'em on command, beat back again;
    By Heaven, I'll tithe 'em all else!

Reg. We'll do our best.   *[Exeunt Drusius and Regulus.*

Pen. Back! cease your bawling drums there,
    I'll beat the tubs about your brains else. Back!
    Do I speak with less fear than thunder to ye?
    Must I stand to beseech ye? Home, home!—Ha!
    Do ye stare upon me? Are those minds I moulded,
    Those honest valiant tempers I was proud
    To be a fellow to, those great discretions
    Made your names fear'd and honour'd, turn'd to wild-fires?
    Oh, gods, to disobedience? Command, farewell!
    And be ye witness with me, all things sacred,
    I have no share in these men's shames! March, soldiers,
    And seek your own sad ruins; your old Penius
    Dares not behold your murders.

1 *Sold.* Captain!

2 *Sold.* Captain!

3 *Sold.* Dear, honour'd captain!

Pen. Too, too dear-loved soldiers,
    Which made ye weary of me, and Heaven yet knows,
    Though in your mutinies, I dare not hate you;
    Take your own wills! 'tis fit your long experience
    Should now know how to rule yourselves; I wrong ye,
    In wishing ye to save your lives and credits,
    To keep your necks whole from the axe hangs o'er ye:

Alas, I much dishonour'd ye; go, seek the Britons,
And say ye come to glut their sacrifices;
But do not say I sent ye. What ye have been,
How excellent in all parts, good and govern'd,
Is only left of my command, for story;
What now ye are, for pity. Fare ye well!   *[Going.*

Enter Drusius *and* Regulus.

Drus. Oh, turn again, great Penius! see the soldier
   In all points apt for duty.
Reg.   See his sorrow
   For his disobedience, which he says was haste,
   And haste, he thought, to please you with. See, captain,
   The toughness of his courage turned to water;
   See how his manly heart melts.
Pen. Go; beat homeward;
   There learn to eat your little with obedience;
   And henceforth strive to do as I direct ye.
                     [Exeunt Soldiers.
Macer. My answer, sir.
Pen.   Tell the great general,
   My companies are no faggots to fill breaches:
   Myself no man that *must,* or *shall,* can carry:
   Bid him be wise, and where he is, he's safe then;
   And when he finds out possibilities,
   He may command me. Commend me to the captains.
Macer. All this I shall deliver.
Pen. Farewell, Macer!   *[Exit.*
Cur. Pray gods this breed no mischief!
Reg. It must needs,
   If stout Suetonius win; for then his anger,
   Besides the soldiers' loss of due and honour,
   Will break together on him.
Drus. He's a brave fellow;
   And but a little hide his haughtiness,
   (Which is but sometimes neither, on some causes)
   He shows the worthiest Roman this day living.
   You may, good Curius, to the general
   Make all things seem the best.
Cur. I shall endeavour.
   Pray for our fortunes, gentlemen; if we fall,
   This one farewell serves for a funeral.

The gods make sharp our swords, and steel our hearts!
Reg. We dare, alas, but cannot fight our parts.   [*Exeunt.*

SCENE II.—*The Tent of Junius.*

Enter Junius, Petillius, *and a* Herald.

Pet. Let him go on.   Stay; now he talks.
Jun. Why,
     Why should I love mine enemy? what is beauty?
     Of what strange violence, that, like the plague,
     It works upon our spirits?   Blind they feign him;
     I am sure, I find it so——
Pet. A dog shall lead you.
Jun. His fond affections blinder——
Pet. Hold you there still!
Jun. It takes away my sleep——
Pet. Alas, poor chicken!
Jun. My company, content, almost my fashion——
Pet. Yes, and your weight too, if you follow it.
Jun. 'Tis sure the plague, for no man dare come near me
     Without an antidote; 'tis far worse, hell.
Pet. Thou art damn'd without redemption then.
Jun. The way to't
     Strew'd with fair western smiles, and April blushes,
     Led by the brightest constellations; eyes,
     And sweet proportions, envying Heaven; but from
          thence
     No way to guide, no path, no wisdom brings us.
Pet. Yes, a smart water, Junius.
Jun. Do I fool?
     Know all this, and fool still?   Do I know further,
     That when we have enjoy'd our ends we lose 'em,
     And all our appetites are but as dreams
     We laugh at in our ages?—
Pet. Sweet philosopher!
Jun. Do I know on still, and yet know nothing?   Mercy,
          gods!
     Why am I thus ridiculous?
Pet. Motley on thee,
     Thou art an arrant ass.
Jun. Can red and white,
     An eye, a nose, a cheek——

Pet. But one cheek, Junius?
     An half-faced mistress?
Jun. With a little trim,
     That wanton fools call fashion, thus abuse me?
     Take me beyond my reason? Why should not I
     Dote on my horse well trapt, my sword well hatch'd?
     They are as handsome things, to me more useful,
     And possible to rule too. Did I but love,
     Yet 'twere excusable, my youth would bear it:
     But to love there, and that no time can give me,
     Mine honour dare not ask (she has been ravish'd),
     My nature must not know (she hates our nation),
     Thus to dispose my spirit!
Pet. Stay a little; he will declaim again.
Jun. I will not love! I am a man, have reason,
     And I will use it; I'll no more tormenting,
     Nor whining for a wench; there are a thousand——
Pet. Hold thee there, boy!
Jun. A thousand will entreat me.
Pet. Ten thousand, Junius.
Jun. I am young and lusty,
     And to my fashion valiant; can please nightly.
Pet. I'll swear thy back's *probatum*, for I have known thee
     Leap at sixteen like a strong stallion.
Jun. I will be man again.
Pet. Now mark the working!
     The devil and the spirit tug for't: Twenty pound
     Upon the devil's head!
Jun. I must be wretched!
Pet. I knew I had won.
Jun. Nor have I so much power
     To shun my fortune.
Pet. I will hunt thy fortune
     With all the shapes imagination breeds,
     But I will fright thy devil. Stay, he sings now.
     [*Song by Junius, and Petillius after him in mockage.*
Jun. Must I be thus abused?
Pet. Yes, marry must you.
     Let's follow him close: Oh, there he is; now read it.

Herald. [Reads.] It is the general's command, that all sick persons, old and unable, retire within the trenches; he that fears, has liberty to leave the field: Fools, boys, and cowards, must not come near the regiments, for fear of their infections; especially those cowards they call lovers.

Jun. Ha?

Pet. Read on.

Herald. [Reads.] If any common soldier love an enemy, he's whipp'd and made a slave: If any captain, cast, with loss of honours, flung out o' th' army, and made unable ever after to bear the name of a soldier.

Jun. The pox consume ye all, rogues!	[*Exit.*

Pet. Let this work;
    He has something now to chew upon.   He's gone;
    Come, shake no more.

Herald. Well, sir, you may command me,
    But not to do the like again for Europe;
    I would have given my life for a bent two-pence,
    If I e'er read to lovers whilst I live again,
    Or come within their confines——

Pet. There's your payment,
    And keep this private.

Herald. I am school'd for talking.	[*Exit.*

Enter DEMETRIUS.

Pet. Now now, Demetrius? are we drawn?

Dem. 'Tis doing:
    Your company stands fair.   But pray you, where's
        Junius?
    Half his command are wanting, with some forty
    That Decius leads.

Pet. Hunting for victuals.
    Upon my life, free-booting rogues! their stomachs
    Are like a widow's lust, ne'er satisfied.

Dem. I wonder how they dare stir, knowing the enemy
    Master of all the country.

Pet. Resolute hungers
    Know neither fears nor faiths; they tread on ladders,
    Ropes, gallows, and overdo all dangers.

Dem. They may be hang'd though.

Pet. There's their joyful supper;
    And no doubt they are at it.

Dem. But, for Heaven's sake,
    How does young Junius?

Pet. Drawing on, poor gentleman.

Dem. What, to his end?

Pet. To the end of all flesh, woman.

Dem. This love has made him a stout soldier.

Pet. Oh, a great one,
  Fit to command young goslings. But what news?
Dem. I think the messenger's come back from Penius
  By this time; let's go know.
Pet. What will you say now
  If he deny to come, and take exceptions
  At some half syllable, or sound deliver'd
  With an ill accent, or some style left out?
Dem. I cannot think he dare.
Pet. He dare speak treason,
  Dare say what no man dares believe, dares do——
  But that's all one; I'll lay you my black armour
  To twenty crowns, he comes not.
Dem. Done.
Pet. You'll pay?
Dem. I will.
Pet. Then keep thine old use, Penius!
  Be stubborn and vain-glorious, and I thank thee.
  Come, let's go pray for six hours; most of us
  I fear will trouble Heaven no more: Two good blows
  Struck home at two commanders of the Britons,
  And my part's done.
Dem. I do not think of dying.
Pet. 'Tis possible we may live; but, Demetrius,
  With what strange legs, and arms, and eyes, and noses,
  Let carpenters and copper-smiths consider.
  If I can keep my heart whole, and my windpipe,
  That I may drink yet like a soldier——
Dem. Come, let's have better thoughts; mine's on your
    armour.
Pet. Mine's in your purse, sir; let's go try the wager!
                                              [*Exeunt.*

SCENE III.—*The British Camp. In the background, the
      Tent of Bonduca, with a raised Platform.*

Enter Soldiers, *bringing in* JUDAS *and his four companions
    (halters about their necks),* BONDUCA, *her* Daughters, *and*
    NENNIUS *following.*

Bond. Come, hang 'em presently.
Nen. What made your rogueships
  Harrying for victuals here? are we your friends?
  Or do you come for spies? Tell me directly,

Would you not willingly be hang'd now?   Don't ye long
     for't?

Judas. What say ye? shall we hang in this vein?   Hang we
     must,
     And 'tis as good to dispatch it merrily,
     As pull an arse like dogs to't.

1 *Sold.* Any way,
     So it be handsome.

3 *Sold.* I had as lieve 'twere toothsome too:
     But all agree, and I'll not [stick] out, boys.

4 *Sold.* Let us hang pleasantly.

Judas. Then pleasantly be it:
     Captain, the truth is,
     We had as lieve hang with meat in our mouths,
     As ask your pardon empty.

Bond. These are brave hungers.—
     What say you to a leg of beef now, sirrah?

Judas. Bring me acquainted with it, and I'll tell ye.

Bond. Torment 'em, wenches (I must back), then hang 'em.
                                   [*Exit.*

Judas. We humbly thank your grace!

1 *Daugh.* The rogues laugh at us.

2 *Daugh.* Sirrah, what think you of a wench now?

Judas. A wench, lady?
     I do beseech your ladyship, retire;
     I'll tell you presently: You see the time's short;
     One crash, even to the settling of my conscience.

Nen. Why, is't no more but up, boys?

Judas. Yes, ride too, captain;
     Will you but see my seat?

1 *Daugh.* Ye shall be set, sir,
     Upon a jade shall shake ye.

Judas. Sheets, good madam,
     Will do it ten times better.

1 *Daugh.* Whips, good soldier,
     Which you shall taste before you hang, to mortify you;
     'Tis pity you should die thus desperate.

2 *Daugh.* These are the merry Romans, the brave madcaps:
     'Tis ten to one we'll cool your resolutions.
     Bring out the whips.

Judas. 'Would your good ladyships
     Would exercise 'em too!

4 *Sold.* Surely, ladies,

We'll show you a strange patience.
Nen. Hang 'em, rascals!
    They'll talk thus on the wheel.

Enter CARATACH.

Car. Now, what's the matter?
    What are these fellows? what's the crime committed,
    That they wear necklaces?
Nen. They are Roman rogues,
    Taken a-foraging.
Car. Is that all, Nennius?
Judas. 'Would I were fairly hang'd! This is the devil,
    The kill-cow Caratach.
Car. And you would hang 'em?
Nen. Are they not enemies?
1 *Sold.* My breech makes buttons.
1 *Daugh.* Are they not our tormentors?
Car. Tormentors? flea-traps!—
    Pluck off your halters, fellows.
Nen. Take heed, Caratach;
    Taint not your wisdom.
Car. Wisdom, Nennius?
    Why, who shall fight against us, make our honours,
    And give a glorious day into our hands,
    If we dispatch our foes thus? What's their offence?
    Stealing a loaf or two to keep out hunger?
    A piece of greasy bacon, or a pudding?
    Do these deserve the gallows? They are hungry,
    Poor hungry knaves, no meat at home left, starved:
    Art thou not hungry?
Judas. Monstrous hungry.
Car. He looks like Hunger's self. Get 'em some victuals,
    And wine to cheer their hearts; quick! Hang up poor
        pilchers?
2 *Sold.* This is the bravest captain——
Nen. Caratach,
    I'll leave you to your will.
Car. I'll answer all, sir.
2 *Daugh.* Let's up and view his entertainment of 'em!
    I am glad they are shifted anyway; their tongues else
    Would still have murder'd us.
1 *Daugh.* Let's up and see it!   [*Exeunt.*

Enter HENGO.

Car. Sit down, poor knaves! Why, where's this wine and
    victuals?
    Who waits there?
Serv. [*Within.*] Sir, 'tis coming.
Hengo. Who are these, uncle?
Car. They are Romans, boy.
Hengo. Are these they
    That vex mine aunt so? can these fight? they look
    Like empty scabbards all, no mettle in 'em;
    Like men of clouts, set to keep crows from orchards:
    Why, I dare fight with these.

Enter Servants *with victuals and wine, and set out a table.*

Car. That's my good chicken!—And how do ye?
    How do ye feel your stomachs?
Judas. Wond'rous apt, sir;
    As shall appear when time calls.
Car. That's well; down with't.
    A little grace will serve your turns. Eat softly!
    You'll choke, ye knaves, else.—Give 'em wine!
Judas. Not yet, sir;
    We are even a little busy.
Hengo. Can that fellow
    Do anything but eat?—Thou fellow!
Judas. Away, boy;
    Away; this is no boy's play.
Hengo. By Heaven, uncle,
    If his valour lie in's teeth, he's the most valiant.
Car. I am glad to hear you talk, sir.
Hengo. Good uncle, tell me,
    What's the price of a couple of cramm'd Romans?
Car. Some twenty Britons, boy; these are good soldiers.
Hengo. Do not the cowards eat hard too?
Car. No more, boy.—
    Come, I'll sit with you too.—Sit down by me, boy.
Judas. Pray bring your dish then.
Car. Hearty knaves!—More meat there.
1 *Sold.* That's a good hearing.
Car. Stay now, and pledge me.
Judas. This little piece, sir.

Car. By Heaven, square eaters!—
    More meat, I say!—Upon my conscience,
    The poor rogues have not eat this month! how terribly
    They charge upon their victuals!—Dare ye fight thus?

Judas. Believe it, sir, like devils.

Car. Well said, Famine!
    Here's to thy general.   *[Drinks.*

Judas. Most excellent captain,
    I will now pledge thee.

Car. And to-morrow night, say to him,
    His head is mine.

Judas. I can assure you, captain,
    He will not give it for this washing.

Car. Well said.

Enter the Daughters *on the Platform.*

1 *Daugh.* Here's a strange entertainment: How the thieves
    drink!

2 *Daugh.* Danger is dry; they look'd for colder liquor.

Car. Fill 'em more wine; give 'em full bowls.—Which of you
    all now,
    In recompence of this good, dare but give me
    A sound knock in the battle?

Judas. Delicate captain,
    To do thee a sufficient recompense,
    I'll knock thy brains out.

Car. Do it.

Hengo. Thou darest as well be damn'd! Thou knock his
    brains out?
    Thou skin of man?—Uncle, I will not hear this.

Judas. Tie up your whelp.

Hengo. Thou kill my uncle? Would I
    Had but a sword for thy sake, thou dried dog!

Car. What a mettle
    This little vermin carries!

Hengo. Kill mine uncle?

Car. He shall not, child.

Hengo. He cannot; he's a rogue,
    An only eating rogue! kill my sweet uncle?
    Oh, that I were a man!

Judas. By this wine, which I
    Will drink to Captain Junius, who loves
    The queen's most excellent majesty's little daughter

Most sweetly, and most fearfully, I will do it.
Hengo. Uncle, I'll kill him with a great pin.
Car. No more, boy!
    I'll pledge thy captain. To ye all, good fellows!
                            [Drinks.
2 *Daugh.* In love with me? that love shall cost your lives
      all.—
    Come, sister, and advise me; I have here
    A way to make an easy conquest of 'em,
    If fortune favour me. *[Exeunt Daughters*
Car. Let's see you sweat
    To-morrow blood and spirit, boys, this wine
    Turn'd to stern valour.
1 *Sold.* Hark you, Judas;
    If he should hang us after all this?
Judas. Let him:
    I'll hang like a gentleman, and a Roman.
Car. Take away there;
    They have enough. *[The table removed*
Judas. Captain, we thank you heartily
    For your good cheer: and if we meet to-morrow,
    One of us pays for't.
Car. Get 'em guides; their wine
    Has over-master'd 'em.

    Enter second Daughter *with a letter, and a* Servant.

2 *Daugh.* That hungry fellow
    With the red beard there, give it him, and this,
    To see it well deliver'd.
Car. Farewell, knaves!
    Speak nobly of us; keep your words to-morrow,
    And do something worthy your meat.—

    Enter a Guide.

Go, guide 'em,
And see 'em fairly onward.
Judas. Meaning me, sir?
Serv. The same.
    The youngest daughter to the queen entreats you
    To give this privately to Captain Junius;
    This for your pains!
Judas. I rest her humble servant;
    Commend me to thy lady.—Keep your files, boys.

Serv. I must instruct you further.

Judas. Keep your files there!

Order, sweet friends; faces about now.

Guide. Here, sir;

Here lies your way.

Judas. Bless the founders, I say!

Fairly, good soldiers, fairly march now; close, boys!

[*Exeunt.*

SCENE IV.—*The Roman Camp.*

Enter SUETONIUS, PETILLIUS, DEMETRIUS, DECIUS,
and MACER.

Suet. Bid me be wise, and keep me where I am,
And so be safe? not come, because commanded?
Was it not thus?

Macer. It was, sir.

Pet. What now think you?

Suet. *Must come* so heinous to him, so distasteful?

Pet. Give me my money.

Dem. I confess 'tis due, sir,
And presently I'll pay it.

Suet. His obedience
So blind at his years and experience,
It cannot find where to be tender'd?

Macer. Sir,
The regiment was willing, and advanced too,
The captains at all points steel'd up; their preparations
Full of resolve and confidence; youth and fire,
Like the fair breaking of a glorious day,
Gilded their phalanx; when the angry Penius
Stept like a stormy cloud 'twixt them and hopes.

Suet. And stopt their resolutions?

Macer. True; his reason
To them was odds, and odds so infinite,
Discretion durst not look upon.

Suet. Well, Penius,
I cannot think thee coward yet; and treacherous
I dare not think: thou hast lopt a limb off from me;
And let it be thy glory, thou wast stubborn,
Thy wisdom, that thou left'st thy general naked!
Yet, ere the sun set, I shall make thee see
All valour dwells not in thee, all command

In one experience.   Thou wilt too late repent this,
And wish " I *must* come up " had been thy blessing.
Pet. Let's force him.
Suet. No, by no means; he's a torrent
　　We cannot easily stem.
Pet. I think, a traitor.
Suet. No ill words! let his own shame first revile him.—
　　That wine I have, see it, Demetrius,
　　Distributed amongst the soldiers,
　　To make 'em high and lusty; when that's done,
　　Petillius, give the word through, that the eagles
　　May presently advance; no man discover
　　Upon his life, the enemies' full strength,
　　But make it of no value.   Decius,
　　Are your starved people yet come home?
Dec. I hope so.
Suet. Keep 'em in more obedience: This is no time
　　To chide, I could be angry else, and say more to you;
　　But come, let's order all.   Whose sword is sharpest,
　　And valour equal to his sword this day,
　　Shall be my saint.
Pet. We shall be holy all then.　　　*[Exeunt all but Decius.*

Enter JUDAS *and his* Company.

Judas. Captain, captain, I have brought 'em off again;
　　The drunkenest slaves!
Dec. Pox confound your rogueships!
　　I'll call the general, and have ye hang'd all.
Judas. Pray who will you command then?
Dec. For you, sirrah,
　　That are the ringleader to these devices,
　　Whose maw is never cramm'd, I'll have an engine——
Judas. A wench, sweet captain.
Dec. Sweet Judas, even the forks,
　　Where you shall have two lictors with two whips
　　Hammer your hide.
Judas. Captain, good words, fair words,
　　Sweet words, good captain; if you like not us,
　　Farewell! we have employment.
Dec. Where hast thou been?
Judas. There where you dare not be, with all your valour.
Dec. Where's that!

Judas. With the best good fellow living.

1 *Sold.* The king of all good fellows.

Dec. Who's that?

Judas. Caratach.
 Shake now, and say, we have done something worthy!
 Mark me, with Caratach; by this light, Caratach!
 Do you as much now, an you dare.—Sweet Caratach!
 You talk of a good fellow, of true drinking;
 Well, go thy ways, old Caratach!—Besides the drink,
  captain,
 The bravest running banquet of black puddings,
 Pieces of glorious beef——

Dec. How 'scaped ye hanging?

Judas. Hanging's a dog's death, we are gentlemen;
 And I say still, old Caratach!

Dec. Belike then,
 You are turn'd rebels all.

Judas. We are Roman boys all,
 And boys of mettle. I must do that, captain,
 This day, this very day——

Dec. Away, ye rascal!

Judas. Fair words, I say again!

Dec. What must you do, sir?

Judas. I must do that my heart-strings yearn to do;
 But my word's past.

Dec. What is it?

Judas. Why, kill Caratach,
 That's all he ask'd us for our entertainment.

Dec. More than you'll pay.

Judas. 'Would I had sold myself
 Unto the skin I had not promised it!
 For such another Caratach——

Dec. Come, fool,
 Have you done your country service?

Judas. I have brought that
 To captain Junius——

Dec. How?

Judas. I think will do all;
 I cannot tell; I think so.

Dec. How! to Junius?
 I'll more inquire of this.—You'll fight now?

Judas. Promise,
 Take heed of promise, captain!

Dec. Away, and rank then.
Judas. But, hark you, captain; there is wine distributing;
  I would fain know what share I have.
Dec. Be gone;
  You have too much.
Judas. Captain, no wine, no fighting:
  There's one called Caratach that has wine.
Dec. Well, sir,
  If you'll be ruled now, and do well——
Judas. Do excellent.
Dec. You shall have wine, or anything. Go file;
  I'll see you have your share. Drag out your dormice,
  And stow 'em somewhere, where they may sleep hand-
    somely;
  They'll hear a hunts-up shortly.
Judas. Now I love thee;
  But no more forks nor whips!
Dec. Deserve 'em not then.
  Up with your men; I'll meet you presently;
  And get 'em sober quickly.   [*Exit.*
Judas. Arm, arm, bullies!
  All's right again and straight; and which is more,
  More wine, more wine. Awake, ye men of Memphis,
  Be sober and discreet; we have much to do, boys.
                                              [*Exeunt.*

ACT III

SCENE I.—*A Temple of the Druids.*

Enter a Messenger.

Mess. Prepare there for the sacrifice! the queen comes.

Music. Enter in solemnity the Druids *singing : the second*
  Daughter *strewing flowers ; then* Bonduca, Caratach,
  Nennius, *and others.*

Bond. Ye powerful gods of Britain, hear our prayers;
  Hear us, ye great revengers; and this day
  Take pity from our swords, doubt from our valours;
  Double the sad remembrance of our wrongs
  In every breast; the vengeance due to those
  Make infinite and endless! On our pikes

This day pale Terror sit, horrors and ruins
Upon our executions; claps of thunder
Hang on our armed carts; and 'fore our troops
Despair and Death; Shame beyond these attend 'em!
Rise from the dust, ye relics of the dead,
Whose noble deeds our holy Druids sing;
Oh, rise, ye valiant bones! let not base earth
Oppress your honours, whilst the pride of Rome
Treads on your stocks, and wipes out all your stories!

Nen. Thou great Tiranes, whom our sacred priests,
Armed with dreadful thunder, place on high
Above the rest of the immortal gods,
Send thy consuming fires and deadly bolts,
And shoot 'em home; stick in each Roman heart
A fear fit for confusion; blast their spirits,
Dwell in 'em to destruction; through their phalanx
Strike, as thou strikest a proud tree; shake their bodies,
Make their strengths totter, and their topless fortunes
Unroot, and reel to ruin!

1 *Daugh.* Oh, thou god,
Thou feared god, if ever to thy justice
Insulting wrongs, and ravishments of women,
(Women derived from thee) their shames, the sufferings
Of those that daily fill'd thy sacrifice
With virgin incense, have access, now hear me!
Now snatch thy thunder up, now on these Romans,
Despisers of thy power, of us defacers,
Revenge thyself; take to thy killing anger,
To make thy great work full, thy justice spoken,
An utter rooting from this blessed isle
Of what Rome is or has been!

Bond. Give me more incense!
The gods are deaf and drowsy, no happy flame
Rises to raise our thoughts. Pour on.

2 *Daugh.* See, Heaven,
And all you powers that guide us, see and shame,
We kneel so long for pity. O'er your altars,
Since 'tis no light oblation that you look for,
No incense-offering, will I hang mine eyes;
And as I wear these stones with hourly weeping,
So will I melt your powers into compassion.
This tear for Prosutagus my brave father;
(Ye gods, now think on Rome!) this for my mother,

And all her miseries; yet see, and save us!
But now ye must be open-eyed. See, Heaven,
Oh, see thy showers stolen from thee; our dishonours,
Oh, sister, our dishonours! Can ye be gods,
And these sins smother'd?   [*A smoke from the altar.*

Bond. The fire takes.

Car. It does so,
But no flame rises. Cease your fretful prayers,
Your whinings, and your tame petitions;
The gods love courage arm'd with confidence,
And prayers fit to pull them down: Weak tears
And troubled hearts, the dull twins of cold spirits,
They sit and smile at. Hear how I salute 'em:—
   [*Kneels.*

Divine Andate, thou who hold'st the reins
Of furious battles, and disorder'd war,
And proudly roll'st thy swarty chariot wheels
Over the heaps of wounds and carcasses,
Sailing through seas of blood; thou sure-steel'd sternness,
Give us this day good hearts, good enemies,
Good blows o' both sides, wounds that fear or flight
Can claim no share in; steel us both with angers
And warlike executions fit thy viewing;
Let Rome put on her best strength, and thy Britain,
Thy little Britain, but as great in fortune,
Meet her as strong as she, as proud, as daring!
And then look on, thou red-eyed god; who does best
Reward with honour; who despair makes fly,
Unarm for ever, and brand with infamy!
Grant this, divine Andate! 'tis but justice;
And my first blow thus on thy holy altar
I sacrifice unto thee.   [*A flame arises.*

Bond. It flames out.   [*Music.*

Car. Now sing, ye Druides.   [*Song.*

Bond. 'Tis out again.

Car. He has given us leave to fight yet; we ask no more;
The rest hangs in our resolutions:
Tempt him no more.

Bond. I would know further, cousin.

Car. His hidden meaning dwells in our endeavours,
Our valours are our best gods. Cheer the soldier,
And let him eat.

Mess. He's at it, sir.

Car. Away then;
    When he has done, let's march.—Come, fear not, lady;
    This day the Roman gains no more ground here,
    But what his body lies in.
Bond. Now I'm confident.   [*Exeunt. Recorders playing.*

SCENE II.—*The Roman Camp.*

Enter JUNIUS, CURIUS, *and* DECIUS.

Dec. We dare not hazard it; besides our lives,
    It forfeits all our understandings.
Jun. Gentlemen,
    Can ye forsake me in so just a service,
    A service for the commonwealth, for honour?
    Read but the letter; you may love too.
Dec. Read it.
    If there be any safety in the circumstance,
    Or likelihood 'tis love, we will not fail you:
    Read it, good Curius.
Cur. Willingly.
Jun. Now mark it.

    Cur. [*Reading.*] " Health to thy heart, my honour'd Junius
    And all thy love requited! I am thine,
    Thine everlastingly; thy love has won me;
    And let it breed no doubt, our new acquaintance
    Compels this; 'tis the gods' decree to bless us.
    The times are dangerous to meet, yet fail not;
    By all the love thou bear'st me I conjure thee,
    Without distrust of danger, to come to me!
    For I have purposed a delivery
    Both of myself and fortune this bless'd day
    Into thy hands, if thou think'st good. To show thee
    How infinite my love is, even my mother
    Shall be thy prisoner, the day yours without hazard;
    For I beheld your danger like a lover,
    A just affecter of thy faith: Thy goodness,
    I know, will use us nobly; and our marriage,
    If not redeem, yet lessen Rome's ambition:
    I am weary of these miseries. Use my mother
    (If you intend to take her) with all honour;
    And let this disobedience to my parent
    Be laid on love, not me. Bring with thee, Junius,
    Spirits resolved to fetch me off, the noblest,
    Forty will serve the turn, just at the joining
    Of both the battles; we will be weakly guarded,
    And for a guide, within this hour, shall reach thee
    A faithful friend of mine. The gods, my Junius,
    Keep thee, and me to serve thee! Young Bonvica "——

This letter carries much belief, and most objections
Answer'd, we must have doubted.

Dec. Is that fellow
Come to you for a guide yet?

Jun. Yes.

Dec. And examined?

Jun. Far more than that; he has felt tortures, yet
He vows he knows no more than this truth.

Dec. Strange!

Cur. If she mean what she writes, as it may be probable,
'Twill be the happiest vantage we can lean to.

Jun. I'll pawn my soul she means truth.

Dec. Think an hour more;
Then, if your confidence grow stronger on you,
We'll set in with you.

Jun. Nobly done! I thank ye.
Ye know the time.

Cur. We will be either ready
To give you present counsel, or join with you.

Enter SUETONIUS, PETILLIUS, DEMETRIUS, *and* MACER.

Jun. No more, as ye are gentlemen. The general!

Suet. Draw out apace; the enemy waits for us.
Are ye all ready?

Jun. All our troops attend, sir.

Suet. I am glad to hear you say so, Junius:
I hope you are dispossess'd.

Jun. I hope so too, sir.

Suet. Continue so.   And, gentlemen, to you now!
To bid you fight is needless; ye are Romans,
The name will fight itself: To tell ye who
You go to fight against, his power, and nature,
But loss of time; ye know it, know it poor,
And oft have made it so: To tell ye further,
His body shows more dreadful than it has done,
To him that fears less possible to deal with,
Is but to stick more honour on your actions,
Load ye with virtuous names, and to your memories
Tie never-dying Time and Fortune constant.
Go on in full assurance! draw your swords
As daring and as confident as justice;
The gods of Rome fight for ye; loud Fame calls ye,

      Pitch'd on the topless Apennine, and blows
      To all the under-world, all nations,
      The seas and unfrequented deserts, where the snow
         dwells;
      Wakens the ruin'd monuments; and there,
      Where nothing but eternal death and sleep is,
      Informs again the dead bones with your virtues.
      Go on, I say: Valiant and wise rule Heaven,
      And all the great aspects attend 'em; Do but blow
      Upon this enemy, who, but that we want foes,
      Cannot deserve that name; and like a mist,
      A lazy fog, before your burning valours
      You'll find him fly to nothing. This is all,
      We have swords, and are the sons of ancient Romans,
      Heirs to their endless valours; fight and conquer!

Dec. Dem. 'Tis done.

Pet. That man that loves not this day,
      And hugs not in his arms the noble danger,
      May he die fameless and forgot!

Suet. Sufficient!
      Up to your troops, and let your drums beat thunder;
      March close and sudden, like a tempest: All executions
                              [*March.*
      Done without sparkling of the body; keep your phalanx
      Sure lined, and pieced together, your pikes forward,
      And so march like a moving fort. Ere this day run,
      We shall have ground to add to Rome, well won.
                                [*Exeunt.*

SCENE III.—*The open Country between the Camps.*

Enter CARATACH *and* NENNIUS.

Nen. The Roman is advanced; from yond' hill's brow
      We may behold him, Caratach.

Car. Let's thither;   [*Drums within at one place afar off.*
      I see the dust fly. Now I see the body.
      Observe 'em, Nennius; by Heaven, a handsome body,
      And, of a few, strongly and wisely jointed!
      Suetonius is a soldier.

Nen. As I take it,
      That's he that gallops by the regiments,
      Viewing their preparations.

Car. Very likely;

He shows no less than general.   See how bravely
The body moves, and in the head how proudly
The captains stick like plumes; he comes apace on.
Good Nennius, go, and bid my stout lieutenant
Bring on the first square body to oppose 'em,
And, as he charges, open to enclose 'em;
The queen move next with hers, and wheel about,
To gain their backs, in which I'll lead the vanguard.
We shall have bloody crowns this day, I see by't.
Haste thee, good Nennius; I'll follow instantly.
                                      [*Exit Nennius.*
How close they march, as if they grew together.
                                          [*March.*
No place but lined alike, sure from oppression!
They will not charge this figure; we must charge 'em,
And charge 'em home at both ends, van and rear;
                          [*Drums in another place afar off.*
They never totter else.   I hear our music,
And must attend it.   Hold, good sword, but this day,
And bite hard where I hound thee! and hereafter
I'll make a relic of thee, for young soldiers
To come like pilgrims to, and kiss for conquests.   [*Exit.*

SCENE IV.—*In front of the Roman Camp.*

Enter Junius, Curius, *and* Decius.

Jun. Now is the time; the fellow stays.
Dec. What think ye?
Cur. I think 'tis true.
Jun. Alas, if 'twere a question,
    If any doubt or hazard fell into't,
    Do ye think mine own discretion so self-blind,
    My care of ye so naked, to run headlong?
Dec. Let's take Petillius with us!
Jun. By no means;
    He's never wise but to himself, nor courteous,
    But where the end's his own: We are strong enough,
    If not too many.   Behind yonder hill,
    The fellow tells me, she attends, weak guarded,
    Her mother and her sister.
Cur. I would venture.
Jun. We shall not strike five blows for't.   Weigh the good,

The general good may come.
Dec. Away! I'll with ye;
    But with what doubt——
Jun. Fear not! my soul for all!
        [*Exeunt. Alarms, drums and trumpets in several*
          places afar off, as at a main battle.

SCENE V.—*Near the Field of Battle. In the Back-ground*
    the Tent of Penius, with a Platform.

Enter DRUSIUS *and* PENIUS *above.*

Drus. Here you may see them all, sir; from this hill
    The country shows off level.
Pen. Gods defend me,
    What multitudes they are, what infinites!
    The Roman power shows like a little star
    Hedged with a double halo.—Now the knell rings:
                    [*Loud shouts.*
    Hark, how they shout to the battle! how the air
    Totters and reels, and rends a-pieces, Drusius,
    With the huge-vollied clamours!
Drus. Now they charge
    (Oh, gods!) of all sides, fearfully.
Pen. Little Rome,
    Stand but this growing Hydra one short hour,
    And thou hast out-done Hercules!
Drus. The dust hides 'em;
    We cannot see what follows.
Pen. They are gone,
    Gone, swallow'd, Drusius; this eternal sun
    Shall never see 'em march more.
Drus. Oh, turn this way,
    And see a model of the field! some forty,
    Against four hundred!
Pen. Well fought, bravely followed!
    Oh, nobly charged again, charged home too! Drusius,
    They seem to carry it. Now they charge all;
                    [*Loud shouts.*
    Close, close, I say! they follow it. Ye gods,
    Can there be more in men? more daring spirits?
    Still they make good their fortunes. Now they are gone
        too,

For ever gone! see, Drusius, at their backs
A fearful ambush rises.   Farewell, valours,
Excellent valours! oh, Rome, where's thy wisdom?
Drus. They are gone indeed, sir.
Pen. Look out toward the army,
I am heavy with these slaughters.
Drus. 'Tis the same still,
Cover'd with dust and fury.

Enter the two Daughters, *with* Junius, Curius, Decius,
Soldiers, *and* Servants.

2 *Daugh.* Bring 'em in;
Tie 'em, and then unarm 'em.
1 *Daugh.* Valiant Romans,
Ye are welcome to your loves!
2 *Daugh.* Your death, fools!
Dec. We deserve 'em;
And, women, do your worst.
1 *Daugh.* Ye need not beg it.
2 *Daugh.* Which is kind Junius?
Serv. This.
2 *Daugh.* Are you my sweetheart?
It looks ill on't!   How long is't, pretty soul,
Since you and I first loved?   Had we not reason
To dote extremely upon one another?
How does my love?   This is not he; my chicken
Could prate finely, sing a love-song.
Jun. Monster——
2 *Daugh.* Oh, now it courts!
Jun. Arm'd with more malice
Than he that got thee has, the devil.
2 *Daugh.* Good!
Proceed, sweet chick.
Jun. I hate thee; that's my last.
2 *Daugh.* Nay, an you love me, forward!—No?—Come, sister,
Let's prick our answers on our arrows' points,
And make 'em laugh a little.   Ye damn'd lechers,
Ye proud improvident fools, have we now caught ye?
Are ye i' th' noose?   Since ye are such loving creatures,
We'll be your Cupids: Do ye see these arrows?
We'll send 'em to your wanton livers, goats.
1 *Daugh.* Oh, how I'll trample on your hearts, ye villains,

Ambitious salt-itch'd slaves, Rome's master-sins!
The mountain-rams tupt your hot mothers.

2 Daugh. Dogs,
To whose brave founders a salt whore gave suck!
Thieves, honour's hangmen, do ye grin? Perdition
Take me for ever, if in my fell anger,
I do not out-do all example.

Enter CARATACH.

Car. Where,
Where are these ladies?—Ye keep noble quarter!
Your mother thinks you dead or taken, upon which
She will not move her battle.—Sure these faces
I have beheld and known; they are Roman leaders!
How came they here?

2 Daugh. A trick, sir, that we used;
A certain policy conducted 'em
Unto our snare: We have done you no small service.
These used as we intend, we are for the battle.

Car. As you intend? Taken by treachery?

1 Daugh. Is't not allow'd?

Car. Those that should gild our conquest,
Make up a battle worthy of our winning,
Catch'd up by craft?

2 Daugh. By any means that's lawful.

Car. A woman's wisdom in our triumphs? Out!
Out, [out,] ye sluts, ye follies! From our swords
Filch our revenges basely?—Arm again, gentlemen!—
Soldiers, I charge ye help 'em.

2 Daugh. By Heaven, uncle,
We will have vengeance for our rapes!

Car. By Heaven,
Ye should have kept your legs close then.—Dispatch
there!

1 Daugh. I will not off thus!

Car. He that stirs to execute,
Or she, though it be yourselves, by him that got me,
Shall quickly feel mine anger! One great day given us,
Not to be snatch'd out of our hands but basely,
And must we shame the gods from whence we have it,
With setting snares for soldiers? I'll run away first,
Be hooted at, and children call me coward,
Before I set up stales for victories.

Give 'em their swords.

2 Daugh. Oh, gods!

Car. Bear off the women
   Unto their mother!

2 Daugh. One shot, gentle uncle!

Car. One cut her fiddle-string!—Bear 'em off, I say.

1 Daugh. The devil take this fortune!

Car. Learn to spin,   [*Exeunt Daughters.*
   And curse your knotted hemp!—Go, gentlemen,
   Safely go off, up to your troops; be wiser;
   There thank me like tall soldiers: I shall seek ye.
                              [*Exit with Soldiers, etc.*

Cur. A noble worth!

Dec. Well, Junius?

Jun. Pray ye, no more!

Cur. He blushes; do not load him.

Dec. Where's your love now?   [*Drums loud again.*

Jun. Puff! there it flies. Come, let's redeem our follies.
                    [*Exeunt Junius, Curius, and Decius.*]

Drus. Awake, sir; yet the Roman body's whole;
   I see 'em clear again.

Pen. Whole? 'tis not possible;
   Drusius, they must be lost.

Drus. By Heaven, they are whole, sir,
   And in brave doing; see, they wheel about
   To gain more ground.

Pen. But see there, Drusius, see,
   See that huge battle moving from the mountains!
   Their gilt coats shine like dragons' scales, their march
   Like a rough tumbling storm; see 'em, and view 'em,
   And then see Rome no more. Say they fail, look,
   Look where the armed carts stand; a new army!
   Look how they hang like falling rocks, as murdering!
   Death rides in triumph, Drusius, fell Destruction
   Lashes his fiery horse, and round about him
   His many thousand ways to let out souls.
   Move me again when they charge, when the mountain
   Melts under their hot wheels, and from their ax'trees
   Huge claps of thunder plough the ground before 'em!
   Till then, I'll dream what Rome was.

Enter SUETONIUS, PETILLIUS, DEMETRIUS, MACER, *and*
Soldiers.

Suet. Oh, bravely fought!
    Honour 'till now ne'er show'd her golden face
    I' the field: Like lions, gentlemen, you have held
    Your heads up this day.   Where's young Junius,
    Curius, and Decius?
Pet. Gone to heaven, I think, sir.
Suet. Their worths go with 'em! Breathe a while. How do
    ye?
Pet. Well; some few scurvy wounds; my heart's whole yet.
Dem. 'Would they would give us more ground!
Suet. Give? we'll have it.
Pet. Have it? and hold it too, despite the devil.

Enter JUNIUS, DECIUS, *and* CURIUS.

Jun. Lead up to th' head, and line sure! The queen's battle
    Begins to charge like wildfire. Where's the general?
Suet. Oh, they are living yet.—Come, my brave soldiers,
    Come, let me pour Rome's blessing on ye; Live,
    Live, and lead armies all! Ye bleed hard.
Jun. Best;
    We shall appear the sterner to the foe.
Dec. More wounds, more honour.
Pet. Lose no time.
Suet. Away then;
    And stand this shock, ye have stood the world.
Pet. We'll grow to't.
    Is not this better now than lousy loving?
Jun. I am myself, Petillius.
Pet. 'Tis I love thee.   *[Exeunt Romans.*

Enter BONDUCA, CARATACH, Daughters, NENNIUS, *and*
Soldiers.

Car. Charge 'em i' th' flanks! Oh, you have play'd the fool,
    The fool extremely, the mad fool!
Bond. Why, cousin?
Car. The woman fool! Why did you give the word
    Unto the carts to charge down, and our people,
    In gross before the enemy? We pay for't;

    Our own swords cut our throats! Why, pox on't!
    Why do you offer to command? The devil,
    The devil, and his dam too! who bid you
    Meddle in men's affairs?
Bond. I'll help all.   *[Exeunt all but Caratach.*
Car. Home,
    Home and spin, woman, spin, go spin! you trifle.
    Open before there, or all's ruin'd—How?
                        [Shouts within.
    Now comes the tempest on ourselves, by Heaven!
Within. Victoria!
Car. Oh, woman, scurvy woman, beastly woman!   *[Exit.*
Drus. Victoria, victoria!
Pen. How's that, Drusius?
Drus. They win, they win, they win! Oh, look, look, look,
      sir,
    For Heaven's sake, look! The Britons fly, the Britons
    fly! Victoria!

      Enter Suetonius, Soldiers, *and* Captains.

Suet. Soft, soft, pursue it soft, excellent soldiers!
    Close, my brave fellows, honourable Romans!
    Oh, cool thy mettle, Junius; they are ours,
    The world cannot redeem 'em: Stern Petillius,
    Govern the conquest nobly. Soft, good soldiers!
                        [Exeunt.

    Enter Bonduca, Daughters, *and* Britons *flying.*

Bond. Shame! whither fly ye, ye unlucky Britons?
    Will ye creep into your mothers' wombs again? Back,
      cowards!
    Hares, fearful hares, doves in your angers! leave me?
    Leave your queen desolate? her hapless children
    To Roman rape again, and fury?

      Enter Caratach *and* Hengo.

Car. Fly, ye buzzards!
    Ye have wings enough, ye fear! Get thee gone, woman,
                      [Loud shout within.
    Shame tread upon thy heels! All's lost, all's lost! Hark,

Hark, how the Romans ring our knells!
> [*Exeunt Bonduca, Daughters, etc.*

Hengo. Good uncle,
Let me go too.
Car. No, boy; thy fortune's mine;
I must not leave thee.   Get behind me; shake not;
I'll breech you, if you do, boy.—

Enter PETILLIUS, JUNIUS, *and* DECIUS.

Come, brave Romans!
All is not lost yet.
Jun. Now I'll thank thee, Caratach.   [*Fight.   Drums.*
Car. Thou art a soldier; strike home, home!   Have at you!
Pen. His blows fall like huge sledges on an anvil.
Dec. I am weary.
Pet. So am I.
Car. Send more swords to me.   [*Exeunt Britons.*
Jun. Let's sit and rest.   [*They sit down.*
Drus. What think you now?
Pen. Oh, Drusius,
I have lost mine honour, lost my name,
Lost all that was my light: These are true Romans,
And I a Briton coward, a base coward!
Guide me where nothing is but desolation,
That I may never more behold the face
Of man, or mankind know me!   Oh, blind Fortune,
Hast thou abused me thus?
Drus. Good sir, be comforted;
It was your wisdom ruled you.   Pray you go home;
Your day is yet to come, when this great fortune
Shall be but foil unto it.   [*Retreat.*
Pen. Fool, fool, coward!
> [*Exeunt Penius and Drusius into the tent.*

Enter SUETONIUS, DEMETRIUS, Soldiers, *Drum and
Colours.*

Suet. Draw in, draw in!—Well have you fought, and worthy
Rome's noble recompense.   Look to your wounds;
The ground is cold and hurtful.   The proud queen
Has got a fort, and there she and her daughters
Defy us once again: To-morrow morning
We'll seek her out, and make her know our fortunes

Stop at no stubborn walls.—Come, sons of Honour,
True Virtue's heirs, thus hatch'd with Britain blood,
Let's march to rest, and set in gules like suns.
Beat a soft march, and each one ease his neighbours!

[*Exeunt*

ACT IV

SCENE I.—*The Roman Camp.   The Tent of Junius.*

Enter PETILLIUS, JUNIUS, DECIUS, *and* DEMETRIUS, *singing.*

> *Pet.* Smooth was his cheek,
> *Dec.* And his chin it was sleek,
> *Jun.* With, whoop, he has done wooing!
> *Dem.* Junius was this captain's name,
>   A lad for a lass's viewing.
> *Pet.* Full black his eye, and plump his thigh,
> *Dec.* Made up for love's pursuing.
> *Dem.* Smooth was his cheek,
> *Pet.* And his chin it was sleek,
> *Jun.* With, whoop, he has done wooing!

Pet. O my vex'd thief, art thou come home again?
    Are thy brains perfect?
Jun. Sound as bells.
Pet. Thy back-worm
    Quiet, and cast his sting, boy?
Jun. Dead, Petillius,
    Dead to all folly, and now my anger only——
Pet. Why, that's well said; hang Cupid and his quiver,
    A drunken brawling boy! Thy honour'd saint
    Be thy ten shillings, Junius; there's the money,
    And there's the ware; square dealing: This but sweats
        thee
    Like a nesh nag, and makes thee look pin-buttock'd;
    The other runs thee whining up and down
    Like a pig in a storm, fills thy brains full of ballads,
    And shows thee like a long Lent, thy brave body
    Turn'd to a tail of green fish without butter.
Dec. When thou lovest next, love a good cup of wine,
    A mistress for a king! she leaps to kiss thee,
    Her red and white's her own, she makes good blood,
    Takes none away; what she heats sleep can help,
    Without a groping surgeon.
Jun. I am counsel'd;
    And henceforth, when I dote again——

Dem. Take heed;
    Ye had almost paid for't.
Pet. Love no more great ladies;
    Thou canst not step amiss then; there's no delight in 'em:
    All's in the whistling of their snatcht-up silks;
    They're only made for handsome view, not handling;
    Their bodies of so weak and wash a temper,
    A rough-paced bed will shake them all to pieces;
    A tough hen pulls their teeth out, tires their souls;
    Plenæ rimarum sunt, they are full of rinnet,
    And take the skin off where they're tasted: Shun 'em;
    They live in cullisses, like rotten cocks,
    Stew'd to a tenderness that holds no tack;
    Give me a thing I may crush.
Jun. Thou speak'st truly:
    The wars shall be my mistress now.
Pet. Well chosen!
    For she's a bouncing lass; she'll kiss thee at night, boy,
    And break thy pate i' th' morning.
Jun. Yesterday
    I found those favours infinite.
Dem. Wench good enough,
    But that she talks too loud.
Pet. She talks to the purpose.
    Which never woman did yet.   She'll hold grappling,
    And he that lays on best is her best servant;
    All other loves are mere catching of dottrels,
    Stretching of legs out only, and trim laziness.
    Here comes the general.

Enter Suetonius, Curius, *and* Macer.

Suet. I'm glad I have found ye:
    Are those come in yet that pursued bold Caratach?
Pet. Not yet, sir, for I think they mean to lodge him;
    Take him I know they dare not, 'twill be dangerous.
Suet. Then haste, Petillius, haste to Penius:
    I fear the strong conceit of what disgrace
    He has pull'd upon himself, will be his ruin;
    I fear his soldiers' fury too; Haste presently;
    I would not lose him for all Britain.   Give him, Petillius--
Pet. That that shall choke him.   [*Aside.*
Suet. All the noble counsel,

His fault forgiven too, his place, his honour——
Pet. For me, I think, as handsome——   [*Aside.*
Suet. All the comfort;
    And tell the soldier, 'twas on our command
    He drew not to the battle.
Pet. I conceive, sir,
    And will do that shall cure all.
Suet. Bring him with you
    Before the queen's fort, and his forces with him;
    There you shall find us following of our conquest.
    Make haste!
Pet. The best I may.   [*Exit.*
Suet. And, noble gentlemen,
    Up to your companies! we'll presently
    Upon the queen's pursuit.   There's nothing done
    Till she be seiz'd; without her, nothing won.
                 [*Exeunt.   Short flourish.*

SCENE II.—*Open Country between the Camps.*

Enter CARATACH *and* HENGO.

Car. How does my boy?
Hengo. I would do well; my heart's well;
    I do not fear.
Car. My good boy!
Hengo. I know, uncle,
    We must all die; my little brother died,
    I saw him die, and he died smiling; sure
    There's no great pain in't, uncle.   But pray tell me,
    Whither must we go when we are dead?
Car. Strange questions!—
    Why, to the blessedest place, boy—Ever sweetness
    And happiness dwells there.
Hengo. Will you come to me?
Car. Yes, my sweet boy.
Hengo. Mine aunt too, and my cousins?
Car. All, my good child.
Hengo. No Romans, uncle?
Car. No, boy.
Hengo. I should be loth to meet them there.
Car. No ill men,
    That live by violence, and strong oppression,
p 506

Come thither; 'tis for those the gods love, good men.
Hengo. Why, then, I care not when I go, for surely
    I am persuaded they love me: I never
    Blasphemed 'em, uncle, nor transgressed my parents;
    I always said my prayers.
Car. Thou shalt go then,
    Indeed thou shalt.
Hengo. When they please.
Car. That's my good boy!
    Art thou not weary, Hengo?
Hengo. Weary, uncle?
    I have heard you say you have march'd all day in armour.
Car. I have, boy.
Hengo. Am not I your kinsman?
Car. Yes.
Hengo. And am not I as fully allied unto you
    In those brave things as blood?
Car. Thou art too tender.
Hengo. To go upon my legs? they were made to bear me.
    I can play twenty mile a-day; I see no reason,
    But to preserve my country and myself,
    I should march forty.
Car. What wouldst thou be, living
    To wear a man's strength!
Hengo. Why, a Caratach,
    A Roman-hater, a scourge sent from Heaven
    To whip these proud thieves from our kingdom.   Hark,
    Hark, uncle, hark! I hear a drum.   [*Drum.*

Enter JUDAS *and his* Soldiers, *and stand on one side of
the stage.*

Judas. Beat softly,
    Softly, I say: they are here.   Who dare charge?
1 *Sold.* He
    That dares be knock'd o' th' head: I'll not come near
    him.
Judas. Retire again, and watch then.   How he stares!
    He has eyes would kill a dragon.   Mark the boy well;
    If we could take or kill him—A pox on ye,
    How fierce ye look!   See, how he broods the boy!
    The devil dwells in's scabbard.   Back, I say!
    Apace, apace! he has found us.   [*They retire.*

Car. Do ye hunt us?

Hengo. Uncle, good uncle, see! the thin starved rascal,
 The eating Roman, see where he thrids the thickets:
 Kill him, dear uncle, kill him! one good blow
 To knock his brains into his breech; strike's head off
 That I may piss in's face.

Car. Do ye make us foxes?—
 Here, hold my charging-staff, and keep the place, boy!
 I am at bay, and like a bull I'll bear me.—
 Stand, stand, ye rogues, ye squirrels!   [*Exit.*

Hengo. Now he pays 'em;
 Oh, that I had a man's strength!

Enter Judas.

Judas. Here's the boy;
 Mine own, I thank my fortune.

Hengo. Uncle, uncle!
 Famine is fallen upon me, uncle.

Judas. Come, sir,
 Yield willingly (your uncle's out of hearing),
 I'll tickle your young tail else.

Hengo. I defy thee,
 Thou mock-made man of mat! Charge home, sirrah!
 Hang thee, base slave, thou shakest.

Judas. Upon my conscience,
 The boy will beat me! how it looks, how bravely,
 How confident the worm is! a scabb'd boy
 To handle me thus!—Yield, or I cut thy head off.

Hengo. Thou darest not cut my finger; here 'tis, touch it.

Judas. The boy speaks sword and buckler! Pr'ythee yield,
  boy;
 Come, here's an apple, yield.

Hengo. By Heaven, he fears me!
 I'll give you sharper language:—When, ye coward,
 When come ye up?

Judas. If he should beat me——

Hengo. When, sir?
 I long to kill thee! Come, thou canst not 'scape me;
 I have twenty ways to charge thee, twenty deaths
 Attend my bloody staff.

Judas. Sure 'tis the devil,
 A dwarf devil in a doublet!

Hengo. I have killed
>A captain, sirrah, a brave captain, and when I have done,
>I have kicked him thus. Look here; see how I charge
>This staff!
>>[*Kicks and beats him with the truncheon of Caratach.*

Judas. Most certain this boy will cut my throat yet.

Enter two Soldiers *running.*

1 *Sold.* Flee, flee! he kills us.
2 *Sold.* He comes, he comes!
Judas. The devil take the hindmost!
>>[*Exeunt Judas and Soldiers.*

Hengo. Run, run, ye rogues, ye precious rogues, ye rank
>   rogues!
>'A comes, 'a comes, 'a comes, 'a comes! that's he, boys!
>What a brave cry they make!

Enter CARATACH *with a Head.*

Car. How does my chicken?
Hengo. 'Faith, uncle, grown a soldier, a great soldier;
>For, by the virtue of your charging-staff,
>And a strange fighting face I put upon't,
>I have out-brav'd Hunger.
Car. That's my boy, my sweet boy!
>Here, here's a Roman's head for thee.
Hengo. Good provision!
>Before I starve, my sweet-faced gentleman,
>I'll try your favour.
Car. A right complete soldier!
>Come, chicken, let's go seek some place of strength
>(The country's full of scouts) to rest a while in;
>Thou wilt not else be able to endure
>The journey to my country. Fruits and water
>Must be your food a while, boy.
Hengo. Anything;
>I can eat moss, nay, I can live on anger,
>To vex these Romans. Let's be wary, uncle.
Car. I warrant thee; come cheerfully.
Hengo. And boldly!
>>[*Exeunt.*

SCENE III.—*The Tent of* Penius.

Enter Penius, Drusius, *and* Regulus.

Reg. The soldier shall not grieve you.
Pen. Pray ye forsake me;
    Look not upon me, as ye love your honours!
    I am so cold a coward, my infection
    Will choke your virtues like a damp else.
Drus. Dear captain!
Reg. Most honoured sir!
Pen. Most hated, most abhorred!
    Say so, and then ye know me, nay, ye please me.
    Oh, my dear credit, my dear credit!
Reg. Sure
    His mind is dangerous.
Drus. The good gods cure it!
Pen. My honour, got through fire, through stubborn breaches,
    Through battles that have been as hard to win as heaven,
    Through Death himself, in all his horrid trims,
    Is gone for ever, ever, ever, gentlemen!
    And now I am left to scornful tales and laughters,
    To hootings at, pointing with fingers, " That's he,
    That's the brave gentleman forsook the battle,
    The most wise Penius, the disputing coward."
    Oh, my good sword, break from my side, and kill me;
    Cut out the coward from my heart!
Reg. You are none.
Pen. He lies that says so; by Heaven, he lies, lies basely,
    Baser than I have done!   Come, soldiers, seek me;
    I have robb'd ye of your virtues!   Justice seek me,
    I have broke my fair obedience! lost!   Shame take me,
    Take me, and swallow me, make ballads of me,
    Shame, endless shame! and pray do you forsake me!
Drus. What shall we do?
Pen. Good gentlemen, forsake me;
    You were not wont to be commanded.   Friends, pray
      do it,
    And do not fear; for, as I am a coward,
    I will not hurt myself (when that mind takes me,
    I'll call to you, and ask your help), I dare not.
                    [*Throws himself upon the ground.*

Enter PETILLIUS.

Pet. Good-morrow, gentlemen!   Where's the tribune?
Reg. There.
Drus. Whence come you, good Petillius?
Pet. From the general.
Drus. With what, for Heaven's sake?
Pet. With good counsel, Drusius,
     And love, to comfort him.
Drus. Good Regulus,
     Step to the soldier and allay his anger;
     For he is wild as winter.   [*Exeunt Drusius and Regulus.*
Pet. Oh, are you there? have at you!—Sure he's dead,
                                 [*Half aside.*
     It cannot be he dare out-live this fortune;
     He must die, 'tis most necessary; men expect it,
     And thought of life in him goes beyond coward.
     Forsake the field so basely?   Fy upon't!
     So poorly to betray his worth?   So coldly
     To cut all credit from the soldier?   Sure
     If this man mean to live (as I should think it
     Beyond belief), he must retire where never
     The name of Rome, the voice of arms, or honour,
     Was known or heard of yet.   He's certain dead,
     Or strongly means it; he's no soldier else,
     No Roman in him; all he has done but outside,
     Fought either drunk or desperate.   Now he rises.—
     How does lord Penius?
Pen. As you see.
Pet. I am glad on't;
     Continue so still.   The lord general,
     The valiant general, great Suetonius——
Pen. No more of me is spoken; my name's perished.
Pet. He that commanded fortune and the day,
     By his own valour and discretion
     (When, as some say, Penius refused to come,
     But I believe 'em not), sent me to see you.
Pen. Ye are welcome; and pray see me, see me well;
     You shall not see me long.
Pet. I hope so, Penius.—   [*Aside.*
     The gods defend, sir!
Pen. See me and understand me: This is he,
     Left to fill up your triumph; he that basely

Whistled his honour off to th' wind, that coldly
Shrunk in his politic head, when Rome, like reapers,
Sweat blood and spirit for a glorious harvest,
And bound it up, and brought it off; that fool,
That having gold and copper offered him,
Refused the wealth, and took the waste; that soldier,
That being courted by loud Fame and Fortune,
Labour in one hand that propounds us gods,
And in the other Glory that creates us,
Yet durst doubt and be damned!

Pet. It was an error.

Pen. A foul one, and a black one.

Pet. Yet the blackest
May be washed white again.

Pen. Never.

Pet. Your leave, sir;
And I beseech you note me, for I love you,
And bring along all comfort: Are we gods,
Allied to no infirmities? are our natures
More than men's natures? When we slip a little
Out of the way of virtue, are we lost?
Is there no medicine called sweet mercy?

Pen. None, Petillius;
There is no mercy in mankind can reach me,
Nor is it fit it should; I have sinned beyond it.

Pet. Forgiveness meets with all faults.

Pen. 'Tis all faults,
All sins I can commit, to be forgiven;
'Tis loss of whole man in me, my discretion,
To be so stupid, to arrive at pardon!

Pet. Oh, but the general——

Pen. He is a brave gentleman,
A valiant, and a loving; and I dare say
He would, as far as honour durst direct him,
Make even with my fault; but 'tis not honest
Nor in his power: Examples that may nourish
Neglect and disobedience in whole bodies,
And totter the estates and faiths of armies,
Must not be played withal; nor out of pity
Make a general forget his duty;
Nor dare I hope more from him than is worthy.

Pet. What would you do?

Pen. Die.

Pet. So would sullen children,
  Women that want their wills, slaves disobedient,
  That fear the law. Die? Fy, great captain! you
  A man to rule men, to have thousand lives
  Under your regiment, and let your passion
  Betray your reason? I bring you all forgiveness,
  The noblest kind commends, your place, your honour—
Pen. Pr'ythee no more; 'tis foolish. Didst not thou
  (By Heaven, thou didst; I overheard thee, there,
  There where thou stand'st now) deliver me for rascal,
  Poor, dead, cold, coward, miserable, wretched,
  If I out-lived this ruin?
Pet. I?
Pen. And thou didst it nobly,
  Like a true man, a soldier; and I thank thee,
  I thank thee, good Petillius, thus I thank thee!
Pet. Since you are so justly made up, let me tell you,
  'Tis fit you die indeed.
Pen. Oh, how thou lovest me!
Pet. For say he had forgiven you, say the people's whispers
  Were tame again, the time run out for wonder,
  What must your own command think, from whose
    swords
  You have taken off the edges, from whose valours
  The due and recompense of arms; nay, made it doubtful
  Whether they knew obedience? must not these kill you?
  Say they are won to pardon you, by mere miracle
  Brought to forgive you, what old valiant soldier,
  What man that loves to fight, and fight for Rome,
  Will ever follow you more? Dare you know these
    ventures?
  If so, I bring you comfort; dare you take it?
Pen. No, no, Petillius, no.
Pet. If your mind serve you,
  You may live still; but how?—yet pardon me:
  You may out-wear all too;—but when?—and certain
  There is a mercy for each fault, if tamely
  A man will take't upon conditions.
Pen. No, by no means: I am only thinking now, sir
  (For I am resolved to go), of a most base death,
  Fitting the baseness of my fault. I'll hang.
Pet. You shall not: you are a gentleman I honour,
  I would else flatter you, and force you live,

Which is far baser.   Hanging? 'tis a dog's death,
And end for slaves.

Pen. The fitter for my baseness.

Pet. Besides, the man that's hanged preaches his end,
And sits a sign for all the world to gape at.

Pen. That's true; I'll take a fitter; poison.

Pet. No,
'Tis equal ill; the death of rats and women,
Lovers, and lazy boys, that fear correction;
Die like a man.

Pen. Why, my sword, then.

Pet. Ay, if your sword be sharp, sir.
There's nothing under Heaven that's like your sword;
Your sword's a death indeed!

Pen. It shall be sharp, sir.

Pet. Why, Mithridates was an arrant ass
To die by poison, if all Bosphorus
Could lend him swords: Your sword must do the deed:
'Tis shame to die chok'd, fame to die and bleed.

Pen. Thou hast confirm'd me; and, my good Petillius,
Tell me no more I may live.

Pet. 'Twas my commission;
But now I see you in a nobler way,
A way to make all even.

Pen. Farewell, captain!
Be a good man, and fight well: be obedient;
Command thyself, and then thy men. Why shakest
thou?

Pet. I do not, sir.

Pen. I would thou hadst, Petillius!
I would find something to forsake the world with,
Worthy the man that dies: A kind of earthquake
Through all stern valours but mine own.

Pet. I feel now
A kind of trembling in me.

Pen. Keep it still;
As thou lovest virtue, keep it.

Pet. And, brave captain,
The great and honour'd Penius!—

Pen. That again!
Oh, how it heightens me! again, Petillius!

Pet. Most excellent commander—

Pen. Those were mine!

Mine, only mine!

Pet. They are still.

Pen. Then, to keep 'em
 For ever falling more, have at ye!—Heavens,
 Ye everlasting powers, I am yours:
 The work is done,   [*Falls upon his sword.*
 That neither fire, nor age, nor melting envy,
 Shall ever conquer. Carry my last words
 To the great general: Kiss his hands, and say,
 My soul I give to Heaven, my fault to justice,
 Which I have done upon myself; my virtue,
 If ever there was any in poor Penius,
 Made more, and happier, light on him!—I faint—
 And where there is a foe, I wish him fortune.
 I die: Lie lightly on my ashes, gentle earth! [*Dies.*

Pet. And on my sin! Farewell, great Penius!—
 The soldier is in fury; now I am glad [*Noise within.*
 'Tis done before he comes. This way for me,
 The way of toil;—for thee, the way of honour! [*Exit.*

Drusius, Regulus, *and* Soldiers, *are heard without.*

Sold. Kill him, kill him, kill him!

Drus. What will ye do?

Reg. Good soldiers, honest soldiers——

Sold. Kill him, kill him, kill him!

Drus. Kill us first: we command too.

Reg. Valiant soldiers,
 Consider but whose life ye seek.—Oh, Drusius,
 Bid him be gone; he dies else. — [*Drusius enters.*]—
  Shall Rome say,
 Ye most approved soldiers, her dear children
 Devoured the fathers of the fights? shall rage
 And stubborn fury guide those swords to slaughter,
 To slaughter of their own, to civil ruin?

Drus. Oh, let 'em in; all's done, all's ended, Regulus;
 Penius has found his last eclipse. Come, soldiers,
 Come and behold your miseries; come bravely,
 Full of your mutinous and bloody angers,
 And here bestow your darts.—Oh, only Roman,
 Oh, father of the wars!

Enter Regulus *and* Soldiers.

Reg. Why stand ye stupid?
  Where be your killing furies? whose sword now
  Shall first be sheathed in Penius? Do ye weep?
  Howl out, ye wretches, ye have cause; howl ever!
  Who shall now lead ye fortunate? whose valour
  Preserve ye to the glory of your country?
  Who shall march out before ye, coyed and courted,
  By all the mistresses of war, care, counsel,
  Quick-eyed experience, and victory twined to him?
  Who shall beget ye deeds beyond inheritance
  To speak your names, and keep your honours living,
  When children fail, and Time, that takes all with him,
  Build houses for ye to oblivion?
Drus. Oh, ye poor desperate fools, no more now soldiers.
  Go home, and hang your arms up; let rust rot 'em;
  And humble your stern valours to soft prayers!
  For ye have sunk the frame of all your virtues;
  The sun that warmed your bloods is set for ever.—
  I'll kiss thy honoured cheek. Farewell, great Penius,
  Thou thunderbolt, farewell!—Take up the body:
  To-morrow morning to the camp convey it,
  There to receive due ceremonies. That eye,
  That blinds himself with weeping, gets most glory.
     [Exeunt, bearing out the body. A dead march.

SCENE IV.—*Before the Fort of Bonduca.*

Enter Suetonius, Junius, Decius, Demetrius, Curius, *and*
  Soldiers; Bonduca, *two* Daughters, *and* Nennius, *on the*
  ramparts. Drums and colours.

Suet. Bring up the catapults, and shake the wall;
  We will not be out-braved thus.
Nen. Shake the earth,
  Ye cannot shake our souls. Bring up your rams,
  And with their armed heads make the fort totter,
  Ye do but rock us into death.   *[Exit.*
Jun. See, sir,
  See the Icenian queen in all her glory,
  From the strong battlements proudly appearing,
  As if she meant to give us lashes!

Dec. Yield, queen.

Bond. I am unacquainted with that language, Roman.

Suet. Yield, honour'd lady, and expect our mercy,
    We love thy nobleness.   [*Exit Decius.*

Bond. I thank ye! ye say well;
    But mercy and love are sins in Rome and hell.

Suet. You cannot 'scape our strength; you must yield, lady:
    You must adore and fear the power of Rome.

Bond. If Rome be earthly, why should any knee
    With bending adoration worship her?
    She's vicious; and, your partial selves confess,
    Aspires, the height of all impiety;
    Therefore 'tis fitter I should reverence
    The thatched houses where the Britons dwell
    In careless mirth; where the bless'd household gods
    See nought but chaste and simple purity.
    'Tis not high power that makes a place divine,
    Nor that the men from gods derive their line;
    But sacred thoughts, in holy bosoms stored,
    Make people noble, and the place adored.

Suet. Beat the wall deeper!

Bond. Beat it to the centre,
    We will not sink one thought.

Suet. I'll make ye.

Bond. No.

Enter PETILLIUS, *who whispers* SUETONIUS.

2 *Daugh.* O mother, these are fearful hours; speak gently
    To these fierce men, they will afford ye pity.

Bond. Pity? Thou fearful girl, 'tis for those wretches
    That misery makes tame. Wouldst thou live less?
    Wast not thou born a princess? Can my blood,
    And thy brave father's spirit, suffer in thee
    So base a separation from thyself,
    As mercy from these tyrants? Thou lovest lust sure,
    And long'st to prostitute thy youth and beauty
    To common slaves for bread. Say they had mercy,
    The devil a relenting conscience,
    The lives of kings rest in their diadems,
    Which to their bodies lively souls do give
    And, ceasing to be kings, they cease to live.
    Shew such another fear, and, by the Gods,
    I'll fling thee to their fury.—

Suet. He is dead then?

Pet. I think so certainly; yet all my means, sir,
  Even to the hazard of my life——

Suet. No more:
  We must not seem to mourn here.

Enter Decius.

Dec. There is a breach made;
  Is it your will we charge, sir!

Suet. Once more, mercy,
  Mercy to all that yield!

Bond. I scorn to answer:—
  Speak to him, girl—and hear thy sister.

1 *Daugh.* General,
  Hear me, and mark me well, and look upon me,
  Directly in my face, my woman's face,
  Whose only beauty is the hate it bears ye;
  See with thy narrowest eyes, thy sharpest wishes,
  Into my soul, and see what there inhabits;
  See if one fear, one shadow of a terror,
  One paleness dare appear but from my anger,
  To lay hold on your mercies.   No, ye fools,
  Poor fortune's fools, we were not born for triumphs,
  To follow your gay sports, and fill your slaves
  With hoots and acclamations.

Pet. Brave behaviour!

1 *Daugh.* The children of as great as Rome, as noble,
  Our names before her, and our deeds her envy,
  Must we gild o'er your conquest, make your state,
  That is not fairly strong, but fortunate?
  No, no, ye Romans, we have ways to 'scape ye,
  To make ye poor again, indeed our prisoners,
  And stick our triumphs full.

Pet. S'death, I shall love her!

1 *Daugh.* To torture ye with suffering, like our slaves;
  To make ye curse our patience, wish the world
  Were lost again, to win us only, and esteem [it]
  The end of all ambitions.

Bond. Do ye wonder?
  We'll make our monuments in spite of fortune;
  In spite of all your eagles' wings, we'll work
  A pitch above you; and from our height we'll stoop

As fearless of your bloody soars, and fortunate,
As if we pray'd on heartless doves.
Suet. Strange stiffness !
    Decius, go charge the breach.   *[Exit Decius.*
Bond. Charge it home, Roman;
    We shall deceive thee else.—Where's Nennius!

Enter NENNIUS.

Nen. They have made a mighty breach.
Bond. Stick in thy body,
    And make it good but half an hour.
Nen. I'll do it.
1 *Daugh.* And then be sure to die.
Nen. It shall go hard else.
Bond. Farewell, with all my heart !   We shall meet yonder
    Where few of these must come.
Nen. Gods take thee, lady!   *[Exit.*
Bond. Bring up the swords and poison.

Enter one with Swords and a great Cup of Poison.

2 *Daugh.* Oh, my fortune !
Bond. How, how, ye whore ?
2 *Daugh.* Good mother, nothing to offend you.
Bond. Here, wench.—
    Behold us, Romans !
Suet. Mercy yet.
Bond. No talking !
    Puff ! there goes all your pity.—Come, short prayers,
    And let's dispatch the business !   You begin;
    Shrink not, I'll see you do't.
2 *Daugh.* Oh, gentle mother !
    Oh, Romans ! oh, my heart ! I dare not.
Suet. Woman, woman,
    Unnatural woman !
2 *Daugh.* Oh, persuade her, Romans !
    Alas, I am young, and would live.—Noble mother,
    Can ye kill that ye gave life ?   Are my years
    Fit for destruction?
Suet. Yield, and be a queen still,
    A mother, and a friend.
Bond. Ye talk !—Come, hold it,
    And put it home.

1 *Daugh.* Fy, sister, fy!
    What would you live to be?
Bond. A whore still?
2 *Daugh.* Mercy!
Suet. Hear her, thou wretched woman!
2 *Daugh.* Mercy, mother!   [*Kneels.*
    Oh, whither will you send me?   I was once
    Your darling, your delight.
Bond. Oh, gods! fear in my family?—Do it, and nobly.
2 *Daugh.* Oh, do not frown then.
1 *Daugh.* Do it, worthy sister;
    'Tis nothing ; 'tis a pleasure: We'll go with you.
2 *Daugh.* Oh, if I knew but whither!
1 *Daugh.* To the blessed:
    Where we shall meet our father——
Suet. Woman!
Bond. Talk not.
1 *Daugh.* Where nothing but true joy is——
Bond. That's a good wench!   [2 *Daugh. drinks.*
    Mine own sweet girl! put it close to thee.
2 *Daugh.* Oh,
    Comfort me still, for Heaven's sake.
1 *Daugh.* Where eternal
    Our youths are, and our beauties; where no wars come,
    Nor lustful slaves to ravish us.
2 *Daugh.* That steels me;
    A long farewell to this world!   [*Dies.*
Bond. Good; I'll help thee.
1 *Daugh.* The next is mine.—
    Show me a Roman lady in all your stories,
    Dare do this for her honour; they are cowards,
    Eat coals like compell'd cats: your great saint, Lucrece,
    Died not for honour; Tarquin tupt her well,
    And, mad she could not hold him, bled.
Pet. By Heaven.
    I am in love! I would give an hundred pound now
    But to lie with this woman's behaviour. Oh, the devil!
1 *Daugh.* Ye shall see me example: All your Rome,
    If I were proud and loved ambition,
    If I were lustful, all your ways of pleasure,
    If I were greedy, all the wealth ye conquer——
Bond. Make haste.
1 *Daugh.* I will.—[*Drinks.*]—Could not entice to live,

But two short hours, this frailty.   Would ye learn
How to die bravely, Romans, to fling off
This case of flesh, lose all your cares for ever?
Live, as we have done, well, and fear the gods;
Hunt honour, and not nations, with your swords;
Keep your minds humble, your devotions high;
So shall ye learn the noblest part, to die.   [*Dies.*

Bond. I come, wench.—To ye all, Fate's hangmen, you
That ease the aged Destinies, and cut
The threads of kingdoms as they draw 'em! here,
Here is a draught would ask no less than Cæsar
To pledge it for the glory's sake!

Cur. Great lady!

Suet. Make up your own conditions.

Bond. So we will.

Suet. Stay!

Dem. Stay!

Suet. Be anything.

Bond. A saint, Suetonius,   [*Drinks.*
When thou shalt fear, and die like a slave.   Ye fools,
Ye should have tied up Death first, when ye conquer'd;
Ye sweat for us in vain else: See him here!
He is ours still, and our friend; laughs at your pities;
And we command him with as easy reins
As do our enemies.—I feel the poison.—
Poor vanquish'd Romans, with what matchless tortures
Could I now rack ye!   But I pity ye,
Desiring to die quiet: Nay, so much
I hate to prosecute my victory,
That I will give ye counsel ere I die:
If you will keep your laws and empire whole,
Place in your Roman flesh a Briton soul.   [*Dies*

Suet. Desperate and strange!

Enter DECIUS.

Dec. 'Tis won, sir, and the Britons
All put to th' sword.

Suet. Give her fair funeral;
She was truly noble, and a queen.

Pet. Pox take it,
A love-mange grown upon me!   What a spirit!

Jun. I am glad of this!   I have found you.

Pet. In my belly,
    Oh, how it tumbles!
Jun. Ye good gods, I thank ye!   *[Exeunt.*

ACT V

SCENE I.—*A mountainous Country.*

CARATACH *discovered upon the Rock in the Back-ground, and*
HENGO *by him sleeping.*

Car. Thus we afflicted Britons climb for safeties,
    And, to avoid our dangers, seek destructions;
    Thus we awake to sorrows.—Oh, thou woman,
    Thou agent for adversities, what curses
    This day belong to thy improvidence!
    To Britanie, by thy means, what sad millions
    Of widows' weeping eyes! The strong man's valour
    Thou hast betrayed to fury, the child's fortune
    To fear, and want of friends; whose pieties
    Might wipe his mournings off, and build his sorrows
    A house of rest by his bless'd ancestors:
    The virgins thou hast robb'd of all their wishes,
    Blasted their blowing hopes, turned their songs,
    Their mirthful marriage-songs, to funerals;
    The land thou hast left a wilderness of wretches.—
    The boy begins to stir; thy safety made,
    'Would my soul were in heaven!
Hengo. Oh, noble uncle,
    Look out; I dreamed we were betray'd.
Car. No harm, boy;
    'Tis but thy emptiness that breeds these fancies:
    Thou shalt have meat anon.
                [A soft dead march within.
Hengo. A little, uncle.
    And I shall hold out bravely.—What are those,
    (Look, uncle, look!) those multitudes that march there?
    They come upon us stealing by.
Car. I see 'em;
    And pr'ythee be not fearful.
Hengo. Now you hate me;—
    'Would I were dead!
Car. Thou knowest I love thee dearly.
  Q ⁵⁰⁶

Hengo. Did I e'er shrink yet, uncle?   Were I a man now
    I should be angry with you.

Enter DRUSIUS, REGULUS, *and* Soldiers, *with* PENIUS'S *Hearse,*
Drums, and Colours.

Car. My sweet chicken!—
    See, they have reached us; and, as it seems, they bear
    Some soldier's body, by their solemn gestures,
    And sad solemnities; it well appears, too,
    To be of eminence.—Most worthy soldiers,
    Let me entreat your knowledge to inform me
    What noble body that is, which you bear
    With such a sad and ceremonious grief,
    As if ye meant to woo the world and nature
    To be in love with death?   Most honourable
    Excellent Romans, by your ancient valours,
    As ye love fame, resolve me!
Sold. 'Tis the body
    Of the great captain Penius, by himself
    Made cold and spiritless.
Car. Oh, stay, ye Romans,
    By the religion which ye owe those gods
    That lead ye on to victories! by those glories
    Which made even pride a virtue in ye!
Drus. Stay.—
    What's thy will, Caratach?
Car. Set down the body,
    The body of the noblest of all Romans;
    As ye expect an offering at your graves
    From your friends' sorrows, set it down a-while,
    That with your griefs an enemy may mingle,
    (A noble enemy, that loves a soldier)
    And lend a tear to virtue!   Even your foes,
    Your wild foes, as you called us, are yet stored
    With fair affections, our hearts fresh, our spirits,
    Though sometime stubborn, yet, when Virtue dies,
    Soft and relenting as a virgin's prayers:
    Oh, set it down!
Drus. Set down the body, soldiers.
Car. Thou hallowed relic, thou rich diamond,
    Cut with thine own dust; thou, for whose wide fame
    The world appears too narrow, man's all thoughts,

Had they all tongues, too silent; thus I bow
To thy most honour'd ashes! Though an enemy,
Yet friend to all thy worths, sleep peaceably;
Happiness crown thy soul, and in thy earth
Some laurel fix his seat, there grow and flourish,
And make thy grave an everlasting triumph!
Farewell all glorious wars, now thou art gone,
And honest arms adieu!   All noble battles,
Maintain'd in thirst of honour, not of blood,
Farewell for ever!

Hengo. Was this Roman, uncle,
    So good a man?

Car. Thou never knewest thy father.

Hengo. He died before I was born.

Car. This worthy Roman
    Was such another piece of endless honour,
    Such a brave soul dwelt in him; their proportions
    And faces were not much unlike, boy.—Excellent nature!
    See how it works into his eyes!—mine own boy!

Hengo. The multitudes of these men, and their fortunes,
    Could never make me fear yet; one man's goodness——

Car. Oh, now thou pleasest me; weep still, my child,
    As if thou saw'st me dead! with such a flux
    Or flood of sorrow, still thou pleasest me.—
    And, worthy soldiers, pray receive these pledges,
    These hatchments of our griefs, and grace us so much
    To place 'em on his hearse.   Now, if ye please,
    Bear off the noble burden; raise his pile
    High as Olympus, making Heaven to wonder
    To see a star upon earth out-shining theirs:
    And ever-loved, ever-living be
    Thy honour'd and most sacred memory!

Drus. Thou hast done honestly, good Caratach;
    And when thou diest, a thousand virtuous Romans
    Shall sing thy soul to Heaven.—Now march on, soldiers.
               [*Exeunt Romans.   A dead march.*

Car. Now dry thine eyes, my boy.

Hengo. Are they all gone?
    I could have wept this hour yet.

Car. Come, take cheer,
    And raise thy spirit, child; if but this day
    Thou canst bear out thy faintness, the night coming
    I'll fashion our escape.

Hengo. Pray fear not me;
    Indeed I am very hearty.
Car. Be so still;
    His mischiefs lessen, that controls his ill.   [*Exeunt.*

SCENE II.—*The Roman Camp.*

Enter PETILLIUS.

Pet. What do I ail, i' th' name of Heaven? I did but see her,
    And see her die; she stinks by this time strongly,
    Abominably stinks. She was a woman,
    A thing I never cared for; but to die so,
    So confidently, bravely, strongly—Oh, the devil,
    I have the bots!—By Heaven, she scorned us strangely,
    All we could do, or durst do; threaten'd us
    With such a noble anger, and so govern'd
    With such a fiery spirit—The plain bots!
    A pox upon the bots, the love-bots! Hang me.
    Hang me even out o' th' way, directly hang me!
    Oh, penny pipers, and most painful penners
    Of bountiful new ballads, what a subject,
    What a sweet subject for your silver sounds,
    Is crept upon ye!

Enter JUNIUS.

Jun. Here he is; have at him!   [*Sings.*

        She set the sword unto her breast,
           Great pity it was to see,
        That three drops of her life-warm blood,
           Run trickling down her knee.

Art thou there, bonny boy? And i'faith how dost thou?
Pet. Well, gramercy; how dost thou?—He has found me,
    Scented me out; the shame the devil owed me,
    He has kept his day with.—And what news, Junius?

    Jun. It was an old tale ten thousand times told,
        Of a young lady was turn'd into mould,
        Her life was lovely, her death it was bold.

Pet. A cruel rogue! now he has drawn pursuit on me,
    He hunts me like a devil.—No more singing!
    Thou hast got a cold: Come, let's go drink some sack,
        boy.
Jun. Ha, ha, ha, ha, ha, ha!

Pet. Why dost thou laugh?
    What mare's nest hast thou found?
Jun. Ha, ha, ha!
    I cannot laugh alone:—Decius! Demetrius!
    Curius!—oh, my sides! ha, ha, ha, ha!
    The strangest jest!
Pet. Pr'ythee no more.
Jun. The admirablest fooling!
Pet. Thou art the prettiest fellow!
Jun. Sirs!
Pet. Why, Junius,
    Pr'ythee, away, sweet Junius?
Jun. Let me sing then.
Pet. Whoa, here's a stir, now! *Sing a song of sixpence!*
    By Heaven, if—pr'ythee—pox on't, Junius!
Jun. I must either sing or laugh.
Pet. And what's your reason?
Jun. What's that to you?
Pet. And I must whistle
Jun. Do so.
    Oh, I hear 'em coming.
Pet. I have a little business.
Jun. Thou shalt not go, believe it: What! a gentleman
    Of thy sweet conversation?
Pet. Captain Junius,
    Sweet captain, let me go with all celerity!
    Things are not always one; and do not question,
    Nor jeer, nor gibe: None of your doleful ditties,
    Nor your sweet conversation; you will find then
    I may be angered.
Jun. By no means, Petillius;
    Anger a man that never knew passion?
    'Tis most impossible: A noble captain,
    A wise and generous gentleman?
Pet. Tom Puppy,
    Leave this way to abuse me! I have found you,
    But, for your mother's sake, I will forgive you.
    Your subtile understanding may discover,
    As you think, some trim toy to make you merry,
    Some straw to tickle you; but do not trust to't;
    You are a young man, and may do well; be sober,
    Carry yourself discreetly.

Enter DECIUS, DEMETRIUS, *and* CURIUS.

Jun. Yes, forsooth.

Dem. How does the brave Petillius?

Jun. Monstrous merry.
    We two were talking what a kind of thing
    I was when I was in love; what a strange monster
    For little boys and girls to wonder at;
    How like a fool I looked!

Dec. So they do all,
    Like great dull slavering fools.

Jun. Petillius saw too.

Pet. No more of this; 'tis scurvy; peace!

Jun. How nastily,
    Indeed how beastly, all I did became me!
    How I forgot to blow my nose! There he stands,
    An honest and a wise man; if himself
    (I dare avouch it boldly, for I know it)
    Should find himself in love——

Pet. I am angry.

Jun. Surely his wise self would hang his beastly self;
    His understanding self so mawl his ass self——

Dec. He's bound to do it; for he knows the follies,
    The poverties, and baseness, that belongs to't;
    He has read upon the reformations long.

Pet. He has so.

Jun. 'Tis true, and he must do't: Nor is it fit indeed
    Any such coward——

Pet. You'll leave prating?

Jun. Should dare come near the regiments, especially
    Those curious puppies (for believe there are such)
    That only love behaviours: Those are dog-whelps,
    Dwindle away because a woman dies well;
    Commit with passions only; fornicate
    With the free spirit merely. You, Petillius,
    For you have long observed the world——

Pet. Dost thou hear?
    I'll beat thee damnably within these three hours!
    Go pray; may be I'll kill thee. Farewell, Jackdaws!
                                    [*Exit Petillius.*

Dec. What a strange thing he's grown!

Jun. I am glad he is so;
    And stranger he shall be before I leave him.

Cur. Is't possible her mere death——

Jun. I observed him,
    And found him taken, infinitely taken,
    With her bravery; I have followed him,
    And seen him kiss his sword since, court his scabbard,
    Call *dying* dainty dear, her *brave mind* mistress;
    Casting a thousand ways to give those forms,
    That he might lie with 'em, and get old armours.
    He had got me o' the hip once; it shall go hard, friends.
    But he shall find his own coin.

Enter MACER.

Dec. How now, Macer?
    Is Judas yet come in?

Enter JUDAS.

Macer. Yes, and has lost
    Most of his men too.   Here he is.

Cur. What news?

Judas. I have lodged him; rouse him, he that dares!

Dem. Where, Judas?

Judas. On a steep rock i' th' woods, the boy too with him;
    And there he swears he'll keep his Christmas, gentlemen,
    But he will come away with full conditions,
    Bravely, and like a Briton.   He paid part of us;
    Yet I think we fought bravely: For mine own part,
    I was four several times at half-sword with him,
    Twice stood his partizan; but the plain truth is,
    He's a mere devil, and no man.   I' th' end, he swinged
        us,
    And swinged us soundly too: He fights by witchcraft;
    Yet for all that I saw him lodged.

Jun. Take more men,
    And scout him round.   Macer, march you along.
    What victuals has he?

Judas. Not a piece of biscuit,
    Not so much as will stop a tooth, nor water
    More than they make themselves: They lie
    Just like a brace of bear-whelps, close, and crafty,
    Sucking their fingers for their food.

Dec. Cut off then
    All hope of that way; take sufficient forces.

Jun. But use no foul play, on your lives! that man
    That does him mischief by deceit, I'll kill him.
Macer. He shall have fair play; he deserves it.
Judas. Hark ye!
    What should I do there then?   You are brave captains,
    Most valiant men: Go up yourselves; use virtue;
    See what will come on't; pray the gentleman
    To come down, and be taken.   Ye all know him,
    I think ye have felt him too: There ye shall find him,
    His sword by his side, plums of a pound weight by him,
    Will make your chops ache: You'll find it a more labour
    To win him living, than climbing of a crow's nest.
Dec. Away, and compass him; we shall come up,
    I am sure, within these two hours.   Watch him close.
Macer. He shall flee through the air, if he escape us.
Jun. What's this loud lamentation?   [*A sad noise within*
Macer. The dead body
    Of the great Penius is new come to th' camp, sir.
Dem. Dead?
Macer. By himself, they say.
Jun. I fear'd that fortune.
Cur. Peace guide him up to Heaven!
Jun. Away, good Macer.   [*Exeunt Macer and Judas.*

    Enter SUETONIUS, DRUSIUS, REGULUS, *and* PETILLIUS.

Suet. If thou be'st guilty,
    Some sullen plague, thou hat'st most, light upon thee!
    The regiment return on Junius;
    He well deserves it.
Pet. So!
Suet. Draw out three companies,
    (Yours, Decius, Junius, and thou, Petillius),
    And make up instantly to Caratach;
    He's in the wood before ye: We shall follow,
    After due ceremony done to th' dead,
    The noble dead.   Come, let's go burn the body.
                    [*Exeunt all but Petillius.*
Pet. The regiment given from me? disgraced openly?
    In love too with a trifle to abuse me?
    A merry world, a fine world! served seven years
    To be an ass o' both sides? sweet Petillius,

You have brought your hogs to a fine market!   You are
    wise, sir,
Your honourable brain-pan full of crotchets,
An understanding gentleman; your projects
Cast with assurance ever!   Wouldst not thou now
Be bang'd about the pate, Petillius?
Answer to that, sweet soldier! surely, surely,
I think you would; pull'd by the nose, kick'd?   Hang
    thee,
Thou art the arrant'st rascal!   Trust thy wisdom
With anything of weight? the wind with feathers!
Out, you blind puppy! you command? you govern?
Dig for a groat a-day, or serve a swine herd,
Too noble for thy nature too!—I must up;
But what I shall do there, let time discover.   *[Exit.*

SCENE III.—*The mountainous Country, with the Rock in the
            Back-ground.*

    Enter MACER *and* JUDAS, *with meat and a bottle.*

Macer. Hang it o' th' side o' th' rock, as though the Britons
    Stole hither to relieve him: Who first ventures
    To fetch it off is ours.   I cannot see him.
Judas. He lies close in a hole above, I know it,
    Gnawing upon his anger.—Ha! no; 'tis not he.
Macer. 'Tis but the shaking of the boughs.
Judas. Pox shake 'em!
    I am sure they shake me soundly.—There!
Macer. 'Tis nothing.
Judas. Make no noise; if he stir, a deadly tempest
    Of huge stones falls upon us.   'Tis done! away, close!
                                [Exeunt.

    CARATACH *appears on the rock.*

Car. Sleep still, sleep sweetly, child; 'tis all thou feed'st on!
    No gentle Briton near, no valiant charity,
    To bring thee food?   Poor knave, thou art sick, extreme
        sick,
    Almost grown wild for meat; and yet thy goodness
    Will not confess, nor show it.   All the woods
    Are double lined with soldiers; no way left us
    To make a noble 'scape.   I'll sit down by thee,

And, when thou wak'st, either get meat to save thee,
Or lose my life i' th' purchase; good Gods comfort thee!
                                                    [*Exit.*

Enter below Junius, Decius, Petillius, *and* Guide.

Guide. You are not far off now, sir.
Jun. Draw the companies
    The closest way through the woods; we'll keep on this
      way.
Guide. I will, sir: Half a furlong more you'll come
    Within the sight o' th' rock. Keep on the left side,
    You'll be discover'd else: I'll lodge your companies
    In the wild vines beyond ye.
Dec. Do you mark him?   [*Pointing to Petillius.*
Jun. Yes, and am sorry for him.
Pet. Junius,
    Pray let me speak two words with you.
Jun. Walk afore;
    I'll overtake you straight.
Dec. I will.   [*Exit.*
Jun. Now, captain?
Pet. You have oft told me, you have loved me, Junius.
Jun. Most sure I told you truth then.
Pet. And that love
    Should not deny me any honest thing.
Jun. It shall not.
Pet. Dare you swear it?
    I have forgot all passages between us
    That have been ill, forgiven too, forgot.
Jun. What would this man have?—By the gods, I do, sir,
    So it be fit to grant you.
Pet. 'Tis most honest.
Jun. Why, then I'll do it.
Pet. Kill me.
Jun. How!
Pet. Pray kill me.
Jun. Kill you?
Pet. Ay, kill me quickly, suddenly;
    Now kill me.
Jun. On what reason? You amaze me!
Pet. If you do love me, kill me; ask me not why:
    I would be kill'd, and by you.
Jun. Mercy on me!

What ails this man? Petillius!

Pet. Pray you dispatch me:
    You are not safe whilst I live: I am dangerous,
    Troubled extremely, even to mischief, Junius,
    An enemy to all good men. Fear not; 'tis justice;
    I shall kill you else.

Jun. Tell me but the cause,
    And I will do it,

Pet. I am disgraced, my service
    Slighted and unrewarded by the general,
    My hopes left wild and naked; besides these,
    I am grown ridiculous, an ass, a folly,
    I dare not trust myself with: Pr'ythee, kill me!

Jun. All these may be redeem'd as easily
    As you would heal your finger.

Pet. Nay——

Jun. Stay, I'll do it;
    You shall not need your anger. But first, Petillius
    You shall unarm yourself; I dare not trust
    A man so bent to mischief.

Pet. There's my sword,   *[Gives up his sword.*
    And do it handsomely.

Jun. Yes, I will kill you,
    Believe that certain; but first I'll lay before you
    The most extreme fool you have play'd in this,
    The honour purposed for you, the great honour
    The general intended you.

Pet. How?

Jun. And then I'll kill you,
    Because you shall die miserable. Know, sir,
    The regiment was given me, but till time
    Call'd you to do some worthy deed, might stop
    The people's ill thoughts of you for lord Penius,
    I mean his death. How soon this time's come to you,
    And hasted by Suetonius! "Go," says he,
    "Junius and Decius, and go thou, Petillius,"
    (Distinctly, *thou*, *Petillius*), "and draw up,
    To take stout Caratach:" There's the deed purposed,
    A deed to take off all faults, of all natures:
    "And *thou*, *Petillius*," mark it! there's the honour;
    And that done, all made even.

Pet. Stay!

Jun. No, I'll kill you.

He knew thee absolute, and full in soldier,
Daring beyond all dangers, found thee out,
According to the boldness of thy spirit,
A subject, such a subject——

Pet. Hark you, Junius!
I will live now.

Jun. By no means.—Woo'd thy worth,
Held thee by the chin up, as thou sunk'st, and showed
thee
How Honour held her arms out. Come, make ready,
Since you will die an ass.

Pet. Thou wilt not kill me?

Jun. By Heaven, but I will, sir. I'll have no man dangerous
Live to destroy me afterward. Besides, you have gotten
Honour enough; let young men rise now. Nay,
I do perceive too by the general (which is
One main cause you shall die, howe'er he carry it)
Such a strong doting on you, that I fear
You shall command in chief: how are we paid then?
Come, if you'll pray, dispatch it.

Pet. Is there no way?

Jun. Not any way to live.

Pet. I will do anything,
Redeem myself at any price: Good Junius,
Let me but die upon the rock, but offer
My life up like a soldier!

Jun. You will seek then
To outdo every man.

Pet. Believe it, Junius,
You shall go stroke by stroke with me.

Jun. You'll leave off too,
As you are noble, and a soldier,
For ever these mad fancies?

Pet. Dare you trust me?
By all that's good and honest——

Jun. There's your sword then;
And now, come on a new man: Virtue guide thee!
[*Exeunt.*

Enter CARATACH *and* HENGO, *on the rock.*

Car. Courage, my boy! I have found meat: Look, Hengo,
Look where some blessed Briton, to preserve thee,

Has hung a little food and drink: Cheer up, boy;
    Do not forsake me now!
Hengo. Oh, uncle, uncle.
    I feel I cannot stay long: yet I'll fetch it,
    To keep your noble life.   Uncle, I am heart-whole,
    And would live.
Car. Thou shalt, long I hope.
Hengo. But my head, uncle!
    Methinks the rock goes round.

    Enter MACER *and* JUDAS *below, and stand apart.*

Macer. Mark 'em well, Judas.
Judas. Peace, as you love your life!
Hengo. Do not you hear
    The noise of bells!
Car. Of bells, boy? 'Tis thy fancy;
    Alas, thy body's full of wind.
Hengo. Methinks, sir,
    They ring a strange sad knell, a preparation
    To some near funeral of state: Nay, weep not,
    Mine own sweet uncle! you will kill me sooner.
Car. Oh, my poor chicken!
Hengo. Fy, faint-hearted uncle!
    Come, tie me in your belt, and let me down.
Car. I'll go myself, boy.
Hengo. No, as you love me, uncle!
    I will not eat it, if I do not fetch it;
    The danger only I desire; pray tie me!
Car. I will, and all my care hang o'er thee! Come, child,
    My valiant child!   [*Lets Hengo down by his belt.*
Hengo. Let me down apace, uncle,
    And you shall see how like a daw I'll whip it
    From all their policies; for 'tis most certain
    A Roman train: And you must hold me sure too,
    You'll spoil all else.   When I have brought it, uncle,
    We'll be as merry——
Car. Go, i' th' name of Heaven, boy!
Hengo. Quick, quick, uncle! I have it.—Oh!
                            [*Judas shoots Hengo.*
Car. What ail'st thou?
Hengo. Oh, my best uncle, I am slain!
Car. I see you,
    [*Caratach kills Judas with a stone, and draws up Hengo.*

> And Heaven direct my hand!—Destruction
> Go with thy coward soul!—How dost thou, boy?—
> Oh, villain, pocky villain!

Hengo. Oh, uncle, uncle,
> Oh, how it pricks me (am I preserved for this?)
> Extremely pricks me!

Car. Coward, rascal coward!
> Dogs eat thy flesh!

Hengo. Oh, I bleed hard; I faint too; out upon't
> How sick I am!—The lean rogue, uncle!

Car. Look, boy;
> I have laid him sure enough.

Hengo. Have you knock'd his brains out?

Car. I warrant thee for stirring more: Cheer up, child.

Hengo. Hold my sides hard; stop, stop; oh, wretched fortune,
> Must we part thus? Still I grow sicker, uncle.

Car. Heaven look upon this noble child!

Hengo. I once hoped
> I should have lived to have met these bloody Romans
> At my sword's point, to have revenged my father,
> To have beaten 'em. Oh, hold me hard! But, uncle——

Car. Thou shalt live still, I hope, boy. Shall I draw it?

Hengo. You draw away my soul then: I would live
> A little longer (spare me, Heavens!) but only
> To thank you for your tender love! Good uncle,
> Good noble uncle, weep not!

Car. Oh, my chicken,
> My dear boy, what shall I lose?

Hengo. Why, a child,
> That must have died however; had this 'scaped me,
> Fever or famine——I was born to die, sir.

Car. But this unblown, my boy?

Hengo. I go the straighter
> My journey to the gods. Sure I shall know you
> When you come, uncle?

Car. Yes, boy.

Hengo. And I hope
> We shall enjoy together that great blessedness
> You told me of.

Car. Most certain, child.

Hengo. I grow cold;
> Mine eyes are going.

Car. Lift 'em up!

Hengo. Pray for me;
  And, noble uncle, when my bones are ashes,
  Think of your little nephew! Mercy!
Car. Mercy!
  You blessed angels, take him!
Hengo. Kiss me! so.
  Farewell, farewell!   *[Dies.*
Car. Farewell the hopes of Britain!
  Thou royal graft, farewell for ever!—Time and Death,
  Ye have done your worst. Fortune, now see, now
    proudly
  Pluck off thy veil, and veiw thy triumph: Look,
  Look what thou hast brought this land to.—Oh, faiɪ
    flower,
  How lovely yet thy ruins show, how sweetly
  Even death embraces thee! The peace of Heaven,
  The fellowship of all great souls, be with thee!

   Enter Petillius *and* Junius, *on the rock.*

  Ha! Dare ye, Romans? Ye shall win me bravely.
  Thou'rt mine!   *[Fight.*
Jun. Not yet, sir.
Car. Breathe ye, ye poor Romans,
  And come up all, with all your ancient valours;
  Like a rough wind I'll shake your souls, and send 'em——

   Enter Suetonius, *and all the Roman* Captains.

Suet. Yield thee, bold Caratach! By all the gods,
  As I am soldier, as I envy thee,
  I'll use thee like thyself, the valiant Briton.
Pet. Brave soldier, yield, thou stock of arms and honour,
  Thou filler of the world with fame and glory!
Jun. Most worthy man, we'll woo thee, be thy prisoners.
Suet. Excellent Briton, do me but that honour,
  That more to me than conquests, that true happiness,
  To be my friend!
Car. Oh, Romans, see what here is!
  Had this boy lived——
Suet. For fame's sake, for thy sword's sake,
  As thou desirest to build thy virtues greater!
  By all that's excellent in man, and honest——
Car. I do believe. Ye have had me a brave foe;

Make me a noble friend, and from your goodness,
Give this boy honourable earth to lie in!
Suet. He shall have fitting funeral.
Car. I yield then;
Not to your blows, but your brave courtesies.
Pet. Thus we conduct then to the arms of peace
The wonder of the world!
Suet. Thus I embrace thee!   [*Flourish.*
And let it be no flattery that I tell thee,
Thou art the only soldier!
Car. How to thank ye,
I must hereafter find upon your usage.
I am for Rome?
Suet. You must.
Car. Then Rome shall know
The man that makes her spring of glory grow.
Suet. Petillius, you have shown much worth this day,
Redeem'd much error; you have my love again;
Preserve it.—Junius, with you I make him
Equal in the regiment.
Jun. The elder and the nobler;
I will give place, sir.
Suet. You show a friend's soul.
March on, and through the camp, in every tongue,
The virtues of great Caratach be sung!   [*Exeunt.*

GLOSSARY

A', on, in; he

ABIDE UPON'T, depend upon it (Dyce); other reading " to bide upon," dwell, insist upon

ABILIMENTS, habiliments, equipment

ABLE, active, vigorous

ABSOLUTE, perfectly fitted and accomplished

ABUSE, deceive, maltreat, insult

ABY, pay, atone for

ACCIDENT, event, chance

ADMIRABLE, wonderful

ADMIRE, wonder at

ADVICE, reflection, deliberation

ADVISED, considerate, cautious, opposite to rash

AFFECT, love; like, care for; move, impress

AFTER-LOVE, future love

AGE, " pleasing —," pleasing season of youth; " present —," " early old age "

ALLOW, approve

ALTER, change countenance

AMBER, a provocative

AMISS, fault

AN, if

ANCIENT, ensign (standard, and bearer)

ANNOY, anything hurtful, or discomforting

ANON, directly, presently

APPEASE, become appeased

APPLE-SQUIRE, pander

APPLY, ply, betake, address one's self to

APPROVED, proved, tested

APT, ready, inclined, willing

ARCHES, prison in the Court of A

ARTICLE, arrange by treaty, stipulate

ARTIFICIAL, artful

ASPECT (astrol.), relative position of heavenly bodies at given times

ASPIC, asp

ASPIRE, reach, attain

ASSURED, affianced

BAFFLE, disgrace, insult, with special reference to the punishment inflicted on a forsworn knight, part of which was to hang him up by the heels (see Nares)

BAIR, bairn

BALOO, see refrain of " Lady Anne Bothwell's Lamentation " (Percy's Reliques), " Balow, my babe, etc."

BANDOG, dog tied or chained up

BANQUET, " running —," a light repast between meals

BASTA (Ital.), enough

BATE, deduct; " bate me the king," with exception of, reduce

BATTLE-RAY, battle array

BAY, laurel, said never to be struck by lightning

BEAR-WARD, bear keeper

BEDSTAFF, (?) wooden pin in the side of the bedstead for supporting the bedclothes (Johnson); one of the sticks or " laths "; a stick used in making a bed.

BEHOLDING, beholden

BEND, aim, purpose

BERAY, befoul

BESHROW, beshrew, " a curse light upon "

BESIDES, aside from the mark; by the side of

BEZZLE, squander

BILBO, sword (Bilboa blade)

BILBOES, fetters fastened to bars of iron for mutinous sailors

BILBO-LORD, BILBO-MEN, sword lord, or men, swaggerers

BILLET, log

BIRDING-PIECE, fowling-piece

" BLACK SANCTIS," burlesque hymn; any confused or violent noise (Nares)

BLANKS, blank bonds to be filled up according to (Arbaces') pleasure

467

BLAZE, blazon, proclaim

BLENCH, start, swerve, shrink

BLOWN, swollen, puffed up with pride

BLURT, treat with contempt

BOB, sneer

BOLT, arrow

BORD, circumference

BOTS, parasitical worms

BOTTOM, dale

BOUND, boundary, limit

BRABBLE, brawl, quarrel

BRAVE, in fine clothes

BRAVERY, show, grandeur

BRAWN, muscle; " brawn-fallen," shrunk, weak

BREAK UPON, break in upon, interrupt

BREATHE, take breath

BREECH, whip

BREWIS, broth, soup

BROOD, watch over

BURN (" their mentions "), *brand* and *blur* have been proposed

BUSKIN, foot-covering reaching high up the leg; a half-boot

BUSS, kiss

BUT, unless, except

BUT IF, unless

BUZZARD, blockhead, coward

BY AND BY, directly

BYE AND MAIN, gaming terms

CALAMINT, aromatic herb

CAMPHIRE, camphor

CANKER, a corrosive disease; a diseased, worm-eaten thing

CAP, arrest

CARD, face of mariner's compass

CARDUUS BENEDICTUS, Holy thistle

CARE, watchful regard

CAREFUL, full of care, anxious

CARK, care

CARRACK, large ship of burden, galleon

CARRIAGE, bearing, behaviour

CARRY, conduct, carry on

CAST, plot, devise, contrive; dismiss, cashier, "— their caps," salute

CENSURE, opinion, judgment

CENSURE, pass judgment, express opinion

CENSURING, criticising, censorious

CERTAINTY, " at a —," certain of not being " encroached " upon as regards price

CHANGE, exchange

CHARM, persuade, induce

CHIBBAL, onion

CHIN-COUGH, hooping-cough

CHIVE, *see* foul

CIRCUMSTANCE, circumlocution, details, ceremony

CLAP, pat

CLEAR, innocent; plain, true; absolved

CLEARER, purer, fairer

CLEARLY, without blame

CLIP, embrace

CLOSE, retired, secret(ly), private(ly); strictly confined

CLOTE, burdock; other flowers, yellow water-lily, etc., also so called

CLOTH, drop-scene

CLOUT, piece of cloth, rag, " men of —s," scarecrows

COALS, " eat —," etc., cats were supposed to do so when angry (Dyce)

CODES! (COADS!), app. an altered or " minced " adjuration: *cf.* ecod! gads! ods! etc. (Oxford Dict.)

COG, cheat, cajole

COME ALOFT, vault, or play the tricks of a tumbler (Nares)

COMFORTABLE, comforting

COMFREY, a healing plant

COMMON, public, generally known

COMMONS, common people

COMPASS, bound, limit

COMPASS, encircle, surround

CONCEIT, idea, conception

CONCEIVE, know, understand

CONDITIONS, qualities

CONSORT, company, band

CONSTANT, unshaken, faithful

CONTAIN, restrain

CONY, term of endearment

COPY, tenure, charter

CORDEVAN, Spanish leather from Cordova

CORONALS, chaplets, garlands

CORPS, living body

COTE, hut

COURAGING, courageous

COURSE, " in —," " by —s," in turn, by turns

COURTSHIP, courtliness, courtly behaviour

COY, disdainful, indifferent

COY, stroke, caress

COURT-STALE; *see* stale

COXCOMB, fool

CRACKNEL, kind of biscuit

CROSS, thwart

CROSS, thwarting, perverse

CRUDDLE, curdle

CULLIS, strong broth

CUNNING, clever, skilful

CURIOUS, fastidious, scrupulous, nice

DARE, scare, frighten

DEAR, expressive of anything that provokes strong feeling or interest

DEBATE, discord, strife

DECEIVE, prove false to

DEEM, judge, think

DEFEND, " gods —," forbid

DELIVER, state

DENIER, old French coin, twelfth of a sou

DENY, refuse

DEPREST, assuaged

DESCRY, reveal, make known

DISCOURSE (King and no King), " transaction," " story of what took place "; perhaps " course of arms or combat " (Oxford Dict.)

DISCOVER, reveal, disclose

DISPLEASE, cause dissatisfaction; cause hurt, pain

DISTEMPERED, deranged in mind, or feelings, disordered, wild

DOCUMENT, lesson

DOG, dog-star

DOR, mock, make a fool of

DORUS, supposed reference to Spenser

DOTTEREL, a bird proverbially foolish, allowing itself to be caught while it apes the movements of the fowler, even to stretching out its leg if the latter does so

DOUBT, dread, apprehend; cause fear, affright

DRAGON'S WATER, medicinal preparation

DRAW, (of wound) to draw " humours " from; move, pass; track, scent

DRESSING, coiffure

DROLLERIES, puppets

DRUM, drummer

DRY BEAT, beat soundly

DRY-FOUNDERED, foundered, lamed (said of horses)

DUNDER-WHELP, dunderhead

EASINESS, indulgence, reverse of harshness

EKE, also

EMBEZZLE, " used here probably in the same sense as *bezzle* " (*q.v.*) (Dyce)

EMPERAL, emperor

END, purpose, resolution; issue

ENDLESS, immortal

ENGINE, device

ENLARGING, release

ENTERTAIN, entertainment

ENVY, hatred, spite

ENVY, emulate, vie with

EQUAL, impartial, just

ERRANT, erring

ERST, formerly

ESTATE, state, order

ETTIN, giant

EVEN, direct; " make even," square (as an account)

EYE, " by the —," (?) in unlimited quantity (Oxford Dict.)

FACE, to show effrontery, confront with impudence

FACER, shameless bullies, braggarts

FACES ABOUT, face about, military word of command

FADING, a dance; " with a — " was the burden of an old song

FAIN, be glad, like

FAIR, beauty

FALSIFY, feign

FANCY, love

FARE, track of a hare or rabbit (Oxford Dict.)

FAST AND LOOSE, a cheating game, played with a folded belt, also known as " pricking at the belt or girdle " (*see* Nares)

FATAL, fateful

FATAL SISTERS, Fates

FAVOUR, countenance

FEAR, frighten; " — me not," fear not for me

FEARFUL(LY), full of fear, timorous(ly)

FEGARIES, vagaries

FELL, cruel, fierce

FEW, " in —," in few words, in short

FIRE-DRAKE, fiery dragon

FIT, ready, prepared; suitable, proper

FITCHOCK, fitchew, polecat

FLAPPET, small flap

FLEER, sneer, mock

FLESH, initiate or inure to bloodshed, etc.; hence " Fleshing "

FLIGHT, light arrow

FLIRT-GILL, light, flirting woman

FLURT, scoff, gibe

FOIL, " grace, beauty, or glorie given unto " (Cotgrave)

FOND, foolish

FOOT, " with the prey in his —," like a falcon (Bond. var. ed.)

FOR, for fear of

FORKS, forked stake used as a whipping-post (Oxford Dict.)

FORMALLY, according to good form, or custom, with precision

FOUL(NESS), ugly(liness)

FOUL CHIVE HIM, ill-luck befall him

FOUNDERED, dumbfoundered

FOX, old English broad-sword

FRATEOUSLY, nimbly

FREE, generous

FULL, complete, fully endowed

FURMETY, frumenty, made of hulled wheat boiled in milk, with sugar, etc.

GALLEY-FOIST, Lord Mayor's barge

GALLIARD, lively dance in triple time

GALLOWS, gallows-bird

GASKINS, breeches

GAUDY, merry

GENT, gentle

GENTLE, nobly born

GENTLENESS, affability

GILL, contemptuous term for a woman

GIRD, jeer, witticism ; gird, scoff

GIVE, tell

GLORIOUS, boastful, vain-glorious, proud

GOLD-WEIGHTS, minute weights, signifying the minutest particular

GOODNESS, potency

GOODS, gifts, virtues

GRACEFULNESS, graciousness

GRATIFY, show gratitude, requite

GRATULATE, recompense

GREASE, gull, cheat

GREEN-FISH, unsalted fish (especially cod)

GREENNESS (of a wound), (?) freshness, festering, or mortification

GRIEF, bodily pain

GRIEVE, grieve over

GRIN, gin, trap

GROAT, four pence

GROSS, " our people in —," the main body of the army

GROUTNOL, blockhead

GRUDGING, secret longing, inclination

GULES, heraldic term for red

HALTER-SACK, gallows-bird

HAMPER, fetter, confine

HAMS, " butter'd —," running footmen used to have their legs greased (Weber)

HAND-WOLF, tamed wolf

HAP, chance

HAPPILY, haply

HARDLY, with difficulty

HARNESS, armour

HARRY, forage

HATCH, inlay or overlay with gold or silver

HAZARD, peril

HEARTY, strengthening ; heartfelt

HEELS UPWARD, allusion to the burial of suicides

HEIGHTEN, elate, exalt

HIGHT, called

HOBBY-HORSE, a figure introduced into the Morris dance (an imitation horse was fastened round the waist of the performer, who imitated the movements of a skittish horse)

HOIT, revel

HOLD, wager

HOLT, wood, copse

HONESTY, good manners or breeding

HOREHOUND, " black —," *Ballota nigra*, a purple-flowered weed

HOUND, set on

HUCKLE-BONE, hip, or haunch, bone

HUFF, HUFFING, swagger(ing)

HUM, strong drink, infusion of spirits in ale

HUMOUROUS, ill-humoured, touchy, moody, capricious ; pertaining to the humours

HUSWIFE, hussy

IDLE, vain, useless

IMPOSTUMED, swollen, festered

IMPROPER, not particular property, common

IMPROVE, raise the price

INDENT, agreed upon, contracted

INEVITABLE, irresistible

INGENIOUS, ingenuous

INGIRT, encircle

INGRANT, ingrate, ungrateful

INSULT, exult, triumph over

INTENT, intention, wish, aim
I-WIS, in truth, certainly

JACK, a low, insolent fellow
JACK OF STRAW, Jack o' Lent, puppet thrown at in Lent
JIG, a merry tune or dance accompanying it
JOHN DORY, hero of a popular song
JOVY, jovial
JOY, rejoice

KEEP, frequent, haunt (Dyce); dwell
KENNING, view, sight
KEXES, dry stalks, properly of hemlock
KICKSHAW (*quelque chose*), trifle
KIND, nature; " in their —," according to their rôle; " use him with his —," meet him with his own weapons
KNACKS, knick-knacks, trumpery
KNOT-GRASS, supposed to hinder growth
KNOWN, acquainted with

LAME, weak, defective
LAMMING, beating
LANCH'D, lanced
LARD, fatten
LARE, " fatten "
LARGELY, without restraint, freely
LAVOLTA, lively dance for two persons, consisting a good deal in high and active bounds (Nares)
LAY, wager
LAWN, glade, or open space in the wood
LEAVE, leave off, desist, give up
LEESE, lose
LEG, " make a —," bow, do obeisance
LESSON, " do his —," teach him
LET, hindrance
LET, prevent, hinder
LEWD, wicked, vile
LIABLE, exposed to the possibility
LIBERALLY, freely
LIKE, please
LINE, bring into line
LINGEL, shoemaker's thread
LIST, pleasure, desire
LIST, like, please
LISTS, enclosed space in which tournaments were held
LIVELY, living

LIVER, supposed to be the seat of the passions
LOADEN, laden
LODGE, track a fugitive to his hiding-place
'LONG OF, along of, on account of
LOOK, look out, look up
LOSE, get rid of
LUNGIES, lout, lubber
LUSTY, merry
LYÆUS, Bacchus
LYSIMACHUS, loose strife

MADDING, mad behaviour
MAINTAIN, defend
MANAGE, management, control
MANFUL, manly
MARCHPANE, confection of almonds, sugar, etc.
MAT, matting
MAW, stomach, inclination
MAZE, confusion
MEACOCK, dastard, a derisive appellation for a meek husband
MEAN, moderation, discretion
MEAN, intermediate; of the rank-and-file
MEASURE, stately dance; dance in general
MEECHER, go between, pander
MERE(LY), entire(ly), utter(ly), nothing but
MEW, shut up, confine; moult
MICKLE, much, greatly
MILAN SKINS, " I think they were fine gloves manufactured at Milan " (Nares)
MILE-END, place for training the citizens
MISCARRY, come to grief
MISLIKE, disapproval
MITHRIDATUM, antidote against poisons
MITTIMUS, warrant for arrest
MONCASTER, Mulcaster, first headmaster of Merchant Taylors' School
MOP, grimace
MORISCO, Morris dance, or dancer
MORRIS, Morris, or Moorish, dance, in which certain personages were represented; part of the merriment on May-day, etc.
MOST, uttermost
MOTION, proposal, request; movement, emotion, impulse; puppet-show; mow, grimace
MOTLEY, patched habit of a fool
MOVE, urge, exhort; rouse

NAPKIN, handkerchief
NAUGHT, good for nothing, bad, evil
NAWL, awl
NEAT, dainty, refined
NESH, delicate, weak
NEW-CAST, form anew
NEW-YEANED, new-born
NICE, fastidious
NIFLES, trifles
NIPITATO, strong ale
NODDY, simpleton
NOTABLE, excellent, fine
NOTELESS, of no worth or note
NUMP, blockhead

OBSERVANCE, homage, devoted service
OBSERVATION, homage, devoted, obsequious, attention or service
OBSERVER, respectful, courteous admirer
OCCASIONS, affairs, business
ON, of
ONE, at one; one and the same
ONLY, nothing but, absolutely; sole; mere; pre-eminent, " par excellence "
OPINION, reputation
ORIGANUM, marjoram
OR ERE, ere, before
OUT, " I'll not —," " I will make one of the party "
OUTBRAVE, defy
OUTLEAP, outburst, sally
OUT-NAME, exceed in fame
OVER - CURIOUS, over - scrupulous, fastidious
OVERGRACE, favour beyond desert
OVERHIE, leave behind by hastening on (Oxford Dict.)

PALLET, palate
PALTER, shuffle, equivocate
PANTOFLE, slipper, or shoe
PARCEL, partly, in part
PARTIZAN, kind of pike or halberd
PARTS, qualities, endowments
PASSING(LY), exceeding(ly)
PASSION, sorrow, affliction
PATCH, fool (from Ital. *Pazzo*; or so called on account of motley dress)
PAY DOWN, balance, " weigh down "
PEAK, pry, peep
PEEVISHNESS, foolishness, obstinacy
PELTING, paltry

PEPPERNEL, " apparently a lump or swelling " (Nares)
PERDU, " set thee —," in ambush
PERISH, cause to perish
PERJURE, swear falsely to
PER'LOUS, perilous, capable of inflicting harm
PERT (PEART), perk
PICKTHANKS, sycophant talebearer
PIECE, person, man or woman
PILCHER, pilchard
PINED, tormented, tortured
PITCH, height of a bird of prey's flight
PITCH-FIELD, field of battle
PLAINLY, honestly
PLUCK DOWN A SIDE, " cause the loss or hazard of the side or party with which a person plays " (Nares)
POINTS, tagged laces for fastening the breeches to the doublet
POLITIC, prudent, judicious
PORT, deportment, bearing
POWDER, salt, season, spice
PRACTICE, intrigue, treacherous device
PREASE, press, crowd
PRECEDENT, example
PREFER, recommend
PRESENT(LY), immediate(ly), forthwith
PREST, ready
PRICK, spur, speed; incite
PRICKANT, PRICKING, spurring, riding
PRICKET, buck in its second year
PRIVATE, " — to herself," belonging to herself, her own mistress
PRIVY COAT, light armour worn under the coat
PROOF, " to the —," to the utmost, last degree
PROPER, handsome
PROPERTIES, stage necessaries
PROVANT, provender
PROVOKE, incite
PURCHAS'D, incurred by his (Jasper's) conduct
PUSILL, pucelle, used in uncomplimentary sense
PUT, commit

QUEASY, fastidious, nice, difficult of handling
QUELL, slay, kill
QUICK, alive, living
QUICKNESS, keenness

QUIT, remit, do away with; acquit, absolve; repay, make return

RACK, clouds driven before the wind in the upper air, drifting vapour

RAND, slice, piece

RASCAL, young, lean, or inferior deer

REACH, arrive at meaning of, understand

READY, READIER, dressed, more dressed

REBECK, three-stringed instrument played with a bow

REBUKE, beat, buffet (Oxford Dict.)

RECLAIM, restrain

RECORDER, kind of flute or flageolet

RECURE, cure, heal

REFUSE, reject

REGIMENT, command

RENT, tax, rate

REPAREL, apparel

REPROVE, condemn

RESOLUTE, convinced

RESOLVE, to be free from doubt, convinced; inform, assure, satisfy

RESTY, lazy, sluggish

RHAMNUS, buckthorn

RID, make away with

RIDE THE WILD MARE, play at see-saw

RIFF-RAFF, trash

RIGHT, forthwith, at once

RING, "cracked in (within) the —," coins so cracked were rendered unfit for currency

ROGUE, vagrant, beggar; hence "rogueship"

ROUND, roundelay

ROUT, company, set

RUDE, inexperienced; rough, uncivilised

RUDENESS, roughness, act of violence

SAD, serious, grave

SAFETY, trust, security

SALLET, salad

SALT, lascivious

SAUCY, bold, proud, overbearing

SAY, "subject for experiments" (Nares)

SCAPE, escape

SCIENCE, "the noble —," fencing

SCOTCH, cut, hack

SCOURING STICK, rod for cleaning the barrel of a gun

SECOND, help

SECURE, safe, protected; over-confident, presumptuous

SENSIBLE, sensitive, capable of feeling; perceptible

SENTENCE, maxim

SERES, talons

SERVANT, lover

SET, setting

SET, stake

SHAMEFAST, shamefaced

SHAWM, musical instrument resembling a hautboy

SHEER, shire

SHEETS, "*The shaking of the sheets* was a favourite dance, generally alluded to with *double entendre*" (Dyce)

SHIFT, change attire

SHORT, short of the mark

SHREWD(LY), mischievous, evil; badly

SHRINK IN, draw in, back

SHUTTING, close

"SILVANUS' BOY," Cyparissus, changed to a cypress because he slew Silvanus' favourite stag

SINGLE, sincere, straightforward

SIR, formerly applied to women as well as men

SIT (AT), stand firm to

SLICK, sleek

SLIGHT, unimportant, insignificant

SLIP-STRING, knavish fellow (Halliwell)

SLUBBER, stain, soil

SMOKE, suffer, be punished

SMOOTH, soft, soothing, flattering

SMOOTHNESS, state of being bland, wheedling, etc.

SNICK UP, hang

SOOTH, flatter, humour

SORT, band, company

SORT, select, choose

SOUGHT TO, courted, solicited

SOUND, swoon

SOWTER, cobbler

SPANIELS, Spanish

SPARKLING, scattering

SPEAK, speak for, proclaim

SPEED, good fortune, success

SPENT, broken, or lost, useless; worn out

SPRINGALD, youngster

SPRITE, spirit

SQUARE, stout, hearty

SQUARE, adjust, regulate

STALE, anything used to decoy or deceive, bait, stalking-horse

STAMP, impression; make impression on

STANDERGRASS, male orchis

STAPLE, market

STARS ("of Rome"), Dyce refers to the song of Deborah, "the stars in their courses," etc. "Shafts," or "darts," has been proposed

STARTUPS, "a sort of rustic shoes, with high tops, galoches, or half-gaiters" (Dyce)

STATE, estate

STAY, halt, stand, delay

STAY, stop, check; await, wait for; bear up under

STIFFNESS, stiff-neckedness

STILL, ever, continually

STOCK, race, family

STONE-BOW, cross-bow for shooting stones

STOOP, drinking-vessel

STOOP, swoop down upon

STOPPING, "— hedges," mending, all. to man in the moon with his bundle of sticks

STORY, history, record

STOUND, amazement

STOUT, proud, stubborn

STRAIGHT, strict

STRAIN, race, lineage

STRANGE, extraordinary, remarkable in some way. "Made it strange," made it a matter of scruple, difficulty

STRANGELY, wonderfully

STRICTNESS, state of being strict in behaviour, manner of life, etc.

STRIKE, produce an effect upon

STRINGER, rake

STYLE, title

SUBURBS, resort of ill-reputed characters

SUFFERANCE, submission, forbearance; suffering

SUFFICIENT, reliable

SURE, safe, secure(ly)

SURQUEDRY, pride, presumption

SUSPECT, suspicion

SUTLER, seller of provisions and drink in a camp

SWADDLE, cudgel

SWARTY, swarthy

SWINGE, beat

SWOUND, swoon

TABLE-BOOK, tablets, notebook

TACK, "hold —," to have sustaining quality

TAINT, disgrace, throw slur on

TAKE IN, conquer, subdue

TAKE ME WITH YOU, "hear me out," "understand me fully" (Dyce)

TAKE UP, take possession of

TALL, bold, brave, fine

TANSY, a dish made of eggs, cream, etc. (see Nares)

TARTARIAN, a cant term for a thief

TASK, tax

TAWDRY-LACE, some kind of cheap necklace bought at the fair held in honour of St. Audrey

TAXES, censures "private —," aspersions on private individuals

TEMPER, calmness, composure

TEMPER, control, subdue

TEMPERED, disposed, conditioned

TENDER, care for, cherish

TERMAGANT, Saracen deity who played a ranting part in the old miracle-plays

THICKS, thickets

THINK, intend

THREE-PILED (protesters), most costly kind of velvet (either wearing such, or used to signify their exaggerated protestings)

THRID, thread

THRIFTY, obtained by thrift

THRUM, finger

TILLER, cross-bow

TIMBER FOR TIMBER, man for man

TIMELESS, untimely

TINE, teen, vexation, sorrow

TITHE, decimate

TO, in addition to

TOD, bush

TOIL, weary

TOLE, draw, entice

TOPLESS, not to be overtopped, supreme

TORMENTIL, supposed to allay pain, hence its name

TORN, torn to death

TOTTER, make totter, undermine

TOUCH, take to task, tax

TOY, fancy

TRAIN, wile, allure, artifice

TRASH, hold back with a trash, a long strap fastened to the hound, which, dragging on the ground, handicapped the too forward animal

TRENCH, cut

TRENCHER, wooden platter

TRIM, array, decking out; gear, equipment

TRIM, gay, fine, pleasant

TROUL, pass round

TRUNK - HOSE, round, swelling breeches

TYMPANY, inflated pride

UNAPT, unfit, unready

UNCERTAINTY, inconsistency

UNCOLLECTED, without control of mind, distraught

UNEXPRESSED, inexpressible

UNHAPPY, UNHAPPILY, wicked(ly), mischievous(ly), wanton(ly)

UNTHRIFT, spendthrift

USE, usage, custom

USE, be in the habit, be accustomed; dwell

VAMP, patch

VASTNESS, boundlessness

VEX, torment, agitate; to be vexed at

VILD, vile

VIRTUE, valour

VIRTUOUS, possessing hidden virtue, or power

VISITED, plague-stricken

WAKE, annual festival of the dedication of a church which gradually became an occasion for mirth and brawling

WALK, wander on earth as a ghost

WANION, " with a —," with a vengeance

WARD, guard

WASH, washy

WASSAIL-BOWL, allusion to custom of going about the village carousing, singing, and dancing (wassailing) at Christmas time, etc.

WASHING, " will not give it for this —," proverbial expression, meaning, it seems, according to Nares, " will not submit to this overbearing insult "

WASTETHRIFT, spendthrift

WATCH, " — of midsummer-day," annual muster of troops

WELKIN, sky

WHIFFLER, one who cleared the way for a procession (originally a fifer), an usher

WHILST, meanwhile

WHIM-WHAM, whim, freak

WHIPT, brocaded

WHITE BOY, term of endearment

WIDE, aside from the mark

WILD-FIRE, " allusion to fable of Phæton "

WINK, close the eyes

WISH, wish for

WITHOUT, unless; beyond

WON, dwell

WOOD, mad

WOT, knows

YCLEPED, called

VERYMAN'S LIBRARY: A Selected List

BIOGRAPHY

ESSAYS AND CRITICISM

FICTION

2

3

RELIGION AND PHILOSOPHY

SCIENCE

TRAVEL AND TOPOGRAPHY